THE RETT SYNDROME HANDBOOK

**In words you can understand
From those who understand**

**by Kathy Hunter
Founder and President
International Rett Syndrome Association**

**and
fellow families everywhere**

W9-CUO-039

IRSA
International Rett Syndrome Association
9121 Piscataway Road, Suite 2B
Clinton, Maryland 20735
Phone: (800) 818-RETT
Fax: (301) 856-3336
www.rettsyndrome.org

Copyright ©1999 by Kathy Hunter

All rights reserved
The purpose of this handbook is to circulate the most up-to-date and correct information on Rett syndrome. Permission to reprint articles from this publication is granted as long as written credit is given to the author and the International Rett Syndrome Association.

First IRSA Edition, 1999

Printed in the United States of America

Library of Congress Cataloging in Publication Data

Hunter, Kathy
    Rett Syndrome Handbook, The

ISBN 0-9669528-0-4

TABLE OF CONTENTS

ACKNOWLEDGEMENTS XI

DEDICATION XIII

FOREWORD BY DUANE ALEXANDER, M.D. XV

CHAPTER 1   I HAVE SO MANY QUESTIONS! 25
WHAT IS RETT SYNDROME? — 25
TESTS TO RULE OUT OTHER STUFF — 26
TYPES OF RETT SYNDROME — 27
DIAGNOSTIC CRITERIA — 28
STAGES OF RETT SYNDROME — 29
WHAT WILL SHE BE ABLE TO DO? — 31
CAUSE OF RETT SYNDROME — 31
DRUG TRIALS — 32
LIFE EXPECTANCY — 34
RESEARCH RESULTS — 35

CHAPTER 2   WELCOME TO RETTLAND 39
NICE PLACE TO VISIT, BUT... — 39
STRETCHING OURSELVES — 40
WHICH WAY TO GO? — 41
GETTING STARTED — 41
YIELD — 41
PACK LIGHTLY — 41
DANGEROUS CURVES AHEAD — 42
CONSULT THE MAP — 42
ASK FOR DIRECTIONS — 42
DRIVE GENTLY — 42
DETOUR AHEAD — 43
ROAD UNDER CONSTRUCTION — 43
REDUCE SPEED — 44
SHARE THE WHEEL — 44
DISCUSS THE ROUTE — 44
SEEK ROADSIDE ASSISTANCE — 45
PLAY ROAD GAMES — 45
GET A TUNE UP — 45
TAKE SHORT TRIPS — 46

DRIVE DEFENSIVELY — 46
PASS WITH CAUTION — 47
SMILE AND WAVE — 47
BEWARE OF BACKSEAT DRIVERS — 48
ENJOY THE TRIP — 48
LOOK IN THE REARVIEW MIRROR — 48
CHECK THE WARRANTY — 49
ARRIVAL: GETTING THERE IN ONE PIECE — 49

CHAPTER 3   FAMILY VOICES 53
ORDINARY LIFE...EXTRAORDINARY LOVE — 53
TALES OF TRIUMPH — 54
THE SAINTS COME MARCHIN' IN — 55
LITTLE THINGS MEAN A LOT — 56
BROTHERS AND SISTERS — 57
HELPFUL HINTS FOR PARENTS — 66
GRANDPARENTS AND RELATIVES — 67
HELPFUL HINTS FOR GRANDPARENTS & RELATIVES — 68

CHAPTER 4   CARE FOR THE CAREGIVER 69
MY COPE RUNNETH OVER — 69
FROM GRIEF TO GOOD GRIEF — 69
RECIPES FOR STRESS — 70
CREATING BALANCE — 71
GETTING BETTER, NOT BITTER — 71
SETTING BOUNDARIES — 71
HELP YOUR CHILD, DON'T HARM YOURSELF — 71
INVEST WISELY — 71
FIND THE RIGHT TIME — 71
STOP, LOOK, LISTEN AND TALK — 72
HAVE FAITH IN YOURSELF — 72
BE GENTLE WITH YOURSELF — 72
HELP IS A HOLLER AWAY — 72
DO SOMETHING DIFFERENT — 72
GET AWAY ALONE — 72
LEARN TEMPORARY INCOMPETENCE — 73
TOSS THE GUILT — 73
KEEP YOUR SENSE OF HUMOR — 73
YOU DON'T HAVE TO BE A HERO — 73
COUNT YOUR BLESSINGS — 73

CHAPTER 5

MAKING SENSE **75**
- INSIDE OUT, UPSIDE DOWN AND BACKWARDS — 75
- SENSORY INTEGRATION — 76
- SIGHT — 77
  - DEPTH PERCEPTION — 78
- SOUND — 79
  - VOLUME CONTROL — 79
- TOUCH — 80
  - PAIN TOLERANCE — 80
- TASTE — 81
- SMELL — 81
- AROUSAL AND CALM — 81

CHAPTER 6

BEHAVIORS **83**
- AIN'T MISBEHAVIN' — 83
- FLUCTUATIONS — 83
- WITHDRAWAL — 84
- CRYING — 84
- TRUST YOUR INSTINCTS — 86
- MOOD SWINGS — 90
- NIGHT TERRORS — 90
- FACIAL MOVEMENTS — 90
- TOOTH GRINDING — 90
- CHALLENGING BEHAVIORS — 91
- SELF-INJURIOUS BEHAVIORS — 92
- MEDICATIONS — 94
- HELPFUL HINTS FOR CHALLENGING BEHAVIORS — 94

CHAPTER 7

THE HANDS **97**
- THE HALLMARK OF RETT SYNDROME — 97
- STEREOTYPED MOVEMENTS — 97
- HAND SORES — 97
- SPLINTS — 99
- INCREASING HAND SKILLS — 100

CHAPTER 8

SEIZURES **103**
- WHAT IS A SEIZURE? — 103
- SEIZURES IN RETT SYNDROME — 104
- ANTICONVULSANT MEDICATIONS — 108
- SPECIAL DIETS — 110
- STATUS EPILEPTICUS — 111

CHAPTER 9   THE NERVOUS SYSTEM 113
CENTRAL NERVOUS SYSTEM — 113
PERIPHERAL NERVOUS SYSTEM — 113
AUTONOMIC NERVOUS SYSTEM — 116
BREATHING — 116
THE HEART — 122
SWALLOWING — 122
SLEEP — 123
CONSTIPATION — 125
CIRCULATION — 133
TEMPERATURE REGULATION — 133
PAIN — 134
DROOLING — 134

CHAPTER 10   DAY-TO-DAY MANAGEMENT 137
DENTAL CARE — 137
TOILET TRAINING — 139
BATHING — 141
LIFTING — 141
SEATING AND POSITIONING — 141
PUBERTY — 143
SEXUAL MATURITY — 147

CHAPTER 11   MOTOR PROBLEMS 149
MOVEMENT — 149
    CRAWLING...SITTING...WALKING
HYPOTONIA AND HYPERTONIA — 151
SPASTICITY — 151
MOTOR APRAXIA — 151
BALANCE — 153
SPATIAL DISORIENTATION — 153
ATAXIA — 154
TRANSITIONAL MOVEMENTS — 154
PROPRIOCEPION — 154
VESTIBULAR STIMULATION —
OSTEOPOROSIS — 155

CHAPTER 12   ORTHOPEDICS 157
THE FEET — 157
THE BACK — 159

THE HIPS — 159
THERAPIES — 162
SURGERY — 163

CHAPTER 13   APPROACHES TO TREATMENT 169
WHAT EVERY THERAPIST SHOULD KNOW — 169
TREATMENT ASPECTS — 170
PHYSICAL THERAPY — 171
OCCUPATIONAL THERAPY — 173
SPEECH THERAPY — 176
MUSIC THERAPY — 177
HYDROTHERAPY — 179
HIPPOTHERAPY — 179
LOVE THERAPY — 180

CHAPTER 14   FRIENDS AND FUN 181

CHAPTER 15   EDUCATION AND LEARNING 187
COMPREHENSION — 187
GOOD DAYS...BAD DAYS — 190
ALL KIDS CAN LEARN — 191
TESTING METHODS — 192
LEVELS OF MOBILITY AND TEACHING — 193
THE TEACHING PROGRAM — 195
SELECTING A SCHOOL —
THE IEP — 197
SERVICES — 199
PLACEMENT OPTIONS — 200
EDUCATION HELPFUL HINTS — 201
A NOTE TO THE TEACHER — 202
INCLUSION: ME, TOO! — 202

CHAPTER 16   COMMUNICATION 209
LOVE SPOKEN HERE — 209
AUGMENTATIVE AND ALTERNATIVE COMMUNICATION — 211
DEVELOPING CHOICE-MAKING SKILLS — 211
USING YES/NO — 212
BODY LANGUAGE — 213
FACILITATED COMMUNICATION — 214
EYE POINTING — 214

Eye Blinks — 215
Communication Boards — 216
Head Pointers — 217
Using Switches — 218
Voice Output Devices — 219
Choosing Vocabulary — 221
Using Words — 221
A Communication Success Story — 223
Computers — 224
Iep Objectives — 225
How To Pay For This Stuff — 226
Communication Catalogs — 227
Laura's Communication Digest — 227
Communication Helpful Hints — 229
The Eye-Gaze Frame — 229
The Eye-Gaze Vest — 230

Chapter 17   Nutrition And Feeding 231

Problems — 231
A Feeding Program — 232
Promoting Weight Gain — 232
Vitamin And Mineral Supplements — 233
Carnitine — 234
Chewing — 236
Swallowing — 236
Gastroesophageal Reflux (Ger) — 238
Importance Of Liquids — 240
Gastrostomy Button — 241

Chapter 18   Genetics 247

Genetic Vs Inherited — 247
X And Y Chromosomes — 247
Dominant And Recessive — 248
X Inactivation — 248
Males With Rett Syndrome — 248
Risk Of Having Another Child — 249
Hope For Research — 250

Chapter 19   When The School Bus Doesn't Come Anymore 253

Future For The Girl With Rett Syndrome — 253
Programs — 254

HOME AWAY FROM HOME — 255
EVALUATING A RESIDENTIAL SETTING — 256
GUARDIANSHIP — 259
SUPPLEMENTAL SECURITY INCOME —
COMMUNITY SUPPORT — 263

CHAPTER 20   LAUGHTER – THE BEST RX 265

CHAPTER 21   PEARLS OF WISDOM 271

CHAPTER 22   WHERE TO GO FOR HELP 277
PROGRAMS — 277
MEDICAID — 277
COMMUNITY RESOURCES — 279
MEDICAL TRAVEL — 280
CHOOSING AND FUNDING EQUIPMENT — 281
INSURANCE — 281
BOOKS AND MAGAZINES — 283
BOOKS FOR CHILDREN — 285
CATALOGS AND DIRECTORIES — 286
PUBLICATIONS, NEWSLETTERS AND PERIODICALS — 287
FREE MATERIALS — 287
ASSOCIATIONS — 288
GOVERNMENT AGENCIES — 289
HOTLINES AND INFORMATION LINES — 290
INTERNET SITES — 291
PARENT TRAINING AND INFORMATION CENTERS — 291
STATE SPECIAL EDUCATION DEPARTMENTS — 293

EPILOGUE 299

COMING TO TERMS

A RETT SYNDROME GLOSSARY 303

INDEX 317

I am the Child

I am the child who cannot talk. You often pity me. I see it in your eyes. You wonder how much I am aware of...I see that as well. I am aware of much...whether you are happy or sad or fearful, patient or impatient, full of love and desire, or if you are just doing your duty by me. I marvel at your frustration, knowing mine to be far greater, for I cannot express myself or my needs as you do. You cannot conceive my isolation, so complete it is at times. I do not gift you with clever conversation, cute remarks to be laughed over and repeated. I do not give you answers to your everyday questions, responses over my well-being, sharing my needs, or comments about the world around me. I do not give you rewards as defined by the world's standards...great strides in development that you can credit yourself. I do not give you understanding as you know it. What I give you is so much more valuable...I give you instead opportunities. Opportunities to discover the depth of your character, not mine; the depth of your love, your commitment, your patience, your abilities; the opportunity to explore your spirit more deeply than you imagined possible. I drive you further than you would ever do on your own, working harder, seeking answers to your many questions, creating questions with no answers. I am the child who cannot talk.

I am the child who cannot walk. The world sometimes seems to pass me by. You see the longing in my eyes to get out of this chair, to run and play like other children. There is much you take for granted. I want the toys on the shelf. I need to go to the bathroom, Oh, I've dropped my fork again. I am dependent on you in these ways. My gift to you is to make you aware of your great fortune, your healthy back and legs, your ability to do for yourself. Sometimes people appear not to notice; I always notice them. I feel not so much envy as desire, desire to stand upright, to put one foot in front of the other, to be independent. I give you awareness. I am the child who cannot walk.

I am the child who is mentally impaired. I don't learn easily, if you judge me by the world's measuring stick. What I do know is infinite joy in the simple things. I am not burdened as you are with strife and conflicts of a more complicated life. My gift to you is to grant you the freedom to enjoy things as a child, to teach you how much your arms around me mean, to give you love. I give you the gift of simplicity. I am the child who is mentally impaired.

I am the disabled child. I am your teacher. If you allow me, I will teach you what is really important in life. I will give you and teach you unconditional love. I gift you with my innocent trust, my dependency upon you. I teach you of respect for others and their uniqueness. I teach you about the sanctity of life. I teach you about how very precious this life is and about not taking things for granted. I teach you about forgetting your own needs and desires and dreams. I teach you giving. Most of all, I teach you hope and faith. I am the disabled child.

Anonymous

ACKNOWLEDGEMENTS

A WARM AND SPECIAL THANK YOU TO

THE AMERICAN LEGION CHILD WELFARE FOUNDATION

 FOR GENEROUSLY
PROVIDING THE
FUNDS TO MAKE
THIS BOOK
POSSIBLE

MIKE BORCHARDT AT CREATIVE MARKETING NETWORK
FOR THE DESIGN, TYPESETTING AND PRINT CO-ORDINATION
AND CHRIS, RICH, HOWARD AND RITA FOR ALL THEIR HELP

CONNIE COUGHLIN FOR HER DANI DOODLES ARTWORK

CLAUDIA WEISZ AND MAUREEN WOODCOCK FOR COPY EDITING

MY FAMILY FOR THEIR CONTINUED PATIENCE AND UNDERSTANDING

FAMILIES EVERYWHERE FOR THEIR CONTRIBUTIONS

AND OUR GIRLS, FOR THEIR GENEROUS GIFTS OF LOVE

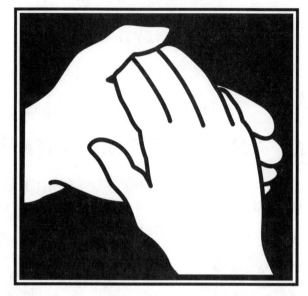

INTERNATIONAL
RETT
SYNDROME
ASSOCIATION

It is most appropriate that this is called a "handbook," for hands are the hallmark of RS. It is with our hands that we touch, we feel, we grasp, we stroke, we carry, we comfort, we give and receive. When we hold hands, we connect, and we double our strength. Our goal is to join our hands together, extending the circle ever wider until the day when others ask, "What is RS?", not because it is unknown, but because it has been defeated.

Kathy Hunter
Founder and President, IRSA

DEDICATION

TO THE MOMS AND DADS IN RETTLAND EVERYWHERE, WHO LIVE ORDINARY LIVES YET MEET EXTRAORDINARY DIFFICULTIES WITH COURAGE AND CONVICTION YEAR AFTER YEAR...

TO THE BROTHERS AND SISTERS WHO HELP CARE FOR THEIR SISTERS WITH COMPASSION AND LOVE EVERY DAY...

TO THE DEDICATED PHYSICIANS, TEACHERS AND THERAPISTS, WHO USE LOVING HANDS TO HELP WHENEVER THEY CAN...

AND TO THE GIRLS AND WOMEN WITH RETT SYNDROME, WHO RISE ABOVE CHALLENGE EVERY MOMENT OF THEIR LIVES, AND THROUGH WHOSE UNCONDITIONAL LOVE WE FIND HOPE AND INSPIRATION.

He & me Creations
DaniDoodles©

Doodles by: Connie
All rights reserved.   Line drawings ©1997-1999 Connie Coughlin

The family is the country of the heart. There is an angel in the family who, by the mysterious influence of grace, of sweetness, and of love, renders the fulfillment of duties less wearisome, sorrows less bitter. The only pure joys unmixed with sadness which it is given to man to taste upon earth are, thanks to this angel, the joys of the family.

Giuseppe Mazzini

FOREWORD

Readers of this handbook should know first of all how fortunate they are that it exists. Whether the parent, relative, family friend, advocate, physician, teacher or care giver, there is much here to help you understand the puzzle that is Rett syndrome and to facilitate your interaction with the girls and women who have this condition.

This handbook could not have been written ten years, or even five years ago. An attempt to compile such a volume would have yielded only a few pages. The fact that it exists now represents two major factors: the amount of knowledge gained from targeted medical research on Rett syndrome, and the labor of love of parents gathering and sharing their observations and insights from years of living with and caring for their daughters.

Compiling this information, organizing it and writing it in the special way she has of telling a story has been the task of Kathy Hunter, founder of the International Rett Syndrome Association (IRSA). This handbook is yet one more contribution from her and this model organization that represents the best in the American tradition of activism and self-help to fill a need and champion a cause. The accomplishments of this organization during its relatively short existence are nothing short of phenomenal, and the quality and value of this handbook further enhance the already outstanding reputation of the IRSA.

In addition to what it actually provides that will benefit all persons with Rett syndrome and their families, there is much more to be hoped for from this handbook. It is hoped that it will be imitated and emulated by other organizations aspiring to provide similar information and guidance for those caring for persons with the condition of their interest. It is hoped that people will be spurred to provide the IRSA with additional information for the next edition that must inevitably follow. And it is hoped most of all that it will be only an interim guide that, while enormously helpful, will be quickly supplanted with new information and be made obsolete as soon as possible as medical research provides discoveries that will develop effective treatments and ultimately, a cure.

Duane Alexander, M.D.
Director, National Institute of Child
Health and Human Development
National Institutes of Health

INTRODUCTION

In 1954, Dr. Andreas Rett of Vienna, Austria, noticed two girls sitting together with their mothers in his waiting room. The girls made the same unusual hand washing movements, and he discovered after examining them one after the other that their clinical and developmental histories were strikingly alike. After consulting with his nurse, he found six girls like them in his practice. He felt certain they had the same disorder. Dr. Rett made a film of the girls and went all over Europe trying to find other cases. He published his discovery in several obscure German language medical journals, which unfortunately never reached the attention of the worldwide medical community. In 1960, Dr. Bengt Hagberg observed several similar girls in his busy practice in Sweden. He put these interesting cases in a special box under his desk, vowing to look further into the nature of this unusual and unknown disorder. In 1978, Dr. Ishikawa and colleagues from Japan described three girls in a brief note which also went unnoticed. Many years went by before Drs. Hagberg and Rett realized they were reporting the same disorder. In a generous gesture, Dr. Hagberg deferred his original descriptive title and submitted the name Rett syndrome for the first English language article on the disorder, published in late 1983. Until his death in 1996, Dr. Andreas Rett worked ceaselessly to unite parents and professionals in a community of care to bring a better life to the girls whose disorder bore his name. Dr. Bengt Hagberg, at the age of 76, continues as a world leader in the field. His energy and enthusiasm in the research arena are only surpassed by his gentle spirit and compassion at the human level of the lives he works to improve.

Shortly before the first paper on RS was published, my daughter, Stacie, who was ten years old at the time, was given the diagnosis of Rett syndrome. She became the 36th known case in the world. She had developed normally until 15 months of age, then began a regression which led to loss of the few words she had developed, aloofness, withdrawal and irritability most of the time. She began mouthing and wringing her hands constantly. Like many of your daughters, Stacie had a number of diagnoses, including autism and Angelman (Happy Puppet syndrome). However, she never fit neatly into any category. She was always one of a kind.

Two important events then happened which changed me forever. To this day, my spirit stays afire to keep the movement alive - just so this will never happen to others. One is the young doctor who told me to just give up, saying that Stacie would never know what it was like to be normal and I had to accept that and try to keep my own life normal. The other was a child psychologist who told me that it was possible I had caused the "autism," according to an outdated theory on autism and "cold" mothers. You can be sure that these were the first two people to receive information about Rett syndrome. Their insensitive comments launched me on a journey to prevent others from ever having to hear the same unfortunate advice.

Since the IRSA began nearly fifteen years ago on my kitchen table, I have longed for this book - a tangible resource to put into the hands of families new to the diagnosis of Rett syndrome. Usually exhausted from the diagnostic process, they ask in so many different ways, "So, where do we go from here? What do we do while we wait for the cure?" As Stacie was growing up, there were no answers for our questions. It was important to direct energy at finding those answers and giving them to families everywhere as they arrived in "Rettland."

Of course, even with a guide, all of our girls are different and there is more than one direction to go. There may be forks in the road, a number of bumpy spots and some rough obstacles. But for all of the low places, there are magnificent high places to round out the view from Rettland. With the experience and suggestions of others who have already been there, we are able to map out our journeys. We can be safe in the knowledge that we are not alone. It may take some time to adjust to the new scenery in Rettland, but once we fully arrive, the vista is spectacular.

Your experience with Rett syndrome will be a lasting journey of love. It may take awhile to realize, but you'll come to know it in time. As you listen gently to the words that come from the hearts of those who have been there, you will recognize how much we share in common.

THE BOOK OF LIFE

It's too bad that the Book of Life doesn't come with a first draft, so you can edit out the bad stuff and double the good stuff. But it doesn't work that way. You didn't choose to have a chapter on RS included in your life. Nevertheless, it is a part of you that you can't edit out – or white out. This is the plot you got. You have to make your own happy ending. Whether your Book of Life is a tragedy, a horror story, a drama or a true life adventure is all up to you.

And you can do that because it's not what happens, but how you choose to look at what happens that makes your life what it is. Attitude is paramount. Every experience can be seen as an obstacle or an opportunity, depending on your outlook. You can choose to remain bitter or you can choose to get better. You can complain because rosebushes have thorns, or you can rejoice because thornbushes have roses. Life is more than what you are handed – it's what you do with what is placed in your hands.

Do you ever wonder why something can happen to two different people with radically different outcomes? I have two lifelong friends who had troubled upbringings. Both were children of alcoholics. Both grew up poor. Both became teachers. One committed suicide, the other built his own successful business. Each had the same difficult childhood, but one was not defeated by it.

You can't choose how you are born or how you die, but you can choose how you live. Your attitude is your most important possession. To say it another way, what happens *to* you is less significant than what happens *within* you.

I often hear from parents when they are at their lowest point, just having learned their daughter's diagnosis. Many times I hear them say, "I don't know what else can happen." I say gently and quietly, "a lot." And the truth is, Rett syndrome is not the worst thing that could happen to them. Someday, down the road a way, after it has had time to settle, they will realize that there are worse things than RS. A lot worse.

WE WITHER

When you hear the words RS for the first time, they bring on bewilderment, confusion, and sadness. Your heart droops, your hopes shrink and your spirit wilts to the ground. You go through the universal stages of grief, no less than if your child had died. You may wonder what you did to make this happen and stay awake at night wondering how to make it go away. And then you have to face a couple of universal truths: 1) you didn't make it happen and 2) it won't go away.

Then, you get angry. Real, deep-down gut wrenching angry. Angry at God, angry at fate, angry at life. But you pull yourself together and keep moving forward, doing what needs to be done. Pretty soon you realize that there are not enough hours in the day to do what you need to do, and guilt enters the picture. There are so many competing emotions it's sometimes hard to separate them out. Many days, its hard to see a patch of blue sky through the heavy clouds, and there seems to be no silver lining, much less one you can see. Over each door to the Rett family home could hang a sign with the the Chinese Proverb: *"No one can say of this house, there is no trouble here."*

RS is hard. It hurts. It bewilders. It confounds. It defies reason. It shouldn't be this way. You would gladly trade a king's riches to take away RS. It will take some time before you realize that, just as Helen Keller said, "When one door of happiness closes, another opens; but often we look so long at the closed door that we do not see the one which has been opened for us."

Many times, I've thought to myself that I'd rather be a rotten person than have to deal with all this growth and greater wisdom stuff that comes from the suffering. But I can't change what RS has done to my daughter. I can only change what it does to me. If I don't choose the growth and greater wisdom stuff, I'm guaranteed to wither.

The playwright Henry Miller wrote, "Life has no other discipline to impose, if we would but realize it, than to accept life unquestioningly. Everything we shut our eyes to, everything we run away from, everything we deny, denigrate or despise, serves to defeat us in the end. What seems nasty, painful, evil, can become a source of beauty, joy and strength, if faced with an open mind. Every moment is a golden one for him who has the vision to recognize it as such." Those golden moments come in time, when we learn to thank God, thank fate and thank life. We learn that the physics of happiness do not require perfection and performance, only acceptance and love. This awareness does not come easily. We don't wake up a few days after the diagnosis and have a revelation. We meet hurt after hurt, challenge after challenge and crisis after crisis. Then we are able to put a real name on hurt, on challenge, on crisis. We learn that the big things in life really are, after all, the little things.

Each of us has to learn to change what we can, accept what we can't and go on. Those of us who have been crushed can attest to this: we grow stronger in the broken places. We gain so many valuable insights and gather so much courage. As one mother told me, "I am no longer afraid of *anything*." At the same time, we learn the true meaning of unconditional love and the see the enormous power of the powerless.

Don't you find it amusing what other people think is a problem? Makes me chuckle sometimes. I just smile and remember my own philosophy about problems... "if little kids don't die from it, it ain't a problem." When I've been in line a long time and have exercised incredible patience with delays or bumbled transactions, the clerk often thanks me for my composure while others are flying off the handle around me. I usually reply, "Well you know, I learned patience in the Hard School. I have a child with multiple handicaps. She can't do anything for herself. I've had a lot of practice. And you know what? This is small stuff. In fact, if this is the worst thing that happens to me today, I'll still be way ahead." It usually brings a surprising calm to others who take a moment to reconsider.

People have always amazed me when they comment about my patience with Stacie. I find it remarkable to begin with, because Stacie is the one with patience. She has to wait to be fed when I think she is hungry, put to bed when I think she is tired. She has to put up with people who either act like she isn't there or treat her like she's an infant. People often remark that "they couldn't do it." I usually smile and say, "Well, what *would* you do?" Of course, love does not diminish with the diagnosis. It grows.

WE GROW

We don't grow overnight. We grow in little spurts. We don't learn it all in books. Experience is the best teacher. When my first child was born, I looked at him and said, "I've never been a mother before. I don't know what to do." The doctor smiled and said, "You'll be fine. He's never been a baby before, either."

The story I am about to tell is true. While I was pregnant with Stacie 25 years ago, I took a college course called Psychology of the Exceptional Child. For some reason, one phrase jumped out from the course textbook with the chilling words, "autism is the most severely debilitating disorder of childhood." I shuddered as I thought about what a wrenching experience it must be to have such a child. Then, with my vast experience as mother of two healthy boys and my newly found education from this informative course, I decided to write my final paper on "How to Counsel Parents of Mentally Retarded Children." I read all the right books, brought together the needed resources, and wrote the paper. I figured I must have said all the right things – I got an "A" on the paper. I was excused from the final exam because I was giving birth, but my good grades earned me an "A" in the class anyway. I thought I knew everything there was to know.

About ten years later, I was cleaning out the basement when I came upon a box of old books and papers. There it was staring up at me: "How to Counsel Parents of Mentally Retarded Children." My mouth dropped open as I stared down at the "A" paper. I started to read what I had written, and then with sudden rage, I tore it into a thousand pieces and threw it in the trash. Bitter tears flooded my face as I realized how prophetic that I would choose this subject so long before, and how preposterous that I could even begin to pretend to know what to say before I had lived through it.

I think this is why as parents, our souls are so connected. Others can think about it, study it, teach about it and write about it, but they don't live it. So they don't really know it. We are a fraternity, a sorority, blood brothers and sisters, unrelated but, so very related.

We come from many roads away and much distance apart, speaking any number of dialects and observing different customs but, we are one. According to the old Swedish proverb: "Shared joy is double joy, and shared sorrow is half sorrow." That's what joins our hearts. It hurts me to know that your child also has RS, but it helps me to know that we can get through it together.

We grow from this experience. Like the trees, we learn to bend with the wind before the force breaks us. And like some of the most beautiful flowers in the garden that bloom even more brilliantly after their blossoms are pinched off, we grow more from living with adversity than when everything is "perfect." When we think we want it all, we should remember the ancient Chinese curse: "May your every wish be granted."

The lucky ones learn to count their blessings instead of their burdens. Have you ever wondered what it would be like to have a child with RS and live in a country where there was little medical care and no special education? No family to help out? It's hard to imagine how some people survive without some life-saving items we all take for granted, like disposable diapers, washing machines, velcro, VCR's, McDonald's French fries, walkman, PL94-142 and Barney. We can't count our burdens without remembering our blessings.

BLOOM WHERE YOU ARE PLANTED

No matter what the circumstances, we can choose to be alive, to thrive and to survive. Choose to grow, and bloom where you are planted. Throughout it all, it is important to always keep your sense of humor. Laughter gets the blood bubbling, swells the chest, jolts the nerves, sweeps the cobwebs from the brain, and cleans out the whole system. Laughter is physical therapy for the soul. You've come a long way when you can laugh at some of life's predicaments.

It's good that we can laugh. And it's healthy for us to cry now and then. Above all, it is important to hope.

Do you know what hope is?
It's magic and it's free
It's not in a prescription
It's not in an IV

It punctuates our laughter
It sparkles in our tears
It simmers under sorrows
And dissipates our fears

Do you know what hope is?
It's reaching past today
It's dreaming of tomorrow
It's trying a new way

It's pushing past impossible
It's pounding on the door
It's questioning the Answers
It's always seeking more

It's rumors of a breakthrough
It's whispers of a cure
A rollercoaster ride
Of remedies unsure

Do you know what Hope is?
It's candy for the soul
It's perfume for the spirit
To share it, makes you whole

Unknown

I'd like to share my hope with you. I hope to soon be out of work. I hope to make RS something no one ever heard of, not because it is unknown, but because it is conquered. I hope the next book I write will be titled, "RS: The Cure."

My hopes are very high. Once I didn't even have ordinary hope, and now I have "high, apple pie in the sky" hope. Hope is faith, reliance and trust. We have every reason to be hopeful. We are so close to finding answers. It hasn't been easy. We've seen the misfortune of RS strike more than once in a family, but have seen the fortunate turnaround of families willing to overlook their own tragedy to participate vigorously in research. We have seen the sadness of girls lost to early death, yet have had our hearts warmed by parents who consented to autopsy so that the rest of us could be spared the same anguish. We've had bake sales, craft sales, car washes, races, dances, dinners, auctions and concerts for the cause. It all adds up to hope. We are closer than we have ever been to solving the puzzle of RS. Just when you are about to give up or lose hope, remember that the world is round—the end is often the beginning. We are going to come full circle. It's going to happen. We are joined hand in hand, by Carl Sandburg's promise, "where there is life, there is hope."

BELIEVE IN YOURSELF: BELIEVE IN HER

The insights we gain are invaluable. While some may see our daughters as powerless, we know of the enormous power she has to change us. She may not walk, yet she helps us walk taller. As she struggles to move, she moves many hearts. She may need to be fed, yet she feeds our spirits. We seek to understand her, yet in so doing, we begin to understand far more. She may not speak to us in words, but she speaks to us in so many ways in the silent language of love.

Your daughter brings many blessings. She may never talk, but she will never talk back. She may never run, but she will never run away from home. She may need drugs to sustain life, but she will never take drugs to escape life. She may never use her hands for skills, but she will not use those hands for violence or evil.

Look into her eyes and you can't help but have hope. She lives through her eyes. She loves through her eyes. As Dr. Alan Percy says, "The eyes have it." Her eyes, windows to the soul, take us to cherished places within her heart. Her eyes do more than see us – they touch us. Every human emotion is whispered, sung, shouted by her dancing, sparkling eyes.

While there may be confusion in her head, make no mistake. There is a lot of understanding in her head. While she may have many obstacles to learning, she can learn many things. Just because she can't show it doesn't mean she doesn't know it. It's in there. She's in there. Keep looking. You'll see.

Kathy Hunter
Founder and President, IRSA

There is Hope! As the parent of a 22 year old child with Rett syndrome, I know there is hope. I, too, worried about my child's future, and wondered how I would ever deal with life as she grew older. Often I grieved for the things that I had dreamed of for her that would never happen – acceptance by society, her prom, her graduation, her contribution to society, and many other hopes and dreams that mothers have for their children. Yes, I grieved as I spent hours at her bedside when she was sick, or as I listened to her screams, or as I walked the floor at night with her. But day by day, and often, hour by hour, I survived. And today I am pleased to inform you that my daughter has grown to be a lovely young lady who has fulfilled many of the hopes and dreams that I had for her.

I dreamed of my daughter having a wonderful personality, adored by people, and when I was really hoping big, I wanted her as a friend with whom I could share my deepest thoughts. My hopes and dreams have been fulfilled. My daughter is known and loved by many people. Whether we are attending church or going to the local McDonald's, our daughter has many friends who go out of their way to talk to her.

At first I was afraid when my daughter, Heidi, was placed in the high school because I feared the comments of the "normal" students. But much to my surprise, the teens accepted her, talking to her and even volunteering to help with her special needs. And though she may not be able to respond with words, her beautiful smile and sparkling eyes communicate more clearly than words ever could. As a result, Heidi has made many friends.

I have found a special friend in my daughter. She never tells secrets, she never complains, nor does she ever condemn me, but listens patiently as I tell her about my life. I wanted to see my child do the things that other students do, such as go to the prom and graduate. My daughter went to her prom and she was beautiful. Heidi had a wonderful time, listening to the music and having people stop by our table to talk to us. Then when we went to pay for our prom pictures, we found they had already been paid for by an anonymous friend.

And the graduation just got better! According to the law where we live, the handicapped students graduate along with the regular students. So in May of 1997, my daughter graduated from high school. That night the audience was told not to applaud until all students had received their diplomas. Sporadic applause occurred anyway. However, when my daughter, physically supported, approached the podium, the crowd roared. In fact, she got a standing ovation that night. And although I had not sent out graduation announcements, family and friends gave her a surprise party and she was showered with gifts.

I wanted to see my child make a contribution to society. I thought this could never happen, because, after all, she is handicapped. Then a few months after graduation, as I stood in a local shop chatting with two individuals that I greatly admire, I realized otherwise. One of the individuals was a friend of mine who has written a number of books while the other was an artist who travels nationwide teaching her skills. As the two talked, one commented that Heidi had contributed so much to society by being a participant in the research at Johns Hopkins Hospital. In fact, she said that Heidi had probably made more a contribution than any of the three of us. It was at this point that I realized that my child had contributed a great deal to society by participating in research.

So to those parents who question what lies ahead, I would have to say that it depends on you. It depends on your attitude toward your special daughter and whether or not you allow her to participate in family, church, and the community. Today, my 22 year old daughter has none of the bad behaviors of her youth nor is she as sick as she used to be. She attends a special school 3 days a week, and regularly attends church. She is a very beautiful, well-behaved young lady who has the touched the lives of many. I am very proud to have her as my daughter.

Joyce Hill

I Have So Many Questions...

What is Rett syndrome?

Rett Syndrome (RS) is a unique developmental disorder which begins in early infancy, seen almost always in girls. It is found in a variety of racial and ethnic groups throughout the world.

She seemed to develop so normally. What happened?

The cause is not yet known for sure, but it is believed that RS results from a chain of events beginning with a genetic mutation, or change in the child's genetic material. Mutations occur naturally in everyone all the time and most do not cause problems, but a specific genetic change, yet unidentified, leads to the condition we call RS. This mutation results in the shortage or absence of some specific "factor" needed for normal development of selected regions of the brain responsible for sensory, emotional, motor and autonomic function. Development appears to be normal in early infancy until the factor is needed for further brain development. Without this factor, selected regions of the brain remain developmentally immature. This explains why the child appears to be developing normally in the first months of life.

If it is a mutation, does this mean I may have another child with RS?

While there is strong evidence of a genetic basis, the chance of having more than one child with RS is very small, less than one percent. This means that 99% of the time the mutation is sporadic, just occurs on its own and is not repeated in a family.

At what age does Rett syndrome begin?

The age when RS begins and the severity of different symptoms may vary. The child with RS is usually born healthy and shows an early period of apparently normal or near normal development until 6-18 months of life, when there is a slowing down or stagnation of skills. A period of regression then follows when she loses communication skills and purposeful use of her hands. Soon, stereotyped hand movements, gait disturbances, and slowing of the normal rate of head growth become apparent. Other problems may include seizures and disorganized breathing patterns which occur when she is awake. There may be a period of isolation or withdrawal when she is irritable and cries inconsolably. Over time, motor problems may increase, while other symptoms may decrease or improve.

After McKenna was born, I knew I was finally being rewarded for all of the pain I had been through. Not only was she incredibly beautiful, but healthy too! All ten fingers and toes! When she started saying "mama" and "dada" at a mere five months old, I was ready to enroll her in a mensa pre-school. She was a very passive baby. She made eye contact and smiled constantly, but never tried to pull up or play with her baby gym. She took forever to roll over and never cried. I worried and my friends told me I was overreacting. I had her evaluated at 13 months and she started P.T. and speech. At 15 months she still was not bearing weight, but crossed and uncrossed her fingers constantly. She stopped babbling and stopped making eye contact. She "army crawled" for a little while during the summer and then stopped. She also stopped looking at her books, which was her absolute favorite thing to do, and started hitting herself in the head. She underwent every test known to man. Most came back normal. Her EEG was very mildly abnormal. In time, her babbling came back as well as her eye contact.

What kind of handicaps will she have?

Apraxia (dyspraxia), the inability to program the body to perform motor movements, is the most fundamental and severely handicapping aspect of RS. It can interfere with every body movement, including eye gaze and speech, making it difficult for the girl with RS to do what she wants to do. Due to this apraxia and her inability to speak, it is very difficult to make an accurate assessment of her intelligence. Most traditional testing methods require her to use her hands and/or speech, which may be impossible for the girl with RS. Her mobility may be delayed and she may have difficulty crawling or walking.

Since she loses skills, is RS degenerative?

Most researchers now agree that RS is a developmental disorder and not a degenerative disorder with continuous downward progression as once thought. Barring illness or complications, survival into adulthood is expected.

How often does RS occur?

RS is most often misdiagnosed as autism, cerebral palsy or non-specific developmental delay. While many health professionals may not be familiar with RS, it is a relatively frequent cause of delayed development in girls. The prevalence rate in various countries is from 1:10,000 to 1:23,000 live female births, making it three times more common in females than phenylketonuria (PKU), a congenital error of metabolism that is tested for in every newborn.

How is Rett syndrome diagnosed?

At this time there is no scientific test that will prove Rett syndrome, but we hope that one will soon be available. The diagnosis is made after excluding other disorders which have "biological markers." Your daughter's doctor will probably order one or more of the following tests to rule out the possibility of a known neurometabolic or neurodegenerative disorder:

Blood: blood count, protein electrophoresis, electrolytes, creatinine, urea, liver enzymes, copper ion, ceruloplasmin, plasma lactate and ammonium ion, proclatin, TSH, thyroid hormones, chromosomes, DNA and DHPR
Urine: mucopolysaccharides, oligosaccharides, organic acids, amino acids, orotic acid, monoamine metabolites
Cerebrospinal Fluid (CSF): immunoelectrophoresis, monoamine metabolites, endorphins, serotonin
Skin: Chromosomes (fibroblast cultivation), electron microscopy
X-Ray: CT scan of brain
Neurophysiological tests: EEG, evoked responses, EMG, NCV
Eyes: ERG, VER
Genetic and Genealogy: Study of family history

What disorders must be ruled out?

Other possible conditions which could look like RS must be ruled out. They include Angelman syndrome (Happy Puppet Syndrome) and Prader-Willi syndrome, metabolic disorders such as OCT deficiency, disorders of organic acids and amino acids; storage diseases, mitochondrial disorders, and Batten Disease. While there are no scientific tests for them, autism and cerebral palsy are often misdiagnosed.

How does RS differ from autism?

While RS occurs primarily in girls, autism occurs much more frequently in boys. In both conditions, there is loss of speech and emotional contact. However, symptoms seen in RS and not in autism include deceleration of the rate of head growth and loss of purposeful hand skills and mobility. While hand "flapping" is seen frequently in autism as visual stimulation, the wider range of compulsive purposeless hand stereotypes common to RS are not seen in autism. The girl with RS almost always prefers people to objects, but the opposite is seen in autism. Unlike those with autism, the RS girl often enjoys affection. While girls with RS often have autistic tendencies at an early age, these features decrease over time.

How is the RS diagnosis made?

Once other disorders have been ruled out, Rett syndrome can be considered. The diagnosis of RS becomes a clinical one, based on signs and symptoms that you can observe. Your child's doctor will look carefully at her early growth and development and will evaluate her medical history and physical and neurological status. In making the diagnosis, specialists rely on a RS Diagnostic Criteria Worksheet, which has been developed by the world's foremost authorities in RS. Your daughter may fall into one of three categories:

Classic RS: those who meet the diagnostic criteria guidelines
Provisional RS: age 1-3, with some clinical evidence of RS, but not enough to meet the diagnostic criteria
Atypical RS: those who do not meet all of the diagnostic criteria for classical RS. The diagnosis of typical RS must include at least three of the primary criteria and five of the supportive criteria. Atypical cases account for about 15 percent of the total of diagnosed cases.

Types of atypical RS include:

Congenital Onset RS: developmental delay is noticed shortly after birth and there is no early normal development; or seizures begin before the regression period
Late Onset RS: signs are delayed beyond the typical 18 month onset, in some cases to 3 or 4 years
Preserved Speech and Hand Skills RS: milder, incomplete symptoms are seen, with age of onset at 3 to 4 years
Male RS: boys with RS may not conform to the same symptoms seen in girls. Researchers are now investigating the possibility that boys with RS may have a more debilitating condition than girls, and thus are not yet recognized.

> Amy is atypical. She was 5 years old before she was diagnosed as mentally retarded/autistic. I just thought that she was quiet, petite, and gentle in her mannerisms. She did not hold a rattle or grab for things like my first child did. She did not "play" with things. She just did things when she was ready. She could count to 10 when she was three. She could snap her fingers. She could ride a tricycle. She could punch her older brother. She did not talk a lot but had an age appropriate vocabulary. She was 4 and in preschool when we asked about her development again. That is the age when most kids learn shapes, colors, etc. Amy couldn't. So, you might say she leveled off at about age 5 and a very slow hand wringing and regression began.

What are the diagnostic criteria for Rett syndrome? How can I be sure my daughter has it?

Most parents know their daughters better than anyone. Often, they know that Rett syndrome fits from the first description. Physicians use the following Diagnostic Criteria Guidelines as a helpful instrument in establishing the diagnosis.

DIAGNOSTIC CRITERIA

All of the following criteria are necessary for the diagnosis of RS:

- Period of apparently normal development until between 6-18 months.
- Normal head circumference at birth followed by slowing of the rate of head growth with age (3 months to 4 years).
- Severely impaired expressive language and loss of purposeful hand skills, which combine to make assessment of receptive language and intelligence difficult.
- Repetitive hand movements including one or more of the following: washing, wringing, clapping, tapping, mouthing and finger manipulation, which can become almost constant while awake.
- Shakiness of the torso, which may also involve the limbs, particularly when she is upset.
- If able to walk, unsteady, wide-based, stiff-legged gait and toe-walking.

SUPPORTIVE CRITERIA

The following symptoms are not required for the diagnosis of RS, but may also be seen. These features may not be observed in the young girl, but may develop with age. By themselves, the supportive criteria do not establish the diagnosis of Rett syndrome. A child with all of the supportive criteria and none of the diagnostic criteria does not have Rett syndrome.

- Breathing dysfunctions which include breath holding (apnea), hyperventilation and air swallowing, which may result in abdominal bloating and distention.
- EEG abnormalities — slowing of normal electrical patterns, the appearance of epileptiform (i.e., not normal) patterns and loss of normal sleep characteristics.
- Seizures.
- Muscle rigidity/spasticity/joint contractures which increase with age.
- Scoliosis (curvature of the spine).
- Teeth grinding (bruxism).
- Small feet (in relationship to stature).
- Growth retardation.
- Decreased body fat and muscle mass (but tendency toward obesity in some adults).
- Abnormal sleep patterns and irritability or agitation.
- Chewing and/or swallowing difficulties.
- Poor circulation of the lower extremities, cold and bluish-red feet and legs.
- Decreased mobility with age.
- Constipation.

It is important to remember that all girls with Rett syndrome do not display all of these symptoms, and individual symptoms may vary in severity. A neurologist or developmental pediatrician should be consulted to confirm the clinical diagnosis.

EXCLUSION CRITERIA

Any one of the following criteria rules out the diagnosis of Rett syndrome

- Enlargement of body organs or other signs of storage disease.
- Vision loss due to retinal disorder or optic atrophy.
- Microcephaly at birth.
- Existence of identifiable metabolic disorder or other inherited degenerative disorder.
- Acquired neurological disorder resulting from severe infection or head trauma.
- Evidence of growth retardation in utero.
- Evidence of brain damage acquired after birth.

I know that Rett syndrome is supposed to be obvious by 18 months to 2 years, but many times we don't know what to look for. Our daughter was different from birth, but we thought she was just quiet and sweet. At 18 months we took her to the pediatrician and he said it was my parenting. Shut me up for awhile. We went on thinking Amy just danced to the tune of the different drummer. At age 4, we couldn't deny any longer that we had a situation that was different. By then we had a younger daughter who was 2 and was already light-years beyond Amy in comprehension and natural abilities. When she was 19, we placed Amy's extensive photo album in front of the researchers. They pointed out signs of RS as early as 3 months. Again all through the photos were the signs we didn't know to look for.

Is Rett syndrome seen predominantly in one race?

No. A statewide population study in Texas has revealed that the incidence of RS in the African-American and Hispanic population in the United States is comparable to that in Caucasian Americans.

What are the stages of Rett syndrome and what do they mean?

Stage 1 begins somewhere between 6-18 months, and is often overlooked, because the symptoms of RS are just beginning and are somewhat vague. Parents and physicians may not notice the subtle slowing of development at first. The infant may have progressed and gained new skills, but at a slower rate or later date than expected. She may have a "floppy" body and a poor suck. Her development then slows down and seems to stagnate. This stage usually lasts a few months, but can last more than a year. The infant may show less eye contact and have reduced interest in toys. She is often described as a "good" baby, calm and quiet. There may be delays in some gross motor milestones, such as sitting, crawling or pulling to stand. Gradually, her lack of attention is noticed and she may have non-specific hand-waving. The rate of her head growth may be slowed, but might not be significant enough to cause notice.

The only difference between Megan and her brother is the way they played. The world acted on Meg, while Connor acted on the world. It's a hard distinction to make, but generally Meg accepted that things happened and didn't try to figure them out.

Stage 2 begins from 1 to 4 years and usually lasts from weeks to months. A general developmental decline is seen with regression and loss of acquired skills. This stage can have a rapid onset or it can be more gradual as acquired finger and hand skills and spoken language are lost. Stereotyped hand movements begin and often include hand-to-mouth movements and clapping first. Movements which follow are most often midline hand wringing or hand washing. These hand movements persist while the girl is awake but disappear during sleep. Hands are sometimes clasped behind the back or held at the sides in a specific pose, with random touching, grasping and releasing. Breathing irregularities may be noticed, and may include episodes of breath holding and hyperventilation (over breathing) associated with vacant spells. Puffing, air expulsion or spitting may precede these. However, breathing is normal during sleep. Some girls appear autistic-like with loss of social interaction and  communication. A lack of imitative or imaginative play is seen. General irritability and sleep irregularity may be seen, and some girls awaken with inappropriate laughing or crying spells. Periods of shakiness may be obvious, especially when she is excited. Gait patterns are unsteady with movements that are uncoordinated and jerky. Initiating motor movements can be difficult. Tooth grinding is common. Further slowing of head growth is usually noticed from 3 months to 4 years, when the girl's head circumference falls on a percentile chart when compared to other children at the same age.

Meg walked at 12 months, the exact same age as her younger brother. Her regression was somewhat slow, first cognitive and then the physical regression happened rather quickly. She was a typically developing child until 15-18 months. She said 15 words or so, including "mama" and "dada." I felt something was wrong, yet I couldn't articulate it. She just couldn't seem to imitate like my friend's child and try as I might, she couldn't get the concept of shape sorting. Gross and fine motor skills were normal or somewhat advanced. By 18 months, she had lost most words and learned one new one, "bubbles." Doctors still didn't think anything was wrong. I believe the cognitive regression happened from 18 months to 30 months. She became autistic-like in that period and was obsessed with coloring. We had crayon marks everywhere. Right around 32-36 months, she started to lose hand use and develop finger rolling. This is when she developed increased muscle tone and lost the ability to squat. She lost all hand use and her gait became very stiff and jerky. She lost the ability to climb stairs, but has since regained them. She developed seizures at 4 years.

Stage 3 usually begins from 2-10 years following the rapid destructive period, and can last for many years. Regression is now over, and she reaches a stable period. Apraxia, motor problems, scoliosis and seizures may be more prominent. However, improvement is seen in behavior with less irritability and crying, less autistic features and good eye contact. She shows more interest in her surroundings, and her alertness, attention span and communication skills improve. Many girls with RS remain in Stage 3 for most or all of their lifetime.

Ashley is in Stage 3. She does not have any eating disorders or serious vascular problems. I am extremely pleased with where Ashley is today. She has continued to advance, however slowly, in areas of communication, alertness, and socially. She is still able to walk, assists some in dressing by raising her arms and pushing sleeves on, and assists in eating and drinking. She can take the utensil with food on it and put it in her mouth, eat and hand back the utensil. She assists in holding a glass and still uses the toilet appropriately. She just seems more overall "with it."

Stage 4, which usually begins after age 10, is characterized by reduced mobility. **Stage 4-A** is used to describe those who once walked and stopped. **Stage 4-B** describes those who were never able to walk. In this stage, muscle weakness, rigidity, spasticity and scoliosis are prominent features which contribute to loss of movement skills. Feet are often swollen, cold and bluish. However, there is no further decline in cognition, communication or hand skills. Emotional contact and eye gaze are improved. Hand movements may decrease in frequency and intensity. Puberty begins at the expected age in most girls. In general, women with RS appear younger than their actual age.

Heather is 22. Her eye contact has increased over the years; it was very sparse in early years, but now she looks at people and especially at men (bats her lashes and flirts shamelessly), which she never did when she was younger. She also hugs people now, which she never did when she was young. She's very affectionate, but it's always on her terms and when she wants to do it. If you infringe on her space unwanted, she will shove you away with a hand or fend you off with a foot. She is particularly possessive about the sofa and will end up nudging people off, one by one, until she has most of it cleared for her personal use, and without most of us realizing it until it's done! She is very savvy about motor planning and I wonder how she does it because clearly her peripheral vision is better than her "straight-on" sight. We delight at every new gain, no matter how minuscule it seems. The affection was something unexpected (developed only in the past two or three years) and she just beams when she hugs us.

Do all girls move through the stages of Rett syndrome similarly?

No. The stages of Rett syndrome are simply provided to help understand the natural history of the disorder. The course of RS is predetermined, and varies from one child to another, including the age when RS begins and the speed and severity of symptoms. Therefore, two girls of the same age can appear quite different.

> Katie did not really regress, she just stopped growing and stagnation set in for about two years. She seemed liked an 18 month old baby, but her eyes told me she understood.

Can the severity be predicted?

Just as in any other disorder, there can be a wide range of disability ranging from mild to severe. It is difficult to predict the intensity of symptoms in any individual child. Many girls begin walking within the normal range, while others show significant delay or inability to walk independently. Some begin walking and lose this skill, while others continue to walk throughout life. Still others do not walk until late childhood or adolescence. The same range holds true for using her hands and other skills she may acquire.

> It is very exciting to me in reading about all the progress being reported in Rett girls of all ages. When I first realized Leah had Rett syndrome, when she was about 2, I felt I was being dealt a double whammy. First all the negatives that she already had, but then also the prospect that she would get worse. She is now 5 and all I have seen is improvements, each of them small steps on a "normal" scale, but large for us.

What will she be able to do?

Although the girl with RS will need help for most activities of daily living, she can learn some independent skills. Most girls can learn to use the toilet and many can learn to feed themselves by hand or with utensils with some assistance. Some girls can learn to use augmentative devices to communicate. Despite their difficulties, girls and women with RS can continue to learn and enjoy family and friends well into middle age and beyond. They experience a full range of emotions and show their engaging personalities as they take part in social, educational and recreational activities at home and in the community.

> I never dreamed that dealing with Rett was going to be so hard and at the same time I can't imagine life without Amelia. I once asked my husband "What is Amelia capable of? I don't know anymore," and Don replied, "love." I never knew what unconditional love was until Rett Syndrome came through our door.

What causes RS?

It is now thought that RS is a genetic disorder of developmental arrest or failure of brain maturation. This is thought to occur when subsets of neurons and their connections (synapses) are disrupted during a very dynamic phase of brain development. This deviation occurs in the first few months of life, when synapses are normally being overproduced, only to be "pruned" later on to the normal adult number. In RS, these synapses appear to be under produced, or possibly over pruned. Researchers are looking carefully at chromosomes and candidate genes whose disturbance could be responsible for faulty maturation of the heart, central nervous system and gastrointestinal tract, which all are affected in RS and could be the result of this disruption.

What are researchers looking for?

Some experts feel that RS may have more than one cause, possibly two or three genetic sites involving two or three biochemical errors. This would account for the varying levels of ability seen in girls with RS, who may have different combinations of error. As an example, there are three types of Down syndrome, and autism is thought to represent at least ten different diseases. Other experts feel that RS is a single gene disorder. With this view, the wide range of severity of symptoms is explained by the differences in X-inactivation patterns in each child, which allows them to "turn off" the Rett gene in some of their cells. (More in Genetics)

What drugs have been tried?

L-Dopa is a synthetic form of dopamine. It has been found to improve rigidity during the motor deterioration stage (4), but otherwise failed to provide improvement on a consistent basis.

Naltrexone (Revia®) is an opiate antagonist, used to alleviate the drug "high" in addicts. It was tried in RS due to the unusually high level of naturally-occurring opium-like brain chemicals called endorphins in the spinal fluid of girls with RS, and their diminished response to pain. The study was limited to the dose of 1 mg/kg/day and did not show dramatic results. However, independent studies have shown that use of naltrexone in higher or lower doses may be beneficial in controlling irregular breathing and seizures, and in alleviating screaming spells. This may be due to the drug's sedative effects. One negative aspect of the study was that performance on the Bayley Scales of Infant Development was significantly worse during the administration of the drug compared to placebo, also possibly due to its sedative effect. Another negative side effect is loss of appetite.

> My daughter has been on Naltrexone and has shown much improvement. She has no more breathing abnormalities and her sweet little personality is back, plus she once again sleeps through the night.

Bromocriptine (Parlodel®) is a drug which improves the functioning of the dopamine system in the brain. One drug trial showed initial improvements in communication, decreased agitation and reduced hand movements in the first phase; however, when the drug was stopped symptoms reappeared, and the reintroduction of the drug did not bring back the initial improvements. The drug was found to be most effective in those girls who had milder symptoms.

> My daughter did nothing but sleep. She seemed "unresponsive" to the world. When she was put on Bromocriptine, she awakened so that others could see she really was responding to her world. We went through a period following her pneumonia/septicemia when her neurologist decided to switch to Permax®- and I celebrate the decision. Mary has remained ambulatory and her affect is very evident. I feel that since we have had these medications, Mary's world has opened so that others recognize her intelligence. She uses the IntroTalker, has shown artistic skills, demanded adult books to read and is starting piano lessons — which she got so excited about when I told her that she almost threw away her french fries.

Tyrosine (dopamine and noradrenalin) and **Tryptophan (serotonin)** are amino acids, used to boost neurotransmitter levels. The study indicated no differences in clinical performance or EEG patterns.

L-Carnitine is a derivative of the essential amino acid lysine, and is often found to be deficient in those who take anticonvulsants. A single case report of one child indicated improvements in language and awareness. However, the child reported was an atypical case of RS, and these results have not been replicated. In another study of 35 girls, carnitine supplements (100 mg/kg/day) did not lead to any major neurological improvements in the group as a whole. However, approximately 75% of the families involved in the study reported subtle, but important improvements to their quality of life while on the drug, including increased alertness, increased mobility, less daytime sleeping, increased energy, and improvement in constipation. Some parents reported their daughter saying a word for the first time in a number of years. L-carnitine has been found beneficial in a large group of girls with RS to increase muscle mass. A beneficial side effect is loose stools. Studies in a large cross-section of girls with RS are currently underway.

Carnitine helped Amanda with fatigue and strength, although she could already stand and walk, but not very well. It took about 2 to 3 months for the strength to build. The fatigue got better right away.

My 32 year old daughter has been taking L-carnitine for more than two years now, and we wouldn't be without it. It enables her to stay awake and alert longer. She can sit through a two hour class awake and alert most times, although there are times when she zzzz's off for awhile! Also she is basically awake in the afternoons now, whereas before she often slept for two or three hours. And on some occasions has actually had enough energy to communicate a little in the afternoon, a feat that was previously only achievable in the morning.

Danielle started taking only two one hour naps instead of sleeping all day. She was more interested in her environment and even in food. Her O.T. and P.T. asked us what we were doing different because Danielle was now trying to do stuff with assistance. She started holding her bottle and over a three month period of time, started standing with assistance. Danielle is again making progress in developing new skills. Her vocalizations have increased, she now stands holding onto the couch, and she holds herself up straighter when sitting. Also, she reaches out to be picked up and is starting to use her hand to activate toys. Best of all, she has gone from the 2nd percentile in weight to the 30th percentile in weight over the past 9 months, is happy all of the time, and is better able to fight off infections. Also, the carnitine seems to have decreased her problems with constipation. Whether all of Danielle's improvements are due to carnitine or the stage of RS I don't know but I would not consider taking her off of the medication at this time.

Two weeks after she started carnitine she became a different person. She now has great eye contact, started to crawl much more, follows us from room to room, smiles and reacts to others and her environment.

Rae Anne had a severe carnitine deficiency. She was taken off the Depakote® and put on Klonopin® and Carnitor® liquid. Rae Anne has been seizure free since. It was suggested that Rae's body may not be producing carnitine naturally as it should so the metabolic testing began. Nothing metabolic was found to be wrong, which suggests it was the Depakote® that caused the problem. Rae Anne responds well to Carnitor®. She likes the taste, and she's eating huge amounts of food. She has gained 10 pounds since last summer. Her hair is healthy and shiny and she's been seizure free!

Danielle has been on carnitine for the past year. The improvements we have seen in her during that time are increased attention span, decreased day time sleeping, more mobility and acquisition of new skills, increased muscle tone, more vocalizations, weight gain, decreased problems with constipation, and fewer seizures.

After 3 months, she is improving incredibly. Everyone who sees her comments on how good she looks and how active she is. She used to lay on her stomach or back all day. She could roll, but never did this to get anywhere. Now she is up on hands and knees rocking, or crawling on elbows or chin and knees. She goes from lying to sitting frequently. She immediately turns to look at you when you enter the room and tracks you as you cross the room. She has started saying "U-uhhh" when she doesn't want something and "U-huhhh" when she does. We hear very loudly the "U-uhhh" for about 20 minutes every night now. She pouts and cries when my husband leaves for work in the morning. She makes choices from 3 picture cards. It could just be a new phase she's in, but we think it is the Carnitor.

What is her life expectancy?

Due to the rarity of RS, very little is known about long term prognosis and life expectancy. Most of those who have been identified are under 18 years of age. It is often difficult to identify older girls and women due to the frequent lack of complete infant and childhood developmental records. However, studies have determined that a girl with RS has a 95% chance of surviving to age 20-25 years. This compares to a 98% survival probability for the general U.S. female population. Between the ages of 25-40, the survival rate drops to 69% in RS, compared to 97% in the general U.S. female population. The average life expectancy of a girl given the diagnosis of RS may exceed 47 years. While there are probably many women in their 40's and 50's who have RS, there have been too few women studied to make reliable estimates beyond age 40. While these statistics show that life expectancy is less in RS, it is not nearly as low as other similar neurological disorders.

What are the causes of death?

It is important to note that only 5% of cases reported to the IRSA have resulted in death. This means that 95% of those diagnosed are still living. The most frequently reported causes of death (one-quarter of deaths) are variations of "sudden death" or "unexplained death," with no apparent underlying cause such as an acute injury or infection. The factors most strongly associated with an increased risk of sudden unexplained death in RS are uncontrolled seizures, swallowing difficulties and lack of mobility. Neither physical or occupational therapy, nutritional status or living arrangements made a difference in the incidence of sudden unexplained death. Ongoing studies will help predict which girls are at greatest risk and which girls might benefit most from new medical or educational interventions. Other deaths have resulted from pneumonia. The factors most strongly associated with an increased risk of death by pneumonia are compromised lung function due to scoliosis and difficulty swallowing. Other causes of death include malnutrition, intestinal perforation or twisted bowel, as well as accidents and illness.

When she dies, what can we do to help find answers?

Although she may be at higher risk for life-threatening events such as pneumonia, choking and seizures, it is very likely that your daughter will live a long life. However, we are all at risk for accidents of many types and illnesses that are unexpected. A time will come when we will all die. Researchers are ready to listen, to learn, and to share. You can participate in research studies that will help us understand RS. Please consider participating in autopsy research, which can be her lasting legacy, and the ultimate gift of help and hope to thousands of families.

> *Never let yesterday's disappointment overshadow tomorrow's dreams!*

What has research taught us about RS?

Studies have revealed that although the brain is 30% smaller than normal, there are no obvious malformations, gross abnormalities or signs of infection. There is increased neuronal cell packing density. That is, cells should be further apart, but in RS they are very close together because cell-to-cell connections are not well-developed along the route. Neurons are reduced in size and there is reduced branching, which interferes with functions such as thinking, doing, and feeling. The number of synapses (brain-cell to brain-cell connections) is about half the normal number. Abnormalities in multiple areas of the brain may account for the following clinical symptoms:

Frontal lobe: Cerebral blood flow appears reduced, particularly in frontal brain regions. This looks like what might be seen in a 7 week old child. This area is much more involved than other brain parts. It is necessary for mood and emotion.
Caudate: much smaller than normal; involved in cognition, awareness and behavior
Putamen: no anatomical change; necessary for movement
Temporal lobe (limbic system): no anatomical change; needed for memory, learning, emotion, behavior
Cerebellum: reduction in some cell populations; needed for equilibrium and balance
Hippocampus: no anatomical change but thinning; necessary for information processing

Substantia Nigra: marked reduction in the pigment, melanin, and degeneration of cells; necessary for movement and critical thinking

Medulla (Brain stem): strong evidence of brain stem immaturity, leading to problems with the autonomic nervous system, such as sleep, salivation, breathing, heart rate, swallowing, bowel motility, blood circulation in hands and feet, and reduced sensitivity to pain

Neurotransmitters: reduced. These include: 1) Dopamine — necessary for movement and critical thinking, 2) Acetylcholine — necessary for memory, cognition, movement control, and 3) Glutamate — necessary for brain plasticity, important in seizures and cell death

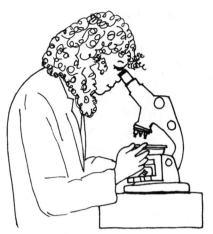

What has research found?

Rett Syndrome was previously described as a neurodegenerative disorder, with very poor prognosis and little potential for learning. Scientific studies have now identified Rett Syndrome as a disorder of developmental arrest, which begins shortly before or after birth at a critical time of brain and synapse formation.

RETT SYNDROME IS A CONDITION OF DEVELOPMENTAL ARREST

Supportive Clinical Evidence
> Early onset
> Normal head size at birth
> Low muscle tone
> Weak cry and poor suck
> Abnormal 4th toe (short)
> Improved learning and gaining new skills

Supportive Neurobiological Evidence
> Small brain (12-33% reduction)
> No malformations, storage, demyelinization, infection or gliosis
> Dendritic arborizations, cell differentiation and neuronal growth affected
> Small neurons with increased neuronal packing, migration not affected
> Thinning of hippocampus
> Significant involvement of caudate nucleus
> Decreased melanin (pigment) in substantia nigra
> Lack of mature olfactory (smell) neurons

Supportive Immunochemical Evidence
> Early cholinergic deficits result in dendritic differentiation
> MAP 2 decreased or absent in inner layer of cortex

These studies reverse the previous hypothesis of brain degeneration, opening doors to educational programs and therapies that will help. Studies have raised speculation that the primary conduction abnormality may be influenced by neurotrophic (growth) factors responsible for maturation of the heart and central nervous system. It is felt that these same neurotrophic factors may drive changes in the intestinal tract. These studies pave the way for treatments that will ultimately lead to a better way of life for girls with Rett syndrome and a method to prevent sudden, unexplained deaths.

Genetic Findings

Rett syndrome has long been felt to be a genetic disorder, as it occurs primarily in girls. The number of candidate genes have been greatly narrowed through research on cases where RS has occurred more than once in the same family.

    9 Families studied
    1 mother/daughter
    2 half sisters, same mother
    1 aunt/niece pair
    4 sets full sisters
    1 set three sisters

Familial recurrences of Rett syndrome comprise only about 1% of the reported cases; these cases hold the key for understanding the genetic basis of Rett syndrome. The X chromosome exclusion map for Rett syndrome has been narrowed to include the distal end of Xq28. These studies bring us closer than ever to identifying the gene which causes Rett Syndrome, which will lead to a biological marker and pre-natal testing.

Autonomic Findings
- Agitation
- Dyspraxia
- Slow responsiveness
- Poor sensory-motor integration
- Disorganized breathing
- Vasomotor changes (blue hands and feet)
- Vacant spells
- Constipation 90%
- Abdominal distention (bloating) 50%

Biochemical Findings
- Transient elevation of plasma ammonia
- Elevated levels of beta-endorphins
- Decreasing levels of dopamine & norepinephrine with age in cerebrospinal fluid (CSF)
- Transient elevation of lactic acid & aline in plasma cerebrospinal fluid (CSF)

Cardiovascular Findings
- Sudden unexplained death, 25% of all deaths
- Immaturity of the atrio-ventricular conduction system (heart)

Nutritional Findings
- Growth failure has many causes, but has a strong basis in nutritional deficit.
- Progressive weight and height failure unless aggressive nutritional rehabilitation is undertaken.
- Repetitive involuntary motor movements are not associated with increased energy expenditure.
- Sleeping metabolic rates are low and are consistent with features of malnutrition; these findings can be reversed with nutritional support.
- Deficits in lean body mass persist despite aggressive refeeding regimens.
- Deficits in lean body mass may be associated with increased rates of amino acid oxidation and urea recycling.
- Preliminary data suggest that the intestinal absorption of calcium and vitamin D status are normal in Rett syndrome, despite the presence of reduced bone mineral density.
- Oropharyngeal dysfunction and gastroesophageal dysmotility are found in 100% and 69% of Rett syndrome girls, respectively.
- Abnormalities of oropharyngeal dysfunction include poor tongue mobility, reduced oropharyngeal clearance, and laryngeal penetration of liquid & solid food during swallowing.

- Esophageal dysmotility, including abnormal wave patterns, delayed emptying, atony, gastroesophageal reflux; gastric dysmotility, including diminished gastric peristalsis or atony.

Neurophysiological Findings

- Seizures are reportedly a common problem.
- Prolonged video/EEG/polygraphic studies confirm that the occurrence of epileptic seizures is overestimated in Rett syndrome.
- Many events were frequently reported as typical "seizures" but were not associated with EEG severe discharge; these events include twitching, head turning, staring, laughing, pupil dilatation, breath holding, and hyperventilation.
- Actual seizures may be under recognized.
- No one characteristic seizure type has been identified in Rett syndrome; both focal and generalized electrographic seizures are recorded.
- Video/EEG monitoring may be necessary to provide definitive information regarding the need for anticonvulsant therapy.

Neuropathological Findings

- Morphologic (anatomical) features are unique, with only decreased brain weight being consistently present. The brain is preferentially involved in this altered growth; other organ weights are appropriate for the individual's height.
- No consistent evidence of a degenerative, inflammatory or ischemic process.
- No evidence of a progressive change in brain morphology over time. MRI and EEG studies support this observation.
- Best hypothesis to fit the fact that there is no recognizable disease process is that RS seems to be the result of a maturational arrest of brain development.
- Golgi studies suggest that arrested brain development affects dendritic size in selected brain regions, namely the frontal, motor, and limbic regions. This change is not seen in Trisomy 21 (Down Syndrome.)
- Alterations in numerous neurotransmitters have been observed, but there does not yet appear to be consistent data suggesting that the primary defect is in any of them.
- Mitochondrial disease ~ is this a secondary effect?
- Morphologic research is directed towards identifying possible deficiencies in neurotrophic factors which could initiate the changes which appear to be an arrest of brain development.

Epidemiology And Survival

- The prevalence of Rett syndrome is 1 per 22,800 (0.44/10000) females aged 2-18 years of age as determined in the Texas Rett Syndrome Registry.
- Rett syndrome has been reported in all races and ethnic groups.
- Rett individuals have an estimated 70% survival at age 35 years; this contrasts sharply with an estimated 27% survival at 35 years for severely retarded individuals.
- The majority of deaths in Rett syndrome are either sudden and unexpected or secondary to pneumonia.

The author wishes to thank the following professionals for ideas and information which was used to develop this chapter: Dr. Bengt Hagberg; Alan Percy, M.D.

WELCOME TO RETTLAND

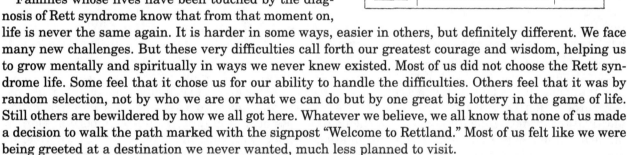

*"A nice place to visit, but I don't know
if I'd want to live there"*

Families whose lives have been touched by the diagnosis of Rett syndrome know that from that moment on, life is never the same again. It is harder in some ways, easier in others, but definitely different. We face many new challenges. But these very difficulties call forth our greatest courage and wisdom, helping us to grow mentally and spiritually in ways we never knew existed. Most of us did not choose the Rett syndrome life. Some feel that it chose us for our ability to handle the difficulties. Others feel that it was by random selection, not by who we are or what we can do but by one great big lottery in the game of life. Still others are bewildered by how we all got here. Whatever we believe, we all know that none of us made a decision to walk the path marked with the signpost "Welcome to Rettland." Most of us felt like we were being greeted at a destination we never wanted, much less planned to visit.

I felt like Dorothy in the Wizard of Oz when I found out that I would be a special needs parent. I didn't know if I had the courage, the wisdom or the heart to do the job. There were so many unknowns and the job description was enormous. And, like Dorothy in the land of Oz, my husband Scott, and I found ourselves tossed like a tornado into a world of confusion and uproar, a world devoid of the safety and security of our beloved hometown, a world that was frighteningly real at one moment and unbelievable at the next. Our friends stayed behind, and not having been where we were, didn't understand our turmoil in this new location.

Oh, how we wished it was just a bad dream. When we first realized something was wrong, we faced denial, then guilt, frustration, and anger. We prayed to God and we shouted at God. We cried alone and we cried together. We searched for answers, begged for a cure, tried everything we could to "fix" our daughter. We tried to "fix" the school system. We tried to "fix" all of the stares, all of the intrusions on our little dream family. We desperately needed to fix it all. But when it all wouldn't fix, we found that we had to fix ourselves.

It seemed like an uphill struggle. In this new land, we didn't find many signs or maps with further directions. The language was very complicated and hard for us to understand. We heard words like *electroencephalogram*, *scoliosis*, and *least restrictive environment*. We struggled to make sense of it all, especially to figure out how we got there and why.

Rettland was very different from anything we had ever experienced. I guess we will always long to be where we started out and wish for the simplicity of the easier route. We have turned down "the road less traveled," and it is not an easy one. It is not well paved and the lighting is poor. It is full of potholes and lots of winding turns. It often leads to a dead end, when we find ourselves searching for yet another obscure road. Rettland has lots of rocks and crags that can make it hard to get around.

We spent a lot of time trying to figure out how to get back home where we started out, far away from Rettland. We thought if we could only be where everyone else was, we would finally be okay. If we just found the magic pill or therapy we'd be able to click our heels and say "there's no place like anyplace but here" and we'd be on our way back to the safety and security of our hometown. We felt that if we just spent enough time teaching her skills, we would cross over to the road that headed back to where we truly belonged.

There are not many travelers on this road, so it's hard to get directions and it's easy to get lost at every turn. But we discovered that we didn't need to stay lost. While we didn't choose this road, each of us can choose where the road takes us. In fact, it makes it a good opportunity to do some road testing to find out what we're made of and where we're really headed. In time we realized that in spite of our struggles, we really had learned a lot in Rettland. After a while, it didn't seem like such a bad place after all. We stopped trying to escape. We made some really good friends, and learned some things about ourselves we might never have discovered had it not been for the tornado that turned us upside down. We learned how to get along in Rettland, and once we arrived back home, we were never the same again. We were okay. In fact, we found ourselves stronger, wiser, and more thankful, a little less judgmental and a lot more spiritual.

We had to draw some of our own maps for uncharted territory. It's not an easy job – we felt like explorers at times. It didn't happen overnight, but with enough time, we found that we could soon manage to look down the road a bit to see beyond the curves to the broader view. When we stayed on course, we made it from the valleys to the mountains, where we found that the view is exquisite. We learned to see our daughter's strengths and found ourselves bathed in the light of her innocence and surrounded by the warmth of her love. We found splendor in ordinary places and joy where others might not even notice. We found times to laugh when others couldn't even find a smile. We learned patience for her many needs and appreciation for her many small gifts. We moved from anger to using that energy constructively, providing better programs for her, learning about Rett syndrome and helping others. We moved from frustration at the lack of a cure to finding ways to support research that will bring it about. While at times it felt like we were traveling by covered wagon, we blazed the trails and still enjoyed the view – learning to minimize the bad and maximize the good. We found the very best of ourselves in the process.

Sometimes we still envy our friends on the super highways - but when we look more carefully to see how they take things for granted, it's really not so bad where we are. It took a long time to fully make our way through Rettland. It took more crying time, more trying times, some falling back into fixing time. Mostly it took time. While it sounds like a cliche, time does heal. It may seem of little importance for you in the beginning of this journey, for you are impatient to make your way. You may have your own itinerary and your own time schedule, feeling that you can't just sit back and wait for the cure. And that's okay. But do take some time to read the following guidelines from those who have blazed the trails to and from Rettland. You are not alone.

Kathy Hunter

Happiness is a way of travel, not a destination.
Roy Goodman

STRETCHING OURSELVES

The growth process for Rett parents and our daughters is so painful yet there is so much to value in that process. There is added dimension to our character, a sense of strength to adjust and accept, a more tender heart to care deeply and lovingly, to love so unconditionally. Our perspective has changed over time. We have grown. I think it's healthy that we have a yardstick to measure our growth. Mine is a song. Jenn was the most beautiful baby I ever saw. I would gaze upon her beauty, relish in the thoughts and dreams of motherhood and life with this beautiful daughter. Joe Cocker's recorded song from years ago expressed so much of what I was feeling. I'd sing it to her as I adored her so: "You are so beautiful to me, You are so beautiful to me, Can't you see? You're everything I hoped for. You're everything I need. You are so beautiful to me." But as the syndrome set in the tears would fall as I sang. The disappointment of what was not to be tore at my heart. Oh, how it ached. You all know that feeling, the sense of loss, the pain. But I never stopped singing that song to Jenn. As time passed I could sing the song without tears, just a numbness. And as more time passed I found I could sing it to Jenn with all the joy and more as I did when she was first born. The RS is still a pain in my heart…and a pain in the you know what! But RS or not, Jenn is Jenn. She is everything I hoped for in a daughter. She is love in a sense I have never known. Her spirit is so perfect, so pure, so full of unconditional love. For that I am grateful. And I am grateful to be at this place in my mind and heart that has accepted and worked with this disorder and seen the real beauty in my daughter. I am not fearful because I have grown so much already, I am encouraged that I will continue on that path and handle our future.

WHICH WAY TO GO?

Each parent makes his/her choices according to his own agenda, situation, preference and philosophy. There is no right way and no wrong way – just different ways to get to the same place. In fact, sometimes we're not even headed for the same place! We may have different goals and dreams for our girls. We all have different expectations and diverse resources.

When we come to a roadblock, we need to ask where we want to be and then make a decision to get there. We come to many choices along the way: types of therapy, kinds of programming, when to medicate, how much, whether to do surgery or not, when to seek alternative placement, whether to and when to take a vacation alone…the list is endless. There will always be some guilt in every decision we make. It is just impossible to always provide what is right for everyone. Remember that we can only do the best that we can do.

It may seem like as soon as one problem is solved, another quickly takes its place. It's sort of like the potholes that you just have to steer around. You might get caught in one or two, but you just have to hold on to the steering wheel and do your best to pull out. Rettland may seem like an obstacle course. Just don't try to overcome too many hurdles at once or you'll find yourself flat on the ground. Try not to dwell on decisions that are well down the road. One at a time is enough.

Remember - when you finally make it through to the first milepost, you can rest with confidence that you are the best expert on your child and your own resources, and you make the best decisions about her. Any professional worth his salt will tell you that parents are the original experts. Take that to heart and believe in yourself. Then, keep on going…

> We all cope in different ways and speeds. But you will move on. I'm not saying it won't hurt, or that it gets easier or less painful, just different. And you will have the strength to deal with it. Trust me. You will.

GETTING STARTED

Before you get started, you may need to focus on the best way to get there. Pay attention to the road markers along the way. They are reminders and warning signs. As you move along, look for these signs and the deeper meaning they may have for your life.

YIELD

Remember the things you can change and those you cannot. Don't waste precious energy for things which cannot be changed. You can change many things…your house, your hair, your job and a million other things. You cannot change the fact that your child has RS. Sometimes it helps to embrace the Serenity Prayer:

> *"God grant me the Serenity to accept the things I cannot change, Courage to change the things I can, and Wisdom to know the difference."*

Change what you can. You can provide good doctors, teachers and therapists and equipment. You can develop a circle of friends to help you keep your lives as normal as possible. You can read, teach others, support research that will bring about the cure. You cannot change yesterday. You can only make the best of today and look with hope toward a better tomorrow.

PACK LIGHTLY

Carry as little baggage as possible. Concentrate on the things that are important. It's easy to be angry about what RS has done to your life, but hostility and aggression make a very heavy load. Leave them behind. Anger is a non-productive emotion and it weighs you down terribly. A good attitude is easier to carry. If you need to vent your anger, do it in a productive way—exercise, write it down, talk about it. When you find yourself getting angry, ask yourself if the anger will change things. Then look for something that can be changed and do it.

You can't expect to prevent negative feelings altogether. And you can't expect to experience positive feelings all the time. The Law of Emotional Choice directs us to acknowledge our feelings but also to refuse to get stuck in the negative ones.

Greg Anderson

Dangerous Curves Ahead

You can deal with anything if you are prepared. You can't see around the curves so you may not see them up ahead, but know that they are there. Keep your eye on the road, your foot ready at the brake and your heart on the journey. Learn all you can about RS so you will be prepared for what may come, but remember that the worst of it may never happen.

> The research papers were so full of doom and gloom. I cried all the time. Then, as time went on, I met other parents with Rett daughters. And, as I learned of all the things my daughter could do, and what other girls could do, it helped to ease the pain. As time goes on, you just start to learn to help your daughter, and be her best advocate. You become a fighter for your daughter! It may not seem like it now, but you will get there. I didn't believe it at first. My daughter has retained a lot of physical abilities, walks very well and has regained a lot of hand function. I never would have believed that in the beginning.

Consult The Map

When you're in unknown territory, it's wise to see what has already been mapped. Look in the library for books by and about families who have made this journey. Call IRSA to join a network of local families so that you can share your concerns and get good ideas that already work. Your doctor is a good source of information. Keep asking him to explain things until you understand.

Ask For Directions

When you don't know where you are or worse still where you are going, don't be afraid to ask for directions. Ask the experts, those with experience and training, or ask other parents, those who have been there. Your child with RS didn't come with an operation manual. When you have a question you can't answer, give us a call at IRSA. If we can't answer it, we'll find someone who can. And remember, there is no such thing as a stupid question.

Drive Gently

Try to have understanding for others who may have taken the easier route, the one you wanted. They can't appreciate your difficulties because they're on the interstate, where the driving is easy. Remember that even you didn't have so much compassion and understanding until you found yourself facing RS square in the face. Your sensitivity came with the territory. Take some time to tell your friends about your RS road, but don't expect them to understand as well as you do. They can't. Your wisdom came from experience.

I don't feel ill will towards those who don't know how to handle Stefanie. I think the reason such people feel uncomfortable around us and our children is because the children are a constant reminder that this could happen to them, too. It's easy to say "That would never happen to me" when you see a crack baby or a fetal alcohol syndrome child, because "I don't drink or I don't do drugs." But when you see a child with RS, you come face to face with the fact that you can do everything right and still have a child with severe, multiple disabilities. There are absolutely no guarantees.

I think that we all need to think back to what we were like before Rett syndrome hit our lives. I remember being sympathetic and caring, but I didn't "know" what it was like, day in and day out, to have to care for someone with such acute needs. And I don't expect others to, either. How can they know? You have to live it to know it.

I use the positive to teach about the negative...I want them to see my Briana, how normal she looks, how brilliantly her eyes shine, how sweet her touch, and how warm the smile...and with all of this I want them to see the daily routine.

DETOUR AHEAD

Be prepared for changes in the route. Make alternative plans. Take along a survival bag with food, wipes, diapers, music and whatever else works at the time. You may be going over the river and through the woods to grandmother's house, but feel like you packed for a whole troop of girl scouts. But it sure makes things easier when you need something to bring your daughter comfort. On the other hand, it's not so easy to plan for the emotional curves that loom ahead when you least expect them. If you remember that detours are inevitable, they won't be so disrupting. When the detour is new and unfamiliar, try to picture yourself soon back on course. In Canada, a detour is called a temporary runaround. Try to see it that way...a temporary runaround. You may have to settle for changes in your daughter's school program while you work out a better plan. You may have to try several seizure medications before you find the right one. Just stick with it. You'll get there.

ROAD UNDER CONSTRUCTION

Sometimes it seems like we're always breaking ground, having to explain things over and over again. Some days, you'll feel like you can take on the world, and other days, you want the world to just go away. You need those days to shut everything off and rest for awhile. Be gentle with yourself. When you've had some quiet time, you'll be refreshed and ready to start again.

Most of us have jobs that call upon us for a variety of skills and we have to keep changing hats. At work I'm counselor, researcher, clerk, secretary, writer, advocate, and lobbyist. When I'm at home I'm wife and mother and I have a number of even more important jobs, so I change hats frequently there, too. When I visit my grandkids, I'm Gummy and I put on still another hat. In each of these roles, I try to wear one hat at a time. But when it comes to being Stacie's mom, it's takes a closet full of hats and too many of them are hard hats. I often have to wear several at once....like teacher, therapist, psychologist, nutritionist, advocate, technology specialist, nurse. This is not only heavy on my head, but it's an expensive wardrobe to maintain. Although I'd like to wear only one hat at a time, it's very hard to do. Now and then, I have to pass some of my hats around. Some time ago, I took inventory of my hat collection and decided some of them just had to go. I sent the teacher hat to school along with the therapist hat. There, they have specially trained experts who wear the hats well. I look to them for advice, but leave the actual teaching and therapy for school hours. This leaves me more time for wearing my favorite, the love hat, which is definitely the most attractive and useful one of all.

REDUCE SPEED

Rettland often seems like the Indianapolis 500. It's part of the world as we know it, the RETT RACE. Try not to speed to solve every problem you think might come up in a lifetime. Your child may not have seizures, and may not need scoliosis surgery. It's best to be prepared with good information, but don't accelerate your worries with potential problems that may not arise. If they do occur, there may be new treatments, or the problem may be mild. When you find yourself getting anxious about how you will handle the future, think about the many challenges you have overcome already and didn't know you could. If you slow down, you minimize the curves and take them with ease. Don't try to do too much. You'll run out of gas a lot faster.

> We are not supposed to deal with it all of this information at once. We have to let a little bit of it seep into our conscious mind each day. But the thing I most want to stress is that even though you have gotten a very hard blow, your precious child is still the same darling daughter to whom you gave birth. She still loves you the same way you loved her at first. And she always will, no matter what. She is just going to do things a little differently than what you had planned. Her love is unconditional. She will forgive all of your mistakes. She will remind you each day that you are not alone in this. None of us like Rett syndrome, but all of us love our daughters beyond description. It is this love that keeps all of us going.

SHARE THE WHEEL

When we share, the burdens are lighter and the blessings sweeter. One partner cannot automatically know when the other needs help. It's up to each of us to ask for help and to give help when it is needed. When one partner feels overburdened, resentment and distance build. You and your partner may grieve the loss in different ways. Mothers are usually more outspoken, while fathers often go inward with their pain. No one form of grief is more acceptable than another. It is sometimes hard to understand each other, but it is of great importance to respect each other's individual way of handling very difficult emotions. If your partner does not show his grief in the same way, it does not mean he is not hurting. It is common for one parent to become wrapped up in the child and for the other parent to retreat. Both are handling it the best way they know how. The parent who is wrapped up doesn't understand the partner's distance and feels a lack of support. The parent who is retreating doesn't understand why their partner is so deeply involved to the exclusion of what may seem like all else. At times a partner may feel he lost his child to Rett syndrome, and then the other parent as well. Spend more time talking openly with one another about your feelings to avoid a lot of unnecessary pain. Your child needs you, but you also need each other - even more now. The couples who seem to manage the best are those who know how to give it their best and still make time for each other. Remember that your child is a very important part of your life, *but not all of your life.* You need to develop outside interests to achieve balance, because RS can sure tip it over the edge at times. It can test your faith, exhaust your mental and physical energies and wear thin your patience. But you can deal with the day to day challenges of Rett syndrome if you have other outlets. Burnout doesn't come from our frantic schedules. It comes from doing too much of the same kind of stuff.

DISCUSS THE ROUTE

Talk with your partner about where you are headed, knowing that men and women differ in how and when they communicate. As a couple, we can get into patterns of holding our feelings in, sometimes to protect our partner from the pain, sometimes to avoid the pain. We can also assume that our partner understands how we feel. One partner may need to talk about it and the other may want to run away from it. Don't expect your partner to read your mind. Resentment builds when one partner feels unheard or misunderstood. Take time to be open and to make your feelings known. Make time to talk to each other. The average American couple spend only two minutes each day in meaningful conversation. We all have busy lives—you may have to schedule times on a regular basis as talk time. Remember that you can't keep a clean house by sweeping the daily dirt under the rug. Take care of things before the pile builds up. This happens in every marriage, but when you have children with extraordinary needs, the problem is so much greater.

> Even though I try to ignore what I cannot control and concentrate on the positives of day-to-day living, I believe we have to express what we're feeling every once in a while in order to continue to heal and cope. No answers or cure will come if we all just sit around in total acceptance. We must be angry and refuse to compromise in order to find answers and make progress, but to keep sane and happy, we do have to mellow out and accept Rett syndrome for what it is.

SEEK ROADSIDE ASSISTANCE

You will find many people willing to help you with your child if you are willing to ask. And that's the key. Family, friends, teachers and therapists want to do what they can to help now and then, but you must be willing to ask. Let them help - it opens the beauty of your child to them and makes them better people. Don't insist they do it your way unless it's absolutely necessary. Let them know that you are comfortable with their own ways. And don't expect them to be perfect! Your child may welcome the time with someone new more than you enjoy the time alone! Your daughter will survive just as well in the hands of friends if they use a different feeding technique and she will not get arrested by the fashion police if she wears stripes and plaid while you're away. Learn to ask for and accept help.

> I never had any help with Jessica until I went to one of our RS support group meetings and the speaker gave names and numbers to different agencies for getting respite hours. I contacted them, they came and assessed Jessica and gave me 12 hours a week respite care. The first agency I was with sent many different people all the time so I switched agencies. I used my hours generally in 6 hour intervals. I now receive 50 hours a week skilled nursing and 20 hours skilled nursing for respite. Everyone that I have working with Jessica I have chosen for her personally. I love my daughter, but work has been a blessing, financially and mentally!

PLAY ROAD GAMES

Look on the light side. Laugh along the way. It makes the trip shorter and much more enjoyable. Your sense of humor will see you through some hard times.

> Once, our son, Dean, was walking Stacie with a harness, which enabled her to walk much better without direct support and kept her out of traffic. When he came upon a group of kids, they stopped and stared. Without breaking stride, he closed his eyes and leaned back, saying, "You're the best seeing eye person I've had yet!" Another time when he held her hand and she walked her dizzy wide based gait, capturing the attention of another group of kids, he said, "Stacie, you just have to get used to this earth atmosphere." Then he glanced at them and winked, saying, "She's an alien, you know." Once in the pool as Stacie jabbered away so loud that no one could ignore, her brother, Jeff, kissed her right on the nose and said, "Those Chinese lessons are really paying off. I'm so proud of you!"

> All those silly songs I learned at camp as a kid have definitely proved more useful than the algebra in college. When Briana and Erica are moody I start singing all those silly songs and things turn around. Having Briana is a blessing because she is teaching us all that simplicity is best most of the time.

GET A TUNE UP

No one can provide limitless care for another human being without paying an enormous price. Families often say that caregivers are hard to find, and/or that they can't afford it. But the truth is, you can either pay now or you can pay later. If you pay now you may sacrifice some material things to afford time away. If you pay later, you may sacrifice a marriage or your sanity. So, it's good advice to pay the babysitter now instead of the divorce lawyer or the mental health professional later. Time away can be an afternoon or an evening a week - it doesn't have to be elaborate. Just make sure that it is time devoted to taking care of yourself and if you have a mate, to take care of your relationship.

We used to have an old, dilapidated '63 panel van which sat sadly in the driveway with four flat tires. It had sentimental value and Scott did love that piece of junk. I put a bumper sticker on the back which says, "rust is my favorite color." When I looked out the window at it, I could remember feeling that way for a long time myself, all deflated and falling apart. I had a long list of priorities and unfortunately, I was at the bottom of that list. I knew that everything on the list was important, but what I failed to recognize was that I could actually take care of all of those priorities much better if I was higher on the list myself. When your daughter has so many needs that are immediate it's hard to see your own. It was many years before I understood that we have to work hard to make time for ourselves. It is one of the most important things we can do for our daughters, for we function better when we take care of ourselves.

Remember that you will never be good for anyone else if you are not good to yourself first. Do whatever it takes. Change your spark plugs and recharge your battery often. Let people help you. If you can't make it to the next rest stop, jump off at the nearest exit and do something just for yourself. It doesn't have to be expensive or time-consuming. Just make sure you do it. You'll get better mileage for the long trip.

My first suggestion is to pick up your little angel, hug her and kiss her and tell her that you are all going to be alright. Next, make a nice hot bath…put your favorite oil into the tub, light some candles, pour yourself the drink of your choice, climb in and cry until it hurts to cry. Then relax…remember all of the wonderful things you were going to teach your little one, and find other ways to teach her. Keep venting, laughing, crying, sharing and loving. But most important than anything else, keep holding your angel close.

TAKE SHORT TRIPS

When you're first starting out, don't try to cover too much ground at once. One day at a time is a good way to do it. In itself, RS can be overwhelming. Trying to figure it all out and plan for the rest of your daughter's life can be immobilizing. Remember that yard by yard, life is hard, but inch by inch, life's a cinch. Pull over when you need to instead of trying to do the trip in one long overnighter.

"I try to take it one day at a time, but lately several days have attacked me at once."

DRIVE DEFENSIVELY

Surround yourself with positive people and look out for others who do not share your philosophy or your dream for her. Find people who believe in your daughter and who recognize her strengths. More than anything, she needs friends who value her just the way she is. Her world will be brighter and yours a lot easier.

One's approach to other people is so important in how they view our children. Ashley has always been accepted by our friends and family, and I feel so fortunate for that. But sometimes people forget to say hello or forget to say goodbye and I know that it is important to Ashley, so I help them remember. We have a cousin who was a great fun-loving gal but I realized that she thought Ashley really was not there…you know what I mean. Then Jan started spending some time at our house and Ashley started laughing at her jokes and Jan got to know her better. Now they are buddies and Jan realizes that Ashley really is there, that it is just difficult for her to show how much sometimes. For me, it is a goal and a challenge that by the time they leave, others will fall in love with her.

PASS WITH CAUTION

It's easy to rush into treatments that might sound promising. We're all anxious for the cure. Check out new or unusual therapies or treatments with experts in the field to help evaluate new directions. See if other families have experience that could help.

SMILE AND WAVE AT OTHER TRAVELERS

Have patience with those who never heard of Rett syndrome. Take a positive approach and try to understand that those who stare do so not to be unkind, but because they are curious. There are some insensitive people in our world, but they really are few and far between. For each person who is unkind, there are dozens of people who are doubly kind. Surround yourself with "up" attitudes, and there's no way to go but up.

Once, I was sitting with Stacie at a mall and noticed an elderly man across the way who kept staring. I said aloud things to Stacie like "I guess his mom never taught him it's not polite to stare." After a while, it got to me and I started to stare back. When that didn't work, I gave a mean glare. He rose to his feet and approached us. I was about ready to slug him when he said, "I'm sorry if you thought I was staring. I have a granddaughter just like yours and I was just admiring how well you interact with her." Now, if he hadn't spoken up, I would, to this day, be telling a story about a mean old man in the mall. Instead, I can tell you that Stacie's sweetness touched a dear old man with a tear in his eye. That probably happens often. I catch myself checking out other handicapped kids looking for RS. Or, I look at their wheelchair to see how comfortable or practical it is. Or, like the old man, I admire the parents or am just interested in the child.

As for people staring at Mary when we are in public, it's just never bothered me. Not to say there haven't been times Mary hasn't made me feel embarrassed, like the first few times she sang loudly during quiet moments at church. Now I just, laugh and thank God she's enjoying herself. I'm always glad people are interested enough to take the time to look. It gives me an opportunity to tell them about this wonderful person and a syndrome named Rett. I can't recall ever having someone "stare" out of much more then pure curiosity. Maybe I don't think much about it because I'm so curious myself. I've always wanted to know the hows, whys, wheres...I remember as a kid, in those rare circumstances when I saw a "handicapped" child, staring and wondering...how do they tie their shoes with no hands...or how do they go up and down stairs in a wheelchair? I remember being told "not to stare because it isn't polite," but I never recall staring out of disgust or anger, just looking with a million questions.

I think another reason some people avoid those of us with special needs children is that they feel embarrassed that their children are normal and they did not suffer as we are and their children don't suffer as many of our girls do. They feel there is nothing they can do or say to help and they feel very awkward. I wish they would know that they are wrong. Kind words, no matter how fumbling, are helpful. And, of course, simply providing friendship keeps us from feeling so disconnected from the world.

I had Josie at a time when it seemed like half the people in my little company were having babies. What a joyful time. Of course, everyone else's baby kept developing normally. I know they were devastated when they found out about Josie, but they all handled it differently. Admittedly, one friend who had developed a habit of inviting Josie and me to the zoo every other Sunday or so with him and his young son suddenly stopped calling. I still talk to this friend, but he never, ever, asks about Josie! He has since had yet another baby, and I ask about his children all the time. Then others ask about Josie on a regular basis. I think they find that once they ask and get their feet wet, it's not so scary to talk about.

BEWARE OF BACKSEAT DRIVERS

Sometimes you have to listen to backseat drivers who want to tell you how and what to do with your daughter, even though they have never been to Rettland. You may have to hear their answers for everything, when you know they don't really have a clue what's going on. Just try to remember that they are only trying to help in their own ways. Then, hold on to the confidence that you know your daughter best, and you make the best decisions when it comes to her well-being. And if you have to say so, say so!

Some days when I'm asked, "how are you?", I don't complain but don't lie either. My daughter has really instilled in me the power of "tell it like it is." Some people shy away from such reality, because their biggest gripe is that the hairdresser was closed on a Monday. Our insight makes us whole. It's okay to share how we feel on some bad days as long as we remember to rejoice throughout.

ENJOY THE TRIP

Avoid asking "Are we there yet?" I don't think we're ever "there." We can always find more ways to grow and learn, more ways to appreciate the delicate beauty of our precious daughters. It works a lot better when we concentrate less on reaching the destination, and more on observing the wonderful scenery we find along the road. If we spend too much time worrying about tomorrow, we miss the beauty of today. Most people don't understand this concept until they have met similar challenge. It makes us put everything in perspective and weigh everything according to different standards. Each of us would gladly give up all of our worldly possessions to have our daughters talk with us, run with us - things that most folks take for granted every single day. It opens us to the precious intangibles in life that couldn't be measured on any scale. It's tough terrain that we must go up, but the climb brings us to a higher appreciation of what really matters.

"Happiness is an inside job. It's not what happens to us; it's what we do with what happens to us. Attitude is our most important possession."

Robert Schuller

LOOK IN THE REAR VIEW MIRROR

When you find it hard to look up, look back at where you have already been and what you and others have already done. Look around you at what has taken place, including some things you may have once thought impossible. Keep it all in perspective.

As the parents of a younger child, we do see a significantly less trying path, thanks to the trailblazing that our contemporaries have been doing. We were referred to Early Intervention Services and have been getting life-saving amounts of respite for several years now. Naomi's primary nurse is a godsend who is constantly finding ways to engage her, draw her out and build her skills. Our last IEP was an upbeat meeting with a team that could not have been more supportive. And our community has surprised us with a fund-raising benefit to help purchase a wheelchair van. I know that we have been very fortunate. But I am also convinced that throughout our society, strides are being made, however halting and imperceptible they may seem.

Services are more widely available. Public attitudes are softening and the strangeness of seeing someone with disabilities out and about is lessening. Sidewalk curb cuts and handicapped parking spaces are literally everywhere now. This is all progress, movement in a positive direction. Every setback and disappointment and frustration stings, but when you are able to step back and see the big picture, you can see that, no matter how far the challenges still line up in front of you, the path you have already traveled is filled with others whose way has been made easier by your struggles.

CHECK THE WARRANTY

There are no guarantees in life. Rett syndrome may not be the worst thing that could happen to your family. Even in "normal" families, situations arise that are out of our control – situations like other illnesses, drug dependence, financial woes, strained family relationships. No family is immune to pain. Remember that life hands out its share of problems to all of us. Others' problems may not be so visible, but they are there and they hurt. Above all, remember that stuff just happens. Rett syndrome is not your fault. You are about as blameless as anyone could be. Check out the good things. One of the absolute guarantees of RS is that there is a rich, rewarding "other side" of the pain – the joy of pure and unconditional love and the ability to recognize what matters and what does not.

My daughter Amy has a cousin 3 months older than she is. It was hard for me to watch Monique develop "normally" as we watched Amy sort of not progress but appear to grow normally. I spent many nights awake trying to remember every detail of my pregnancy and delivery. What pills I might have taken? Was it the sip of wine at the wedding reception (days before we knew about alcohol's affect on fetuses)? Did I have a cold? I had the Hong Kong flu at 7 months and no telling what I took to relieve the symptoms. Anyway, 28 years later I still wonder and at times continue to blame myself.

ARRIVAL — "GETTING THERE IN ONE PIECE"

We all start on this journey at a place called Loss. We may find ourselves in locations like Shock and Denial, where we feel numb head to toe. Further along the road, we may arrive at Fear, Guilt, Anger and Depression, and we may get stuck for awhile. Those who have made the trip before us know that after a time, we will make our way to higher places, Understanding and Acceptance, and we will be able to move on. But, we need to remember that we all move at different speeds and every stage of the journey is necessary and natural as part of the healing process. It may be hard to see at the start, but every painful moment leads us to greater growth. Those who have already traveled this way tell us that after a stay in Rettland, we learn that the soul is without rainbows if the heart is without tears. We discover that what takes the most work brings the most joy, and what we appreciate most is what does not come easily.

We are all different people from our experience with RS, yet we are the same. We learn about priorities and the very simple, most important things in life. In the process, we find ourselves stronger in the broken places and more resilient. We learn patience, wisdom, courage and strength. In the classroom of life, we find that our daughters are not the students. They are the teachers, for they face the real tests and give the real lessons. Our daughters are far braver, far stronger, far more patient than we are. And we now know that when God measures a person, he puts a tape around the heart, not the head. Their beautiful, searching, penetrating eyes dance with glee, sing with laughing abandon, and speak to us with their own endearing language of love. These eyes sometimes flash with anger, flood with tears of frustration and widen with fascination and wonder. They perk up with enthusiasm and fall downcast with disappointment. These eyes express in silence what language cannot, reaching out to capture warm places in our hearts. Our journey with them is jeweled with priceless treasures if we stop to look along the way.

We laugh, we cry, and even yell once in a while, but ultimately we work together and do what needs to be done. It's a tough job but I want to believe the rewards of our little angel's smile and her positive warm fuzzies are what keep us hanging on. She has taught us many things, among them patience, understanding, health tricks and most of all, love and affection.

The remarkable thing is we have a choice every day regarding the attitude we will embrace for that day. We cannot change our past...we cannot change the fact that people will act in a certain way. We cannot change the inevitable. The only thing we can do is play on the one string we have, and that is our attitude....I am convinced that life is 10% what happens to us and 90% how we react to it. And so it is with you...we are in charge of our attitudes."

Charles Swindoll

I have a different perspective, because our daughter is adopted. I don't think Rett syndrome rules our life, but it definitely changes our life. My family's life may have been changed by choice, but don't we make choices everyday? We may make a choice to have another baby, or we may make choice to change jobs. Those choices then change the path of our lives. Sometimes it may be good, and other times it may cause us to struggle. Kristas was one of our best decisions, but sometimes I wonder how it might be without her. However, I also wonder how it might be without my two year old son...a whole lot easier, I'm sure. But I would not trade either of them for the world. Yes, at times I get frustrated or tired or whatever, but the little smile I get from any one of my kids makes it all worthwhile.

Our family has moved beyond what I call Phase One of "Life with Mary." It was a time of drowning, a time of struggling to survive as a family, a time primarily focused on Mary within the context of Rett syndrome, a time of grieving, tremendous adjustments, confusion and anger. Now, in Phase Two we are more able to focus on Mary as a person first, and less on the fact that she has Rett syndrome. We have hope now; we have dreams. We have begun to feel some of the needed energy to work to make those hopes and dreams come true.

The bend in the road is not the end of the road.

Life's Tug of War

Life can seem ungrateful — and not always kind...
Life can pull at your heartstrings — and play with your mind...
Life can be blissful — and happy and free...
Life can put beauty — in the things that you see...
Life can place challenges — right at your feet...
Life can make good — of the hardships we meet...
Life can overwhelm you — and make your head spin...
Life can reward those — determined to win...
Life can be hurtful — and not always fair...
Life can surround you — with people who care...
Life clearly does offer — its Up and its Downs...
Life's days can bring you — both smiles and frowns...
Life teaches us to take — the good with the bad...
Life is a mixture — of happy and sad...
SO...
Take the Life that you have — and give it your best...
Think positive, be happy — let God do the rest...
Take the challenges that life — has laid at your feet...
Take pride and be thankful — for each one you meet...
To yourself give forgiveness — if you stumble and fall...
Take each day that is dealt you — and give it your all...
Take the love that you're given — and return it with care...
Have faith that when needed — it will always be there...
Take time to find beauty — in the things that you see...
Take life's simple pleasures — let them set your heart free...
The idea here is simply — to even the score
As you are met and faced with — Life's Tug of War

           Author Unknown

FAMILY VOICES

ORDINARY LIFE…EXTRAORDINARY LOVE

Most women become mothers by accident, some by choice, a few by social pressures and a couple by habit. This year, nearly 100,000 women will become mothers of handicapped children. Did you ever wonder how mothers of handicapped children are chosen? Somehow I visualize God hovering over earth selecting His instruments for propagation with great care and deliberation. As He observes, He instructs His angels to make notes in a giant ledger. "Armstrong, Beth, son. Patron saint, Matthew. Forrest, Marjorie, daughter, patron saint, Cecelia. Rudledge, Carrie, twins, patron saint…give her Gerard. He's used to profanity." Finally, He passes a name to an angel and smiles, "Give her a handicapped child."

The angel is curious. "Why this one, God? She's so happy." "Exactly," smiles God. "Could I give a handicapped child to a mother who does not know laughter? That would be cruel." "But has she patience?" asks the angel. "I don't want her to have too much patience or she will drown in a sea of self-pity and despair. Once the shock and resentment wear off, she'll handle it. I watched her today. She has that feeling of self and independence that is so rare and so necessary in a mother. You see, the child I'm going to give her has her own world. She has to make her live in her world and that's not going to be easy."

"But, Lord, I don't think she even believes in you." God smiles. "No matter. I can fix that. This one is perfect. She has just enough selfishness." The angel gasps, "Selfishness? Is that a virtue?" God nods. "If she can't separate herself from the child occasionally, she'll never survive. Yes, here is a woman whom I will bless with a child less than perfect. She doesn't realize it yet, but she is to be envied. She will never take for granted a "spoken word." She will never consider a "step" ordinary. When her child says "Momma" for the first time, she will be present at a miracle and know it! When she describes a tree or a sunset to her blind child, she will see it as few people ever see my creations. I will permit her to see clearly the things I see…ignorance, cruelty, prejudice…and allow her to rise above them. She will never be alone. I will be at her side every minute of every day of her life because she is doing my work as surely as she is here by my side." "And what about her patron saint?" asks the angel, his pen poised in midair. God smiles. "A mirror will suffice."   **Erma Bombeck**

There are as many stories in Rettland as their are families, and each learns to develop their own ways to cope with the diagnosis and the way it affects their lives. Reactions may vary in intensity or in their pattern, but in general most parents go through similar stages on their way to acceptance. It may sound trite and completely inadequate during the time that you hurt the worst, but time does make things better.

"Friendship is born at that moment when one person says to another, "What you, too? I thought I was the only one."

C.S. Lewis

TALES OF TRIUMPH

With this diagnosis, nothing changed, but it helped us in many ways to understand Brittany and the disease. A lot of unanswered questions were finally answered. Ironically, there are still a lot of unanswered questions. Rett syndrome is very mysterious. One thing I know, despite Rett Syndrome, our lives are richer because of Brit. If you could see her smile and eyes, you'd be a goner. This is how she communicates and does it so masterfully. I' m so proud of her. She keeps me grounded to what is important, and when I get the "busy life syndrome," she reminds me to slow down, step back, breathe and look at what is important, sort of smell the flowers, look at the sky and read her a story and snuggle. The diagnosis of Rett Syndrome has opened up a whole new road to travel – one not as dark nor as bumpy as the first long road.

When Ann was about four, a teacher suspected Rett and gave us some information to read. We took her for an assessment, and they said she didn't have enough autistic symptoms and ruled it out. From the devastating literature I was given, I was thrilled and left. The subject came up again when she was about eleven. I immediately went to her neurologist who was unsure but suggested I take her for another evaluation. I remembered the literature and asked him if that would change anything we were currently doing for her he said "no," so I didn't take her. I think this is called denial. Then our son's karate instructor told me he had an older sister like our daughter and she had Rett syndrome! He could have knocked me over with a feather. That is when I found IRSA and it was like reading Ann's life story even though no one had met her. She is now 15 and we have come to terms with this diagnosis.

I am embarrassed to admit I don't remember the doctor's name who diagnosed Sarah. I don't feel really good about our experiences. We only had two appointments. The first was when Sarah was around 18 months. I knew something was wrong with her when she was born. There was nothing physical, just a mother's gut feeling. When she was 10 months I took her to the doctor because she wouldn't use her legs. She wouldn't bear weight and wasn't pulling herself to stand. Lots of tests of were negative, and she was diagnosed as developmentally disabled and placed in our local Birth to 3 program. She eventually learned to crawl. I got tired of no answers so we got a referral to Children's. She was given a cognitive test, hearing test, that sort of thing. No diagnosis the first visit, but Rett syndrome was mentioned by the doctor. He gave us no literature. The only thing he told us about Rett was that the major indicator was the loss of major skills. I didn't feel this fit her at the time…Six months later we went back for our follow-up. By then she was clapping a mile a minute. The doctor felt she met all the requirements for a Rett diagnosis. He gave us copies of some really clinical articles and that was the end of the appointment. I will never forget reading these horrible clinical articles in the lobby. The phrases "profoundly retarded" and "uncertain life expectancy" still haunt me. We came home and have never gone back. We did take Sarah to see another specialist, who was great, and she confirmed the diagnosis.

Jessica adores her sister, where Leah sees her as a bother. Noah loves to help her eat. She enjoys going to their dance competitions, but hates soccer and t-ball. So then we run into the baby-sitter dilemma. But once everything is figured out, it tends to run fairly smoothly. I believe we have as "normal" a family as is possible with having a disabled child. But then who is to say what is normal? I don't believe there is a normal family anymore. What's important is that we are happy.

"When we long for life without difficulties, remind us that oaks grow strong in contrary winds and diamonds are made under pressure."

Peter Marshall, "To Each His Own"

To Each His Own

God made me different
You know I really try
He said I am unique
and I never ask him why.
If I appear peculiar,
there's nothing I can do
You must accept me as I am
as I accept you.
God made a casting of each life,
then threw the old away.
Each child is different from the rest,
unlike as night and day.
So often we will criticize,
the things that others do.
Do you know, they do not think
the same as me and you.
So God in all his wisdom,
who knows us all by name
didn't want us to be bored,
that's why we're not all the same.
Author Unknown

THE SAINTS COME MARCHIN' IN

Society tells us since we have special kids, we're special parents and most of us take that to heart. We think that everything we do has to be heroic – and the world keeps reminding us what saints we are. We have to give ourselves permission to be human, and that means asking for help now and then. We have normal resources, and our kids have exceptional needs. Most people don't know what it is like to "live the Rett syndrome life." They are willing to help, but don't know where to begin.

LITTLE THINGS MEAN A LOT

A Letter To Family And Friends

It must be hard for you to understand what we are going through since our daughter was diagnosed with Rett syndrome. Sometimes her behavior can be very upsetting, as she screams for hours. Once alert and attentive, she now often looks away and avoids our gaze. She no longer shows interest in toys she once loved. Our lives have become complicated with a future for which we were not prepared.

Raising this child is the greatest challenge we will probably ever face. We have gone through the same stages of grief that one would experience at the death of a loved one. All of our resources, emotional, physical and financial, have been at times taxed beyond measure. However, we know that with love and patience, we can overcome the challenge and provide the best possible for our beloved child, and for our family. We try to take it one day at a time. Some days are good and some bad. On the good days, we appreciate the beautiful way she has touched our lives with her precious innocence and taught us the true meaning of love. On the bad days, we need your help. Our lives will never be the same again, but in so many ways we are enriched.

I am sure there are times when you don't know how to respond to our situation. Your support and loving care can make such a difference in the way we are able to cope. You probably don't know just how much the little things mean. These suggestions may be helpful:

1) Don't be afraid to ask about our daughter. We have spent many hours with specialists to learn about her condition. It helps to know that you are interested.

2) Respect our decisions about her care. We have listened carefully to the recommendations of many doctors and therapists, and have based our decisions on what we feel to be the best for her.

3) Treat our daughter as a part of the family. Include her in the other children's activities. She may not be able to do everything that the others do, but it is important that she does take part. Nothing hurts more than having your child overlooked because she is different.

4) Teach your children about her. Explain her condition in terms they can understand. Tell them it is okay to ask questions. Ten questions are better than one stare. When your children see that you treat her first as a child, they will respond in the same way.

5) Don't forget to say hello. Although she cannot talk, she does love to be spoken to. It may take her a moment to respond, but she will. Good things come to those who wait.

6) Please understand that family gatherings, particularly birthday parties, can be very difficult at times. No matter how accepting we are, we still agonize for the milestones our daughter will not achieve. With time, the pain will ease. Try to be sensitive.

7) Ask if you can help once in awhile, but don't be surprised if we don't accept your offer at first. It is hard to let others help when society has taught us that as special parents we have to do everything "special." Keep asking until we let you help. It isn't that we don't need the help; it's just that we don't want to burden you if your offer is not sincere.

8) Offer to care for our daughter sometime so that we can get away together. Remember that everything we do and everywhere we go is much more complicated than the ordinary. There is no such thing as sleeping in on Sunday morning, or any morning for that matter.

9) Offer to feed our daughter at the next family gathering. It does not take a special technique that you do not have, nor will she eat better for us. It will be a good break for her and for us.

10) Don't leave our daughter out when you buy little gifts for the children. If the gift is something she cannot chew or a toy she cannot play with, find something that she can be happy with.

11) Don't tell us that we were specially "chosen" for this child. We are ordinary people who are striving against sometimes extraordinary circumstances to provide a "normal" family life. We were not singled out for the job. It just happened at our house. It could just as easily happen at yours, and you would carry on as we have, like ordinary loving parents who care.

12) Don't underestimate the power of your caring. Everything you do to try to understand will help more than you will ever know.

BROTHERS AND SISTERS

Rachel is small, Rachel is quiet.
The silence of Rett is pain in the heart.
Her smile is happiness to me.
Her hands are wet, her hair is a mess!
But she is special to me.

Steve Meisner

All families experience occasional problems between and among siblings. Brothers and sisters of girls with RS experience a number of their own special concerns. The impact of growing up with a sister with RS has far-reaching consequences. Families have to readjust their expectations and increase their focus on the child with special needs. Brothers and sisters can get overlooked or overindulged. Each year at our annual IRSA conference, we invite a panel of siblings to discuss what it's like. Parents sit on the edge of their chairs as they listen to stories and feelings that are recollected and shared. We all want to be good parents. We don't want any of our children to suffer, yet we're so often pulled in so many different directions that it's impossible to provide what everyone needs. We learn from brothers and sisters that their experiences are a mixture of many emotions, and they have the same basic needs ~ openness, sensitivity, guidance from someone who can understand them and freedom to vent their feelings, both good and bad. They want parents to recognize that they are needed as much as their sister needs them. They need time and attention. While many issues surface, most brothers and sisters worry less than their parents about the outcome of growing up in a family that is different. They seem to exceed all of our expectations in the way they are able to accept and adjust in time.

> Once upon a time, Jeff and Dean were Stacie's brothers. When she became handicapped, they became *siblings*. Such a cold, clinical term, not nearly adequate to describe their loving relationship. She owes much to them, but they owe more to her.

How can I explain my daughter's need for extra attention to her younger brothers and sisters?

It is not an easy thing to do. It helps to give as much individual attention to each of the children as possible. Acknowledge their feelings of being slighted at times, and let them know that all of their feelings are real. Try to schedule in some "alone" time. Remember that your other child needs you as much as your special child, just in different ways.

> No matter how we explain it, little ones don't understand like we wish they would. That's why they're kids and we're adults. I realize this when I ask my two year old grandson to stop acting like a child!

> It was Kim's younger brother who showed the sibling rivalry, just as he had become able to do more than she could. Previously, he had adored her, and loved being with her. But for a few months he couldn't stand her. It all passed, of course, as all these things do, and he is a most loving and helpful brother.

Should I enroll my other child in a sibling discussion group?

If your child is willing, it may help him to learn how to be more comfortable sharing feelings. On the other hand, if he feels that this is just one more way his family is different, it may be wise to put it off until another time when he is more receptive.

What are the things that influence a child's outlook?

- Birth order of the sister with RS
- Age of the well child in relation to his sister with RS
- Whether a single parent family
- Family resources
- Family closeness
- Family size
- How the family views the handicap
- Whether or not one or both parents work outside the home
- The family's religious views
- Whether the child is institutionalized or in special classes
- The severity of the handicapping condition
- Whether or not the healthy child is of the same or different gender

How can my child adjust to the embarrassment when people stare or make negative comments?

Your other child may feel different from his friends. He may deal with embarrassment by becoming the center of attention as the class clown or troublemaker. He may pretend that he is not embarrassed, or try to escape it by concentrating on outside interests as a distraction. He may overcompensate by trying to be the best student or the best athlete at school. In most cases, however, kids pick up their cues from parents, and their attitudes generally reflect parental attitudes. So, if you can handle embarrassment, he will probably learn to handle it, too.

> Anger does not get you where you want to go when you have a child like ours. Sometimes people just do not think. I try to involve Ashley in the conversation, sometimes answering for her, sometimes using a smile for a yes. It has been amazing how this has brought people around.

> My sister Michelle can't walk. When she was about 4 or 5 I took her to the park. We were sitting on the bench. I noticed two little girls, staring that, "what's wrong? How come she can't" stare. I asked Michelle loudly (so the little girls could hear) if she wanted to dance again? "Oh yeah," I said, "she is a ballet dancer; she is just tired."

> It used to make me feel uncomfortable when people stared at Jenn. But somewhere along the line years ago I found that people often took their cue from me and how I handled the situation. I would introduce Jenn to those staring at her. And once I did so, they were transformed; facial expressions softened from a hard stare to a compassionate smile. With being introduced to them, Jenn became a real person to them. Conversation would flow and I found those "gawkers" to be very sensitive and caring people.

> I can remember when I was young and had a handicapped person down the street who was a sibling of a friend of mine. When I would go down to her house I did not know how to treat her brother, so I would just pretend that he was not there. Now, of course, I feel so sad about that and realize my mistake in making that choice. I try to remember that when someone new comes into our home. I always make a point to have Ashley say "hi" to them by holding her hand up and saying, "Ashley talks with her eyes and says hi." That always breaks the ice and they begin to talk to her and she begins to smile. I refuse to allow anyone to ignore Ashley, but I mean that in a positive way. Rather than "stewing" because someone has ignored her or holding a grudge against them, I look and act in a positive, kindly way.

How should I teach him to respond to inquisitive people?

There will always be inquisitive people. Explain that curiosity is a natural reaction. Most people simply want to understand something they are not familiar with. Work together on a response that he can use which is easy for him to explain and easy for others to understand. When he encounters someone negative, tell him that sometimes, other people are as handicapped as his sister, by their attitudes.

> I always appreciate people talking to Angie. When they ask questions of her, I just smile and say, "She can't talk, but she understands you." I think people feel awkward, not knowing what to say—I felt that way, too, in my pre-Angie days. I agree it's hard in most situations to give explanations of RS, especially while standing in line somewhere. I don't like to get into discussions about RS in front of Angie, because I think it must be embarrassing for her. I think most people want to be kind. At times, it is hard to come up with an appropriate response until much later, when it is too late.

> My youngest daughter is now in school full time and with more children who are "normal." She is now facing the other kids who are asking her about her sister, "Why she is like that?," "Will you get like that?" For being only 6, she is also very mature and got tired of all the questions. So she now just answers that Cynthia is her "baby sister," and that she is an angel that was sent here to bring us smiles.

Does he feel guilty?

He may feel guilty about a number of competing emotions—anger, jealousy, sadness, frustration, fear and hostility. He might feel guilty because his sister has the disability instead of him. He can walk and talk and enjoy activities his sister cannot participate in. He may feel shame if he would rather not be so involved in caring for his sister. He might feel some guilt when money is spent on him that could be used for equipment for his sister. He might want to downplay his own intelligence or good looks, thinking that it would make his sister feel bad to be compared. The negative aspects of guilt are low self-esteem, hostility, difficulty with relationships, and a desire to deny himself things which he deserves. On the other hand, there are many positive aspects: he may be a good child as thanks for the gift of health. He may be obedient, sensitive, helpful to others in need, and learn to be expressive to others. For these reasons, many brothers and sisters are drawn to helping professions, such as teaching or nursing.

How can we help him avoid resentment?

There are many ways for resentment to creep in. Parents may be overprotective for the sake of their daughter, not allowing him to do something if she cannot do it, too. Outside activities might be restricted when he is needed to help with his sister. She may require lots of time and attention. There may not be enough time to go around so that he does not get time alone. He may have to sacrifice some things so that money, time and energy can be spent on his sister. He might feel that her needs come first, and he may resent the fact that he has chores and she does not. He may feel that her presence and her needs dominate everything in the household. He may feel undue pressure to perform with higher expectations for success to compensate for the heartache of what his sister cannot do. He might feel that you love her more because you do more for her. He may resent the fact that he is scolded more because he is more capable. The negative aspects of resentment are anger, frustration, rebellion and withdrawal. At the same time, if he is given a lot of reassurance, he learns how to deal positively with resentment, and he will find that he is able to vent his feelings and still be a good person.

> Many people used to ask if I've ever felt cheated or deprived of a "normal" relationship with my sister. My answer was always, "No, not at all." Why would I? I have never felt any anger toward anybody or anything about Leesa. Now, I would answer "Yes," with no anger in my voice. I was deprived of a normal relationship with my sister. I never had the chance to have conversations with her or have her tell on me (which worked out for the best sometimes!). But this is not my sister's fault, my parents' fault, or mine. I would never want anyone other than Leesa as my sister.

Late at night after everyone was asleep, I was relaxing and my other daughter got out of bed and came to sit on my lap. She looked at me with big serious eyes and asked if I loved her. I said I loved her very much. She then asked if I would love her more if she were like her sister. My eyes filled with tears as I realized that with all the concern I had for Cynthia's health, I had failed Cameron. We then decided it was time to make changes in our home. We decided Cameron needed a day once a week where she was the center of attention. So we go to lunch once a week where we talk about anything she wants. This is also her time to ask questions that sometimes get overlooked.

My daughter can eat for over two straight hours, so we were not only not doing things that we liked, but we weren't even able to leave the house. We found that we were all getting crabby at each other for not being able to do the things we liked so we started using respite care even though my daughter is only 3 years old. It has been a godsend. Now for about six hours every weekend, my husband and my 5 year old daughter go on a hike, mountain biking, or even get a play date for my 5 year old so that my husband and I can go out on a date. We are all much happier now. Stephanie is always happy, and we feel like our sanity has returned.

Bridget doesn't do well at all in crowds, so my sister will babysit her when I go to the kids' basketball or school programs. I spend a lot more time with Bridget than the other two but I try to make up for that by eating at the dinner table and talking to them about their day and reading to them. I like to spend time with each one of them at bedtime. Instead of talking to them, it seems they always do the talking. Kelly is very motherly to Bridget and plays with her often. Zach keeps his distance most of the time but is also very protective.

How will it affect his self-image?

A brother or sister may question their own intellectual abilities, feeling that others may say they are "smart" only in comparison to their sister. He may feel unworthy of his own accomplishments, whether they are acknowledged or ignored. A sister may secretly wonder if she also has RS without knowing it, since she and her sister came from the same parents or she may worry that she will someday have a child with RS. He may unconsciously be waiting for something bad to happen to him, as it did to his sister. Negative self-images can lead to unhappy relationships, destructive lifestyles and lack of confidence. On the positive side, the majority of brothers and sisters are well-adjusted, happy, productive and caring. It is important to be honest and fair in evaluating brothers and sisters, being careful not to overstate or understate their abilities. This builds trust and eliminates confusion. Brothers and sisters need to know that every compliment and every criticism they hear about themselves is true and honest.

Leesa and I have something that is very unique—a relationship that no one else can see or feel. After all the years together, I seem to be able to sense her feelings, make her laugh, tell what kind of mood she's in, and know what she's thinking through her big blue eyes. This is a girl who has taught me more than anyone else, without even saying a word. She has taught me caring, understanding, compassion, open-mindedness, and brotherly love. She's shown me humility and self-giving. Leesa has made me appreciate what I have, including her, my parents, and what my parents have been able to provide for me. I believe my family and I have grown from her.

From her I have learned not to judge people and to be strong in my beliefs, to be myself by myself. She has taught me tolerance toward others as well as patience. Many things are difficult for my sister—things that many people do without thinking, are beyond her grasp. Taking care of her has helped me in many ways. I have learned a great deal of patience toward others. Lila has no prejudices. The appearance of other people does not faze her in any way. As long as a person is kind to her, that is all that matters. I have learned to judge people by how they act and not how they look. My sister more than anyone else in the world has taught me that outward appearance is only part of what makes a person attractive. It is hard for me to pinpoint any one incident with her that has changed my life – there are so many things. She has daily, in her own sweet way, helped shape my attitudes and personality.

My Inspiration

A smile, a glance, a cry.
This is how she communicates.
Every moment, every verbalization,
a further attempt to communicate.
Her love expressed in her eyes.
Her eyes the gateway to her soul.
Those who know her, love her.
Her friends, like you and me.
Though she is special, very special!
Everyone tries to teach her,
But those who know her
know she is teaching them.
Patience, caring, kindness,
there is no limit to her lessons.
My gratefulness for all she has taught me
This will never fully be expressed.
Due to her, I am me!
For who I am is a result of her teachings.

Those who take the time to know her,
receive the most angelic gift.
Her love!
The richest, most blessed love!
The love expressed in a smile,
expressed in her eyes!

My sister's courage, her determination,
are my inspiration.
Though life has been cruel to her,
her passion for life - unceasing.
Life is always worth living-
this lesson is the greatest my sister has taught me.
Yet "Thank You" will never be enough!

Amanda Payton

Do brothers and sisters blame themselves?

Like their parents, brothers and sisters must sometimes wonder why "bad things happen to good people." He may wonder if getting a sister with RS is some kind of punishment. He may blame himself for getting a healthy body instead of his sister. He may pass the blame around from himself to his parents to God and back again. He may use his sister as an excuse to get out of trouble by getting others to feel sorry for him. Usually, he is actually not mad at his parents, but at the situation. Experiences are out of his control and they hurt. He hates the feelings, but usually feels that his parents did what they had to do. A child may feel neglected even if in reality he is not. Getting short-changed from time to time is inevitable in any family. But when we have a child with RS, parents may find themselves guilty of benign neglect. We thank goodness he can take care of himself, leaving him to fend for himself. This isn't always bad. We just need to learn to reverse it sometimes and neglect the child with RS in harmless ways to give him the support he needs. When they look back, some brothers and sisters tell us they feel their sister received more attention, but knew it had to be that way. Some were jealous of the attention she got, and others felt that they did not lack attention at all. Happily, their thinking matures in time as they are able to put things in perspective.

> I'd give anything if there was one certain thing I could point my finger at and say, "That's what caused it." But in doing so, I feel like I'd have to point my finger at God. And I can't do that. I feel like everything happens for a reason. I don't always understand the reason why. I don't think I ever will on this one, except maybe that's it helped me to slow down, not to take so much for granted and to become closer with God himself.

How can we help him adjust to our situation?

It may depend on his age when his RS sister came to the family. If she was born first, he may feel that "this is the way it's always been." If he is older and watched her regression, he may feel the pain of loss. Or he may deny his sister's limits or the severity of his sister's condition and its effects on the family. He may wish that it wasn't there and pretend that it will go away. Again, he will take cues from the attitudes of his parents. If he is like most brothers and sisters of girls with RS, he will find extra strength and sensitivity and in the end, develop a deeper, more meaningful understanding of life.

> Many of us have had the experience of a doctor who recommended that we institutionalize our daughters for the sake of the rest of the family. I think this is particularly true of those of us with older girls. I hope it doesn't happen as often anymore. In our case, Angela was 3 years old and our neurologist sent her for a psychiatric evaluation. The doctor spent a few minutes with us and observed Angela while we talked. He then pronounced that she had no ego, that I was too attached to her and that we should institutionalize her so that we could have a normal family life. Needless to say, our family has not had all that unusual a time. My other three children, including Angela's twin brother, are successful and well-adjusted young adults. They have told me that they never felt deprived of my time or energy because of their sister. I was a den mother, went to all their sports events and school programs. I managed to finish my undergraduate degree and law school and work almost full time and Angela has been with us through it all.

> I do have two other exceptional children. John, a graduate of the Naval Academy and top 20% of his graduating class, a superb human being with sensitivity and highly developed family values. He was the older brother and Amy's idol. Melissa is an exceptionally good teacher and her students love her. She is firm and loving and believes a mind is a terrible thing to waste. Wonder where she got that attitude? Amy made us a strong family for sure, but protecting the individuality of each member is very important. It was okay in this house to say "This is a low down dirty deal we got, but we will go on and make the best of it and no one member of this family is more important than another."

How much responsibility should we give him?

One of the issues that sometimes comes up is missing out on childhood. Brothers and sisters often must assume adult-like roles without the maturity or experience they need to handle them. He may feel that he missed his place in the family, because his sister will always be the youngest child. He may accept extra responsibility and avoid making waves because everyone is already so upset, but excessive responsibilities may cause him to miss out on opportunities and friendships. If you must require your other child to include his sister with RS, let him choose the activity. Also, he may feel anxious as his parents grow older and can't do as much for his sister. It will help everyone involved if you include others in your daughter's circle of friends who will help care for her best interests when you no longer can. When children are growing up, they always have to do some things they don't like. There is no doubt that having a sister with RS brings added responsibility. Luckily, it also brings great enrichment and helps brothers and sisters feel needed and important.

> Although the responsibilities placed upon me because of Lila are sometimes difficult to deal with, and though sometimes I wish I did not have them, I can think of nothing else in my life that has helped me as much as those responsibilities.

How much should we explain to him?

Some questions are not easily answered, but try to be sincere and honest. Let him know that his thoughts and feelings are important, and that emotions and tears are okay. He needs accurate information in a way he will understand. Try to listen carefully to the kind of questions he asks, and tell him what he needs to know, taking into consideration his age and level of understanding. Start at the beginning and take your time. Explain your own feelings. Have an open attitude. He will soon learn to trust and confide in you. He needs your attention, special time all alone with you. He needs to know all about his sister now and what the future may hold.

How can we help him avoid worrying about the future?

Serious concerns about long-term care can arise when parents are no longer able to provide it. Young children can worry that they, too, will be "sent away." Adult siblings are often in a delicate balance between responsibilities to themselves, their spouses and children, parents, other siblings and the sister with RS. Parents should plan ahead to reduce the burden of worry. Programs such as guardianship, conservatorship and estate planning are aimed at allowing the woman with RS to live as independently as possible without undue hardship on her siblings. Brothers and sisters can be excellent advocates, making sure that all of her needs are met and appropriate services are provided.

> I don't know what the future will bring for Leesa and my family. Sometimes I'm scared of the unknown ahead, yet sometimes I'm very confident. I think many people in this situation go through this. I have to keep my head up and take what comes. It scares me now that I can't be home all the time to help with her. My parents have put their lives into making sure Leesa's life is the best it could possibly be. I want to make sure that I can help them so they can rest a little easier about Leesa's future.

> Stefanie's sister, Jenny, asked me one night who would take care of Stefanie when Mark and I died. The question caught me off guard, because Jenny was only 7 at the time. I told her that we hoped there would be a nice place for Stefanie to live when she becomes an adult, where there would be things for her to do and nice people to take care of her, but that Jenny and her brother Christian would need to look out for her and make sure Stef was being taken care of nicely and properly. Jenny has since decided that she will need to take care of Stefanie someday the way I do, and likes to "practice" for that day. Mark and I have been extremely careful not to "parentify" our two other children or otherwise insinuate that Stefanie would be their complete responsibility when we are gone, whether they like it or not. I am very thankful that the desire to take care of her sister has developed independently.

How will he react if we choose residential placement?

This is a very difficult decision. It is important to reassure him that she is not going away because she is "bad." Let him know that you love her just the same, but are looking for a place for her to get the kind of treatments she needs to be the best that she can be.

> I was only 4 years old. Dawn was 5. We are 14 months apart in age. My best friend. The doctors told my parents that there was nothing they could do to help her and there were no schools that were "appropriate" for Dawn. They told them that the only decision that would be good for Dawn would be to put her in an institution, where she would get help. My parents were in shock, but did as the doctors said. My best friend left home. We visited often, but it wasn't the same. My mom has never forgiven herself for this decision, not saying it was a bad one, just so hard. There was no such thing as "Rett syndrome" then. Years went by and visiting just became the "normal" thing. Always regularly. Each visit, no matter how often, I would cry when it was time to leave. Dawn is now 30 years old and is in a group home and even if I see her every day of the week, I still get choked up when it is time to leave. She is so beautiful and how I wish she didn't have Rett syndrome. I often wonder how different our lives would have been. I love her as she is of course, but still wonder.

I'm so worried about the effect this will have. What can I expect?

Expect some good stuff. It may not always be a rose garden, but it's definitely a place where beautiful things grow. There are many good qualities that come from having a sister with RS, like maturity, patience, awareness and acceptance, tolerance and compassion. There is a heightened sensitivity to prejudice and its consequences and a better sense of values to be gained. Brothers and sisters learn to set priorities based on qualities of goodness toward helping others, appreciation and respect for good health. From their special relationships with their sisters, they learn the most important lessons in life.

> Ten year old Julie's best friend became an aunt and Julie asked me how she could become an aunt. I told her that one of her brothers or sisters would have to get married and have a baby. Then I went on to say that all things considered, she'd probably be the first in the family to have a baby. Then she looked at me and said, "What about Mary?" I replied that Mary probably wouldn't get married unless God healed her of Rett syndrome. She looked at me for a few seconds and I could see the wheels turning. With all sincerity, she said, "Why wouldn't someone want to marry Mary? She's such a nice person." "It's obvious that in Julie's eyes, there is nothing wrong with Mary, only with those who couldn't love her. It's moments like these that make me extra glad Mary has sisters and brothers.

> I took Leesa to one of my last high school dances in my senior year. Leesa would have been a freshman that year and I felt this would be her last chance to do what she should he doing. When one of the senior football players came up to her, asked her if she'd like to dance, and then carried her out onto the floor to dance, I knew I was not the only one touched by Leesa.

> For a few years, Christmas was not a very big time of joy in our household. It was the time of year we always associated RS with, and still do. Three years ago my sister was going through one of her major screaming fits. I remember Reba being miserably sick and regressing. Through the long hours, we would walk the floors with her, trying to get her to stop crying and we noticed that Christmas tree lights would soothe her bellowing cries. To this day, there are Christmas tree lights strung ALL over the house...a daily reminder of Christmas! That year we even thought that it would be best to postpone, or even cancel it for the year! The long faces were seen lurking behind the Christmas tree, and muffled cries were heard behind closed doors. You could almost hear the pain in each cry that said "why me Lord, why my family, why my beautiful sister?" Now I've come to realize that my sister is a blessing, an angel if you will. Each of us has had our own wars along the way, not easy by any means!

Take a long look at your sister. Look at the beauty that sits before you. Think how much different life would be if she had not entered your life. I think of this often and it makes me quickly realize that for one second I would not give up this precious gem. I love her more than my life itself! I think of all the funny stories she's brought my way, and I think of all the laughs that she's given me! I think of the not-so-good times, too, but that is what molded me and my family to what we are today, and for that I would not trade anything!

My sister, Mariana, has a beautiful, happy angel face. People think she is short but she is very tall. I think it's because she can't stand up. She is handicapped. She has something called Rett syndrome. I try and communicate with her by trying my best to learn her language. My sister is the best of all.

Ben is the most sensitive, compassionate and affectionate 11 year old boy I know. When anyone is hurt or upset, he is right there with his arms around the child or adult, doing everything he can to help. He sees right into people's hearts. There is no fooling him when it comes to feelings or character. At his age, when kids are conscious of being "cool," Ben will still hold his daddy's hand in public. He still climbs onto my lap when he gets out of bed in the morning. And he would rather spend an hour with me than with his friends. I can't believe all of this is a coincidence. Our "special" daughter has brought changes in all of us, but especially Ben. The best words I can put on what it has done to my wife and I: it has made us more human, and I think this effect has been amplified in Ben.

I'm almost always guaranteed a smile or a giggle if I say, "I missed you today." Well, I said that to her in her ear and she started giggling. How precious her laugh is! Just a giggle from her is enough to wipe out all that made my day bad! After that, I always say to her and say, "Where's my favorite girl?" and then, "Reba's my favorite girl." She smiled at that one, too. What came next threw me totally off guard! She was looking up and me and I was looking down at her...with that I said, "You know Jennifer loves you soooooooooo much." She smiled so I pushed my luck again, but this time I leaned and whispered in her ear "I love you." With that I looked at her and she said "I love you." I couldn't believe it! Reba never said that before. I didn't realize that my dad was sitting on the couch right behind me. He said, "did Reba just say I love you?" I started crying because I was so happy and excited! Her words were not spoken very clearly but I sure understood what she said. After that she just held my eye gaze and smiled at me, almost talking with her eyes and saying, "Yeah Jennifer, I did say that!"

Our other children are both very special people. They have a compassion for others which is heartening. They always champion the underdog and save other kids from being bullied. They are very thoughtful of their parents and they strive to make success of their own lives. I really believe they are such people because they are Kirstyn's sisters. She, as the oldest, has always been in their lives, and they have had to view the world a little differently from families which do not have anyone with a disability.

If I had to pick the one person in my life that has taught me the most or had the greatest influence, I would have to choose my sister, Lila. There are many things that she cannot do that many people take for granted. She cannot talk except through her attitudes and actions. Lila is almost always happy. I do not think that there is a person whose spirit cannot be lifted when she comes into the room. She does not judge anyone, she seems to love everyone, and she is afraid of nothing. If everyone had my sister's spirit, the world would be a perfect place to live.

When he was about 15, my son, Matt, was a member of a sibling panel at an IRSA conference. Someone in the audience asked him if it was difficult living with a sister with Rett Syndrome. Without missing a beat, he responded, "Not as difficult as living with my other two sisters."

I Have The Courage

I cannot speak,
but you understand me.
I cannot walk,
so you push me.
I cannot sing,
but I love music.
I cannot crawl,
so you carry me.
I cannot tell jokes,
but I love to laugh.
I cannot wash myself,
so you bathe me.
I cannot play with Barbies,
but I can push a switch.
I cannot wave bye-bye,
so you wave for me.
I cannot dress myself,
but you make me pretty.
I cannot read,
so you tell me stories.
I cannot touch,
but I can feel.
I cannot go up the stairs,
so you put me on the lift.
I cannot tell you how much I love you,
so look into my eyes and you will see.
I cannot tell what the future will hold,
but I have the courage to go on.

Jennifer Ann Robles

HELPFUL HINTS FOR PARENTS

- Recognize your place as your child's most powerful teacher
- Listen carefully and provide straight answers
- See each child's individual value and uniqueness
- Limit caregiving responsibilities; use respite care and support services
- Accept your daughter's disability, but also recognize your other child's ability
- Plan special time alone
- Welcome others to the home in an accepting environment
- Give abundant praise to siblings
- Be honest about their accomplishments
- Involve siblings in decisions that may affect them
- Recognize times of special stress:
    Birth of another child
    Sister with RS goes to school
    Friends reject the sister
    Friends ask questions about the sister
    RS sister becomes critically ill

Family keeps secrets about the child
Parents divorce
Parents die
Siblings marry
- Provide a normal family life
- Don't expect siblings to act like adults if they are still children

GRANDPARENTS AND RELATIVES

Just as you never expected to parent a child with special needs, your parents never expected to be placed in this different role. Their hurt is double; they ache for their child and for their grandchild. They may go through the same stages of grief you experience. What is supposed to be a joyous time turns to one of great concern.

How can we make it easier for grandparents?

Just as you need understanding, they need a sympathetic ear. Try to understand how they must feel.

> The feelings are very much the same as those of the parents, with two big differences. First, a child of my child is twice my child. I hurt twice, once for my daughter and again for my granddaughter. Not just emotional hurt, but physical hurt too, deep heartbreaking hurt. Like any parents, my husband and I worked diligently to provide our daughter with advantages we never had. When she married, she held these same hopes and desires for her family. I hurt when I see my daughter thin, and over-tired, knowing she is being robbed of the carefree years of youth. I hurt when strangers "treat her funny" because her 4 year old is in diapers and drinks from a bottle, while physically she looks totally normal. I hurt when I see my daughter struggle with well-meaning doctors, therapists, and even equipment manufacturers, who fail to trust a mother's instinct as to what is best for her child. I hurt when I see my daughter go through the stages of denial, then "Why me," then the frustration, bitterness and finally acceptance. I feel pride when she faces each day with optimism, patience, and a smile. I feel guilty that I live so many miles away and can't be of much help. I feel frustrated that I can't take Megan home with me because of the seizures, sleeplessness, and constipation. I feel sad when I see my grandsons running, playing, growing, learning, and seeing them explore life with such wonder and delight. I grieve that I will never bake cookies with Megan Ann. We will never shop till we drop, sing songs, share secrets, ride bikes, or buy prom dresses, nor will she marry. The list goes on and on. Secondly, a grandparent is once-removed from the situation, as far as offering guidance, opinions, and suggestions. She must bite her tongue many times because, after all, the decisions concerning this child are not hers to make. The parents are already bombarded from many directions with well-intentioned advice.

My child's grandparents won't accept the diagnosis.

It may be hard for them to face the facts. They may want to think the doctor made a mistake or that it is not so serious. This is their own denial, and it is a necessary part of the growth process. They are not with you day in and day out, so they don't see the problem as you do. Give them some information to read and some time to take it all in.

My parents try to make decisions for us. We want them to respect our choices for her care.

Grandparents are dealing with a problem they probably have never had to face before. They want to make sure the best decisions are made. Be patient with their suggestions, but be firm about how you want to handle things.

My parents don't help at all. They seem to be uncomfortable around our daughter.

This attitude usually comes from not knowing what to do or how to do it. They may be afraid they will do something wrong or harmful. Help them develop confidence. They don't know what you need unless you tell them. They may see you doing everything perfectly, and assume you don't want any interference. Do ask them for help, letting them know how much it means.

> I was at my sister's house around Christmas, as she was putting ribbons around stocking stuffers. She started with the other nieces and nephews, and handed me Michelle's, with no name tag and no ribbon. I hesitated a minute, handed it back, and said, "Oh, I'm sorry, Michelle wants the ribbons and all the works, too." She happily prepared Michelle's the same if not better than the others. I just don't let anyone overlook Michelle. If her cousins or any guests greet or say goodbye to everyone and not Michelle, I kindly ask Michelle, "Did you tell So and So hi, or bye?" And they come around every time.

Do grandparents learn to cope as we do in time?

Every person is different and there is no formula for growth or acceptance. Chances are, though, that they will be touched in the same way you have been.

> Many good things have come from our hurt. We are closer to God, for Megan is like an angel sent for a little while to teach us, strengthen us, and set our priorities straight. With her chubby little cheeks, black eyes, and long curly hair, she has taught us perseverance, and that you can still have a smile when all else has gone wrong. She has taught us patience and humility. She has taught us to listen more closely with our hearts to others less insulated from life's problems and hurts. She is a constant reminder that all persons need love and praise. Megan Ann can no longer crawl, walk, talk, or feed herself, but her face lights up when we praise her or hold her close! Is the hurt lessening? No, but acceptance is just around the corner. God's plan is perfect, and one day He will take Megan Ann home where she will walk and talk, and play. Even though the tears are just below the surface, I don't question God's plan or feel bitter anymore.

HELPFUL HINTS FOR GRANDPARENTS AND RELATIVES

- Listen with love. Try to be non-judgmental and sincere.
- Give us time to adjust. We need time to work things out.
- Respect our choices. You may have a different opinion, but we need mutual strength and support.
- Respect our schedules. We're more overwhelmed than ever.
- Be available. The most precious gift you can give is your time.
- Balance your time and attention among all of the children and grandchildren.
- Don't leave our daughter out. Include her in conversation, games and fun.
- Love her. She is first a child. Recognize her strengths.

CARE FOR THE CAREGIVER

"MY COPE RUNNETH OVER"

It is so important to place this chapter near the front of the book, and not leave it for the end – just as it is important to put ourselves first in the care pyramid, at the foundation. Taking care of all of someone else's needs for a lifetime is a task. No matter how much you love her, no matter how strong you are, no matter how good an attitude you may have – it is a task. Most of us do what we can to provide for her needs first, because there is little time for everything. All too often, we find ourselves at the bottom of the priority list. Just as the stewardess advises us on a flight, we need to put on our own oxygen masks before helping our children. This is lifesaving stuff we're talking about. It is nearly impossible to provide everything that is needed for someone else when our own basic needs are not met.

There is no getting away from the all-out demands of the role of caregiver. While other family members can "fend" for themselves now and then, our daughters with RS count on us for every aspect of daily living. We didn't get any job preparation for this role. The hours are long and the vacations too few and far between to make up for the energy drain. We must schedule doctors visits, therapy appointments and IEP meetings while providing enrichment and stimulation for our special daughters, making sure not to overlook the needs of the other children. It's not always easy to just dial up a babysitter or find a substitute. And there are many deep emotions to balance at the same time. Love is the easy part. Sometimes it's hard to see beyond the sadness and pain. Finding the strength to meet these everyday challenges can overwhelm us at times.

FROM GRIEF TO GOOD GRIEF

The first step in caring for ourselves is to understand that we all live with a mix of emotions from joy to despair. Grief is a natural response to loss. We need to give ourselves time and permission for it. In a sense, we are mourning the death of lost dreams for our girls. When we find ourselves particularly sad, we can remember to look at our daughters and see that they are happy most of the time. While she struggles with the limits of what she can do, the grief really is ours, not hers. Grief runs in cycles and may return when we think we are doing well, such as during holidays or birthdays. We're better prepared when we realize that this is inevitable. Grieve the loss naturally. Sharing feelings is a good way to resolve the grief. Write it down – put it in a poem, or talk to loved ones and friends.

> The frustrations of Rett are so insidious at times…you think you're going along smoothly and handling it when all of a sudden it hits you like a brick wall. *My daughter has Rett syndrome!* And some of the initial shock and pain resurfaces and leaves you with that knot in the pit of your stomach. I suspect that most of us all have this knot in our stomachs, the lump in our throats and the pain in our hearts. No matter the specifics, we are all connected. So that is where our strength lies.

Some days we're angry at everyone for everything, when actually we're angry about RS. People stare, people don't help, and everything we do seems difficult. It makes us mad! It's okay to be angry about it, but it's not okay to let anger take control. Anger can consume us. It is non-productive and just weighs us down terribly. Anger should be aimed not at her, but at her disability. We are all angry about what RS has done to our girls and to our lives, but hostility and aggression are cumbersome. Get rid of emotions that won't help. If you need to vent your anger, do something about it. Find constructive ways to deal with your anger so that it doesn't cripple you. Take a walk, ride a bike, shoot hoops, write it down, talk about it. Accept that some people are ignorant and will stare. Sometimes you might stare back. Another time you might stop and politely explain about your daughter. Every now and then you just have to let loose and tell the staring person he's rude. When you find yourself getting angry, ask yourself if the anger will change things. Then look for something that can be changed, change it and move on.

> I find my days to be an emotional roller coaster, completely tied to Nikki's emotions. When she has a good moment, so do I. As her mood changes, so does mine. I try to stay strong, believing that as I feel her, she feels me. Today, sadness overcomes me. She once again has an upper respiratory thing going on. All sorts of emotions are flying out of her – anger, frustration and sadness. Sadness for what I believe, she knows she cannot do. The everyday occurrence of banging into a wall, which normally doesn't even faze her, is sending her into a river of tears.

Too much caregiving can lead to exhaustion, depression and resentment. If you always fill the glasses of everyone around you first, when it finally is your turn, the pitcher is empty. Make sure to re-fill your own glass often. You need strength to pass the pitcher.

> Moms of girls with Rett syndrome and other handicapping conditions really have to work at acheiving balance in their lives and at keeping their sanity. We deserve to have lives of our own, and we will only have this if we are willing to step forth and claim it by doing those things we know we must.

RECIPES FOR STRESS

by Claudia Weisz

Take an unlimited amount of obligations, and fit them into a limited amount of time. Combine with any number of things over which you have no control. Add a sedentary lifestyle and several hands full of junk food, and mix well. Add a family member who needs constant attention and care. Refuse all offers of help. Add several hours of sitting in hospitals and doctors' offices, several hours of nighttime caregiving, a handful of unexplained screaming spells, a dash of explaining to others why she is crying. Be sure to mix in a container where no one understands and stir with a spoon of solid tension. Add self-pity, to taste. Serve with loneliness and isolation. Variations of this basic recipe can be created from the following optional ingredients:

Some sort of medication can add flavor to your stress recipe. Telephones (especially flavorful if your phone number is very close to that of a local real estate office with rental and sale signs all over town, or better yet, a teenager.) Just as a little sugar and spice added to vinegar makes a delectable sauce, certain ingredients added to your recipe for stress balance its flavor.

The first thing to remember in any recipe is the importance of weighing the ingredients. Weigh upsetting events on a scale of one to ten. Get support. Even great chefs have their assistants. Reach out for help. Give support. Again, watch quantities.

Animals can add to stress or relieve it. Stroking a pet can lower blood pressure: damaged furniture or carpeting may raise it. Squabbling siblings (these are nice served with a sprig of anger). Demanding or complaining spouse or boss (best drawn and quartered or filleted. Avoid marinating, especially in wine). Malfunctioning office machines (most effective if served with a deadline). Vomiting dog (most effective combined with a light colored, deep pile carpet, preferably new). Constantly meowing cat (adds a nice touch, especially one with fleas). Any pet, as long as it needs constant feeding, and letting in and out.

Share yourself, but don't give it all away. Eliminate unnecessary ingredients. Often the finest sauces are those with the least ingredients. Simplicity can be elegant. Do you really need the pet, or should you keep the pet and get rid of the carpeting?

Take stock of your ingredients. Make a list of the things which upset you. Are you really upset at the dog or at the kids who said they'd take care of him? Do you have "isolation" mislabeled "privacy?"

All recipes are easily altered. If you are too heavy handed with any one ingredient the result will lack balance. Remember, you are the chef!

> Being a caregiver 24 hours a day 7 days a week will make you neurotic. I know, because I am and I will probably always be a little crazy. As time goes on and your life patterns change you will make different decisions. I haven't had a vacation in 18 years that hasn't been to care for someone else. I am not complaining, I feel blessed that I have the skills to give comfort to others. But I am tired. And on the days that we feel less than perfect we should be able to say so.

CREATING BALANCE

GET BETTER...NOT BITTER

Manure stinks but it makes great fertilizer. Try to look on the bright side. For every negative, there is a positive...it just takes a harder look and a good attitude.

SET BOUNDARIES

Realize that you can say "no" once in awhile and still be a good parent. Let others take responsibility for refreshments for the baseball team now and then. Since you can't do it all, do what is the most important. Set limits on what you have to do and what you really want to do.

HELP YOUR CHILD, BUT DON'T HARM YOURSELF

Too much helping can be bad for your health. When your life is organized totally around the needs of others, you are always compromising and this leads to distress. It is very important to learn to take care of your own needs. You don't have to stop being helpful altogether. Caring and nurturing are very important traits. Just make sure that taking care of others doesn't interfere with taking care of yourself.

INVEST WISELY

To see how your investments balance, fold a piece of paper in half. On one side, list the things you do for others. On the other side, list what you do for yourself. Do your lists balance or even come close to it? If not, it's time to start getting some equilibrium.

FIND THE RIGHT TIME

Choose a good time to discuss your daughter's needs with your partner. Avoid making it the first or only topic of conversation after work or when you are both tired.

STOP, LOOK, LISTEN AND TALK

Men and women differ in how and when they communicate. As a couple, we can get into patterns of holding our feelings in, sometimes to protect our partner from the pain, sometimes to avoid the pain. We can also assume that our partner understands how we feel. One may need to talk about it and the other may want to run away from it. Listen carefully and then talk about it. Don't expect your partner to read your mind. Recognize that while it probably IS the biggest issue at your house, it is not the only issue.

HAVE FAITH IN YOURSELF

Don't think that you have to know how to do everything perfectly or the way that others suggest might be right. You ARE the best expert on your child. Listen to your own heart.

BE GENTLE WITH YOURSELF

When you get Rett lag, reach for the oxygen. A twenty minute power nap does wonders. Meditate, stare out the window or go for a walk when you can. When you've had some quiet time, you'll be refreshed and ready to start again.

HELP IS A HOLLER AWAY

Don't hesitate to ask someone else to help. Basically, you have two choices. You can GIVE IN and get help, or you will reach the point where you GIVE OUT and then GIVE UP. It happens all too often in families who have taken first rate care of their daughters and neglected themselves. They wake up one day and say, "I can't do this one day longer." It's better to get help than try to do it alone. Get help when you first need it rather than waiting for a crisis to build. Where can you find help?
- family members
- teachers
- friends, neighbors or church members
- doctors, nurses and other health professionals
- support groups
- parents of other children with special needs

DO SOMETHING DIFFERENT

Develop interests outside your special parent role so that you avoid burnout. Find a healthy outlet that has nothing to do with your child's condition. Do something physical if you can. The following rules apply: Do it – Do it today – Do it with gusto – Do it without guilt.

GET AWAY ALONE

You need to nurture and foster your relationship with one another if you plan to be together for the long haul. Plan some time away just for yourselves. If you are a single parent, the same applies. Don't consider it a luxury; consider it a necessity and budget for it. Do without something else, not time alone together. There may be many things you need, but you need yourself first. Then you need each other.

LEARN TO BE TEMPORARILY INCOMPETENT

People never want to help when they think they can't do it as well as you. They are less likely to want to help when they see you do everything perfectly. Be willing to settle for less once in awhile. Sometimes, less is more.

TOSS THE GUILT

Recognize this as soon as you can. It's impossible to get away from the guilt. In your own eyes, you may feel that you can never do enough. Stop trying to do the impossible. If your child is cranky and you take her to McDonald's with the other kids, she may spoil the All American Dinner Out. So you're guilty. If you leave her home and take the other kids, you've left the poor disabled child at home. So you're guilty again. Guilty no matter what. Accept that and toss the guilt out the window. When she's in good spirits take her. When she's cranky, leave her at home where she will probably be happier anyway. Everyone wins once in awhile. Do the best that you can do.

KEEP YOUR SENSE OF HUMOR

If you don't have a sense of humor, you're doomed. Laugh at each other, but also laugh at yourselves. Laughter is exercise you need to survive. To others who don't walk in our shoes, what we are able to laugh at may seem warped. It's all part of learning about what's important and what's not.

YOU DON'T HAVE TO BE A HERO

Give yourself permission to be human – to be sad, to be mad, to be fed up, to be un-special. At times you may care as much as Mother Theresa and you can try as hard as Superman, but you don't have to always be special. We are not helpful to anyone around us if we are tired, emotionally drained, sleep deprived and have no social outlet.

COUNT YOUR BLESSINGS

When you add it all up, you have much to be thankful for.

> *A life hemmed in respite is less likely to unravel.*

MAKING SENSE

INSIDE OUT, UPSIDE DOWN  AND BACKWARDS

Many girls with RS are reported to be less in tune with their senses as babies and more inactive than their brothers and sisters. Some seem uninterested in the world around them. Others have strong reactions to particular sights or sounds. In infancy, these responses are not seen as a dramatic sign that something is wrong. But when a girl enters the regression phase of RS, there is no mistaking it. It becomes obvious to everyone that her world has turned upside down, inside out and backwards. Something is wrong. She may cry inconsolably and act frightened at sights and sounds that were not a problem in the months before. She may become hysterical at any change in her environment. She may reject being handled, not wanting to be touched. Foods that she once liked best may be rejected. She may look away and refuse to make eye contact.

All of this is terribly confusing for parents. We wonder what in the world is happening. Everything that worked before fails. Our child is miserable, and we are equally upset. It is one of the most bewildering aspects of RS – knowing that something is wrong, and not knowing where to turn. All too often, we feel that in her misery, she has rejected us, too.

While it is a stressful time for parents, it is an even more difficult time for her. Something is wrong. During the regression period, she is terribly confused by the sensory input she receives. She cannot make sense of things that look, sound, taste, smell, and feel differently than they did a short time ago. Sounds that may seem normal to you may all of a sudden be painfully loud to her. The distance from the high chair to the floor may seem like she's looking down from the rooftop. Sensory chaos is all around her. She may go from hyperactive to unresponsive for days. Her world does not make sense.

During this time, it is most helpful to recognize that she is not rejecting you; she's rejecting the chaos. Understanding this and providing structure and security to her world will reduce her anxiety and yours, as well. When she begins to lose skills, our first inclination is to rush out and buy every book on therapies we can find in an attempt to head off the pending disaster. We want to bombard her with stimulation from every corner – rocking, stroking, singing, even spinning her to stimulate those senses which seem to be refusing or amplifying input. It goes against our theories about the need for brain stimulation and early intervention, but in RS, providing too much stimulation is probably not the most helpful thing to do at this time. It's better to provide emotional security and soothing comfort so that she can adjust to the calamity. When her sensory impressions have been moderated, she'll be in a more responsive mood for therapies that can really help.

In time, she seems to get better. Either she learns how to sort out and handle these sensory highs and lows or her sensory impressions normalize to some degree. Even so, she will always have some difficulty perceiving, interpreting and integrating sensory stimuli – and this may cause her to become distressed or panicked. One parent said her daughter can tune out a train running through the family room at times, but she always bolts straight up in bed from a sound sleep at the first light touch of her doorknob.

Sometimes using two senses at once can be overwhelming, so she unconsciously chooses to concentrate by "looking" over "listening" or chooses to "smell" before she "tastes."

Situations affect our girls in scary ways, like crossing from light floor color to dark floor color. Amy doesn't look particularly scared but can't do it on her own – she needs a slight nudge to tell her it's okay. Her teacher found she got very upset when changing activities if they didn't give her any warning that this was happening. So now they tell her and show her photos of the new activity well before changing and this has helped enormously.

SENSORY INTEGRATION

Leah used to get sick and throw up any time she was on a swing, but with more experience she got used to it and now enjoys it. We took her to a specialist in Sensory Integration about 3 weeks ago and got exercises which are supposed to help. The notion is that people with vestibular problems need help in setting their proprioceptive (touch, joints, position sense) inputs. We are supposed to do leg and arm rubbing, push in on her shoulder joints, hands on shoulder, leg weights, ace bandage wraps and several other exercises several times a day for a month. We are supposed to see improvements, both physical and in her focus and concentration. Once the exercises were done, she became much calmer. She actually said "Mo" (for more) since she liked it. When I do it to her, however, she tries to get away, probably reflecting how skillfully I do the exercises.

We have had Katie in all types of therapies including Sensory Integration. I can tell you, it has really worked with Katie. She is very aware of her hands and uses them very well. Swinging on a platform swing has brought back her depth perception and equilibrium. We still see occasional problems in this area, but they are quicker to go away. We are also trying the brushing now, on the palms of her hands. She has never been a hand wringer, but she is a fist clencher. She can now relax her hands when asked to and will actually hold her hand out to you when she knows she is going to have them brushed! Katie has always tickled the palms of her hands and the bottom of her feet. She still does but not as intensely as she used to. We also give Katie a good rub down twice a day. She loves it! I believe all of this together has made her more coordinated, a better walker and better skilled with her hands. The program of exercise we were given for her involves leg and arm rubbing, hands on and off her shoulders, joint compressions, ankle weights, ace bandage wrapping, hand rubbing, etc. The goal is to improve her sense of touch, movement and proprioceptive input. We are supposed to see improvement in six weeks. The short term goals are to improve play skills, decrease mouthing and teeth grinding, improve awareness of her hands, move from two inch mat to carpet more quickly and improve her balance.

We do the rubbing, deep pressure, weights, and lots of balance activities with Corinne. She loved the exercise ball so much, we bought one for home. Much of this activity is also good for muscle isolation and strengthening—her P.T. explained that what she was doing on the exercise ball was something I could also do at home and that it would help to strengthen the back muscles and help to prevent scoliosis. What works most for Corinne is the deep pressure/joint compressions, especially when on her arms and shoulders. I have found that pressure on her shoulders will allow her to move her arms/hands more accurately without me having to guide her so much. This gives me a more accurate understanding of what she is reaching for. It also enables her to push her walker better and not have me push for her.

Initially, they worked on all of the sensory issues. Her therapist said they needed to desensitize her by brushing her arms and legs, and get her to feel all sorts of different textures. It was very difficult for her to withstand this and she cried and cried. Now she has no problems at all with this and she has begun reaching for food objects and accepting hand-over-hand play. She still grinds her teeth constantly even with the oral stimulation from the gum care brushes. Yet, I personally believe that children can learn and understand so much about the world around them through touch, and Sensory Integration can only benefit them.

When Corinne is sitting (or standing sometimes – she needs to hold onto something) we press downward on her shoulders giving her a better awareness of where she is. They call this deep pressure and it seems to have a lasting (albeit short) effect – for some time afterwards she is better able to take her hands apart and to use them functionally. This also helps with her learning to push her walker – she tends to lean back but by pushing downward she "gets" the forward motion. Unfortunately it disappears too quickly!

I like the idea of wraps and joint compression. I think our kids are loose and cannot support weight sometimes and that this might help. Putting orthotics in Amanda's shoes definitely helped straighten her feet and helped her walk better – basically took some of the support off her body.

We use deep pressure with Shanda and we make it a game. We call it the "cookie game." We wrap Shanda in a blanket and then tell her we are going to eat the Shanda cookie. We use deep pressure on her shoulders, arms and legs. She just loves this game!

Kim has been doing Feldenkrais functional integration (FI) all this year. There is much pressing on the shoulders while Kim is lying down on her back (eventually she was able to do that, with just small bolsters under knees and ankles, head back resting on folded towels). It is in short rhythmic pulses, and very gentle. Any slight resistance and the physical therapist tries another way. The idea is that it is felt through the bones down to the feet. It is also done in the other direction, i.e. from the feet towards the shoulders. It must feel very good, because Kim just loves it.

The way you look at your daughter changes and the therapists are all pros, so they'll have a lot of positive things to say. So initially things seem to help. The true test is after you have done a therapy for 3 to 6 months, stop and look at her current level of functioning. Measure her level of functioning in several areas with concrete toys, environments, tasks, social issues, etc. Then, after 6 more months, see if she has actually improved or has stopped regressing compared to prior 6 month point in time, not from the initial starting point. Anyone can say she improved from the initial point, just from changing the way you look at something.

We went through Sensory Integration therapy for about 2 years, did the platform swing in the house, swinging outside, brushing, shaving cream, massaging, and all that stuff. It was fun for us and Amanda, and we needed some fun things to do. She loved the platform swing in the house with a mirror, and she loved to kick balls and balloons on the swing. It was hilarious, some of the sessions, we really got her "cooking." Like all therapies, it seemed to help socially in some ways initially but overall, after 2 years, she actually walked worse and did not seem more or less tactile defensive. I know other kids, personally, that this approach really helped, but they were more tactile defensive to begin with.

SIGHT

Most girls with RS have normal vision with the exception of near and far sight, which can be corrected with glasses, and crossed eyes, which can be corrected by patching and surgery. Often, she will look at an object she wants to pick up, then glance away before she reaches for it. She may look from the corner of her eye or use a side-glance instead of looking straight on. When approaching something new and unfamiliar, she often looks quickly, glances away, and looks again several times before she finally settles on the object of her attention. Then, she often leans forward to visually inspect the object carefully. Some parents describe their daughter's vision as "either-or" – shifting quickly from things close to far away, but not taking in what is between the two. Sometimes she cannot visually follow an object except in short jerky movements, while at other times she can follow smoothly.

It seems Lisa can't process what she sees and look at it the same time. She will see something she really likes then look away for awhile than back at it. It always seemed very strange to us when Lisa first started walking. We still had to hold on to her hand. She closed her eyes most of the time we were walking on the sidewalk but she always knew when we came back to the curb, and would step down without prompting.

Before Katri began to loose her hand grasping, she would always look at her food on the tray and look away before she took the food and put it to her mouth. At the time Ilene and I thought that she wouldn't use the utensils because she wasn't concentrating and looking at what she was doing. Now I think she was focusing on the task, but to do so she had to look away.

When something interferes with Kim's view of an object, she will adjust her gaze to improve that view. It happens so frequently – either she looks away, or turns her head, and when ready will look directly at the object in question. I think that it is a genuine attempt to improve a situation that has gone bad.

Objects with a distinct figure-ground effect with sharp contrasts or clear outlines (white door on a painted wall) seem to catch her attention more quickly. The combination of lights and motion, such as mirrors, glitter or candles is also attractive. Many parents report that their daughters are drawn to eyes, whether in person, on a doll or a photograph. These preferences are seen in infant development. As she gains experience, she may learn to discriminate in more sophisticated ways than using sensory impressions.

Karina used to close her eyes the moment anyone came in her line of vision. That was also during the regression period and lasted about two years. During regression, Kim would not look anyone in the eye. If we came too close, she would shut her eyes rather than look at ours. I didn't understand, but now think it may be related to seeing in bits, and there may have been something unpleasant about looking at our eyes. This went on for about 3 years.

It's as if looking at the object would be painful, so instead she will risk soulful glances, quickly, quietly, fearful that if they were to hit their target the object would disappear.

Dani has often not been able to look right at an object she really wants to pick up. Even when she's finger painting, she doesn't look at the canvas until it's finished.

Visually, Leah may be both defensive to some visual information and have difficulty coordinating her eyes together to know where she is in space. This can add to her fearfulness of moving on uneven surfaces.

Depth perception is altered, and the girl with RS who is able to walk often hesitates when she must go up or down. Going up steps is difficult enough, but going down steps is often impossible. This is because she perceives the distance from one step to another as much higher or lower than reality, and she fears falling. It is the same when she changes level, grade or texture.

Meghan will have problems with changes in the floor or ground. She is not always looking down, so many times she misses them. But, every now and then in unfamiliar territory, she will come across a change she doesn't know how to negotiate. We try to help her by telling her verbally – "it is a step" or "it is not a step." Sometimes, she just needs to look at it for a minute and then she will go over it. It can be just paint on a parking lot.

Maria is quick to go up stairs, but very hesitant to go down. Part of it is the fear of falling and being unsure about stepping down, but one thing I never considered was what Maria's P.T. told me. Maria started to go down the stairs sideways instead of forward. She would rotate her hips, and I thought it made her feel more secure. That may have been part of it, but we also discovered a new term called "passive insufficiency of the hamstrings muscles." This means that Maria was rotating her hips forward to side-step down the stairs because of her tight hamstrings, which weren't supporting her weight on the back leg as she was stepping with the front leg.

Going up stairs requires a weight shift slightly forward. Meg tends to want to extend backwards which is very dangerous on the stairs. We hold her left hand (standing behind her) and pull her ever so slightly forward at about waist level to get the weight shift we need for climbing stairs. This helps her to initiate the movement. Sometimes, she also needs a physical prompt at her right hand to hold the railing. If we stand too close, she will lean on us for support and not do the work. It's a delicate balance and she has good and bad days. On really good days, she will even alternate her feet!

It really helps Becky if there are no steps and if the difference between the kitchen floor and the carpeted floor is as even as possible. Also helps if the colors are similar so she doesn't feel as if she will "fall off" from one room to another.

SOUND

Hearing is normal in Rett syndrome, except for mild problems which may result from recurrent middle ear infections. The young girl with RS may have a larger incidence of these infections and fluid in the middle ear, which could lead to hearing problems later. She uses sounds to associate various elements of her environment. While she can concentrate on visual images by continuing to look at them, sound images are here and gone. For her to concentrate, they must be repeated. Sights and sounds are very important in making sense of her surroundings. Noisy surroundings are very uncomfortable for some girls and they become very agitated and irritable. Others may react by laughing, or even going to sleep to shut the noise out. Unexpected, loud, shrill or high-pitched sounds may frighten or confuse her. She may have a preference for a particular kind of music or rhythm.

When Stephanie was 2 years old, she could hardly deal with being touched. Also, the sound of running water from the water faucet, the vacuum cleaner, lots of people making the same sounds such as cheering, clapping, or singing would make her tremble. Now that she is almost 4 years old, she loves to be hugged and cuddled, likes running water to be falling on her head, still hates the vacuum cleaner, but thinks people clapping are cheering her on.

At times she almost seems angry until the noise is resolved. When she was younger, crowd noise seemed to affect her more than now. Her teacher at school has noticed and voiced that she is "sensitive" to a lot of "noise stimuli" – except music.

Amy gets overstimulated by children crying. She gets very tense. She will sometimes escape to her room or she will start yelling her own version of rett-rap or she will have a seizure. It's too many stimuli coming her way at one time and she can't handle it. Although Amy loves to be the center of the party, she can only handle so much.

Briana is especially sensitive to other children who scream and cry. She has not yet ever had a seizure, but the loud noises of another student screaming make her become agitated and tremulous. When a new student came into her class this past fall, and would spend the better part of each day screaming and crying, Briana became a ball of frustration. Her skills fell short of her usual productivity, and her emotions were all knotted up. When Briana arrived home from school, it took me close to an hour each day to get her to relax and be comfortable. I started having trouble getting her ready for school in the mornings, as she protested wanting to be there. She covered her ears before she even got on the bus, and her little fists would be clenched. The trouble stopped only when the other child was removed from the class during her crying fits.

TOUCH

Many girls are sensitive about their faces – they don't like having their faces washed or teeth brushed and hate being splashed by wind, rain or snow. They often rub their eyes or scratch their faces. They may look at food for a long time on the spoon before they take it to their mouths. They prefer food at room temperature rather than hot or cold, and texture is frequently more important than taste and smell. They swallow solids more readily than liquids.

Although it may vary, most girls have a high sensitivity to pain and difficulty expressing their pain in conventional ways. They may tense up and freeze instead of crying out loud. There may be a delay in feeling pain. Often, "external pain," such as a bump on the head or a shot, does not seem to hurt as much as "internal pain," like a stomachache or gas. Some parents report that their daughters feel pain differently in various parts of the body – a fall on the front of the head may seem to cause great pain, while a fall on the back of the head may not cause any reaction at all. Sometimes a child's fracture is not discovered until two days later when swelling sets in.

This poses serious problems when trying to identify the source of crying – is it pain or is it boredom or frustration or anger? The chapter on Behavior offers a check-list to help sort it out.

> She also hated being touched. I remember her sitting on my lap with my arms around her but not touching. Still, when she noticed my arms, she would push me away. She never did this with her brother. Quite the contrary. He could hug her and play with her. So I think it was not all sensory input problems. She made her choices of input.

> Leah appears to be both insensitive to some types of touch and hypersensitive to others. A good sense of touch is important to emotional development, hand skills and attention. Leah would use her hands more if she was more aware of them. She is defensive to light touch stimulation and has some lack of registration. She has a problem differentiating protective versus discriminative information. Protective touch gives withdrawal or defense, while discriminative touch provides the brain with precise information on size, shape and texture of objects and environment. The ability to separate whether touch is harmful or not is essential for tool use, attention, many aspects of social and emotional development and tolerance of self care activities including grooming and eating. Leah constantly mouths objects to give her more information. The mouth has the largest touch representation area in the body.

> We play a game called "Jiggle the Bones." Bri loves it and we all walk away smelling good. We all put lots of lotion on our hands and little Bri, then we tickle her, or as I call it Jiggle her Bones…It's a fun way for Erica to help in some of Bri's therapies.

> In my experience it is very useful to stimulate her sense of body and hands: by massage, tickling, stroking gently, all sorts of body games, also the rough ones. Karina has gone a long way in accepting others to touch her and in touching objects herself. It did come very slowly and gradually. Do not expect to see progression in a few months; do not evaluate the use of therapies after a short period. Sometimes hopeful changes do not last long, but they can return later, sometimes after years.

TASTE

Girls with RS seem to have normal taste senses. Just like any other child, they have likes and dislikes.

> I always thought it was strange that McKenna would grab the lemon slice out of my iced tea when she was a year old and suck on it. McKenna has always been able to pack away a ton of food, but she also eats almost anything. She sucks on lemons, eats dill pickles, loves all of her veggies, and even eats the baby food meats! She can be picky though…she will only eat hamburgers from

McDonald's. She likes chicken sticks from Burger King, but won't touch McDonald's nuggets. She will eat the canned macaroni and cheese but not the "good stuff" like Kraft! She will eat rice with veggies but won't touch rice pudding! Go figure! She will drink anything, milk, juice, pop, even coffee. I wonder if she has taste buds?

SMELL

Shanda can smell food a mile away! She gets lots of enjoyment out of eating new foods.

AROUSAL AND CALM

The nervous system moderates our level of arousal. When everything is working right, we are able to remain awake and alert, provided that we have had enough sleep, without becoming upset or hyperactive. Many younger girls with RS seem to get over-excited easily and end up screaming and crying in situations that involve too much sensory input. On the other hand, many girls fall asleep frequently during the daytime. It may be that their quality of sleep is poor and they are simply tired or it may be the effects of medication. Or, it could be a problem with sensory modulation, which is regulated in part by the level of serotonin in the brain.

Following are some exercises to either rev her up or settle her down:

Calming Sensations:
- Slow, rhythmic, back and forth movement. Most calming when eyes are righted with the horizon
- Deep pressure or steady compression
- Slow stretch (avoid using with children who have low muscle tone)
- Wrapping tightly in a blanket
- Firm stroking over large areas
- Warm temperatures
- Simple shapes with rounded contours
- Unchanging visual stimuli
- Subtle or subdued patterns with pastel colors
- Gentle, sing-song rhythms
- Simple melodies and low tones
- Dim light
- Weighted vest or blanket

Arousing Sensations:
- Activities which involve rapid, jerky movements that involve a change in direction. The most arousing are movements that are unpredictable and involve a change in direction.
- Hanging upside down (inverting the head)
- Swinging on suspended equipment
- Spinning around (watch for autonomic reactions such as increased perspiration, nausea, flushed or pale skin, hiccups. These signal overarousal!)
- Light touch
- Cold temperatures
- Bright colors or lights
- Red and yellow shades of color
- Black on white or white on black patterns
- Loud music with rapid tempos
- All odors
- Rough textures
- Objects with irregular shapes and angular edges
- Touch to the face

Proprioception is a sense which allows the girl with RS to know where her body is in space without having to look. The **vestibular system** lets her identify movement – whether her body or something near her is moving. These systems will be discussed in Chapter 11, Motor Problems.

The author wishes to thank the following professionals for ideas and information which was used to develop this chapter: Barbro Lindberg; Jan Townsley, OTR/L.

BEHAVIORS

"AIN'T MISBEHAVIN'"

Whether it is performance or mood, when it comes to typical behavior in RS, the one thing that is consistent is inconsistency. We all have moods, influenced by internal forces (headache, constipation, fatigue) and external influences (weather, activity). In RS, moods can fluctuate to extremes within the space of an hour when nothing else in the environment has changed. The girl with RS may be laughing one moment and screaming the next, without explanation. One parent described her daughter as a "tornado waiting to land." One of the most difficult aspects of this behavior is not knowing what to do to return her to calm. Or, she may waken in the night laughing uproariously for hours and be impossible to quiet. It is easy to call this misbehavior, but a closer look tells us that much of it is out of her control.

> Jocelyn does not imitate and has no fine motor skills at all and very poor gross motor skills. What we have found is that for her to do a task it has to be very important and be more spontaneous than learned. For instance, if something she may want is just out of her reach and I want her to try to get it, if I ignore her (or seem to) she may well reach on her own. On the other hand, if I try to model or break down the task into simpler steps it seems that she either can't or won't do it. So we just try to make things look fun and have her participate at her level, when she is ready. When I feed her, sometimes she won't open her mouth. If I try to "force" even gently she resists (and will win every time), but if I pull the spoon away and say "Okay, whenever you are ready," she'll usually open up readily. Sometimes, especially in the morning she won't open 'til I test her hot cereal first and make sure that it's not too hot! I've given her a too hot bite once too often! I think letting her know she has some control over a situation helps, too. The other side of this is that acceptance is very important to her and sometimes she will begin to cry out when she feels left out. If her peers are comfortable with her they can understand this and help her be more involved. There are also times when there seems to be nothing that will make her happy, but this is part of understanding Jocelyn and her need to "vent."

FLUCTUATIONS

> We have noticed these patterns all of Amy's life. We call it "earth to Amy" days. When she is locked out, she is locked out. Then she will be very responsive, verbal, walk, and be in tune. These are the days when she initiates conversation, smiles, laughs appropriately, and gets the joke. They follow no rhyme or reason, are not cyclic, are not related to weekends or weather. When she has the good days, it's God's gift, the other I call the Rett Demon.

> Shanda has her on days and off days too. She has days when everything she tries to do goes great, and other days when she can't do anything right. On the "off" days we just read her favorite books and watch Barney movies. On her "on" days she is a bubbling fountain of joy! I notice Shanda's "off" days usually occur when she has been up during the night. She has many more "on" days than "off" days since she turned five.

WITHDRAWAL

Many girls with RS go through a period of social withdrawal during the regression period, which can be one of the most trying aspects of the disorder. While it may seem like bad behavior, it most likely the result of her confusion. She may be irritable and sleepless, cry for long periods of time and resist your attempts to hold her. She may become very upset if things in her surroundings are changed and she may turn her eyes away to avoid eye contact. She may have a higher tolerance to pain. It is a difficult time for her as she adjusts to many changes. Her bewilderment is understandable. She has lost her ability to use words and to make sense of the world around her. Her body does not move as freely as it used to. She has lost the security and control she was just beginning to master. During this difficult time, it is hard to know just what she needs. The security that comes from structure and routine, and the comfort that flows from love and understanding are very helpful. She needs to experience success in spite of her handicaps. As she comes out of the regression stage and learns to cope with this new unpredictability, she gradually makes better eye contact, and regains emotional balance and interest in people and her surroundings. In fact, many parents call their daughter a "social butterfly" in middle childhood.

> I can tell you the screaming/crying spells don't last forever. The main thing, I think, is not to let it drive you crazy. My husband said he just had to put Sherry down and get away from her a little – nothing he did seemed to help and it was horribly frustrating for him.

CRYING

Crying has a purpose. It signals anger, sadness, frustration or pain. Babies learn shortly after birth that crying brings a response, and mothers learn quickly to distinguish the kind of cry they hear. Crying is the only form of communication that babies can use to indicate their discomfort, hunger or thirst. Because girls with RS have difficulty communicating any other way, crying becomes a logical choice. We try to read her many forms of body language and understand her expressive eyes, but we don't always consider her crying as a form of communication. But if she is uncomfortable from sitting in one position for too long, hungry or mad, crying seems a logical choice when nothing else works to get the message across. Never underestimate her ability to understand. Talk to her and tell her you know she is doing the best that she can.

> Maria is 12 and has had crying spells that have lasted for up to two hours a couple of times a day. She has always been very happy in the past. We saw the pediatrician, the neurologist, and had our first appointment with an orthopedic. We also saw the gastroenterologist, who did an endoscopy to rule out stomach problems. We returned to the pediatrician, who ran several blood and urine tests, and found nothing. We feel like pulling our hair out!

Parents have described it this way:

- She acts like she is in acute pain.
- Sometimes she cries as if her heart is breaking.
- She cries as if she wants desperately to say something.
- She cries bitterly, sobbing at times.
- Sometimes it appears to be a tantrum.
- She is inconsolable, with giant, sad tears.
- Sometimes she is crying one moment and laughing the next.
- She cries when she is somewhere where she doesn't want to be, or doing something she doesn't want to do.

> She just gets very upset and starts yelling and eventually has a total "meltdown." As you can imagine, a flipped out, 85 pound 10-year-old and a cart full of groceries does not make for happy times, not to mention her sister and brother who seize the moment to pull a few stunts of their own. We have just learned to respect Stefanie's limitations in these areas and try not to take her into a place that will provoke a "meltdown," kind of like you learn not to wear perfume around someone who has asthma.

Some people suggest that girls cry just to be crying. Common sense tells us that no one cries for fun. If she is crying, you'd better believe something is wrong. Maybe it is physical; maybe it's emotional. Maybe she's trying desperately to tell you something and crying is her only way of communicating. Chances are, it isn't entirely under her control. Paying careful attention to her non-speech cues about her needs may alleviate some of the distress. Don't assume she is crying just because she has RS. The first priority is to make sure nothing is physically wrong. Here is a list of things to have her doctor rule out:

- Is she constipated or impacted? Has she had a regular BM?
- Does she have a toothache? Does she refuse food, sweets or cold?
- Could it be a headache? Does she squint her eyes or hit her head?
- Could it be a sore throat? Does she refuse to swallow?
- Could it be an ear infection? Does she pull at her ear?
- Is it heartburn or reflux? Does she burp or regurgitate? Cry after eating?
- Does she have cramps? Is it time for her period?
- Is she limping or favoring one part of her body?
- Does she cry when she is moved?
- Does she have vaginal discharge?
- Does she wiggle and squirm like she itches?
- Is her brace too tight? Does she have red marks?
- Does she have leg or foot cramps?
- Does she have allergies?
- Does she have a urinary tract infection? Does she have strong or scant urine?
- Could she have gallstones?
- Could there be an ovarian cyst?

> When I ask Lauren on her talker where it hurts she lets me know her stomach hurts, head doesn't, and it's her upper stomach that hurts. When she eats late in the day, she takes a couple of bites, then breathes deeply and pushes away. This all started quite suddenly, so I don't think its an allergy. We're stumped. She had dental surgery during this, and I think he would have noticed if it was teeth. I'm feeling totally frustrated and hopeless. The GI specialist told us to see our neurologist – it's not neurological in any way other than that pain is. I feel like maybe they think I'm just manufacturing something because things were going OK. One doctor asked me how I'd feel if her symptoms went away suddenly even if we didn't figure out the cause. I immediately replied, "Delighted!" I tried to impress on them that our girls don't just act like they're in pain for no reason, and Lauren loves to eat when it feels safe and won't make her hurt worse.

Caregivers stop at nothing in trying to get to the bottom of what is making her cry. Sometimes they are able to help. Their suggestions include the following:

- Give her food or drink
- Change wet clothes
- Treat constipation
- Massage her arms, hands, legs
- Remove her from a crowded situation
- Put her in a quiet room or a dark room
- Change her routine or return to an expected routine

- Avoid excessive cold or heat
- Avoid becoming emotional or upset in front of her
- Take her to the toilet
- Play her favorite music or video
- Adjust her seating
- Cuddle her
- Distract her
- Take her for a car ride
- Put her in a warm tub
- Rub her tummy
- Stroke her forehead
- Wrap her in a warm blanket
- Talk to her soothingly
- Use a weighted blanket to comfort her
- Use a communication system

Angela would have bad crying fits when she would hide behind a chair, or anything she could hide behind. We had never seen her shed a tear. She would cry, but only have tears when she was hurt so bad, and then the tears would come. We now know she has low blood sugar, so we feed her orange juice or peanut butter very soon, and in less than 3 minutes, her mood is back to normal. It sure has made Angela feel so much better. We make sure to feed her three good meals a day and get in at least three snacks.

Sometimes Maria wakes up crying, and sometimes laughing. We always have a real hard time trying to figure out what is wrong. When she cries, we check the obvious – diaper, fever, a drink. Living in Vegas, we also got used to checking for ant bites...a lot of times we were never able to figure out what was wrong. My doctor suggested giving her Tums, in case she was having stomach problems or heartburn. We also put a stereo system in her room so we can play music real low, and we tell her she has to be quiet to hear it. Sometimes that works, too. The problem is that this is all too common a problem, and sometimes she has to work thru it herself. The hardest thing about it is not knowing why she is crying and not being able to help.

Trust Your Instincts
by Claudia Weisz

There are a few things you can do to figure out why your daughter is crying. For example, if she starts to scream just before dinner every night, you could try feeding her a half hour earlier, or giving a light snack after school. That's an easy one. But let's say she's been screaming whenever you want to take her for a walk. You get her coat on and she starts. Because you don't want to tug her around the block screaming, you take the coat off and don't go. She stops. What are the possibilities? She could simply not like going for a walk, and is telling you so. Or she could have pain, or perhaps her shoes don't fit properly, or her braces are tight, or perhaps her toes curl under or other foot deformities are becoming painful to her. To figure this out, you need to see how she walks the rest of the day, and in other situations.

If she's in a wheelchair and reacts that way, maybe it hurts to breathe cold air, or perhaps she doesn't like the extreme cold or heat. Maybe the neighbor's big dog scares her. To determine if something is serious, you need to keep track of the frequency, duration and intensity of the crying or screaming spells. Occasionally, you will misjudge the seriousness of the need, or perhaps never figure out her problem. Failing to recognize a serious problem prolongs the discomfort and can overwhelm you with guilt. Don't let it get you down.

It's inevitable to step in puddles of guilt from time to time, but the danger comes when we decide to lie down and soak it up. Just step through, empty your boots if you need to, and keep walking.

In other situations, especially "out of the blue" ones, you must use all your senses – eyes, ears, touch and smell – and a lot of intuition. You can learn to interpret your child's cries.

Look to see the expression on her face. Check her eyes for fear or anger. Are there tears? Look at her schedule. Are you late with her lunch or snack? If she uses the toilet, does she appear uncomfortable during urination or elimination? When was her last bowel movement? Is she chafed in areas that seldom see the light of day, and are seldom dry? That could make anyone cranky.

Feel her forehead for fever, feel her tummy to see if it's distended. If you keep a Food/Mood Chart, you'll perhaps make a connection if there is a food that repeatedly disagrees with her. Or, perhaps she's been swallowing air, which is common in our kids. Run your fingers around her waistband – are her clothes binding? Does she wear a belt or jeans that are cute, but miserable to wear when her abdomen expands from air swallowing? Feel her hands and feet. Is she cold? Hot? Feel her limbs for hardness, (cramping?) and compare left with right. Check her shoes for pebbles or bits of cereal…you never know! Check her hair clips and rubber bands. Tight pony tails can give a headache, and sometimes a hair clip can pull hair quite painfully. Is a label from her shirt scratching the back of her neck?

Do you smell vomit on her pillow in the morning? This could signify a reflux problem, causing a burning sensation in her esophagus. Is she passing gas, but having difficulty eliminating? Does her breath smell unpleasant – perhaps from infected tonsils, strep throat, stomach trouble or bad teeth? Is there a distinctive odor you can describe to her physician?

Listen to the intensity of her cry. Is it an irritating, constant whine, or an ear-piercing, heart-stopping scream? Does it start suddenly or slowly build? How long does it last and how does it stop – with or without your help? How often does it occur? Same time every day? All day once a month? Three times a week? How long does it last? What helps? Tylenol? Antacid? Laxative? Enema? Massage? Music?

You're the expert. If she has a normally sunny disposition and suddenly begins to have screaming spells, your task is to determine why. You are likely to be the person best acquainted with any changes in her life, as well as her normal disposition. We must remember just because these girls have Rett syndrome does not make them immune to all the other discomforts common to mankind.

There is a reason it disturbs us so to hear our children cry. It's been built into us, motivates us, and ends with us madly searching for answers. There is a danger in assuming that because these girls can't talk, we can't find out what's wrong. Don't believe it. We are their advocates, their connection with the rest of the world. Their cries are supposed to produce stress in us, so we can come to their rescue. It's one of the basics of human nature.

To try to figure out what she is trying to communicate by her behavior, we do a process known as "functional assessment." We write on index cards every time she has a tantrum – what was going in the classroom (what activity was going on, what Shanda was doing, who, if anyone was interacting with her immediately prior to the tantrum). The tantrum is briefly described and then (this is important) we write down what was done by adults and peers when the tantrum happened. After we have collected a number of recordings, we and the teacher and any other relevant individuals (therapists, aides) can look at the cards and try to form a hypothesis about what Shanda is accomplishing with this behavior. The most common functions of "negative" behavior are gaining attention, escaping from a task or situation, and gaining something she wants. Shanda usually tantrums when the teacher is working with another child, and this is for gaining attention. When she tantrums during lunch, music class, and other noisy times of the day, they take her out in the hall, so she is using tantrums to escape from a situation she doesn't like. The behavior may have several different functions. Once we have identified what function the behavior serves for Shanda, we can work on teaching her another behavior (such as activating a switch or doing some kind of vocalizing that is not a tantrum) to accomplish the same function. This is more effective, not to mention more humane, than just trying to stop the tantrums.

Nothing is worse than having a miserable child when you can't figure out the misery. It seems like the "cry button" is stuck in the "on" position and there is no way to turn it off. In fact, it is difficult for her to stop. It can drive you to distraction trying to figure out what is wrong and trying to make it better. Sometimes, trying to soothe her only makes the crying escalate. When you've tried everything from both lists, try to remember the following:

1) She doesn't want to be this way.
2) She is doing the very best she can do.
3) It will be over before long and she will be her sweet self again.

Laura has been experiencing major crying bouts. She has always had fussy periods in the past, but never really cried any tears. She is now crying tears in unnerving crying sessions that literally last for hours. When when Laura went to her eye doctor last week, one of these episodes started up – and the doctor was so shaken by it that he called the emergency room! Laura's crying spells are not seizures. She appears to be very aware of things around her during these spells. We've tried everything imaginable to comfort her but to no avail. The sessions eventually come to an end on their own. The feeling of helplessness is absolutely overwhelming!

We find two separate kind of outbursts. Sometimes in the past Ashley will just have had too much...too much of people trying to do things to her, for her, whatever. It is clear to me that she just does not want to be messed with. At those times I have simply left her in a chair by herself and let her listen to music or watch TV. She would quickly become composed and be fine afterwards. However, there is another kind of outburst where nothing seems to console her. I believe these outbursts are more serious. These outbursts went on for weeks...not constantly, but periodically for weeks. Again, we did not know why they started or why they stopped. They did stop, but, it was because of nothing that we did.

Leah occasionally has crying spells, heavy on tears, where we find it difficult to console her. Sometimes these are "night terrors" and we wonder if they are bad dreams. She has always had tears, but like her "normal" sister, she has two types of crying – upset crying which can be from having her feelings hurt, being hungry, wanting to go the bathroom, versus the type of crying when she is really hurt or something is really bothering her. There is a different tone, cadence and temper to the crying and we can easily tell the difference when things are really wrong. I think crying is one of the ways of communicating that the girls use, but sometimes it gets past a point where they lose control of it.

Jocelyn often times goes thru "bad days" when she cries or screams. Most of the time though, it will tend to only be a short bout, part of the day, or often solved by a change in activity. I found often that when it's time to leave, she begins to cry, but as I ignore it and continue to put her in the car and turn the music on, she begins to calm herself again and is fine. Other times I feel that its truly an emotional frustration that causes the tears. These times, after I've determined that its nothing I can "fix," I let her know that I'll give her some "space" to work it out herself. Again, she seems to get over it better on her own. I try to think of my own bad days. Sometimes I don't want everyone trying to make it better either, but would rather be left alone.

> Over the last 27 years we have gone through episodes of crying/screaming/hand-biting spells. The early years were difficult. I think maybe the frustration at loss of skills was a big part of the early spells. In later childhood, we discovered acid reflux, where the stomach acid backs up into the esophagus and burns it. Eating became very painful for her, yet she was hungry, as the acid and empty stomach made for more pain. Zantac® and Maalox® helped and a change of medication seemed to help, as well. In other years it was sensitivity certain foods: tomatoes, chocolate, eggs, citrus, and a lactose intolerance – each time requiring a search and rescue technique by keeping records of what she ate each day. The last time, and the thing it took us the longest to figure out, involved shortened heel cords as a cause for her feet and calves cramping several times a day. The foot problems may be caused by Angie curling her toes when she walks, in an effort to hold on to the floor with her feet. When lifting her out of the shower – where she stands – her little flat feet act like suction cups, and I hear a sound similar to pulling a suction cup off a window. Also, long periods of sitting, letting the feet drop, will shorten the heelcord over time. She now wears AFO's and has very few cramps anymore.

Some parents report that the use of Naltrexone (Revia®, formerly Trexan®), is very effective in reducing anxiety and screaming spells. The dose has to be tailored to the child, as some do better with a smaller dose and others with a higher dose. The pill has a very bitter taste, but can be "camouflaged" in chocolate ice cream. One negative side effect of Revia® is loss of appetite, which can lead to weight loss.

As she gets older, she may continue on a much more even emotional level than at an earlier age. The majority of girls do get better in time. However, a small number of girls seem to go through a second emotional decline, usually after the age of 8 years. Crying, screaming and whining can accompany sleeplessness. Self-injurious behaviors such as face-slapping, face-hitting and hand biting may occur. Parents report that their daughter hasn't cried for years, which makes it even more puzzling. Schools are concerned that something serious is going on, and parents are convinced of it. Unfortunately these crying spells are not uncommon although they usually get better as the girls get older.

> We went through them a bit when Jocelyn was very young. Then again when she was in 5th grade and even put her on seizure medicine in case it was seizure related. It was not, and we found that it was an emotional response to something happening at school. Once we identified it, and the situation changed, the crying stopped. We are going through it again at 19 years old, but now it seems to be pain related, we think abdominal. I believe these crying episodes can be caused by many things, emotions, pain, frustration. I try to determine the cause by trial and error, and as a last resort try to make her comfortable and get away, because the more I try to help with something I can't "fix" the more frustrating it is for both of us.

> Kayla used to have crying spells that would last for hours on end. She would just scream and scream. Nothing we did calmed her unless she was being held or rocked and that didn't always work. During the time when she was crying she would hit herself and pull her hair out. That lasted for about 6 months and it was awful. When we found out about Rett syndrome we just concluded that she was going through a regression stage. I'm not sure what made her stop but we now know when she gets to crying and becoming self-abusive, put a Barney tape in the VCR and it's all over.

> Becky Sue, 17, has had those crying spells off and on for many years. Since she is so good and happy most of the time it broke my heart to see her so upset. But at the same time it was wonderful to see another emotion. There are a million things that could cause her to be upset or hurt. So we go through the list to see what it might be; toes in shoes wrong, sticker somewhere, not enough sleep, too much sleep, medication, or pre-menstrual symptoms. I always talk to Becky and ask her what's wrong and how can I make it better? Sometimes just the talking and hugs soothe her, sometimes not. She does have mood swings that are related to her menstrual cycle.

MOOD SWINGS

The pendulum can swing quite dramatically in a short period of time. She can go from tears to laughter without explanation.

> She will be lying on the floor as quiet as a mouse and then she will burst out in this hysterical laughter that just puts everyone in a good mood. These are my best times with her. She can be so "iffy" at times. We never know whether or not she will "allow" us to play with her. We respect her space and leave her alone, but when she begins laughing like that, we take it as an invitation! Her little brother, now 15 months, can't resist her whenever she laughs. He will bring her a toy and pat her belly, sit on her, pounce on her, and she LOVES it! She's even backhanded him before, but he still comes back.

> What's funny, or aggravating, about all of this is her mood swings are so violent sometimes. Just the other day, she went from hysterically laughing to screaming at the top of her lungs so loud she set off the glass break sensors on our security system. I would love to know what goes on in her mind.

NIGHT TERRORS

Sleep or night terrors are most often seen in typically developing toddlers, usually around age two. They occur when the child goes into deep sleep very quickly. Often these episodes begin with a scream and an abrupt awakening, and are followed by disorientation. They are different from routine nightmares. Night terrors are considered a sleep disorder, much like sleep walking. Stress can increase the likelihood of sleep terrors.

> Kristas scared us one time when we found her in her window sill banging on the window. We tried some sleep medications, but they didn't help much. She eventually outgrew the sleep terrors.

> When she was a toddler she frequently woke up with nighttime terrors/tantrums and it was very difficult and emotionally draining for both of us, because they would last for hours. But we came across something that has been a lifesaver and has been extremely beneficial to our Rosie. It's called a Kelliquilt, a 25 pound, weighted blanket. We wrapped Rosie in it like a cocoon during those times and the deep pressure calmed her down and also protected her. It costs around $149 and has been the best purchase we ever made. We still use it now when she is very anxious and her engine is too revved up and needs to come back to neutral.

FACIAL MOVEMENTS

Other body movements and behaviors can be seen. Facial grimaces, such as stretching, twisting movements of the lower jaw, lips and tongue, are common in the younger girl. She may chew or bite her lips or blow bubbles. Sometimes these grimaces get worse when her hand movements are interrupted. These movements are thought to be involuntary, something she cannot control.

TOOTH GRINDING

Bruxism, or tooth-grinding, can be an annoying problem. It is described as a "creaking" sound, like uncorking a wine bottle. Some parents have reported success using jaw massage to relieve the grinding. Others have had orthodontic appliances made by the dentist with varying rates of success. Some feel that anxiety medication helps. Another tactic is to give her a soft towel or object to chew on in place of the grinding. Tooth grinding usually reduces drastically when the permanent teeth come in. Children usually do not grind their teeth to the point of exposing the nerve root or pulp.

> Dani's speech therapist showed us how to massage the inside of Dani's cheek – you could feel how tense the muscles were – and it relaxed her. Now we give her a pacifier to chew on and she rarely grinds her teeth.

> Ashley's teeth grinding got so bad that I took her to a dentist and he made a soft mouthpiece for her to wear when the grinding appeared. Apparently it worked because she stopped grinding her teeth. That was about 2-3 years ago. Then out of the blue, she began grinding her teeth again about a month ago. Ashley is 17 now. I have not figured out what the cause of the grinding is but I think that it is probably due to some discomfort.

> Sherry pretty much outgrew the constant, severe teeth-grinding and now only does it occasionally. We can sometimes get her to relax her jaw by rubbing very gently in little circles around where the jawbone connects, and near the temples – that whole area. She likes that a lot.

> Maria used to grind her teeth so badly we could hear it across the room! It used to drive me crazy, until I learned to tune it out, then it only drove everyone else crazy.

> Angela grinds her teeth when she is pain. It may be just a headache. Tylenol always stops it after a short time so I am certain that it is discomfort that starts the grinding. She does not do it often. We made a "chewing necklace" from aquarium tubing with an infant teether. She wears it around her neck and can put it in her mouth when she wants to chew or grind. It even looks "cool" like some of the jewelry her friends wear.

CHALLENGING BEHAVIORS

Challenging behavior is any behavior which is difficult to manage, disruptive, or harmful. It can be hard to determine why the behavior began and how to change it. In general, we know that behaviors have a specific function. Sometimes, she may engage in this behavior simply out of habit or as a tension reliever, much the way a young child might suck her thumb. Other behaviors may be her way of sending important messages. Until we discover the meaning of her behavior, we may not be able to change it. More importantly, until we know why she is doing the behavior, she will not get the response she seeks. Hand or wrist biting can mean more than being frustrated. It can mean, "I hurt and need to belch," or "I need attention," "I am constipated," or "This is too hard for me."

To determine why she is engaging in the behavior, consider these factors about her:

- her physical state, including illness, seizures and neurological status
- the situation in which the behavior occurs
- a knowledge of her usual concerns

Many typical toddlers go through a brief phase of biting, hitting, or spitting because it gets attention. As they develop language, they find more effective ways of getting attention and having their needs met. Girls with RS do not develop language and it may take a long time, even with an intensive, highly structured teaching program, to teach them acceptable ways of responding.

> Stefanie occasionally hits or pulls hair. She gets a time out at her desk, while the rest of the class is doing something cool. At the After School Center Stef has been put in the "time out corner" for hitting and pulling hair. It is effective if it's done consistently. Stefanie definitely knows that these behaviors are not acceptable, but does them anyway to get a reaction. It may sound harsh, but I have sat Stef down and explained to her that just because she has Rett syndrome does not mean

she can get away with bad behavior. I know she understands from the look in her eyes, but sometimes she is just a little stinker. In all honesty, it's usually not the Rett syndrome stuff that drives me crazy with Stef. It's the normal kid stuff!

Amanda used to bite. We let her bite pillows or have a doll she could bite – but generally she wanted to bite other people. The best way we distinguished behaviors was to give her alternative behaviors and this takes much time. Eventually, we have taught Amanda to say "you me" for "you meanie," or "I'm mad." It took about a year, with lots of practice and animation to show her. Then one day she just said it in a rage, and is still able to when she is mad.

Briana went through a biting phase. It was her way of telling people they were overstepping their boundaries with her. It shocked the school when my response was, "Dear Lord, I hope that other child is disease free." As it turned out, Jamahl had pulled Briana's hair, maybe more than once, so she bit him. I didn't condone her biting, though I was very happy that she had defended herself, and had to keep telling Bri no biting. She has even lockjawed me a couple of times when she didn't get what she wanted.

Studies have shown that if you can teach a new behavior that accomplishes the same task as the old, undesirable one, the child will leave the old behavior behind and use the new one. So if hitting is her way of saying hello, try to replace the behavior. As soon as someone approaches for a greeting, gently put your hand on her hand. Say a cheery "Hi" for her and have the friend make eye contact, touch her hand gently and warmly, and say "Hi" in return. In this way, you have taught her how to greet people appropriately. You may have to set up situations in which she can greet someone perhaps dozens of times each day, continued over several weeks. Another major factor in changing the behavior is learning to change our own response to it, which can actually reinforce the negative behavior.

It is easier to change the environment than to change the behavior. People who work with her should be tuned into her needs, and be able to read her signals. These can be very subtle and easily overlooked. It is important for everyone to remember that her behaviors are challenging for her, as well. It is not her, but the disorder that drives the behaviors. Structuring her environment to decrease her anxiety level does not mean letting her get away with whatever she wants to do. It means that expectations should be within her ability. She should have frequent pauses and many pleasant interactions. If you use a positive approach, seeing her as capable, she will develop self-confidence. Keep a positive attitude and treat her with sensitivity and respect, seeing her first and the disability second. You may be surprised at how well she responds.

It is important to bring people in her life into a "circle of support." This can include parents, relatives, friends, as well as school or community professionals and anyone who is committed to affecting a change. In this supportive environment, you can share different perspectives and ideas for helping her in various aspects of her life. The "circle" can also be a very comforting resource for her and those she relates with, who often have a strained relationship. It is natural to feel angry when aggressive behaviors are aimed at you.

SELF-INJURIOUS BEHAVIORS

Some girls with RS injure themselves. Most often, this takes the form of biting or hitting themselves. Some medications have been found effective in treating these episodes, probably due to their sedative effect. It is important, however, to rule out any physical cause or source of pain or frustration first. Experts feel that girls who injure themselves may do so because they have a high threshold for pain. Girls with RS often have high circulating levels of B-endorphins, one of the body's natural painkillers which is chemically related to opiates, like heroin or morphine. It is possible that endorphin levels are elevated because of the self-injury. No one is certain which comes first.

After much deliberation and anxiety, we put Stefanie on Tranxene® because she was very agitated and getting worse. It seemed like any little thing set her off. Sometimes it was that she was not feeling well and we weren't picking up on it. Other times it was due to general frustration, and other times we just didn't know what was the trigger. She was yelling, hitting herself in the head constantly and had significantly thinned out her waist length hair from the ears forward. We were at our wits end, and more importantly, Stefanie was obviously not happy. I read somewhere that drugs in the Valium® family can become habit-forming, but if the choice is a miserable child who hits herself in the head and is so incredibly miserable that she screams all the time, or the habit-forming drugs, I go for the drugs.

While at times a girl may appear to have an increased tolerance to pain, sometimes her pain threshold is less than normal. Little things like a scratchy clothing tag or a wrinkle in a sock may seem terribly irritating and cause her to bite her hand. Surely sensation is distorted, but it seems selective. We have instructed caregivers to assume that something gentle like a range of motion exercise is causing a painful response if she reacts negatively, such as biting her hands. Then we back off until she can tolerate some more exercise. We don't want to deprive her of part of her therapy time, but don't want her to feel that we are hurting her.

Maria slapped her chin, then across her cheek repeatedly. When she was upset, she would punch herself in the jaw. Because we had no insurance, no diagnosis, and no intervention, we got creative. We made her first arm brace for her, out of a potato chip can! My husband cut the metal ends off, cut it longways down the side, lined it with foam padding and velcroed it around her elbow so she couldn't bend her arm to hit herself. I always had to laugh when she wore it at the grocery store. They always wanted to charge me for the Pringles, and stared at me dumfounded when I handed it to them! If nothing else, it made a good conversation piece!

No matter what you do, even changing her diaper, Brit begins to hit herself in the chin and eye, cheek and temple area. Her arm splints have been on more than off, and I try to put them on before changing her, etc. I purchased water wings to use in the bath tub. She bites herself very hard when mad or agitated. We saw a whirlwind of these behaviors for a period of five months about a year ago, and then one day they were gone.

Stephanie slaps her body, usually her thighs, when she is angry, frustrated or tired. She also pulls other people's hair occasionally and says "ow." This is usually to see the reaction from the other person. When she was younger, around age two, she used to pinch herself and anyone who got in range, too.

Her new method is a very loud, and I do mean LOUD, scream followed by slapping motions. Anyone in the way will get a good pop. Mom gets one from time to time. I don't discourage this behavior as it is one of the few ways for her to let people know that they have stepped in a bit too closely. I'm trying to teach her a better method of showing her disapproval. A nice scream in the ear doesn't hurt too terribly.

Kim used to take very deliberate aim at my nose and hit it hard with her forehead. Having no means of communication in those days, she did all she was able to do. However, I did not understand. I think some things that might help other girls are holding her close and reassuring her, playing some music with a strong rhythm and melody, but not too loud, and perhaps rocking gently with it. If this helps, it might be worth trying some form of communication system if you don't already have one – even for her to answer "yes" or "no" to questions you would ask her, to help relieve her frustration at not being able to make the actions she wants to make.

Jessica bangs her head when she is mad, and if you are holding her she will head butt you if she can. She has really hurt me before and herself as well. Also she will kick and if she hits her shin she will just keep on kicking or what ever it is, such as hitting her elbow or smacking something with the back of her hand. She doesn't seem to mind that kind of pain...But let me get a brush to brush her hair and she tries to run!

> We do not have a lot of problems with this anymore except for scratching the moment you remove Angela's clothes and occasional rocking which results in head banging but can be controlled. When she was going through the regressive period at two she pulled her hair out constantly. We had to keep a bonnet on her at all times. She even pulled out her eyelashes. She was so miserable at this time, crying inconsolably and vomiting if touched. Even after these symptoms stopped, the hair pulling continued for about another year.

MEDICATIONS

Naltrexone (Revia®) has been found useful in treating some children who are self-injurious. Because they have a higher than normal pain threshold, girls with RS may not "feel" the hitting or biting as intensely. Naltrexone blocks the "natural" occurring opiods in her brain and therefore she "feels" the pain and may no longer self-injure. Tranzene® has also been used with success.

> Heather took Naltrexone. We had tried it because of self-injurious behavior and aggression. Her condition worsened and she became more aggressive. We did not keep her on it for more than a period of a week though. It scared us and we took it away under the doctor's approval. Be prepared for anything, as different girls respond differently to medicines.

> Naltrexone does work for her, but it took a good two, almost three weeks to see results. We basically started it for the extreme fussiness and lack of sleep. I never linked her hand movements to this, but since she started a year ago, her movements have gone from a hard hit to the face, even sometimes biting her hands, to a gentle flicking and definitely a more calmer hand movement. Now she only wears splints when at school or when we are out and about.

> Heather's self-injurious behavior did decrease and we use the arm bands even less now than before. We don't have to use them now for more than a few hours at a time, maybe twice a month. It is great. We use Tylenol® when she gets fussy and that is it.

SUGGESTIONS FOR CHALLENGING BEHAVIORS

- Look for a quiet time to interact. Positive times reinforce caring relationships.
- Believe in her ability and desire to "be good."
- Provide adequate support and respite time for caregivers.
- Try to determine if she is bored and provide more stimulating activities.
- Allow her to participate in choice-making to give her some control.
- Go beyond letting her watch what is going on. Include her in normal experiences of daily living.
- Physical restraint should be a last resort. Make it as brief as possible but long enough to provide safety.
- In severe cases, medications might be helpful. There is no one drug that works best for everyone.

Some anti-convulsants, such as Tegretol® or Depakote®, are helpful in mood control. Ask her physician what might be recommended. Don't hesitate to ask for referral to a specialist such as a developmental pediatrician, pediatric neurologist or child psychiatrist. Try each drug one at a time and monitor their effectiveness. It can take several weeks for a concentration of the drug to build up in the body, several weeks to see if it works, more time to adjust the dosage, and still more time to take her off the drug to see if it has been helpful. Be patient.

- The use of "aversives," such as squirting her face with cold water to interrupt the behavior, are not recommended. They are damaging to her self-concept and self-esteem, and are too easily abused.
- Explore various communication methods.

The author wishes to thank the following professionals for ideas and information which was used to develop this chapter: Tina Iyama-Kurtz, M.D.; Claudia Weisz.

THE HANDS

"Her hands are instruments of her heart, not her head."
Barbro Lindberg

Repetitive hand movements are the hallmark of Rett syndrome, usually one of the first things noticed. However, hand movements are also seen in other disorders. In making the diagnosis of RS, what she does with her hands is not as important as what she does not do with her hands compared with what she once could do. The combination of normal hand use followed by loss of purposeful hand use must be present for the diagnosis of RS to be confirmed. The degree of loss of hand skills will vary with the age when her regression began. This is more difficult to show when the onset is early, because as an infant, she has not yet developed a repertoire of hand skills. When home movies of infants who are later diagnosed with RS are viewed, it is evident that even before regression, some girls show subtle signs that hand use is not entirely normal in infancy. She may lose most or all of her hand and finger skills, yet she may be able to regain some skills after the regression period.

As an infant, she may develop a normal pincer grasp, allowing her to pick up small objects with the thumb and forefinger. This ability gradually diminishes to a palmar grasp, where the palm and fingers are used in a raking motion. Sometimes her grasp is lost entirely and a striking movement is used instead. Often, as an infant, she can hold a cup or other object, but gradually, she loses the ability to keep her grip on the object. It is as difficult for her to keep holding an object as it is to grasp it to begin with, so it is common for a girl with RS to succeed in picking something up, only to lose her grip and drop it soon after. Hand and mouth movements are often synchronized and when she opens her mouth, she may drop the spoon or piece of food.

> If Amy's bottle is within reach, even almost behind her, she can find it, pick it up right away, and drink it. She's pretty good with a small fork loaded with food lying on her plate. She can pick it up, put the food in her mouth and most times place the fork back down, but cannot load it yet. However, she has extreme difficulty picking up anything else. She will look hard at what she wants, rock and hyperventilate and sometimes, but not often, the hand will come flying out and swipe at it.

Characteristic hand movements change over time, but usually begin with non-specific waving or odd postures of the hands. Often, the next movement seen is hand mouthing or clapping, followed by mid-line hand washing, hand wringing, or hand rubbing and squeezing. Some girls hold their hands apart, rolling or manipulating the fingers.

These hand movements are repeated over and over again the same way. Each hand follows its own distinct pattern of movement. The speed or rhythm of hand movements can sometimes be useful in "reading" her mood – excitement, anger or happiness. As she gets older, the hand movements are slower and less intense, but they still remain. An older girl may sit with her hands folded in a tight grip that is hard to break open, tapping or strumming her fingers. Joint contractures may prevent her from bringing her hands together at midline. Increased spasticity may make grasping more difficult but allow her to increase her grip. Girls who remain mobile tend to have more intense and active hand movements.

> Malia put her hands in her mouth for all different reasons. When she was upset she would do it one way, bored another way, happy another way. It was kind of a barometer on how she felt. Once you got to know her, you could read her moods.

> Jenn mouthed her hands constantly for a long time. She would insert one hand into her mouth and within two seconds replace it with the other, and then two seconds later she'd switch again. About age 4-5 it was not only periodic, but different in form. She would just pat her mouth with her right hand while her left patted her chest. Both hands moved quickly. Then as she got older, they slowed down. And now she very gently pats them as before or pats her hands together in her lap.

In addition to stereotyed hand movements, the girl with RS has a significant degree of **apraxia**, which interferes with her ability to perform intentional motor movements with her hands. She has the desire and will to move her hands, but cannot make them do what she wants them to do. She may also have hand **tremors**, which make using her hands even more difficult. **Spasticity** and **uneven muscle tone** can also affect the hands. In some girls, the thumbs are pulled in across the palm and it is very difficult to bring them back out. This can make difficult grasping absolutely impossible.

She often acts as though she perceives sensory input from her hands differently. She may resist hand-over-hand assistance and may dislike having her hands touched. Some girls bite or lick their hands or hold them in distinctive postures. Due to her apraxia, ataxia and stereotyped movements, it is often difficult for an observer to determine the intentions of her uncoordinated movements, which appear to be random.

The stereotyped hand movements increase when she is stressed or bored. It is important to recognize that she is not causing the repetitive hand movements to happen. They are happening to her. They are not due to self-stimulation. Even in situations where she wants to, she is usually unable to break up these movements on her own. They may be subdued, but the hand movements are continuous during waking. They increase in intensity when she is under stress, whether positive (happiness, eagerness) or negative (discomfort, anger). It is possible to reduce the hand movements by distraction (using the hands in an activity), holding the non-dominant hand to increase use of the dominant hand, and using various splints to immobilize the hands and/or elbows. Tolerance for inhibiting her hand movements differs from one girl to another.

Voluntary hand use is increased when she is relaxed and strongly motivated in non-demanding, interesting or pleasurable activity, such as eating. Some girls can finger feed, while others can use a spoon or fork with assistance to scoop the food. Often, she is motivated to use her hands during music therapy. When the music therapist sits close and an instrument is easily within her reach, she is interested and strongly motivated to strike the instrument, even though her actions may be jerky and uncoordinated.

> Hand use to some extent can definitely be relearned. Before Meg's regression, she could use her hands for anything. She was feeding herself, coloring, turning pages in a book, manipulating objects, climbing, all the things a two-year old should do. Then, she wouldn't use her hands for anything. Now at 5, she will hold your hand when she needs help stepping up on a step and even holds a hand rail independently to climb stairs. We just stand behind her and hold her free hand. The key is that she needs to be highly motivated.

Eye-hand coordination is usually poor because looking (input) and reaching (output) are difficult to coordinate at the same time. Often, she has to look first, look away, and then reach without looking. If she is very motivated and anxious to touch an object, she may have to "gear up" her body for action, but there is always a delayed response. If standing, she will begin to rock back and forth or lean forward. If sitting, she may begin rocking, hyperventilate, grind her teeth or make facial grimaces. Her hand movements may increase in intensity and she may tense her body, sometimes staring closely at the object, sometimes staring off. This can last for a few minutes. Then, she may suddenly lunge at the object without looking at it. She may succeed in picking up the object, but all too often she results in knocking it to the floor instead.

> Kim can feed herself using a fork with a built-up handle that has been molded to her grip, provided we spear the food. She can pick up the fork and put the food into her mouth, but then the fork falls. I sit on her left side, and make a warm cradle of the palm of my left hand, and she rests her left hand, which is holding the fork, in it. I follow her movement up to her mouth and down

to the table, and have been finding that Kim can retain her grip on the fork for the duration of the meal. I'm doubtful that warmth is all there is to this, but I heated the MediPak (liquid-filled bag) in the microwave and laid that beneath her left hand (with the fork). She was able to retain the grip for a few mouthfuls, but not as completely as with the cupped hand.

She has sores on her hands. How can we prevent them?

Skin breakdown and infection can be a significant problem in the girl who puts her hands in her mouth routinely, or whose hand movements are aggressive. Creative therapists and parents have come up with a number of good solutions – holding one hand, distracting her, massaging her hands, providing stimulating hand activities, or putting gloves, wristbands or tube socks on her hands. Sometimes, these methods do not work well enough, and the next step is to devise arm/hand/elbow splints for her to wear periodically during the day. Home made arm splints can be made with rolled up magazines or soft pliable plastic. One parent successfully used a leather golf wrist brace with velcro closure. When these are ineffective, specially fitted splints can be made.

Should we try to discourage or stop her hand movements?

She does not have conscious control over her hand movements, so it is impossible for her to stop them at will. The role of her compulsive hand motion is not entirely understood. It could be a need for extra stimulation to make up for something the brain is lacking, a different or strange sensation in the hands which is relieved by the movements, or the product of a need for motion that does not have a normal outlet. Studies have shown that when the hand movements are blocked completely, the feet often take up the movements. Sometimes, when the hand movements are blocked for a time, they return with double intensity. It is hard to say whether we should or should not discourage these movements when we do not fully understand them. However, when the hand movements are inhibited, many girls are more social and interact more with the environment while they decrease hand to mouth movements and hand wringing behavior. Splinting the hands may allow for greater concentration and more functional use of her hands.

Anca actually seems relieved at times to have the wringing and hand-to-mouth behavior stopped. When we take her elbow braces off, after a while if she becomes fussy. We then put them back on and it calms her tremendously. About 4 years ago she had a custom-made hinged elbow set made. She soon broke them. Now she has some that are very comfortable, washable, and are made in different colors to match a lot of her clothing. Since we have been using these for about 3 years, Anca is quite successful in going long periods without her old behaviors.

Angie seems greatly relieved to have her arm splints on. When she has a screaming spell, she hits herself in the mouth and bites hard on her fingers. As long as she can still get her hands together, she is not stressed about the splints.

Before using a method to reduce the hand movements, consider and respect her own needs. Does she use these movements to express anger or excitement, happiness or sadness? Will she have a way to express these feelings without using her hand movements? What is her reaction to having the hand movements restrained? Some girls are irritable, while others seem relieved to have their hands splinted. If the hand movements create a type of sensory input needed by girls with RS, hand splints may provide this input or alter the need for it in some way. For some girls who are frustrated by arm splints, hand splints can be used. In some cases, a combination of the two techniques used simultaneously or in sequence may be more beneficial. Hand splints may be used to keep the hands open. The thumb is held in an abducted position (away from the body) while the wrist is kept in a neutral or extended position. This allows her to make better use of her hands, or helps to keep the hands from reaching the mouth, avoiding injury. Inhibiting the hand-to-mouth behavior allows more appropriate visual input, which encourages increased eye contact and interaction. Reaching and grasping may be easier. Sometimes, the splints have an overall calming effect.

We finally found arm splints that are wonderful. The are inflatable and zip up the arm. You can make them as "full" or as "soft" as needed. We find that Taylor seems to enjoy having one arm at a time splinted for about thirty minutes each in the morning and afternoon. We use them for concentration purposes.

Alyssa's movements are more intense when there is something on her mind and she is trying to get you to figure it out. When we see her doing it more frequently, we try to see what might be going on that is causing it, and sometimes just putting the splints on for a little bit gives her a breather and a big sigh of relief! Sometimes I think that she doesn't like doing the movement either, but doesn't know how to stop it.

Rachel constantly has her hands in her mouth, and this causes skin breakdown and swelling of her fingers. Some of her fingers are twice the size they should be. Arm splints keep her hands out of her mouth but allow her to wring them. We use antibiotic cream for the skin breakdown. The plastic comes in some really nice colors – Rachel's are a pretty purple.

When Jocelyn was five, we used frozen concentrate orange juice cans, then added a sock with the toe cut out to help keep it in place. Later, we went to homemade splints and eventually now we have splints that are hinged, so that she can bend her arm but not enough to put to her mouth. She seems to be able to focus better when her hands are away from her mouth. She still taps them together but has no problems with skin breakdown around her hands, fingers or mouth. This also eliminates drooling and wetness. Jocelyn does not seem to mind the splints, although we do remove them when she is very agitated at home to allow her to "stim" her hands. This seems to help her cope with things we can't figure out or "fix."

Can the hand movements be modified by splints?

Splints should not be viewed as restraints, but as an aid to treatment. They work most effectively to reduce hand movements in those girls who have mid-line hand movements. Her orthopedic specialist and occupational therapist should be consulted to determine the kind of splints which would be most helpful.

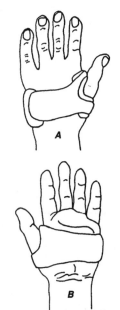

Now she still hand mouths but it is much "lighter" and there are longer periods when she actually puts her hands down, especially when eating. We find that we have to put splints on her when doing P.T. exercises so she will sit for longer periods and actually bear weight on them.

I notice a calming effect when Brittany wears her elbow splints for 15-20 minute increments. This eliminates biting and self abuse and allows her to use her hands and concentrate.

What kind of splints can be used?

Full hand splints extend from immediately below the wrist to immediately above the finger tips on the palm side of the hand, with the thumb protruding in a comfortable position to the side and the fingers slightly bowed inward toward the thumbs. **Half hand splints** are molded in the same way as the full hand splints, but extend from below the wrist to the middle finger joints. **Elbow splints** extend from the forearm, around and just above the elbow, maintaining a comfortable bowed position.

Basic Hand Splint Design
A) dorsal view
B) palmar view

How are the splints made?

They are made from various kinds of plastic which are thin, smooth and rigid, but moldable when heated, such as Theraplast or Polyform. The splints are fitted to the child's contours. They should have a washable soft foam liner that does not absorb odors or bacteria. Elbow splints should allow for twenty to thirty degrees of elbow flexion. Both ends should be flared to prevent pressure sores. The straps should be adjustable to allow the arm to extend, but prevent it from flexing toward the face. Hand splints should leave the pads of the index and thumb exposed so that she will get the necessary sensory feedback when the splints are worn.

Should the splints go on both hands?

It's best to see her reaction and tolerance for the splints. Some girls enjoy having both hands or elbows splinted, while others prefer one at a time. When trying to encourage more purposeful hand use, it is best to splint the non-dominant hand, leaving the other hand free for her to use.

Are there other ways to reduce the hand movements?

Providing an environment that is not too stressful or demanding and the use of vibrators and gentle hand massage can be helpful. It is important to remember that it is probably not wise to limit the hand movements completely unless they are interfering in some way – for instance, greatly limiting her functional hand use or causing sores on her hands or mouth. Moderation is best.

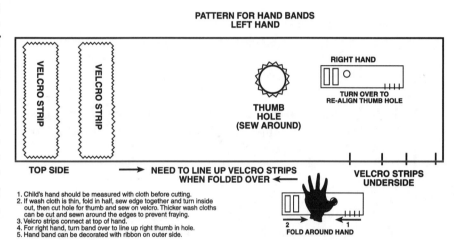

PATTERN FOR HAND BANDS
LEFT HAND

VELCRO STRIP   VELCRO STRIP

THUMB HOLE (SEW AROUND)

RIGHT HAND

TURN OVER TO RE-ALIGN THUMB HOLE

TOP SIDE → NEED TO LINE UP VELCRO STRIPS WHEN FOLDED OVER ←

VELCRO STRIPS UNDERSIDE

2   1
FOLD AROUND HAND

1. Child's hand should be measured with cloth before cutting.
2. If wash cloth is thin, fold in half, sew edge together and turn inside out, then cut hole for thumb and sew on velcro. Thicker wash cloths can be cut and sewn around the edges to prevent fraying.
3. Velcro strips connect at top of hand.
4. For right hand, turn band over to line up right thumb in hole.
5. Hand band can be decorated with ribbon on outer side.

We have discovered a very simple way to keep Angie's hands still. We put a hot water bottle filled 2/3 with very warm water (with the extra air squeezed out) either on her lap or on the table in front of her. She loves the feel of it and will let her hands rest on it relaxed and still for 15 to 20 minutes. She likes to squeeze it.

We've had good luck putting long white athletic socks on one and sometimes both hands. I think Chelsea still has the movement in her hands without feeling constricted by gloves, and she doesn't put her hand in her mouth at all when the sock is on.

Roselyn puts her hands to her mouth constantly. When she was younger we did use elbow splints, but she got very frustrated. For years now I have made little bags of terry toweling with elastic that just slip over her hand. She only thrusts her left hand into her throat, the right hand just the finger tips a bit. But she manages to get the bag off many times in a day, and is very triumphant when she does.

We have used brushing on Amanda and have seen results in tactile awareness. It is just a soft brushing with a surgical brush and massaging after with a terry towel or just your hands. We use a loofa sponge in the tub at bath time, and we go over the whole body, some area with giggles and some areas with resistance. Amanda's right hand is pretty good but when we put texture on the left hand, it's pulled away. Little by little, it's getting better. Hand usage and awareness is what we are after, and it's tough, but we see her carry her bookbag, purse, and pick out groceries at the store. Sometimes they make it to the cart and sometimes not. We eat a lot of funny toast, because Amanda gets the bread at the store, and what a grip! We dare not put it back because she's always watching us!

> When Dani started mouthing her hands at age two we started giving her a pacifier or gummy bears sewn into polyester organza, with a long tail so she couldn't swallow. We also used a special hands free baby bottle and she learned to hold the nipple, attached to a long flexible tube, in her mouth for long periods of time.

Spasticity and uneven muscle tone can also affect the hands. In some girls, the thumbs are pulled in across the palms and it is very difficult to bring them back out. This can make difficult grasping absolutely impossible. Uneven tone can also pull the wrist off to one side.

There are also soft thumb abductor splints which are made out of a dense cell foam and velcro. They don't prevent hand wringing or mouthing but can be used to increase function and reduce the chance of deformities. They do this by gently pulling the thumb out and away from the palm of the hand, which places it in a better position for grasping objects.

How can we increase her hand skills?

The use of a splint on the non-dominant hand may increase her ability to concentrate, and to use the dominant hand in functional activities. Adapting materials so that she can more easily succeed provides good reinforcement. Encourage her to use her hands by using activities or rewards that are attractive to her.

> Velcro is a life saver. I use it so that Briana can hold things: spoon, dolls, new adaptive paintbrushes, and even sippy cups. It helps her maintain her grip, and has even helped her get better at grabbing and holding onto items she wants. She has been reaching more, and retrieving items she wants both at school and at home with less frustration.

> I made a designer grip glove – a velcro catcher's mitt of sorts. Briana and I play catch with one of those fuzzy balls and have a blast. Now I just have to teach her to throw forward. She makes me fetch for the most part, but it's so much fun, and according to her P.T., great reflex training.

> I find Sarah is more willing to try things if her extremities are warm. She tends to have cold hands and feet most of the time, so I try hard to keep her warm and cozy if trying to do something requiring her to respond.

> Over the years I have done many things to stimulate Karina to use her hands, find better balance and play with things. I have coached everyone around her. She did improve greatly on these things, and still does. I must say that one of the things that does not happen is the decrease of hand-mouthing and tooth grinding.
>
> Karina began using her hands again at about 5 years. She has slowly progressed all these years. She eats with a fork now and can pick the food with it herself. She tries two times: if she fails to get something on her fork then she uses her hands. Then she places the fork next to her plate (or throws it), always in my direction. She takes the fork again to eat, etc. She does the same with the cup. I found out that when there is no table in front of her, she keeps the cup in her hand. She used to drop it to the ground, but learned that is not a good idea.
>
> She cannot hold objects for long, but she is improving on the time span. It does help to practice with her. I let her bring me things like books, or let her help to set the table and bring the spoons. She does that remarkably well. She can walk the length of the room carrying things now. She needs a verbal prompt. I "talk her to me." As soon as I look the other way, she drops things.
>
> It is really the other way round: the better she functions, the more alert she is, the more she will do the stereotypies. She takes things in her mouth, but in my opinion it is not to gain information on the objects. She cannot help herself; it is involuntary behavior, and nothing can stop her. I do not put on restraints; she has an arm splint, but hates it. If it is really bad, I hold her hand down, or put a band around it to keep her hand on her chair at mealtimes. But only short periods. I hate to restrain her, as there is a relation between her alertness and stereotypies. There

are moments, and they occur more and more over the years, that she is calm and interested in activities, holding her hands in her lap. That is a hopeful development.

She has to practice a specific movement over and over to have it "installed" in her system. That may take years. For example, Karina has a lift for going upstairs. It has a tiny button for on/off, and she has been able to handle that for three years. During all this time, I practiced with her to teach her to use the big yellow button for going up and down. She has to push it sideways and keep it there, and as soon as she releases her grip, the lift stops. You can understand how difficult it is for a girl to hold a firm grip. For three years I held her hand on the button, pushing it together. Last week she did it on her own for the first time. She is only capable of going downstairs, pushing left to right, which is easier for a left-handed girl than pushing right to left. But she sailed down the stairs all by herself, big smile, making four or five stops, but pushing the button again. How proud we were. Now I try to get her to do it always, which is not her idea of an easy life! Our next goal is a ride downstairs all at once, without stops. And upstairs as well. I want to explain to parents with a young child that Karina did not use her hands for anything between 2 and 5 years. She was completely apraxic, screaming with fear if we put something in her hand. So never give up!

Look for more ideas for promoting and improving hand use in Chapter 14, Occupational Therapy.

All God's kids got a place in the choir
Some sing low, some sing higher
Some sing out on the telephone wire
And some just clap their hands...

The author wishes to thank the following professionals for ideas and information which was used to develop this chapter: Susan Hanks, PT; Barbro Lindberg; Linda Reece, OTR/L; Jan Townsley, OTR/L.

SEIZURES

Seizures can be simply described as a lightening bolt in the brain, and the first time we see it happen, it may frighten us more than the worst electrical storm we've ever seen. Learning what happens during a seizure reduces our anxiety and helps us learn how to react with calm and understanding. Your daughter with RS may never have a seizure in her life, or she may have seizures that are well controlled with medication. Knowledge is your best ally.

Epilepsy is a broad term that is used to describe recurring seizures or the potential for recurrence of seizures. Seizures are called by various names including fits, spells, convulsions and attacks. A seizure is a sign of a disorder and in and of itself is not an illness or a disorder. You can not "catch" epilepsy. It does not cause mental retardation, is not a mental illness, and is not anyone's fault.

The cause of seizures in RS is unknown. We do not understand why some children with RS have seizures while others do not. However, since RS involves the nervous system, it is not surprising that seizures occur. If seizures do occur, the onset tends to be between 2 years and 10 years of age.

Should my daughter see a neurologist?

If you suspect that your daughter is having seizure activity, it is wise to consult with a doctor who specializes in the treatment of seizures. It will put your mind at ease and it will assure that she gets a thorough evaluation of her seizure status. A child neurologist should be familiar with RS.

> Jenn's neurologist is one who is thorough in evaluation and treatment. He has the utmost confidence in parental input and works as a team with parents. He is extremely sensitive to our daughters as human beings and not just another medical case. I know that I have to report my every observation to the neurologist so that he can build his database of information on Jenn in order to continue to provide excellent treatment. I know that neurological treatment is an evolutionary process, peculiar to each individual. What works for one doesn't necessarily work for another. What worked three years ago for someone may not work for them now. I know that unchecked seizure activity induces more seizure activity.

What is a seizure?

Every brain cell is an electrochemical unit that generates a very small electrical current. The brain sends out electrical signals through our nerves. The brain receives signals along the nerves from all parts of the body. Normally, this electrical activity is well regulated and organized. Sometimes there is sudden excessive or erratic electrical activity. When this happens, it may result in a seizure. The electrical disturbance that accompanies this seizure may arise from any part of the brain. The kind or type of seizure may indicate the area in the brain where the electrical disturbance arises.

Can we tell when she is having a seizure?

A *clinical seizure* results from the excessive, synchronous discharge of brain cells (neurons), which brings about a change in movement or behavior. If no change is seen in behavior or movement, it is not considered a clinical seizure. Rarely, a seizure discharge may be recorded during an EEG (electroencephalogram, the recording of ongoing brain activity) without any obvious clinical change in a person. More frequently, random EEG abnormal discharges are recorded in many girls. These are not seizures and in themselves do not require anti-seizure medication.

In RS, it can be difficult to determine whether she is having a clinical seizure or autonomic responses which look like a seizure. Often, seizure-like behaviors are seen, but are not seen on the EEG when they occur. Girls with RS have vacant spells which resemble absence seizures, but are not. Often there are jerky movements and eye rolling which are associated with seizures, but in RS they are involuntary movements that are not seizures. In some cases, it is necessary to obtain a 24 hour EEG with video to see if the behavior correlates with EEG seizure discharge.

How are seizures diagnosed?

The diagnosis of epilepsy (seizures) is made on the basis of the parent's description of seizures, physical and neurological examinations and the EEG findings. An EEG is a test to measure and record the electrical activity generated by the brain. It does not measure intelligence. Small electrodes are placed over the scalp and held in place with tape or a special paste. Your daughter will experience no pain or discomfort during an EEG recording, but she must remain still during placement of the electrodes. Therefore, she may become upset and cry. She may need medication to make her drowsy in order to record her brain activity during sleep.

How is an EEG helpful?

The EEG will show changes that may indicate an abnormality in one or many areas of the brain, localize the specific area of the brain that is involved, help determine the type of seizure, and reveal the kind of medication that can best control the type of seizure.

What does an EEG tracing look like?

In individuals who do not have epilepsy, the EEG recordings resemble squiggly lines with waves that are similar in height. In most people with seizures, abnormalities are seen as little bursts of electrical activity, called "sharp waves" or "spikes," which interrupt normal rhythm.

Does the EEG pick up seizures every time my daughter has a seizure?

The EEG records only the electrical activity present at the time the EEG is being recorded. Therefore, a seizure will not be recorded unless she has a seizure during the recording. However, if she has had a recent seizure, the EEG tracing may show changes that are helpful to the physician in determining appropriate treatment. An EEG measures waves on the surface and outer layers of the brain only. If the EEG does not show seizure activity during what you think may be a seizure, it doesn't mean that seizures are not occurring. It could be that they are taking place deep within the brain and cannot be measured by conventional means.

When should the EEG be done?

The neurologist will determine if an EEG is necessary. The EEG should be recorded in both the awake and sleep states since the abnormal activity may be seen in either or both. With medication, the seizures will probably decrease in frequency or be completely controlled. This does not mean the EEG will necessarily be normal.

Why does the EEG need to be done when she is both awake and asleep?

The EEG looks different when she is awake and asleep, and some abnormalities may only be seen when she is drowsy or sleeping. Some children have a normal waking EEG and a very abnormal sleep EEG.

How often should my daughter have an EEG?

Routine repetition at periodic intervals is not necessary, but repeating the EEG may be necessary if seizures change in character, severity or frequency. Children with RS frequently have abnormal EEG patterns. This abnormal pattern may include activity called epileptiform abnormalities that may be recorded in persons who have seizures. The information supplied by the EEG may help define the specific seizure type. The physician can then choose the most appropriate anticonvulsant drugs. However, a normal EEG does not rule out the diagnosis of epilepsy or mean that seizures have not occurred. On the other hand, if there is no history of a seizure, an abnormal EEG does not make the diagnosis of epilepsy.

What abnormalities on the EEG are of importance for the diagnosis and management of seizures?

The EEG can pick up "artifacts," such as muscle twitches and eye blinks that are not coming from the brain. It is not abnormal to see these on an EEG. The abnormalities which are important include spikes, slowing, and evidence of seizures. They may be either **focal** (localized to a specific area of the brain), or **generalized** (seen all over the brain).

Spikes are abnormal discharges from brain cells. The abnormal discharges may involve many brain cells and may result in an EEG seizure discharge and seizure. When spikes are seen in a specific area of the brain, it may indicate where the seizure began. Multi-focal spikes give an indication that there are many abnormal areas of the brain.

Slowing of the EEG is determined when it is compared to the normal rhythm of the EEG, which varies with the age of the child and whether she is awake, drowsy or asleep. Generalized slowing is often seen in children with chronic brain dysfunction.

Evidence of seizures refers to the association of specific abnormalities on the EEG with specific seizure types.

What EEG patterns are seen in the girl with RS?

While the EEG is usually abnormal in RS, there is no diagnostic pattern. EEG patterns frequently seen in RS include generalized slowing, rhythmic slow activity (reported as "theta" activity), and focal and generalized spikes and sharp waves.

What types of seizures are commonly seen in Rett syndrome?

Episodic electrical events can occur in different parts of the brain. The type of seizures they produce will differ depending on what area of the brain is affected and the direction and speed as the event spreads. Each type of seizure may require a different medication. Girls and women with RS may experience generalized and partial seizures, but there is not one specific type of seizure seen in RS. Your child may have only one type of seizure or she may have more than one type. It is important to remember that some children with RS never have seizures. Most seizure disorders respond well to medication.

> Chelsey's seizures are what I guess you could call a focal type. I'm a nurse and I didn't even realize that's what they were for awhile. It's hard to explain what she does. Her breathing pattern will slightly change. She can't open her mouth and she drools.

GENERALIZED SEIZURES

Tonic/Clonic Seizures: These seizures have been called grand mal and are now referred to as generalized tonic/clonic seizures. When the EEG is recorded during a generalized seizure, the seizure activity seems to start all over the brain all at once. Since the whole brain is involved, the seizure may involve all muscles and motor functions with loss of consciousness. Generalized seizures can be "large" and convulsive, with muscle movements like jerking or stiffening, or "small" and non-convulsive with alteration of consciousness but no jerking movements. If she loses consciousness, she may fall and may then have rhythmic jerking of all extremities or stiffening followed by rhythmic jerking. The **tonic phase** is when stiffening occurs. Since all the muscles are contracted, the chest muscles also contract, and breathing may become difficult. She may cry out because of air rushing out of her lungs, but she is not in pain. Lack of oxygen causes a bluish tinge around the lips and face. Saliva may cause a gurgling sound in the throat. The jaw becomes tightly clenched. The **clonic phase** then begins with rhythmic jerking and tightly clenched fists. The arms, legs and head may flex and then relax. This usually lasts no more than a few minutes. When she regains consciousness, she may be sleepy for 1-2 hours afterward. After rest, she should be able to go back to her usual activities.

Absence Seizures: This type of seizure, which has been called **petit mal**, starts suddenly. It is characterized by brief staring spells without a preceding warning. There may be head-bobbing or eye-blinking. Absence seizures generally last just a few seconds and end as abruptly as they began. Afterward, she returns to her usual activity without a period of confusion or sleepiness. Absence seizures can be confused with complex partial seizures because they both involve staring. It is important to differentiate the type of seizure to determine the type of medication that will work best.

Chelsey doesn't have any shaking or tremors during her seizures. She will get very still, her hands clasped together and her jaws clamped shut. Her breathing pattern is different, more on the rapid side. She drools during the seizures. But her pupils are unchanged and you can go up and sit down beside her and talk to her and she looks at you with her eyes, while nothing else moves. I've found if I very calmly talk to her and tell her everything is alright and gently rub the side of her face, she comes out of it in a few seconds. I have seen her seizures last up to 30 minutes. Usually after a really long one she goes to sleep. We've finally got them partially under control with Tegretol® and Dilantin®.

Myoclonic Seizures: Formerly called minor motor seizures, these events consist of abrupt jerks of muscle groups and involve brief, sudden twitch-like movements of one or more extremities. They may take many forms. A foot may kick out, a hand may fly forward. Myoclonic seizures may arise from deep structures in the brain stem that control tone and posture, causing an abrupt increase in a muscle group which brings about a sudden movement of that part of the body. However, myoclonic jerks are not seizures. When falling asleep, most healthy individuals experience a sudden jerk and awaken with a startle. This is a normal sleep phenomenon.

Akinetic/Atonic Seizure: This type of seizure is as sudden as a myoclonic seizure. However, it is characterized by a sudden loss of tone or posture. If standing, the child may suddenly become limp and drop to the floor. If sitting, one may simply see loss of tone with the head falling forward or backward. These seizures are brief. The child returns to her usual activity immediately afterwards. These seizures may also be referred to as "drop attacks."

PARTIAL SEIZURES

The seizure is called partial when at the beginning of the seizure the electrical disturbance is limited to one part of the brain. The electrical disturbance may spread to involve the whole brain. If this occurs, the seizure has become secondarily generalized.

Simple Partial Seizure: These seizures may involve movement with rhythmic jerking of one extremity of one side of the face or body, or they may involve the senses, with a particular tingling, burning or abnormal sensation in any part of the body. There is no alteration of consciousness.

Complex Partial Seizure: During this type of seizure there is some alteration of consciousness. The child is unable to make meaningful responses or her usual responses. The seizures may be characterized by confusion, loss of alertness, and staring episodes, either alone or combined with automatic behavior such as picking at the clothes, smacking the lips, or random nonpurposeful movements of the arms or legs.

How do I know if it is a seizure?

It is sometimes difficult to tell the difference between autonomic responses associated with RS and seizure activity. Some breath holding episodes, cyanotic spells (turning blue), jerky tremors, inattention and eye-rolling movements ordinarily associated with seizures are not seizures in RS. You should observe the sequence of events that occur. For example, does breath holding occur followed by jerky movements or vice versa? Observe the movements. Are they rhythmic or random? How long does the episode last? Does she sleep afterwards? Observe her eyes. Does she stare vacantly or have eye rolling? Does her head drop? All of these events have been observed during breath holding episodes as well as during seizures. Report these observations to your physician. It may be necessary to obtain an EEG with video monitoring of the breathing or movement pattern to establish whether or not the events are seizures and need to be treated with drugs. This is very important to establish, because in addition to their beneficial effects, all anti-convulsants have potential side-effects.

In Ashley's case, severe breathing episodes and seizures do have some similar characteristics, but generally, are quite different. Her eyes are a big clue to seizures. Her eyes will freeze, and have been known to roll upwards, or in one direction only, but, freeze, nevertheless. In breathing episodes, her eyes are free to move around. Ashley's face becomes quite flushed during seizures. There is more movement in her arms during seizures. There is a tightening during breathing episodes, but not as much movement as there is in seizures. Ashley appears frightened or stressed during seizures. I do not notice this during severe breathing episodes. Also, her lips will often turn blue in a seizure but not in a breathing episode. She has had severe apnea where her lips will turn blue, but these episodes do not resemble a seizure.

Karina has this sort of shaking her body, grimacing her face, stiffening and jerking her arms and legs. It lasts one, two minutes, then she relaxes again. She tends to bend over forwards when she is walking, and sideways when she is sitting. It happens frequently, many times a day, but some days more than others. She started this when she was about 8/9 years old. It is not epilepsy. She has that, too, and it definitely is different. My neurologist says it is Rett-related. Anti-epileptic medicines make no difference: on it or off it she "Rettdances." I never tried anything else. It is part of her and although it is not nice, it is not really disruptive to her. She just "sits it out." She needs constant attention when she has these episodes, to prevent her from falling, which by the way never happened. But I take no risk. I put her in a chair with a safety belt.

We took video of a student during her "seizures" and the neurologist said most of what we were seeing was "involuntary motions" dealing with a breathing problem. This girl looks like a falling tree when she has these involuntary movements. Her seizures are a little different.

Can seizures be brought on by activity?

If too much comes at Dani too fast, or if we leave the TV on with no lights (and the light from the TV blinks), she will have a seizure. She is sensitive to loud noises, too.

Brit has had seizures since 4 months, however, never evoked by sound, visual or tactile stimuli. I remember this because we could take her anywhere and we would play games and scare her like "boo" and hide around a corner and she would giggle. Now, however, ripping a paper towel off in front of her has given a seizure, along with a glimmer of sunlight on a therapist's watchband, even a cough or sneeze. Closing the car door is hard to do quietly. Going over the bumps in the side-walk triggers a seizure as well. She began this hypersensitivity at age 5½.

Should she take medication for seizures?

EEG abnormalities are common in RS. The goal is to treat the seizure disorder, not the EEG. If your child has an abnormal EEG but does not have a history of seizure-like activity, she does not necessarily need to take anti-convulsant medication. Even some individuals who have no neurological problems and never have seizures may show abnormalities on the EEG at some time. In research studies of RS, near-ly all girls with RS showed an abnormal EEG, while only from one third to one half of them had true clin-ical seizures.

If she does have seizures, there are many different anticonvulsant drugs which are used for specific seizure types. There is not a specific anticonvulsant drug for the treatment of seizures in RS. A pediatric neurologist needs to know what type(s) of seizure a child is having before prescribing medication. The pri-mary objective of drug therapy is to control the seizures with the least possible drug side-effects. Fortunately, anticonvulsant drugs are generally safe and severe side-effects are rare or very infrequent. All side-effects should be reported to your physician. Any change in behavior, including slowing (over sedation), hyperactivity, incoordination or other behaviors of concern to you are appropriate to bring to the physician's attention.

> Either we don't medicate and Jenn has lots of seizures and is "out of it" most of the time, or we medicate and her seizures are minimized, but the trade-off is the side effects and her not being "with it" some of the time. Nothing's perfect and I can't expect the impossible. I know there's an adjustment phase with new medications, as the body needs time to learn how to work with them.

> Lisa Joy was having trouble with seizures and Tegretol made them worse. About three years ago Felbamate came out and Lisa Joy's neurologist put her Joy on it. There was an amazing change in her – no seizures! He was as pleased as if he had invented the medicine himself. She contin-ues to do really well, with seizures only occasionally, mostly related to lack of sleep. This is a con-troversial medication, but she is doing well, and the doctor has confidence that this is the medicine for her.

How do anticonvulsant drugs work?

There are many drugs to prevent and treat seizures, but it is not entirely clear how or why they work. We do know how these drugs are absorbed and metabolized, and we know about their side effects.

Some drugs are more effective than others for different seizure types. Once the seizure type has been identified, the choice of drugs is made on the basis of the drug's effectiveness, cost, the child's age and other drugs she may be already taking and any drug allergies or sensitivities.

What are some medications that are used?

The objective of anti-convulsant therapy is to use the lowest dose of drug with the least number of side effects to achieve the best seizure control. Sometimes higher doses are necessary, and more than one drug may have to be used to achieve seizure control. It is important to remember that all drugs, including aspirin, have side effects along with their beneficial effects. Side-effects may occur during the first few days on the drug until the body adjusts. Some drugs may require dose adjustment or discontinuation if the side effects are unpleasant.

The Benzodiazepines (Valium®, Klonipin®, Tranzene® and Ativan®) are grouped together as a class of anticonvulsants. Valium® and Ativan® are used to treat status epilepticus (discussed later). Klonopin®, Tranxene®, Valium® and Ativan® are also used in long-term treatment of seizures. The drugs in this class are useful for absence seizures, but are most effectively used to treat myoclonic, atonic and complex partial seizures. Since each of these drugs can cause drowsiness, irritability and hyperactivity, they are usually chosen as "add-on" drugs when other drugs do not bring the seizures under control by themselves. The body can develop tolerance for drugs of this type, so the dose must be regularly increased to maintain a therapeutic effect.

Carbamazepine (Tegretol®) is used for simple and complex partial seizures and tonic/clonic seizures. It does not interfere negatively with behavior and learning and has no cosmetic side effects. Tegretol should be started at a low dose and increased each week for the first several weeks until the appropriate therapeutic blood level is reached. Side effects include drowsiness, dizziness, blurred vision, lethargy, nausea/vomiting, incoordination, decreased white blood count and decreased platelets. One good side effect of Tegretol® is elevation of mood.

Divalproex Sodium (Depakote®) and **Valproic Acid (Depakene®)** are used for tonic/clonic, absence and myoclonic, and simple and complex partial seizures. These two drugs seem to work better after the child has taken them for a couple of weeks. When either of these drugs is stopped, they continue to work for several weeks. Each of these are very safe drugs, but should be used with caution in children under the age of two, and preferably alone. Side effects include nausea/vomiting, indigestion, sedation, dizziness, hair loss, tremor, incoordination, weight loss and/or gain, changes in liver function.

Ethosuximide (Zarontin®) is used for akinetic/atonic seizures and is valuable in treating absence seizures. It has no effect on partial seizures. Side effects include drowsiness, dizziness, GI upset, headache, hiccough, hyperactivity, and nausea/vomiting. Zarontin® can cause allergic reactions, but these complications are very rare. In most cases, it is safe, well tolerated and effective.

Felbamate (Felbatol®) is used for myoclonic seizures, and difficult seizures. It has a rare side effect of liver failure and aplastic anemia. For this reason, it isn't used often except as a last resort and only after the parents have been thoroughly informed of the potential lethal side effects of the drug.

Lamogitrine (Lamictal®) is used as a primary drug or as an "add on" drug, used in combination with other drugs for the treatment of partial and generalized seizures, but should be used cautiously with Depakote®/Depakene® because of a possible likelihood of hypsensitivity reaction (skin rash). It is useful for patients who cannot control their seizures adequately with current medication or who experience unacceptable side effects. Side effects include skin rash, dizziness, headache, double vision and unsteadiness.

Gabapentin (Neurontin®) is a well tolerated "add on" medication for partial complex and tonic/clonic seizures. It does not interfere with other medications, so it is helpful for those on multiple drugs. The most common side effects are sedation, fatigue, dizziness, ataxia, nystagmus, headache, nausea and weight gain.

Phenobarbital (Luminal®) is used for tonic/clonic, and simple and complex partial seizures. Phenobarbital is ineffective for absence seizures. Since it is metabolized slowly, it is usually given only once per day. Allergic reactions are possible, so the child should be observed carefully for skin rashes. The most important adverse side effects are in behavior and learning. Other side effects include drowsiness, lethargy and hyperactivity, which can result in changes in behavior and learning.

Phenytoin (Dilantin®) is used for tonic/clonic and simple and complex partial seizures. This drug can cause allergic reactions, so if a skin rash develops after the first two to three weeks, the child should be seen by the physician immediately. Dilantin® may cause mood changes and lethargy. Overgrowth of the gums reportedly occurs in about half of the children who have therapeutic blood levels. When taken over a long period of time, Dilantin® can cause the development of coarse facial features and more extensive growth of body hair. Side effects include tremor, anemia, loss of coordination, double vision, nausea/vomiting, confusion and slurred speech.

Primidone (Mysoline®) is used for tonic/clonic and simple and partial complex seizures. It is metabolized by the body into phenobarbital. The child should be carefully observed, as the drug can cause hyperactivity and behavior problems. To avoid sedative effects and personality changes, Mysoline® must be started at a low dose and increased very slowly over several weeks. Side effects include drowsiness, appetite loss, irritability, nausea/vomiting, dizziness, and loss of coordination.

Topiramate (Topamax®) is used for partial or partial complex seizures. When Topamax® is combined with Dilantin®, the dose of Dilantin® may need to be increased. If Dilantin® or Tegretol® are added or withdrawn, the dose of Topamax® may need adjustment. Side effects include lethargy, agitation, headaches, drowsiness, incoordination, nervousness, dizziness, and arm/leg tingling. At higher doses, loss of appetite and weight loss can be seen.

When can she stop taking medication?

The medication should never be stopped abruptly. Your child should continue with her medication even if she has not had a seizure for quite awhile. She may continue to be at risk for having seizures. She will not become dependent on the drug; anticonvulsant medications are not addicting. If she can keep control of the seizures for a number of years, she may be able to be taken off these medications without recurrent seizures. But stopping the drug must always be done slowly and with a doctor's careful supervision.

> Over time, we built Jenn up to dosages of 800 mg Tegretol®, 200 mg Phenobarbital®, and 20cc Zarontin® in one day just to control the seizure activity. Now, Jenn needs only 5cc of Tegretol ®per day.

Are there other treatments for seizures?

Special diets may be recommended by your daughter's physician as a last resort when anticonvulsants have proven ineffective. The **ketogenic diet,** one of the oldest treatments for epilepsy, is one which is very high in fat. The diet provides the minimal amount of protein necessary for growth and virtually no carbohydrates. Most of the calories consumed come from fat, using butter or cream. It is a very restrictive diet and can be difficult to begin and maintain. The diet begins with several days of fasting. ***The ketogenic diet must not ever be attempted except under strict medical supervision.*** The diet can be dangerous if not done properly. Food on the diet is strictly limited and not always appealing. A typical meal might consist of a small amount of meat, fish, poultry or cheese, a serving of fruit, an additional serving of fat such as butter or mayonnaise and a serving of heavy whipping cream. While some say the family ends up eating in the closet and the diet is too restrictive, others say the effort is worth it when seizures are under control for the first time.

> Katie has been on the ketogenic diet for almost two years now, with wonderful results. However, when she gets sick, she can sometimes have breakthrough seizures.

John Freeman, MD, Director of the Pediatric Epilepsy Clinic at Johns Hopkins University, has written the following statement for the Child Neurology Society:

The ketogenic diet is a high-fat, very low carbohydrate diet used in some children who have epilepsy that is difficult-to-control with conventional drugs. Although the diet was first developed in the 1920's and widely used through the 1940's, it fell into disuse as new medications for epilepsy became available. Recent widespread media attention to this treatment has increased its use by many centers, and child neurologists are increasingly being asked about the diet.
A made-for-TV film dramatized a true story about a child successfully treated by the diet, and can be expected to generate considerable discussion and many questions. The Child Neurology Society is developing this position statement to assist with responses to this anticipated demand.
• The ketogenic diet is a carefully and individually calculated dietary program that may be useful in children with difficult-to-control epilepsy.

- The diet simulates the effects of prolonged starvation by causing the body to burn fat rather than carbohydrate as its main energy source. The ketone bodies, which are the result of this fat metabolism, are utilized as an energy source by the brain. Why this results in improved seizure control is unknown.

- The diet has never been evaluated in a scientifically controlled manner. However, less rigorous studies done over many years suggest that 30% of children treated with the ketogenic diet will have their seizures well-controlled (>90%). Half of those children will be seizure-free. An additional 30-40% will have their seizure frequency decreased by more than 50%. Approximately 25-30% of patients who try the diet will find that it is not sufficiently effective, and discontinue the diet and return to the use of medications. Some children may be able to decrease or discontinue their medications while on the diet.

- The diet has not been adequately studied in adults.

- The major side-effect of the diet is kidney stones, in some patients calcium oxalate, and in others uric acid stones, which can be successfully treated with adequate fluid intake and acidification of the urine. Increases in plasma lipids have been reported, but their significance is not clear.

- The proper role of the diet in the management of children with difficult-to-control seizures remains to be fully defined. Most children with few seizures will have their epilepsy controlled with one medication. Even when the first medication fails to control the seizures, it is easier and more reasonable to attempt control with a second medication. The diet should be considered only for children who have more than two seizures per week despite treatment with at least two different anticonvulsant medications. The diet is also used when the frequency of seizures, despite medications, interferes with the child's function, or when the medications themselves cause substantial adverse reactions.

- The diet should only be used under proper medical supervision, and by a team which can provide support for the family during the difficult period of adjustment after the diet is initiated. The decision about whether the diet is or is not appropriate for an individual child should be the result of discussions between informed parents and their physician. The diet is not a cure-all, nor is it intended for everyone with epilepsy.

A form of diet less disruptive to family eating is the **MCT diet,** in which a special oil is added and she can eat most foods.

What is status epilepticus (SE)?

A seizure that lasts a very long time is referred to as **status epilepticus. Convulsive status epilepticus** refers to **tonic/clonic seizures,** and **nonconvulsive status epilepticus** refers to an episode of absence spells, staring spells, or periods of confusion that last for more than a half hour. In most children who have SE, the cause is not known. The most common cause of convulsive status in a person who already has seizures is a blood drug level which is too low to control seizures. Status epilepticus may occur from a missed dose, interaction with another drug that has interfered with the drug's effectiveness, or substitution of a generic drug that is not well absorbed in the bloodstream.

Very prolonged SE can cause brain damage. However, it may not be the seizures themselves, but the underlying cause of the seizures, such as infection, trauma, or tumors that may cause brain damage. Most children with SE recover without significant new deficits.

When convulsive SE occurs, it is important to bring the seizures to an end as quickly as possible. Most likely, this will take place in the emergency room of the hospital. Here, she will be observed, blood will be drawn, and oxygen will be given if needed. She will probably get an IV (intravenous line) to supply fluids and to give anticonvulsants into the vein if it becomes necessary. This is the fastest way to get medicine to the brain where it is needed. A number of medications may be used, but Ativan® and Valium®, which are quick-acting anti-convulsants, are usually given first. Their effectiveness may wear off quickly, within minutes, and another seizure may occur. An additional drug such as Dilantin® is then given, which is slower to start acting but lasts longer.

Most of the time, the SE can be controlled within a half hour to an hour of arrival at the hospital. In prolonged cases, it may be necessary to give large doses of medication or give general anesthesia, which usually stops the seizures. While these episodes are frightening to watch, most children recover well and do not have lasting damage, even from prolonged seizures.

When nonconvulsive SE occurs, it is more difficult to detect, because it does not involve body movements. The child may seem detached or just "not herself." The only way to know if nonconvulsive status is happening is to do an EEG, which will show constant spike-wave abnormalities. It is treated with anticonvulsant given into the vein, and the child then returns to her normal state.

The author wishes to thank the following professionals for ideas and information which was used to develop this chapter: Daniel Glaze, M.D.; Rebecca Schultz, RN, MSN, CPNP.

THE NERVOUS SYSTEM

To understand RS, it is necessary to understand the nervous system, which is the body's message and information center. The nervous system is made up of three parts, the **central** nervous system (brain and spinal cord), the **peripheral** nervous system, and the **autonomic** nervous system. Each part controls some aspect of our behavior and affects how we experience the world.

CENTRAL NERVOUS SYSTEM

The central nervous system begins to form during the third week of pregnancy into the three basic regions of the brain: the **cerebral hemispheres**, the **brain stem** and the **cerebellum**. The cerebral hemispheres are located on top of the brain stem, and the cerebellum lies behind it. The cerebellum is still immature at birth. By the fourth month of pregnancy, the brain, although small looks structurally much as it does at birth. But very dynamic changes are taking place within the structure of the brain cells.

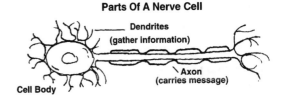

Parts Of A Nerve Cell

Dendrites (gather information)

Axon (carries message)

Cell Body

Nerve cells, called **neurons**, make up the basic structure of the nervous system. Each neuron has a cell body containing a nucleus, and material called **cytoplasm**. Each neuron has a single long fiber extending from the cell body, called an **axon**, and many shorter branch-like limbs known as **dendrites**. Axons carry impulses away from the cell body, while dendrites receive impulses from other neurons and carry them to the cell body.

The nerve cells of the mature cerebral hemispheres are arranged in six layers. The number and complexity of these nerve cell layers increase as the brain grows. The nerve cell bodies migrate from the bottom layer toward the top and spread their projections as they move. If these nerve cell bodies do not move at the right time and make normal connections with other neurons, there can be resulting developmental delay or abnormality.

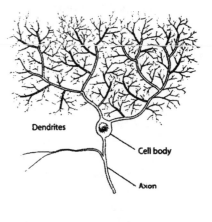

Dendrites

Cell body

Axon

The brain and spinal cord are separated into two different regions. The **gray matter** contains bundles of nerve cell bodies and their dendrites and appears grayish in color. The **white matter** is made up of axons which are covered by an insulating material called **myelin**. This myelin coating is developed after birth and aids the rapid conduction of nerve impulses. The dendrites also increase in number and complexity during the first two years of life.

The neuronal signal is passed from one neuron to the next across a space or synapse. The axon of one neuron is almost touching the dendrite or cell body of another neuron but there is a space to be bridged. This bridge is achieved by the release of chemicals called **neurotransmitters**. A neuron can release one or more of these neurotransmitters and different neurons may release different neurotransmitters. Neurotransmitters are stored in packets called vesicles and released into the synaptic space when a neuron is sufficiently excited and an electrical signal called an action potential reaches the axonal terminal. Neurotransmitters can be excitatory (e.g. glutamate) or inhibitory (e.g. GABA, glycine) to other neurons or have direct effects on muscles, glands, organs and blood vessels (e.g., acetylcholine, dopamine, norepinephrine). The effects of the transmitter are mediated by specific receptors at the other end of the synapse in the receiving neuron or cell. A receptor can have different sub-types so that a neurotransmitter such as acetyl-choline can have a very different action in different places depend-ing on which sub-type of its receptor it binds to.

the forebrain

These chemicals are found in packets at the edge of the axon, called the presynaptic membrane. When they are stimulated by an electrical impulse, the packets open and release the chemical, which then crosses the synaptic space where it stimulates the receptive neuron at its postsynaptic receptor.

the midbrain

The brain and spinal cord make up the central nervous system. All parts of the brain work together to achieve various behaviors but they each have their own special characteristics and functions. The brain can be divided into three basic regions known as the **forebrain**, the **midbrain** and the **hindbrain**.

the hindbrain

The hindbrain consists of the upper part of the spinal cord, the brain stem and the cerebellum. It controls the body's vital functions like heart rate and breathing. The midbrain lies above the hindbrain, and it controls some reflex actions and movements. The forebrain consists of the cerebrum and the structures hidden beneath it. It is the largest and most developed part of the human brain.

CEREBRUM

When people see drawings of the brain, they usually notice the cerebrum. It sits at the top of the brain stem and is the source of intellectual activities such as memory, imagination, planning and thinking. The cerebrum is the largest region of the brain, consisting of two parts joined together in the middle by the tough tissue of the **corpus callosum**. Although the cerebrum is splint in two halves, its two parts (**hemispheres**) communicate with each other. The two hemispheres look exactly alike, but they are very different in the functions they control. For example, the left hemisphere controls the ability to form words, while the right hemisphere seems to control many abstract reasoning skills. Both hemispheres are divided into four lobes. The **frontal lobe** is located in the front (anterior) third of the hemisphere. It

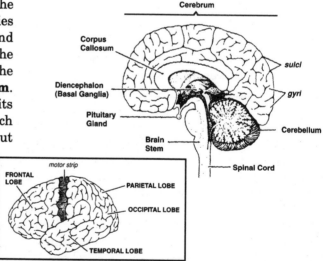

participates in voluntary muscle movement and in memory skills. **Broca's area,** located on the left frontal lobe, allows thoughts to be transformed into words. The **occipital lobe** lies in the back (posterior) fourth of each hemisphere. It processes images from the eyes and links this information with images stored in memory, then passes them to the parietal lobe. The **parietal lobe** sits in the middle-upper part of the cerebrum. It integrates sensory stimuli such as vision, auditory, touch, pain, smell and temperature sensations, so that they can be interpreted. The **temporal lobe** occupies the lower-middle area. Its main function is to regulate communication and sensation, while other parts of this lobe integrate memories and sensations of taste, sound, sight and touch.

In early pregnancy, the surface of the cerebrum is very smooth, but as the brain grows, indentations appear. By birth, the surface has become very rugged, with crevices (**sulci**) and bumps (**gyri**). The brain region which lies just underneath the surface of the cerebrum is called the cerebral cortex. It is made up mostly of nerve cell bodies, or gray matter. The cortex is gray because the nerves in this area do not have the insulation that makes most other parts of the brain appear white. The folds in the brain increase its surface area and the amount of information that can be processed. Just below the gray matter, nerve fibers, or white matter, is found. The cerebral cortex is the area of the brain which controls motion and thought, and may regulate some effects of the brain stem.

Other structures which lie deep within the brain and hidden from view control emotions, perceptions, responses and involuntary movements. The **hypothalamus** contains several important centers which control body temperature, thirst, hunger and eating, water balance and sexual function, emotional activity and sleep. The **thalamus** is a clearinghouse for information to and from the spinal cord and the cerebrum. The **hippocampus** sends memories out to the appropriate part of the cerebral hemisphere for storage and retrieval. The **basal ganglia** modulates motion and thought, and regulates the effects of the brain stem. In addition to the basal ganglia, the **labyrinth** in the inner ear and the cerebellum are also involved in movements. These parts acting together provide a series of checks and balances for motor activities and balance.

CEREBELLUM

The cerebellum lies just below the cerebral hemispheres and hangs behind the brain stem. It coordinates the action of the voluntary muscles, allowing movements to be smooth and accurate. The cerebellum coordinates learned (rote) movements. When the cerebellum does not work properly, a condition called **ataxia** results in jerky, uncoordinated movements.

BRAIN STEM

The brain stem (**medulla, pons** and **midbrain**) connects the two hemispheres of the brain to the spinal cord. It contains cranial nerves which control important body functions such as breathing, heart rhythm, swallowing, sleep, bowel motility, circulation, taste, salivation and sensitivity to pain, vision and hearing, facial expression and eye and tongue movement. Dysfunction of the brain stem can lead to problems in any of these areas.

SPINAL CORD

The spinal cord extends from the brain stem to the lower back in a cylindrical structure, which is surrounded by three layers of covering called **meninges**. The cervical (neck) area and the lumbar (lower back) area are enlarged to enable the peripheral nerve fibers to leave the spinal cord and go to the arms, legs and other body organs. If the spinal cord is injured, motor and sensory messages are interrupted, which results in loss of sensation and movement.

CEREBROSPINAL FLUID

The cerebrospinal fluid is referred to as **CSF**. It is a clear, watery liquid that surrounds and protects the spinal cord and the brain and flows through the four ventricles of the brain. It prevents sudden pressure changes within the brain and is constantly recirculated.

MOTOR SYSTEMS

In order for thoughtful movement to take place, nerve impulses are carried by the pyramidal tract from the motor cortex to motor neurons in the brain stem or spinal cord. The motor neurons then project out to the muscles via cranial and spinal nerves. This motor pathway involves only two sets of neurons (pyramidal tract neurons and motor neurons) and so is called the **Direct Pathway**. Effective motor function, however, requires not only activation of this direct motor pathway, but preparing muscles for activity, coordination of activity within muscles and between muscles, as well as integrating sensory and motor activity. This involves several other "indirect" motor pathways and brain structures including the cerebellum, basal ganglion, red nucleus and striatum. In RS there appears to be both a lack of effective activation of the direct pathway as well as less effective sensory-motor integration and coordination.

SENSORY SYSTEMS

Sensory systems provide information on the external environment to the brain. Spinal and cranial nerves carry information from external receptors on modalities such as touch, pain, joint position, muscle tone, as well as the special senses (e.g. vision, hearing, taste, smell, balance) into the central nervous system. Sensory information is processed, used in reflexes, in sensory-motor integration and when it gets to the sensory cortex, reaches our consciousness.

THE AUTONOMIC NERVOUS SYSTEM

The autonomic nervous system controls automatic body functions like heartbeats, respiratory, digestive, endocrine, urinary and reproductive functions. The nerve impulses can begin in either the brain stem or spinal cord and spread toward the organs. In RS, many functions regulated by the autonomic nervous system are improperly controlled, irregular or erratic, such as breathing, sleep, salivation, heart rate, swallowing, bowel motility and vasomotor control.

The autonomic nervous system is important in a classic situation known as the "fight or flight" response. When we are frightened, several physiological responses take place at the same time. The heartbeat quickens, blood pressure increases, pupils dilate, bronchioles of the lungs expand and the function of the digestive system nearly stops as blood is redirected to the brain and muscles, allowing us to react to the situation.

The activities of the heart and lungs are influenced by nerve cells in the brain stem. They form part of the autonomic nervous system which supplies the digestive tract and blood vessels everywhere in the body. The autonomic nervous system is made up of two parts. The **sympathetic** nervous system raises blood pressure and heart rate (pulse) to cope with sudden challenges. When the sympathetic system is stimulated, we become excited, red faced and alert, ready for "fight or flight." In response, the **parasympathetic** nervous system acts like a natural brake to keep the sympathetic system from excessive effects.

BREATHING

Episodic, abnormal breathing patterns are common in RS. Breathing irregularities may be pronounced, or in some cases may be so subtle that they are not even noticed by parents. These patterns appear to be more exaggerated when the girl with RS is agitated. Irregular breathing patterns often begin at preschool age and may change character in adulthood.

Abnormal breathing patterns may include **hyperventilation**, **breath holding**, **apnea**, and **rapid** and **shallow** breathing. These abnormal breathing patterns may be different in each girl, both in type, frequency and intensity.

Breathing is usually abnormal during wakefulness and tends to be normal during sleep. Breathing becomes more irregular under emotional or physical stress. It appears that these abnormalities result from poor coordination into the respiratory center of the brain stem.

HYPERVENTILATION

The most striking breathing patterns often noticed by parents are periods of overbreathing with fast, deep breaths. Such hyperventilations are often interrupted by cessation of breathing, known as apnea. When she overbreathes in this way, she may seem agitated with increased hand movements, dilated pupils, increased heart rate, rocking body movements and increased muscle tone.

BREATH HOLDING

During periods of breath holding, she takes in breath and holds it, at which time breathing is stopped. Oxygen saturation in the blood, normally 97% or higher, can be greatly reduced in RS, sometimes as low as 50%.

> The breath holding and the hyperventilation are two separate actions. When she holds her breath, she takes in air, holds it and her tummy sticks out. When she hyperventilates, she takes in air and blows it out quickly and repeatedly. My daughter has done both, and there is a definite difference.

> When Katie holds her breath, she smiles while her tummy is pooched out, and looks around like she is fully enjoying herself! The only thing we see is that she cannot concentrate on anything while this happens and when she lets the air out, she becomes a little disoriented for a few seconds. Then she hyperventilates. We have never had her turn blue, but we sure can't believe how long she can hold that breath in! I tried to match her one day and nearly passed out!

AIR SWALLOWING

Most people swallow small amounts of air routinely when they are under stress or eat rapidly, swallow unchewed food or chew gum. Any time there is gastrointestinal discomfort such as heartburn, frequent swallowing of air and saliva may bring some relief, resulting in substantial amounts of air in the stomach. Most of the air that is swallowed is either burped and passed out of the mouth or passes into the small bowel. Once air is out of the stomach, it must travel the whole length of the intestines before it is passed as intestinal gas. In most people, this does not cause a problem. However, if the volume of air is very significant, it can cause complications.

Aerophagia is the swallowing of air. Many girls with RS swallow an excessive amount of air during breath holding, which results in abdominal distention. Their tummies become very bloated and hard.

> Meghan holds her breath and sticks her stomach out. She also hyperventilates. When she is holding her breath, she will not do anything else. If she is working with her teachers, they know to wait until she exhales or they don't get any response. It's as if she needs to tune inward for a few moments to regain her strength or concentration.

> Sherry used to swallow a lot of air. Her little sides would protrude and she would almost have "points" sticking out at her sides — I mean her little tummy would end up almost diamond-shaped. We could expel the air by gently pressing her tummy/sides (with her sitting up, so she wouldn't choke if she "sour-burped") or rubbing in a slightly upward motion to produce a huge belch. This gave her some relief. She doesn't swallow air like that anymore and she hasn't in a number of years. It was mostly a problem up until she was around 5 or 6 years old.

APNEA

Central apnea occurs when she lets a breath out and fails to take another breath, causing a temporary cessation of breathing. This occurs often in girls with RS when they are awake. It usually does not cause serious problems. When she holds her breath, her oxygen levels fall. Sometimes her lips may turn blue and she may even lose consciousness briefly. However, she usually begins breathing again on her own. Apnea would be serious if her oxygen level fell low enough to a level known as anoxia. This is typically not seen in RS.

> Ashley has had lots of apnea and breath holding. In my opinion, breath holding is fairly insignificant, compared to apnea. In breath holding, Ashley will normally pooch out her stomach, then release the air and her stomach will go back to normal. In apnea, she has no pooching of the stomach. Her lips are always blue and she gasps when she starts to breathe again. Her fingernails may also turn blue. Her apnea is much more severe, and she appears to be in distress, but when she holds her breath, she usually appears quite fine, even smiling sometimes. Apnea leaves Ashley incapable of doing almost anything while it is occurring.

VALSALVA'S MANOEUVER

Valsalva's manoeuver takes place when she takes in long inspirations and tries to force them out while the airway is shut. This causes a sudden change in blood pressure and heart rate.

How can breathing be so abnormal when she is awake and normal when she sleeps?

In Rett syndrome, irregular breathing occurs only when she is awake and does not usually occur during sleep. When she is awake, the periods of abnormal breathing result from probable immaturity of neurons regulating breathing mechanisms. During periods of sleep, the changes in body function allow us to breathe regularly and continuously. When abnormal breathing is seen in some girls with RS during sleep, it is usually of the obstructive type, usually from enlarged tonsils. Airway obstruction may be caused by mechanical problems in the breathing passages. Mouth breathing, snoring and frequent ear infections may be signals that your daughter has a problem which should be evaluated by an ear, nose, and throat specialist.

Are the breathing problems dangerous to her health?

They can be alarming to watch, and may make her somewhat uncomfortable, but they are not felt to cause permanent damage. It is not known why the normal breathing during sleep brings out EEG abnormalities, while abnormal breathing during wakefulness causes the EEG to normalize to what is often seen in RS. Cessation of breathing during sleep is not typically seen in RS. However, if your child stops breathing for short periods of time while asleep, you should talk with her physician. She may need testing to rule out airway obstruction. This is a separate problem from RS, for which there is treatment.

Should we use an apnea monitor?

Since her breathing is normal during sleep, the monitor is not necessary. During the daytime, the apnea can occur so often that it would be difficult to keep up with. However, some families choose to use monitors when she sleeps for peace of mind.

Does she need to take oxygen for her breathing problems?

If chronic and prolonged, lack of oxygen can be life-threatening. Most girls with RS who hold their breath do not have dangerously reduced oxygen flow. However, when there is chronic oxygen deprivation and the oxygen levels fall more than 15 times an hour, oxygen can be beneficial. It is probably not necessary, but for peace of mind, it can be helpful.

> Lauren's oxygen saturation has been as low as 17%. She was terribly unhealthy as a result. She also had no energy, she fainted and hurt herself. She needed 3 liters per minute of oxygen 24 hours every day for over 4 years. Lauren needed oxygen. She was much healthier with supplemental oxygen. Almost everything she did she did better with the oxygen. The oxygen never got Lauren even close to 100% saturation of oxygen. Still, it was necessary and a tremendous help to her. We are very glad we found out about it. As I have said many times before, we hope every girl gets tested occasionally for oxygen saturation. Now that Lauren no longer needs supplemental oxygen she is still not at 100%, but she has good healthy pink lips most of the time. However, we don't want anyone to get the impression that oxygen somehow made the Rett Syndrome "better." It simply did a great job of lessening the problems Rett caused in Lauren's breathing. We did not give her oxygen just to relieve apnea and hyperventilation symptoms either. We gave her oxygen to lessen the problems caused by the breathing symptoms. It made her much healthier and alert. But, you need a good reason to do it because it is difficult to accomplish (like so many of the things we all do) and it put our Lauren on a leash made of the oxygen hose. She never was happier than the day she ended its use. The reason we try to be so clear about this is that some Rett families have heard about Lauren's oxygen use, and her success with it, and they get the wrong impression that giving oxygen makes "Rett" better. It doesn't. It does provide an excellent and recommended therapy for the problems associated with low oxygen saturation (a very serious problem) which is a result of some of the bad breathing symptoms that may occur in most Rett girls (sometimes it's always noticed), but not always as seriously as in Lauren.

How can I tell if she is swallowing air?

Air swallowing can be difficult to detect. Air can be swallowed inadvertently in significant amounts each time she eats. It can also occur throughout the day in small amounts. Sometimes it is easy to hear air as it is being swallowed. If her upper abdomen is distended shortly after she eats it could be that she is swallowing air. Here are some signs and symptoms associated with air swallowing:

- Audible swallowing at any time, including sleep
- Severe dysfunction of swallowing with air swallowing apparent during eating or drinking
- Abdominal distention, usually following feedings or episodes of hyperventilation and breath holding
- Frequent burping (may be beneficial)
- Large amounts of gas passed through the rectum

If a large amount of air stays temporarily in the stomach, it will lead to sudden distention of the upper part of the abdomen. The stomach stretches, creating significant tension. If the girl with RS is unable to burp or pass gas, the bowel wall may become thin over time. This is especially true in individuals who have a poor nutritional status. Extreme distention of the wall of the stomach may lead to rupture. Several cases of gastric rupture have been reported in girls with RS. Once the stomach or any part of the intestine is torn, this will lead to peritonitis, an acute inflammation and infection of the abdominal cavity. Without immediate attention, peritonitis may lead to death. However, severe problems are infrequent, even though gastrointestinal problems are common in RS.

If air is passed into the intestine adequately, gastric distention will be less of a problem. But it can accumulate in the mid intestine, causing distention of the abdomen and uncomfortable cramps. Constipation and medications that slow down the passage of stool can worsen abdominal distention.

I asked the GI doc about her breath holding and he said as long as her stomach is the same size in the morning as in the evening, i.e., she's not bloated, then she isn't swallowing air. The act of pushing her stomach out is not damaging as long as she is not bloating with air. It does make getting a diaper on tough! I've found if I tap on her stomach, I can sometimes stop the holding.

How can air swallowing be minimized?

If you suspect that she is swallowing air, there are a few things you can do. Decrease the length of mealtimes if it appears she is swallowing air while eating. Minimize stress and discomfort. Sit her in an upright position after she eats to help her burp and decrease the amount of gas in the stomach that is passed into the bowel. Keep on top of constipation so that gas does not accumulate in the mid intestine. In some situations, even the frequent use of enemas (not routinely recommended) may be preferred to severe episodes of abdominal distention.

If these measures are not adequate and her abdominal distention is severe, you may need to ask the advice of her physician on more aggressive methods. This might include the placement of a tube through her nose into the stomach (nasogastric tube) or the placement of a tube through the abdominal wall into the stomach (gastrostomy button). This will help to decompress the bowel and allow the gas to flow out. It will prevent gas from advancing into the intestine. However, once the air is beyond the stomach, the bowel cannot be decompressed with any of these tubes. Some surgical interventions to prevent reflux, such as the Nissen fundoplication, in which the opening from the esophagus to the stomach is closed, may help in GE reflux, preventing heartburn or intermittent vomiting. At the same time, they can also increase the chances of a complication from air swallowing, since she is now unable to burp to get rid of gas.

The risks and benefits of such surgery should be weighed carefully in each patient prior to making this decision. In rare situations, the placement of a colostomy (opening the bowel into the abdominal wall) may help in allowing adequate flow of intestinal contents and decrease the complications from inadequate passage of stool.

Early detection as well as consultation with a gastroenterologist are extremely important to avoid progression of the problem and to manage it as early as possible, thus preventing more severe complications.

What happens when she hyperventilates?

Deep breathing expels more carbon dioxide from the body than usual, so her hyperventilation causes her carbon dioxide level to fall. Carbon dioxide is one of the body's normal waste products carried in the blood. Its purpose is to maintain the acid/alkali balance so that cells can function normally. When her carbon dioxide level falls, cells cannot function normally. Hyperventilation may cause her to feel dizzy and her fingers to tingle.

What happens when she holds her breath?

When she holds her breath, her oxygen level in the bloodstream falls. This may cause her to feel faint.

Are the abnormal breathing episodes or tremors related to seizures?

The abnormal breathing episodes can resemble epileptic seizures, but they are not. Sometimes, what is thought to be a seizure is not, and some seizures may fail to be recognized when she is asleep or even awake. Vacant spells are brief interruptions of awareness that may resemble seizures but are not.

Will she always breathe this way?

For the majority of girls, irregular breathing patterns become less noticeable as they get older. The younger girl with RS appears to have more hyperventilation while the older girl has more of a type of breathing known as Valsalva's manoeuver.

> Ashley was one of the worst hyperventilaters around. When she was younger she would hyperventilate all day long, every day, every month, every year. As she has grown older, Ashley 17, rarely hyperventilates.

> Meg's breath holding and hyperventilation increased dramatically right around the time she was developing seizures at age 4. She's almost 5 and both have slowed significantly.

> Katie is almost 8, and has been hyperventilating since about 4 years old. In the beginning, it was very heavy and constant, and it really seemed to upset her. Now, she doesn't do it as often, and it doesn't seem to stress her as much. She still has her moments, though. I have had people ask me if we just ran a marathon. Katie will also hold her breath, and it's at those times that we can't get her to follow through on a request. She always has a big grin, though, and I usually call it "Earth to Katie" time!

What should we do about her irregular breathing?

Although episodes of breath holding produce great anxiety for parents to watch, they are always followed by regular breathing. Observing the irregular breathing can cause great concern, but experts in RS recommend a low key approach, taking comfort in the fact that girls do become accustomed to the irregular breathing and regular breathing will soon return. While it may seem like forever, it is important to stay calm and in control. There is a lot of research at present directed at answering these questions.

> Meg does a lot of breath holding. She sometimes even starts to turn a little blue. She always tenses her stomach - pushes it way out when holding. It is sometimes like she needs to do this to get herself together. She is not easily interrupted when she is breath holding although sometimes if we make her laugh or rub her stomach she will stop. We've learned just to wait her out on these episodes.

Are there any medications that can help?

Buspar® has been used by the Glasgow Autonomic Research group with success in carefully selected situations. This group recommends its use only on an individual basis under close medical supervision. Respiratory and autonomic function should be recorded before and during treatment and if no measurable benefit is seen, the drug should be stopped. The dose must be related to the specific case and situation. At best, this medication may improve breathing rhythm. It cannot be expected to reverse the underlying immaturity of the brain stem in RS. The importance of the limited success with this substance is just that it confirms our suspicions that serotonin deficiency is an important part of the disorder and it helps us to plan more effective therapeutic approaches. Note: Buspar® should not be looked at as a cure-all. Even in situations where it is effective, it must be treated with the same caution as any other drug. Because it is new and largely unevaluated, there is no general recommendation. For further reading on this drug: Kerr, AM, Julu, POO, Hansen S, Apartopoulos F. Serotonin and Breathing Dysrhythmia in Rett Syndrome. Perat MV ed, New Developments in Child Neurology Bologna: Monduzzi Editore, 1998 191-95.

Naltrexone (Revia®) is an opiod antagonist that was tried in girls with RS and found to have beneficial effects on breathing. In the study, the dosage was 1mg/kg, but can be adjusted by her physician according to her response.

Use of magnesium citrate or magnesium orotate for treatment of the hyperventilation seen in Rett syndrome was reported as a letter to Lancet in 1992 by Joseph Egger et al., from the Children's Clinic at the University of Munich. They initially used magnesium to treat refractory seizures in a child with Rett syndrome and were surprised to see that her hyperventilation/apnea improved. They then tested low-dose magnesium for treatment of the respiratory irregularities in six other children with stage 2-3 Rett syndrome (ages 4-9). They used an initial dose of 4 mg/kg/day divided into three doses, then increased the dose as tolerated to a maximum of 10/mg/kg/day or until diarrhea developed.

The parents recorded numbers of severe hyperventilation/apnea with cyanosis (turning blue) occurring in a thirty minute period on a daily basis for five days before treatment and after one month of treatment. They found that apnea with cyanosis decreased from 15 episodes (range 12-25) to 5 (range 1-8) and that hyperventilation also decreased from 21 to 5 episodes in six of the children. The seventh child had some decrease in the length of the apneic episodes but became agitated. There was also a reported decrease in seizures.

Over the course of the next 1-4 years, magnesium was stopped three times in five of the patients and in each time, hyperventilation recurred within six weeks and decreased within 3 weeks of restarting treatment. Blood levels of magnesium were essentially unchanged.

It is unclear why this treatment worked so well in this report. Dr. Carolyn Schanen says, "In my experience, some children respond well and some not at all. I have not been able to tell which ones will respond ahead of time so try it with the children with severe problems with hyperventilation/apnea." Magnesium citrate is available over-the-counter as a 'sparkling' laxative that costs about $1 per 10 oz bottle. The concentration is 58.1 mg/ml so for a child who weighs 25 kg (55 lb) the MAXIMUM daily dose is 1.4 cc (1.4 ml) per dose, three times a day.

> We use Magnesium Citrate, which is bought over the counter and kept in the refrigerator. Start at 1 tsp. at AM and PM. Increase to the point of diarrhea, then drop back 1 dosage AM and PM.

THE HEART

The autonomic nervous system controls heart rate. Studies have shown that the atrio-ventricular conduction (transmitting) system of the heart is developmentally immature in RS. Reduced heart rate variability stops the heart from speeding up adequately during periods of excitement, stress, agitation or exertion and also keeps it from slowing down adequately as it should during periods of rest and calm. Abnormal heart rhythms (**arrhythmias**) are sometimes seen, and these seem to become more pronounced with advancing stage of disease.

In healthy people, the cardiovascular system is under increased vagal tone during hyperventilation, in an attempt to balance the effects of over breathing on the heart. In girls with RS, the vagal tone is not increased, so the effects persist, causing irregularities. The sympathetic nervous system is on "high" during breath holding in anyone, but in RS its regulation of heart rate and blood pressure is very poor. This low vagal tone during breath holding and hyperventilation creates an imbalance, which is known to predispose individuals to cardiac arrhythmias and possibly sudden death. It is felt that these irregularities of the heart may account for the sudden unexplained deaths that occur in RS.

Should she have an electrocardiogram (ECG)?

As your daughter enters adolescence, you may wish to have an ECG performed.

What can be done about the heart irregularities?

If irregularities are noted on the electrocardiogram, a cardiologist may be consulted. Nonspecific ECG changes probably do not warrant medications.

SWALLOWING

After food is chewed, it passes to the back of the mouth, the **pharynx**, and into the **esophagus**. A small flap of tissue, the **epiglottis**, covers the **trachea** so that no food will be delivered into the lungs, or **aspirated**. The food passes from the esophagus to the stomach. The swallowing process requires coordinated muscle contractions. Poor coordination of these contractions can interfere with adequate nutrition and may also increase the risk of **aspiration pneumonia**, when food goes into the lungs and sets up infection.

Girls with RS often have difficulty chewing and swallowing, with difficulty closing the mouth during swallowing. If problems are suspected, a video fluoroscopy study during swallowing is recommended. Sometimes, switching to foods that are chopped, mashed or pureed and easier to swallow will take care of minor problems. However, if the swallowing study indicates that she is prone to aspiration, a feeding tube (G-button) may be considered. This will avoid aspiration and pneumonia. See Chapter 18, Nutrition, for swallowing hints.

SLEEP

Sleep problems are relatively common in girls with RS. They often take a long time to fall asleep and have several interruptions in sleep during the night. As a result, their total sleep time is reduced. They may cry at night, but the majority of girls awaken laughing or "talking." Studies have shown that girls with RS sleep less at night as they get older and more during the daytime. When they do have a "bad" night, they generally increase their sleep the next night to make up.

Sleep problems in RS can be disruptive for the whole family. Both the girl with RS and her family need healthy sleep to be at their best. Some use ear plugs, a VCR with earphones in her room or give her sleep medications. Some try soundproofing her room with a "white noise" machine or a fan. One family even covered the walls with thick cotton batting to muffle her nighttime noises. One study measured the effectiveness of the hormone melatonin in girls with RS. While melatonin did reduce the time it took her to fall asleep, it did not reduce the night wakenings.

Many girls with RS awaken during the night laughing. These episodes can last from a few minutes to more than an hour. They seem to come and go, but persist in some until middle age or later.

Here are some suggestions to promote better sleep:

- Have a standard bedtime routine every night. This will give your daughter a "signal" that it is time to relax and get ready for sleep. Try to pick an activity that is not done at any other time of the day. Avoid rough play before bedtime.

- Encourage her to fall asleep independently. If she learns to fall asleep with assistance such as being rocked to sleep, having you in bed with her, having the radio on, or drinking a bottle, she will have difficulty falling asleep under any other circumstances. She becomes dependent on your assistance and can't fall asleep without it. It may seem like a good idea, since it works to get her to sleep, but in the long run in can actually worsen sleep problems and can lead to a vicious cycle. When she awakens in the night, she will be unable to go back to sleep without some intervention.

- Going to sleep and waking up should take place about the same time every day, including weekends. Allowing her to sleep at irregular times imbalances her body's natural biological clock. When she goes to sleep later at night and sleeps later in the morning, you are actually feeding into her body's natural tendency to be out of sync with the demands of daily living. She will continue to fall asleep later at night or awaken at night. If she has the opportunity, she may catch up by sleeping during the day. While catch-up sleep may be okay on the weekends, she loses school time when she naps during the week. Children who don't have the opportunity to sleep during the day often adjust by simply getting less total sleep. Reduced or disturbed sleep may result in irritability and daytime fatigue and increases in challenging behaviors such as tantrums and self injury. So, the way to improve sleep patterns is to regulate the timing of sleep, not just to allow her to sleep at any time of the day.

- Naptimes should occur at the same time and for the same length every day. Most parents want to allow their daughter to get some extra sleep if she did not sleep well the night before. But, letting her sleep at irregular times will only maintain or worsen an existing sleep problem. If she cannot stay awake every day at the same time, allow her to sleep every day at this time. Many girls take "cat naps." Try to allow these at the same time every day and attempt to keep her awake at times outside of the regularly scheduled nap times. Keep track of her sleep-wake pattern for a week and see if there are any times in which sleep is likely. If so, try to make those sleep times as consistent as possible by keeping her awake at all other times and allowing her to sleep only at the scheduled nap times.

- If she does not sleep consistently at the same time every day and you want to encourage more regular sleep, begin by making a schedule of sleep-wake times. First, allow her to sleep at those scheduled times and wake her up at the end of the scheduled nap. Second, choose a time interval in the day when you will definitely keep her awake. Continue to allow her to cat nap throughout the rest of the day. As your daughter begins to tolerate the awake time, extend that interval by one-half to one hour. Gradually continue extending the wake interval until she is only sleeping during the scheduled nap times. If she continues to have sleep problems at night, you may want to consider further decreasing the length or frequency of daytime naps.

- Try to minimize the amount and type of intervention you provide during night wakings. This may be hard because you are missing sleep, too, while you're trying to figure out why she is awake. You are anxious that she may be awake because of a bad dream, a wet diaper, an upset stomach or some other problem which she can't correct. Unfortunately, going to her room and interacting with her during night wakings may only make the problem worse. She may continue to waken during the night in situations where she has a valid reason for being awake but also in situations where she just wants some company. It is hard to know how to respond to her real needs without contributing to the sleep problem. The best solution is to provide the minimal amount of attention necessary to take care of her needs--change her diaper or give a drink without a lot of fuss, place her back in bed, and leave the room. If there doesn't seem to be a valid reason for her to be awake, reassure her that everything is alright, and then quietly leave the room. If you do check on her, do it as soon as she begins to cry. If you only go into her room after she has been crying for a period of time, she only learns to cry harder and for longer periods of time to get your attention. The most important thing to remember is that she needs to go back to sleep by herself.

Changing her sleep pattern may not be easy. If you do make a change, you can expect her sleep to worsen before it gets better. Unfortunately, there are no magic cures. If she has had a sleep problem for years, the problem will not change in just a few weeks. Development of good sleep patterns takes time, effort and consistency on your part. Ear plugs and prayer help, too!

> I cannot remember that Laura has ever slept through the night. When she was about six years old, she had what I would call night terrors and would scream out as if in extreme fright. I thought she was dreaming of falling. She would also wake during the night and 'thud" her forehead on her crib railing. Sometimes she would laugh and chatter. When she was no longer sleeping in a crib, I bought her a sleeping bag and she didn't seem to move around so much and lose her covers. This worked really well.

> The past two years, we have had some changes which we think are due to her trying to communicate. If she gets the least bit too warm, she awakens and cries. This crying is also taking place in the daytime right now. We seem to have much better nights since we are keeping the house cooler, feeding her ice cream just at bedtime, giving her extra water, and leaving the music ready to play if she does awaken. She also seems to enjoy the quiet of her room somewhat earlier than previously.

Here are some suggestions that parents have reported work!

Medications (Benadryl®, Atarax®, Elavil®, Ativan®, Tranxene®, Melatonin®, Chloral hydrate®)
Snack before bed
A warm/cool dark, quiet room
Deep massage
"White sound" machine or fan
A waterbed
Car rides
Soft music
Warm socks on feet

An egg crate mattress
A soft blanket
A warm bath before bed
Settle down time with quiet talk
Warm milk
A warm water bottle on her abdomen
Relaxing audio tapes
No sweets before bed
An active day with exercise
Quiet stories before bed
A bowel movement

> I have found a new product called "Calms" by a company called Hyland Homeopathic. I get it at the health food store. It tastes terrible to chew the tablet, but I crush it and put it into her mouth with a quick "chaser " and she drinks it down. I have also tried the pill and I slept wonderfully. With homeopathic medicine one is supposed to take any medication on an empty stomach 1/2 hour before a meal and 1 hour afterwards.

> I give Taylor (3-1/2 yrs. old, 40 pounds) about 1-1/2 mg of Melatonin. I cut a 3 mg. pill in half. I crush the half between two spoons, and put the powder in a little soda about 1/2 hour before we want her to go to sleep. Taylor used to be a horrible sleeper. She does pretty well sleeping now. Still once in a while we have a tough night, but before the melatonin it was awful!

> My 4 year old daughter takes 2 mg of Melatonin daily and it has made a huge impact on her sleeping patterns. Before she started the Melatonin, she would wake up at all hours of the night and stay up for many hours at times. Then she expected to be able to nap whenever she wanted to throughout the day. After she began the Melatonin, it took 3 weeks before we noticed a change, but the change was like night and day. Her sleeping patterns are almost normal, and she is a much happier child, and we are much happier since we can now sleep!

> We give our daughter 3 mg of Melatonin. Her problem was not so much waking in the night but not being able to fall asleep. She would be up until midnight and then up for the day at 6 am. She gets the Melatonin in capsule form which we open and pour into juice or on food. I have noticed that we are all much happier.

CONSTIPATION

Chronic constipation is one of the most common gastrointestinal problems, experienced by more than 85% of girls with RS at one time in their lives. Most have at one time had difficult to pass, large, hard, and dry bowel movements, which occurred every three or more days. Constipation occurs often in Rett syndrome due to a number of factors which include: lack of physical activity, poor muscle tone, diet, drugs (especially anticonvulsants), inadequate fluid intake, scoliosis, and pain and discomfort associated with elimination. Bowel movements occur less frequently and may become large and hard if the problem is not addressed.

Constipation can cause severe discomfort, pain, and even bleeding due to small anal tears. Some girls express their discomfort by increased anxiety, hand biting and even seizures. Constipation in RS can appear at any age, as early as the first or second year of life or it may be delayed until her early teens. The good news is that appropriate management leads to improvement, and in many cases complete normalization of bowel movements.

How does constipation begin?

When food leaves the stomach, it moves through the intestine (bowel) until it is passed as stool. First it passes through the small bowel, then the colon (large intestine) and finally through the sigmoid and

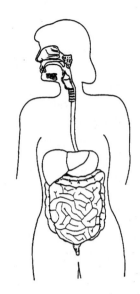

out of the body through the rectum. The intestine is made up of an elastic tube with muscle fibers that produce churning movements, which makes the contents move along until they are passed. In RS, it appears that nothing is wrong with the muscle and nervous components of the large intestine, rectum, and anus. Reflexes which produce bowel movements are normal. There appear to be no anatomic problems, such as a blockage, or organic condition, such as diseased bowel. This type of constipation is called "functional." We do not understand why, but the girl with RS has a tendency for stool to travel slowly through her bowels and for bowel movements to be infrequent. This leads to a large accumulation of stool at the sigmoid and rectum.

Normally, the accumulation of stool at the rectum triggers the need for a bowel movement, which results in emptying of the rectum. However, when the rectum is enlarged by a large volume of stool for a long period of time, the urge to have the BM is lost. When this happens over time, it makes it much more difficult for her to recognize when she needs to have a bowel movement. The prolonged distention of the rectum and the sigmoid from large amounts of stool will cause loss of muscle tone. Consequently, the bowel becomes large and "baggy." This makes it even more difficult to for her to pass the stool.

The large intestine and the sigmoid can absorb a lot of water from the stool, so the longer the stool stays in the intestine, the drier it becomes. This causes bowel movements to become less frequent, larger and harder, becoming more uncomfortable and painful. She may then begin to associate bowel movements with discomfort and pain, and begin withholding stool. The vicious cycle has begun.

How often should she have a bowel movement?

What she eliminates is relative to what and how much she eats, so this can vary. She should be able to pass a stool without pain or distress. Many people think that once a week is "normal for her," but once a week is not normal for anyone! If she is not having a bowel movement after adequate fluids and fiber, and requires frequent laxative use, the physician should be consulted. She should not go longer than three days without a bowel movement.

How can we encourage regularity?

The best way to manage constipation is to prevent it or avoid the vicious cycle described above. Chronic constipation can be a source of serious discomfort and irritability, so it is important to treat it aggressively. She should empty her intestine and rectum completely and regularly with each bowel movement so that they regain their normal size and tone. Daily exercise, occupational and physical therapy may help the problem. Develop a bowel program that stresses the following:

- Increase fluid intake.
- Modify diet with high fiber intake.
- Distribute fiber throughout the day.
- Provide "laxative" vegetables: pears, prunes, apricots, squash.
- Limit "constipating" foods: apple juice, white rice, cooked carrots.
- Give unprocessed bran (1 serving = 1 tablespoon). Make sure to give it with increased fluids.
- For those girls who are able sit on the toilet, sitting once a day at a specific time, especially after the largest meal of the day may sometimes be useful in achieving regularity.

What happens if the constipation is not treated promptly?

If constipation is left untreated, it can lead to **fecal impaction** (blockage of the bowel). This is a serious situation and needs to be treated with **colonic lavage** (washing out the intestines) or even manual removal of the stool under sedation or anesthesia.

FUNCTIONAL FECAL RETENTION

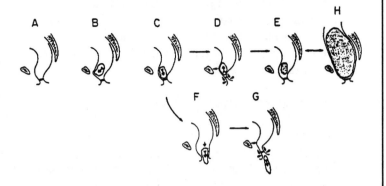

Schematic representation of normal function and chronic stool withholding. (A) The rectum is empty; there is no urge to stool. The internal sphincter is closed. The resting tone of the pelvic floor muscles holds the sides of the anal canal in apposition, keeping it closed. (B) Stool enters the rectum and presses on the rectal wall, causing a sense of fullness. (C) Distention of the rectal wall causes reflex relaxation of the internal anal sphincter, allowing the stool to descend into contact with the upper end of the anal canal. This causes conscious awareness that passage of stool is imminent. (D) The pelvic floor muscles contract to maintain continence, moving the stool upward. (F) If the stool remains in this higher location after the pelvic floor returns to its resting tone, stool will no longer be in contact with the anoderm. Accommodation by the smooth muscles lessens rectal wall tension and the urge to defecate abates. (F) Defecation occurs when the pelvic floor relaxes below the level of resting tone: this opens the anal canal to intrarectal pressure. The accompanying valsalva manoeuver propels the stool down the short, wide anal canal. (G) An "automatic" contraction of the pelvic floor occurs when the stool is no longer in contact with the upper end of the anal canal, and this propulsive force expels the stool completely. (H) If a child repeatedly responds to the defecatory urge by withholding (C to D) a fecal mass accumulates. It becomes more difficult to pass, especially if it is too firm to be extruded without painful stretching of the anal opening. It is too bulky to be shifted upward out of contact with the anoderm. As the pelvic floor muscles fatigue, anal closure becomes less competent and retentive fecal soiling with soft or liquid stool occurs. The child resorts to retentive posturing, attempting to preserve continence by vigorous contraction of gluteral muscles.

> We have found that something works for awhile, and then it stops. The one piece of advice that I can give you is stay on top of constipation every day, never missing one day! If you miss a day, you get behind and you know what that means. You have to start all over again.

How does a high fiber diet help?

Fiber is an effective laxative that can be used over a long period of time. It absorbs water and prevents the stool from becoming dry and hard, even if it stays in the colon for a long time. There are several ways of doing this. First, encourage her to eat green vegetables and fruits every day. Second, use unrefined flour in all baked products. Whole grain bread or dark breads are better than white bread and whole wheat or bran muffins are better than muffins made with white flour. *It is very important to remember that fiber can only be effective if it is given with adequate fluid. When you increase fiber you must increase fluids accordingly.*

> Stacie has Metamucil powder mixed in with 8 ounces of fruited yogurt each morning. Since she doesn't drink enough, the yogurt provides extra fluid.

Some dry cereals or other sources of fiber may be difficult for girls with RS to chew. To make it easier to chew and swallow, fiber can be added to or mixed with foods, and cooked without losing its effectiveness. The amount of fiber cereal during the day can be divided into two or three portions, and given with milk, juice, fruits, or included in other foods.

> For breakfast, I give Ashley either oatmeal with tons of raisins added or Great Grains with raisins added, 4 oz. of orange juice and 6 oz. of prune juice. The prune juice is very important. Ashley gets two or more glasses of prune juice daily, one during the day and one at dinner. She also has at least two pieces of fruit per day, usually more. The only milk she receives is the small amount on her cereal or oatmeal. She has another 20 oz. of juice a day in addition to the prune juice. I try to give her pears and watermelon, as they aid in BM's. Sometimes we have used castor oil, which works.

What about fiber supplements?

Fiber supplements are often recommended for adults, but are often ineffective in children because they usually don't like them. There are many products which can be bought over the counter which are fiber derivatives or similar bulk forming agents. These include methyl cellulose (Citrucel and Maltsupex), or psyllium (Metamucil, Fiberall). Most of these supplements come in a powder form which can be mixed in any liquid. In general, girls 2 - 6 years of age need between 1/4 to 1/3 the recommended adult dose, from 6-12 years, 1/3 to 1/2 the dose and over 12 years the usual adult dose. It is important to introduce the fiber gradually since at first some temporary bloating, gassiness and discomfort may occur. These symptoms usually disappear. Caution should be used when gastrostomy feedings are in use, as fiber supplements can clog the tube. Prune juice is a source of fiber which has an excellent laxative effect and be used daily or every other day.

> Rebecca was immobile and very prone to constipation, but we mostly had it under control. At one stage it was so bad that the strain gave her a prolapsed bowel and anal fissures, which was very upsetting. Then we consulted a colo-rectal specialist who prescribed Metamucil (natural fiber) and lactulose syrup. Rebecca wasn't too keen on Metamucil, so I used to make it into a "dessert." I'd puree a tin of fruit (like peaches) and mix it with a complementary fruit-flavored jelly (using less water to allow for the fruit juice). It made about six servings, so I'd put six doses of Metamucil and lactulose into the jelly and fruit and set it all together in plastic cups.

> I consulted with our pediatrician about dosing with calcium and magnesium for constipation. He said to start with 2 tsp/day and play around with it until we found what worked. Our daughter responds very well to just 1 tsp/day. We buy it at a local health food store. It's made by Nature's Life. It can be taken in milk or juice or added to many recipes.

> If she misses even one day having a bowel movement, she gets constipated, which always leads to impaction. We have discovered something that is working very well for her though! It's called Liquid Calcium-Magnesium. We give her one teaspoon in a small amount of juice each morning with her breakfast. It's completely natural, with some citrus flavoring added. She drinks it fine and it works great. She's been regular since we started this! We cleared this with her pediatrician, since magnesium can affect the heart. He said that she was getting a very small amount and that most of what she did get would come out anyway, and that it was in no way dangerous.

What kinds of food are high in fiber content?

- Whole grains, breads and cereals are high in fiber. Use hot cereals including oatmeal, and cereals with seeds, bran and nuts. High fiber cereals in amounts of .5 - 1 ounce a day in girls from 2-6 years of age, 1 - 2 ounces a day in girls between 6 and 12 years of age, and 2 - 3 ounces in children over age 12 supplies most or all of the dietary fiber requirement.
- Raw fruits and vegetables are better than processed ones. Leave skins on when possible and serve dried fruit, or fresh prunes, pears, peaches and apricots.
- Dried peas, beans, seeds, nuts and popcorn. (Use these cautiously if she chews poorly.)
- Use unprocessed bran in foods or liquids throughout the day. Gradually increase the amount given.

Dawn started on something called Power Pudding. It has worked wonders. I got the recipe and almost barfed! Then I saw it after it was made and really almost barfed! But, she loves it and individually, the only thing in it she will eat is applesauce, but, made like this she chowed it down. Each time she had it, she had a BM within 12 hours. Here goes: 2 lb. bag of pitted prunes, 2 cups of prune juice--chop in blender. Stir in 2 cups of applesauce and 2 cups of All Bran cereal. Stir it all together. That's it.

How can I increase her fluid intake?

Fluids are very important. Water helps to keep the bowel contents soft and easy to pass. If you give fiber without adequate fluids, it increases bulk without lubrication, which means a painful trip down the alimentary canal. Any fluid is helpful; milk, juice, flavored drinks, soups or plain water. Fresh fruits, vegetables and some cooked foods contain fair amounts of water. A minimum of 2 glasses of fluid a day is recommended for girls less than 2 years of age, 3 - 4 glasses for those 2 - 5 years, 4 to 6 glasses for those 5 - 10 years of age and 6 - 8 glasses in girls greater than 10 years of age.

Peppermint tea seems to work well with our daughter along with good fiber. The peppermint is very soothing to her tummy and she loves to drink it so it really helps to increase her fluid intake. I heard that ground flaxseed mixed with juice is helpful.

Do suppositories and laxatives work?

Suppositories are acceptable and can be used on an occasional basis. They act as mild stimulants and lubricate the rectum, but are usually ineffective in the long run since only a small part of the end of the intestine is cleaned. The use of laxatives such as Cascara and Castor Oil can help occasionally.

I lie her down and give her one or two glycerine suppositories every night. If that doesn't work, I use a Microlax laxative as well. Sometimes the bowel also needs some gentle stimulation. Doing this every night means that the stool never becomes hard and difficult to pass. It also means that she doesn't have dirty pants at school which I think is important for her dignity.

We occasionally use suppositories when we absolutely have to but I am adamant about her trying to have a natural BM with no help from outside sources. I just do not want her to become dependent upon these.

Should I give her enemas?

Enemas are good for clean-out procedures and occasional problems, but are not advised to be used routinely. Their constant use may interfere with rectal muscle control, leaving her dependent on them to move her bowels. If enemas are required more than once or twice a month, it is likely that other changes need to be made in the diet or the dose of mineral oil.

Occasionally, Angie will go two days without a bowel movement, and is obviously uncomfortable. We keep a chart of "the action" on the bathroom wall. When we suspect she needs an enema, we ask her if she wants one. She will reply "yes" (by holding her eyes closed) almost 80% of the time. When she doesn't close her eyes, we wait for a few hours or until the next day before asking her again. Usually she has gone by then.

What should we do if she is already constipated?

If she already has hard, dry bowel movements which she has difficulty passing, and if bowel movements come no more often than every 3 days, more aggressive measures are called for. The first step is to assure that the rectum, sigmoid and the distal portion (end) of the large bowel are completely cleaned out. Laxatives taken by mouth do not work effectively if there is a large amount of stool in the distal intestine. The best way to get started is by cleaning this portion of the intestine with enemas. Pediatric Fleet enemas can be used in girls up to 6 years of age. Beyond this age, adult size enemas are necessary. The clean-out should be done with one enema a night for 2 or 3 consecutive nights. Fleet enemas are inexpensive, can be bought over the counter and have easy-to-follow instructions.

Once the colon has been cleaned out, the measures which follow will be much more effective. The next step is to soften the stools by increasing the amount of dietary fiber in the diet as described above. This will assure that the stool remains moist and soft for a longer time, making it easier to pass.

Next, it is important to lubricate the intestinal contents so that it is easier for the intestine to move things along. Mineral oil is the best product to use for this purpose. Flavored mineral oil preparations, such as Kondremul and Haley's, are sold over the counter. The dose is usually determined by her weight and adjusted up or down as needed. A dose of 1 - 2 teaspoons twice a day in girls less than 6 years of age, 1 tablespoon twice a day up to 12 years of age, and 1 - 2 tablespoons twice a day in older girls is usually effective. These doses are only rough estimates of what is needed, so the dose may need to be increased or decreased by 1/3 or 1/2 depending on the results.

How long can she take mineral oil?

Mineral oil is used to help her achieve regularity, which may take from weeks to months. Not enough mineral oil may be ineffective, and too much mineral oil will cause a significant amount of leakage into her underwear or diaper. After 4-8 weeks of regular daily or every other day soft bowel movements, the dose of mineral oil can be gradually decreased by about 1/3 every two weeks and hopefully discontinued completely. It is not recommended for frequent or chronic use due to the irritating effect it has on the colon.

Is mineral oil safe?

Mineral oil is safe as long as your child doesn't have a problem with choking or aspirating food that passes accidentally into the lungs. The oil is very difficult to remove from the lungs and can cause serious complications. However, it can be used for prolonged periods of time without causing nutritional problems or creating any habit or dependency.

Can she be constipated and have diarrhea, too?

It is possible for her to be constipated and have diarrhea intermittently. This happens when newly formed stool passes over the hard stool and "leaks" out.

When a child repeatedly resists the urge to defecate, a mass of stool accumulates in the rectum. Fecal material from high in the colon then trickles around the obstruction, and soiling results whenever the external anal sphincter is relaxed.

What is impaction?

Fecal impaction occurs when the stools become so hard and dry that they cannot pass through the rectum without special measures. Several methods can be used, which include manual removal of stool, special enemas, irrigation with a rectal tube, and giving a special "clean out" preparation through a tube inserted into the nose. In very serious cases of fecal impaction, surgery is necessary.

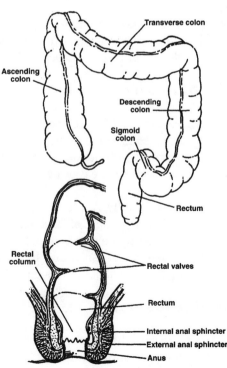

How long will it take for her to become regular?

Patience and perseverance are important. Constipation takes a long time to develop, so it may also take a long time to achieve fully satisfactory results. Some improvement will usually be evident by the first or second week of treatment. However, it is very easy to go back into the vicious cycle even after initial improvement, if you are not persistent with the treatment. If the frequency of bowel movements starts decreasing in spite of adequate diet, fluids, exercise and fiber and three or four days go by without a bowel movement, it may be necessary to again clean out the colon while continuing the other measures. Constipation is a difficult problem in RS, and may require persistent medications.

What is the goal of treatment?

The goal of bowel management is to allow the intestine to return to its normal size and tone by regularly emptying all its contents. In this way, she learns that bowel movements need not be difficult or painful. This realization will encourage her to stop withholding, and as a result, bowel movements will be regular, soft and comfortable. These measures can be helpful to manage most girls who have constipation problems. However, it may be necessary to consult her pediatrician or pediatric gastroenterologist to tailor the treatment to her individual needs. Constipation can be a debilitating and distressful condition, but it is treatable.

Can massage help relieve constipation?

Certain massage techniques, when done on a routine basis, can be helpful. They are used as part of the comprehensive treatment regimen, not to replace it. Check with her doctor to see if massage is recommended.

How is the massage done?

The following two massage techniques are recommended in Pediatric Massage for the Child with Special Needs for an effective constipation massage routine:

Water Wheel
Put one hand in the middle of her abdomen, below the rib cage. Slide your hand down toward the groin area. Then, repeat with the other hand in paddling movements. Continue alternating hands, making sure that one hand is always in contact with the stomach.

Sun-Moon
In this exercise, both hands move in a clockwise direction. This is very important as it follows the natural movement through the intestines. Your left hand is the "sun." Move it in a continuous clockwise circle. Then, visualize a clock face on her stomach. When your left hand gets to 6 o'clock, your right hand (the "moon") will move in a semicircle from your left (9 o'clock) to your right (5 o'clock). Lift your right hand over your left to return to the 9 o'clock position. Repeat in a continuous motion.

For the relief of constipation, these two exercises can be done together in the following sequence:

Water Wheel 6 times. Push knees together into tummy and hold (no longer than 5 seconds in children with special needs because it can interfere with breathing).

Sun-Moon 6 times. Push knees together into tummy and hold (again, no longer than 5 seconds). Gently bounce legs. Repeat three times.

My daughter has a lot of gas. What can we do?

Gas pains can be terribly uncomfortable. Keeping her bowel movements regular and avoiding "gassy" foods will help. If she is unable to pass gas regularly, it may be helpful to sit her on the toilet so that she will strain and release some gas. Over the counter preparations such as Milk of Magnesia®, given daily, can also help. Maalox® contains simethicone and can also be helpful.

Decrease the amount of carbonated beverages and other foods that increase gas formation in the large bowel, such as beans, corn and broccoli. Some laxatives work by increasing the amount of gas and fluid in the colon (lactulose-Chronulac®), and this may make abdominal distention worse, especially when constipation is not already under control. These should be avoided if there is a history of recurrence of air swallowing or abdominal distention.

> I have successfully tried Aloe Vera Gel for gas pains-from 2 to 4 Tablespoons daily. It really helped Lisa Joy. Another good thing to try is Acidophilus--I break open the pill or you can get it in liquid form at the health food store.

> We give Michelle Mylicon drops via G-button after each feeding. If you can crush the tablets it's cheaper, but if you have a G-button the finest particles of the crushed version can cause the button to malfunction. We give the drops alone if she is having a lot of gas pains. We sit her on the toilet and it's easier for her to pass the gas. If that doesn't work we give her digital stimulation and sit her back on the toilet. If that doesn't work we give her a suppository and sit her back on the toilet. If that doesn't work we give her an enema as a last resort; that always works. We give the enema as a last resort even if she has had large bowel movements prior. This is the only thing that works for severe gas and cramping pains. Having the G-button we also use the decompression tubing in combination with a large syringe to suck the air out. I think burping her just like you do a baby after feedings may help, too. Michelle never burps on her own.

> Our daughter is very unhappy due to gas and abdominal upset if I don't give her Acidophilus. I found her to be much better when using it. By the way, yogurt does not contain nearly the amount of beneficial bacteria and not nearly the spectrum as is found in Bifidus and Acidophilus. I buy mine at the health food store, as it tends to be the best quality. Always refrigerate.

> Lisa Joy woke up screaming in pain. My husband gave her a drink of Aloe Vera Plus and she stopped crying in just a few minutes. We think there must be a clear correlation between the relief of her stomach pain and the drinking Aloe Vera Plus.

> Angie has been helped by mixing a tablespoon of Mylanta® which contains the anti-gas ingredient, simethicone, to a large glass of water and a heaping teaspoon of Metamucil® or similar psyllium fiber, in orange flavor. This makes a rather pleasant orange/vanilla "Orange Julius" taste which she likes. We continue stirring as she drinks it through a straw, so as to keep the fiber from settling on the bottom. Incidentally, if you add fiber to a liquid and find it is sitting in the bottom of the glass, you haven't given your daughter fiber, and it doesn't help the plumbing in your house as much as it does your daughter's plumbing.

> Lynn suffered tremendously, screaming for hours at a time. We even took her to the hospital, thinking she may have appendicitis. It turns out her pains were always caused by trapped gas either in her stomach or intestines or both. She has always been an air-swallower, but even hyperventilation can cause this problem. What's worse, she tensed up with pain so gas can go nowhere, and she doesn't know how to burp. We tried every product on the market. We came to the conclusion that we need to avoid it before it became a problem and I am pleased to say it worked.

Gastrointestinal Crises

Gastrointestinal problems are important components of many signs and symptoms seen in RS. These can be not only persistent and cause a significant level of discomfort for many girls, but a small number can eventually become a life threatening problem. While the likelihood of these situations is not frequent, it is wise to be educated.

Intestinal **volvulus** can occur when a loop of bowel twists on itself. This happens sometimes from birth in otherwise normal individuals. When volvulus occurs, there is a sudden blockage of the passage of intestinal contents. This will lead to a rapid distention of the abdomen and backing up of fluid and gas, usually causing vomiting, which can be violent. This will also lead to inadequate supply of blood to the twisted segment and gangrene (death and tearing) of the intestinal wall, spillage of contents into the abdominal cavity, peritonitis and infection.

In a condition known as **intussusception**, the bowel may telescope upon itself (like the finger in a glove). This leads to all the signs of intestinal blockage that occur in volvulus, but additionally, the lining can slough off, causing bloody stools. Fortunately, these latter complications are rare.

Severe impaction, volvulus and intussusception can all cause complete intestinal blockage. Signs of intestinal obstruction are:

- sudden appearance or marked worsening of abdominal distention
- vomiting, usually violent and sometimes containing bile (green or yellow)
- sudden onset of severe unremitting pain or discomfort
- decreased passage of stools when constipation was not previously present
- diarrhea and/or bloody stools

Circulation

Peripheral (away from the trunk) circulation appears to be impaired from an early age. The feet are often cold and blue or red, and do not grow as they should. At a later age, the feet become purplish and swollen with skin that looks like it is shrinking. The feet and legs are often several degrees cooler than the rest of the body. It is important to keep her feet and legs covered well so that they will stay warm and comfortable.

Shanda loves a foot massage with warm lotion or warm baby oil. And this really helps with the circulation in her feet.

To keep Michelle's feet warm, we never let them hang, but provide a small foot stool. We put cotton or cotton blend socks next to her skin in layers. Wool hunting socks work well. We try to walk her if at all possible and check her feet often for warmth.

Temperature Regulation

Girls with RS sometimes have difficulty keeping an even body temperature. They may run a fever with no source of illness. This is not a cause for alarm. They often do not sweat when they are hot, or they sweat in patches instead of all over. They tend to prefer moderation in temperatures, particularly with food.

My daughter always tests her food before completely committing herself and opening her mouth wide. She doesn't like anything too hot or too cold and she won't have a warm drink. She does like ice cream but only because it is sweet. It has to be almost melted and then she is very hesitant, makes faces with the cold but enjoys it. Quite a sight to watch.

Roselyn will not drink anything that is warm. If she senses that the cup is warm she refuses to open her mouth. She does eat warm foods, but tests them first.

It seems many RS girls are very sensitive to heat and really have a problem with over-heating. We always keep a small fan and cool wet cloths on Jenn whenever the temperature outside starts to rise. Otherwise we see a significant increase in her seizure activity and her withdrawing from us.

Angie gets so hot she becomes listless, red, and doesn't perspire. We have to keep her cool with wet washcloths, which is a difficult thing to keep up all day. We use a portable air conditioner on real hot days. That helps a lot.

Amanda can only eat room temperature food. She turns really red if it's warmer outside, and tremors if she gets too cold. She does well between 70 and 74 degrees in the winter and 76 degrees in the summer.

PAIN

Some girls with RS seem to show a high tolerance for pain. They do not react to a needle stick for blood, for instance. Many have high levels of beta-endorphin, the body's own natural pain killer, so this may explain why. However, response to pain is sometimes inconsistent. A girl may not cry when she bumps her head, but cry loudly when she has gas pains. So, her insensitivity to pain is erratic. It could be that she feels internal pain more deeply than external pain. Or it could be that she has a delay in reacting to pain that is mistaken for tolerance. It is likely that she has some disorganization of pain input and processing.

Sherry would sometimes throw herself backwards when she was sitting alone on the floor, and really konk her head. She usually wouldn't cry, and in fact sometimes she would laugh. Mostly, she wouldn't react at all.

Shanda never cries when she is hurt, but this in no way means she does not feel pain the same as everyone else.

As far as her responses to pain, sometimes she is oblivious to it and sometimes she screams and screams. It just depends on the day.

DROOLING

Excessive saliva and drooling are a common problem in RS, especially in girls who have difficulty closing their mouths. Therapies aimed at reducing drooling include tapping around the outside of the lips, rubbing ice around the outside of the lips before a meal and using battery operated vibrators for extra stimulation. A taste of lemon or vanilla on the lips will stimulate lip closure, as will sucking through a straw. Many girls with RS wear colorful bandannas that are color matched to their clothing to catch the wetness. They are stylish, easy to change often, and washable. When drooling becomes a very serious problem, a medication called Artane® can be taken, or a Scopolamine® patch can be worn. An ear, nose and throat specialist can be consulted to see whether surgery will help. The types of surgery done include salivary gland removal, parasympathetic nerve surgery and salivary duct adjustment and/or re-routing.

My daughter has some drooling. What has been helpful to her is some of the oral work she received from sensory integration therapy, to help her be more aware of her tongue, cheeks, palate, etc. They do this by massaging and stretching the insides of the cheek; brushing and applying upward pressure on the palate; brushing and pushing in and backward on the tongue; pressing down on molars; stimulating taste receptors on her tongue and cheeks with intense sour, strong mints, spicy, and cold popsicles or sucking with Mr. Freezies. The mouth is such a strong sensory place and also provides a calm and more organized state when it is stimulated and she is more aware of her mouth and placement of tongue. Even with the low tone my daughter was initially hypersensitive in her mouth, especially on the insides of her cheeks and could only tolerate a few seconds of the therapist doing the stretching and massaging. But over time she was able to tolerate longer times to the point where she would request more, especially having pressure applied to her upper palate. She still hates toothbrushing but I feel this oral work has greatly benefited her. She sucks great from a straw, imitates lots of facial expressions, vocalizes and able to stick out her tongue which before was hard to do.

Over the years we've had lots of drooling, some from seizures, some from reflux, some just from the loss of swallowing skills. During seizure activity there's periodic loss of control in swallowing. And apparently with reflux the body tries to compensate by increasing the production of saliva. With the deterioration of swallowing skills this can become a constant messy problem. Jenn wears neckerchiefs to fashionably catch the drool.

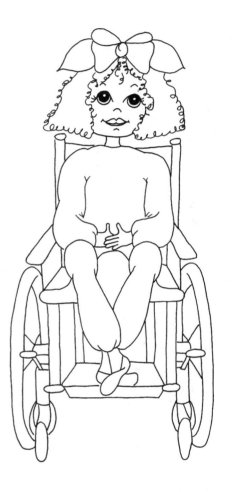

Jocelyn used to drool a lot when she was younger, but using arm splints helped that a lot. It was more the stimulation of tapping her mouth that made her salivate more and swallow less. Anyway now she rarely drools, but I have noticed that she drools more when she seems to be coming down with something. I use it as a guide now, if Jocelyn is drooling, lots of rest, liquids, etc. and usually we are able to avoid illnesses.

Some friends of ours who have a daughter with RS are using a Trans-Derm Scop® patch on Audrey for drooling. This patch is primarily used for motion sickness, but works for drooling, as it does dry out the mouth. It does have some side effects, but they have encountered none with Audrey.

Our OT has shown us some exercises to do to Kelli's face, which really aids in lessening her drooling. We do them before mealtimes, snacktimes, and just throughout the day if we see excessive drooling and they really seem to help her.

The author wishes to thank the following professionals for ideas and information which was used to develop this chapter: Daniel Glaze, M.D.; Peter Julu, M.D.; Alison Kerr, FRCP, FRCP & CH; Merry Meek, CCC, MS; Alan Percy, M.D.; Jose Saavedra, M.D.; Rebecca Schultz, RN, MSN, CPNP; Richard Altschuler, Ph.D.

DAY-TO-DAY MANAGEMENT

DENTAL CARE

Keeping her teeth clean is very important to avoid cavities and pain that can interfere with eating. Tooth grinding can wear the teeth down considerably, and over a long period of time, this may cause pain, as the roots are closer to the surface. The first visit to a dentist, preferably a specialist in dentistry for children, should be done after the appearance of all 20 primary teeth, around the age of 3. If the dental staff is patient and skilled, they will be able to care for her teeth with the least anxiety.

Tooth decay is often caused by excess sugar consumption of all types including drinks, chocolate milk, tea, and juices or milk, especially when given at night in the bottle. Cavities develop when food debris collects, leaving an accumulation of thick yellow plaque. Proper brushing is essential to remove it. It is best to brush while she is lying down, so you can see while brushing. There is no need for toothpaste in the beginning, and only a small amount of toothpaste is necessary when it is used. This is especially important because toothpaste is not made to be swallowed, and she may not be able to spit it out. Swallowing a small amount of toothpaste is okay, but low fluoride toothpaste is best, such as the kind that is made for baby's first teeth. Plain or salted water or mouthwash can be used to wet the toothbrush. Regular fluoride treatments are a must. The toothbrush should have soft bristles and should be the right size for her mouth. Toothbrushes come in a variety of styles including musical ones that can make the job easier. Electric toothbrushes with a small head are effective. If she resists using a toothbrush, a damp washcloth is a good substitute.

Often, it is not tooth brushing, but proper positioning and keeping the mouth open that is the main problem. For some girls, the stimulation of a toothbrush triggers a bite reflex and it can be very difficult for her to let go. To keep her mouth open, try taking a few tongue depressors and stacking them together. Wrap the stack in gauze to provide some padding, and cover the whole thing with adhesive tape to make it somewhat waterproof. Place the stack of tongue depressors between the molars on one side of her mouth while you brush the other. She will be free to chew on the tongue depressors and you will be free to brush. Try to experiment with different ways to find out how she is most comfortable and relaxed, and what position allows you to best see what you are doing.

> Keeping the mouth open to avoid your fingers from being bitten can be done with the aid of two simple items: 1) rubber door holder, and 2) wooden tongue sticks wrapped with gauze, a bundle of 4-5-6, according to the size of her mouth.

> We used the handle of a wooden spoon to keep Rachael's mouth open for tooth-brushing. (I soaked the handle in vanilla extract, and rinsed it with an antibacterial mouthwash after use) Another mom told me she found a vanilla-scented nylon doggy chew bone worked well, after whittling one end down a little. I let Rachael chomp on the left side while I brushed on the right, and vice versa. Rachael seemed to enjoy chomping on the spoon handle. She now cooperates very well with brushing, but when we did have problems, I got a honey-comb weave blanket, spread it on the floor, and rolled Rachael up in it, being sure that her hands were together. Rachael thought this great fun, so I never had a problem. Then I bundled my "Rachael-sausage" into a recliner. More giggles. About once a week, after brushing her teeth (I used a Reach compact-head toothbrush; when I can't find that, I snip some bristles off the handle end of the brush head) I massaged around her gums with my finger covered in a baby's face cloth.

Improper teeth cleaning can lead to **gingivitis** and **periodontis**, diseases of the supporting tissues of the teeth which can eventually cause the loss of bone and teeth. Proper tooth brushing and regular cleaning are important for her continued health. Keeping a regular tooth brushing routine is helpful. It is important to explain to her what you are doing as you go along so she knows what to expect. Counting or singing a familiar tooth brushing song will help her get used to the routine.

Melinda came out of the room wearing two bracelets and a sticker, and holding a new toothbrush. She was one proud, happy little girl! I could hear everyone talking to her the entire time, telling her what they were doing, and she was responding with her eye signals. That was one of those occasions when Rett syndrome temporarily ceased to exist for us. She was just a little girl visiting the dentist.

We got lots of neat dental toys – a dental mirror, which will come in very handy next time I'm trying to figure out what's going on inside her mouth, and a gum stimulator and neat little flossers with handles. I was explaining how Sherry is just now beginning to spit the water out effectively to rinse the toothpaste out of her mouth and the dentist said she didn't even have to use toothpaste anyway.

We have been using the Dentrust toothbrush and it is really great! I don't get bitten anymore when I brush Sherry's teeth and I don't have to hold her mouth open with my fingers. This toothbrush brushes all three surfaces of the teeth in one pass because it's got three brushing surfaces and you run it along the teeth as though it is a train and the teeth are tracks. You can get it at the grocery store for around $3 or so. I have seen similar toothbrushes in catalogs for people with disabilities but they are more expensive and are basically the same thing.

Our dentist has a TV screen mounted above the dental chairs, and cordless headphones to go with them. We bring our own videos. Kim loves the dentist! The only problem is that she laughs so hard sometimes she expels various instruments they've stuck into her mouth. Also, when the inexperienced dental helper leans over her in such a way as to block the video screen, she lets out quite a complaint and sometimes gives them a shove to get them out of the way.

We used lemon-glycerin swabs to moisten and clean her mouth. Heather seemed to really appreciate the moisture they provided and the taste as well. These swabs come in several flavors and can be obtained at any medical supply place. They really help the comfort level of anyone in the hospital or having any kind of mouth or dental work.

When Kim was younger and before she was diagnosed, we worked with a speech therapist who would try to use word sounds to demonstrate mouth positions – just modeling the physical part of speech. So, she would say, "OOOOOpen" a lot when she was talking about open mouths. I picked up on this, and started to say "OOOOOpen" when I wanted Kim to open her mouth for tooth brushing. This was not, as you may imagine, very effective. However, when I evolved this strategy into singing a rousing rendition of "OOOOOOOKLAHOMA," it worked wonders! Now, every night and morning, you can hear us belting out "OKLAHOMA", and Kim laughs and opens her mouth without hesitation every time! Can't imagine what the neighbors think!

Our dentist told us to let our daughter chew on a toothbrush even when it isn't tooth brushing time. Just the chewing and saliva created by it will help to clean the teeth.

ORTHODONTICS

Crystal's dentist who also specializes in handicapped children told me that he did not recommend braces because just trying to do the monthly tightening, keeping her mouth very clean, and the pain associated with normal brace wear is usually not worth it unless her teeth were so bad that she really needed them. I have had braces and I have to agree is no picnic.

It no longer occurs to me that her teeth are not as perfect as I wanted them to be. After all, Anne Stuart is not what I expected her to be in the beginning and I have learned to accept that, too. Just hang in there and let nature takes it course. It's a process we all have to deal with and with our girls it is just tougher to realize we really don't have control about these things. Just try to take it one tooth at a time!

TOILET TRAINING

Girls with RS understand what the toilet is for. Their handicap is in not being able to communicate their needs. It may take some trial and error, some time training and careful observation of her non-verbal signs, but it is possible for her to be toilet trained. You may need to make some adaptations, such as a seat reducer so she can sit on a standard toilet or a specially fitted seat support. A foot stool is important to give her some stability and to keep her feet from getting uncomfortable dangling. Sitting her on the toilet may also help her pass uncomfortable gas.

Jocelyn was having accidents daily, and they always happened as she was either being placed on the toilet or getting off. This was very unusual for Jocelyn. I did not know what to make of it, but would try to make suggestions, none of which seemed to help. Her chiropractor asked how things were going and I told him of this new problem. As I was talking to him, Jocelyn had been looking down at the floor. I told him something I had not said out loud to anyone before that point. I told him that I felt that she was perhaps doing this on purpose to "show who is really in charge." At the moment that I said this she looked up at us with this devilish grin. No delayed response here! She knew we were on to her tricks. The next day as we waited for the bus, I told her I would talk to her aide and try to teach her to back off and not be so controlling if Jocelyn would also try to be more cooperative. I never told anyone at school of my discovery, but the notes from school indicated that the accidents stopped from that day on. I did talk to the aide to make suggestions on relating better to Jocelyn and the year went better.

We have learned that Kristas uses going to the bathroom as a punishment to her care providers when she is mad. She most often urinates on the floor at school. Her teachers said they were trying to sit her down when she wet herself standing up. We did not feel like Kristas liked her placement, and neither did we, so we had her put in a new class. She is now not having very many accidents.

We began toilet training Lauren when she was 5 using the same method used with our other daughter. She eventually seemed to get the idea, with a big smile when she was successful. For several years she sometimes was wet as close as 20 minutes after she used the toilet, while at other times she was dry for two hours. She has never given us a clear signal of when she has to go and I think we confused her by using her communication device when we were about to take her showing her "yes" that she needed to go even when she really didn't. She does wear an Attends pad at night, but not a daytime diaper. She doesn't care if she has accidents, but will generally use the toilet when she needs to.

Jocelyn will cry out unrelentingly when she needs to go to the bathroom until someone understands. I asked her to do this several years ago when I noticed that she was having lots of "accidents" that really weren't her fault. She was vocalizing but I was usually busy or thought it was something else. I asked her not to give up on me, but to try to be patient and keep on vocalizing until I got the message and I would try to be better at interpreting. She did and I did and now she won't quit until I take her to the bathroom. Since a bout with constipation problems after surgery she still often cries on the toilet. Sometimes I leave her alone for a while and I find that she will stop crying easier than if I am there cheering her on. I guess I would rather not have my mother in my face as I try to go, either!

We take Meg to the toilet on a timed basis and she clearly knows what it is for and tries to go at each sitting. Sometimes though, she has just urinated and doesn't have any more to go, but we can see that she tries to push something out. Last night I took her to the bathroom, no diaper on, and while I was looking for the potty seat, she wet the floor. She clearly knew it was the bathroom and time to do her business, but the waiting is what we can't get her to comprehend.

We use a strict time schedule and also follow natural times she might have to go. So after meals, upon waking, even naps, and then at 10 AM, 2 PM, etc. This cues her to use the toilet at those times and to hold until the next toileting time. I have the toilet on Mary's IntroTalker, but also pick up when she gets a panicky look on her face that she needs to go.

We put Michelle on the toilet at certain times of the day, beginning with the times we noticed she would have a bowel movement. We got a toilet adapter which is just a back support with a seat belt that attaches to a regular toilet. Michelle has a little Casio electric piano, that plays tunes with or without striking the keys, on a stand in front of the toilet. We started toilet training when Michelle was about four or five. The more times we placed her on the toilet the better. We leave her on the toilet for 15 minutes at a time. The biggest problem is not being able to place Michelle on the toilet every time she needs to go because she can't tell us.

After about a year of taking Katie to the bathroom on a regular basis she will let us know when she has to go. She walks into the bathroom. She still will forget at times but she knows!

Jocelyn has been going on the toilet for a long time. I know we began to work on it about 4 years old. It took a long time but the option was to continue diapers, so what did we have to lose! Don't give up, keep your expectations high, and don't be afraid to take risks. We often brought Jocelyn "out" without a diaper long before she was mostly "trained." I found that she also did not like to have accidents and would try to hold it, but I think my putting panties on her was a show of confidence that I believed she could do it. Sometimes she did have accidents, then I told her that I thought she did her best and I'd try better to "listen" to her messages. We continued to work together; I believe that success was as dependent on my understanding as her bladder control and it was a team effort in success and failures. She started the fourth grade in panties and still wears them. She does wear Pull Ups at night, but usually is dry anyway.

We leave a "Cheap Talk" device with "I want to go to the bathroom" in convenient places. Leah will use it when it suits her. Given a choice and a chance to communicate she will use the toilet. When we are on top of things she will stay dry the whole day. There are times she is working so hard to hold it in that she will urinate right before I get her on the toilet.

When we faithfully put Rachel on the potty every two hours she keeps a dry diaper. We leave her on it for 3 minutes to give her plenty of time. Most of the time she wears Pull Ups to make it easier for us. She was going on the potty before her severe Rett symptoms showed, but I think with practice many girls can do it. In the past, we have also run water to make her go and sang "Twinkle, Twinkle, Little Star." For some reason she always tinkles when she hears that song!

> I hung a musical crib toy on the cupboard near the toilet, and when Angie would go (I stayed to hear her tinkle) I pulled the string and praised her. The music and action of the toy was a terrific reward. She caught on immediately and always tries to hold it for us.

TOILETING HELPFUL HINTS

School staff should be advised not to leave the girl with RS on the toilet too long. She may become cold and uncomfortable and may show aversive behavior.

- Have the toilet ready before you get her there.
- Make sure she is seated comfortably with proper support for her back and feet.
- Use a seat belt if necessary.
- Give extra fluids and put her on the toilet at regular intervals.
- Give her a lots of praise and a reward that she will look forward to when she is successful. Food always works!
- When she begins to gain success, gradually increase the intervals between toileting.

For bowel training:
- Put her on the toilet when you notice her strain.
- Put her on the toilet after meals, especially after dinner.

BATHING

If she does not sit without support, it may be hard to get her in and out of the tub, and also keep her stable and safe while you wash her. There are a number of waterproof bath chairs available, ranging from mesh sling-back styles to rigid plastic benches and chairs. A hand-held shower hose can be very useful in the tub, especially for hair washing. Waterproof wheelchairs are available for use in roll-in showers. A mesh table that hooks into the back of a roll-in shower provides a safe way to bathe without undue bending by the caregiver.

LIFTING

It is important to learn how to lift correctly, so that you place the least amount of strain on your body, particularly your back. Always lift with your knees bent, which reduces back strain. There are a number of mechanical devices when lifting becomes too difficult. Ramps, platform lifts, stairway lifts and elevators increase accessibility and decrease back strain. Bathtub and bedside lifts can be invaluable.

SEATING AND POSITIONING

Proper seating and positioning are very important for her comfort, and also allow her to participate and use her body in the best way she can. Seating should include a solid seat and solid back to insure upright, level pelvic alignment. Lateral support can be added if necessary to keep her from slumping or leaning to one side. She should be well-seated in the high chair, car seat, stroller, at the table and in her wheelchair – wherever she sits. Comfort, balance and safety must be taken into consideration when choosing seating equipment or positioning.

An evaluation should be done by a team of qualified professionals including physical or occupational therapists, an orthopedist or rehabilitative medicine physician, a rehabilitation technology supplier and parents. If she is in school, her classroom teachers may want to join the team. Together, they should consider a number of issues beginning with her home, school and community environments and the type of seating and positioning she needs to function at her optimum level. Different seats and backs should be combined to simulate different positioning options. A pressure mapping system should be used to identify areas which might be conducive to pressure sores, which can occur when she sits in one position for long periods and cannot shift her weight to relieve the pressure. Cushions should be provided for any areas that might cause a problem. She may need additional supports depending on her ability to sit and hold her head independently.

Seating and positioning strategies should take into consideration her use of technology, such as computers or communication devices. She should be able to have full access to these in a comfortable seating position that enhances her use of technology.

If the equipment is not customized, you may be able to try it out at home before purchasing it. Equipment can cost from hundreds to thousands of dollars. Most health insurance companies or Medicaid will cover most or at least a portion of the cost if the equipment is ordered by the physician and justified by the evaluation team. If health insurance is inadequate, equipment dealers may be able to give you a list of resources, such as local service clubs, which might help with the cost.

PUBERTY

In healthy girls as well as girls with RS, puberty begins around the age of 8 when the pituitary gland begins to secrete hormones. These hormones travel through the bloodstream to the ovaries, where they trigger growth and change. The first observable change is breast budding. One breast may start growing before the other, and they may grow at different rates so they may appear unequal in size at first. Eventually, they will be the same size. Next, she develops pubic hair, and later, underarm hair. She goes through a growth spurt and her hips and breasts become more rounded.

Menstruation (menarche) usually begins about two years after the breasts begin to bud. It is considered "normal" if a girl begins her period after 9 years and before 16 years. Most healthy girls begin menstruating around the age of 13. This is usually the case in RS, but menstruation is delayed in some cases when the girl is very thin. Before hormonal changes can begin, she must reach a critical body weight which some girls with RS may never achieve. She must also have the right amount of body fat and body water for menstruation to begin. In spite of this, many girls with RS begin their menstrual cycles at the expected time. Others may begin their period earlier or later than usual. Some girls have noticeable pubic hair earlier than what is typical. The first few years after menstruation begins, it is normal for her cycle to be irregular. She may skip a period now and then.

> Our daughter started her periods very early, at 7 or 8. This coincided with the other sorts of bodily changes one would expect from puberty. We have not experienced any serious management problems with her period, as she is diapered anyway.

When should she see a gynecologist?

The need for a woman with RS is the same as any other woman. Most maturing girls should have a physical every year after the age of 18, unless they are taking birth control pills, the use of which requires an examination regardless of age. She should see the gynecologist if a vaginal infection is suspected. The examiner should be gentle and patient, and the parent should stay with her, giving reassurance and comfort.

How can we maintain good hygiene?

Menstrual flow is odorless until it comes in contact with air and bacteria. Bathing and the use of disposable wipes are helpful. Sanitary napkins can be used in the panties or can be inserted in the diaper for extra protection.

Should she have a vaginal discharge?

The effect of increased estrogen in her system is a thin, whitish, mucus-like discharge. This causes no discomfort and should not have an odor, cause itching, redness or lesions on the skin.

How can a vaginal or yeast infection be recognized?

A vaginal infection will usually have an odor. It may be very white, thick and cottage cheese-like, or yellowish or greenish in color. It may cause itching and may produce redness. Yeast infections will usually cause a bright red diaper rash with itching. If she has any of these symptoms, her doctor should be contacted.

Can she have an infection or irritation of the vagina even before puberty?

Vaginal irritation is common in girls over 3 years for a number of reasons. Inadequate bathing, wiping from back to front or washing too vigorously may cause problems. Sitting on the ground without protection, using bubble baths, and high sugar diets may also contribute to difficulties, as well as wearing clothing that is too tight and does not let air circulate. Pinworms and anal scratching are other sources of vaginal irritation. To avoid these problems, change her diaper frequently, give warm baths (avoid using bubble baths) and use bland lotions or ointments to protect the skin.

Can she use tampons?

Slim tampons which have been developed for teens can be used, and are most easily inserted when she is lying on her side, legs drawn up. Be sure to insert the tampon completely into the vagina, as it will be uncomfortable if it is only partly inserted. If tampons are used, it is important to change them often. As with anyone who uses tampons, it is important to recognize the signs of toxic shock syndrome, which occurs most often in women younger than 30. TSS is a rare but potentially dangerous disorder which is caused by bacteria which find a breeding ground in the absorbent nature of the tampon and moisture of the vagina. Sudden fever of 102 or more, vomiting or diarrhea, dizziness and rash are the symptoms to watch for. A physician should be consulted immediately.

> Stacie puts her hands in her pants. This was a problem when she began having her period. Although she was frightened at first, we calmly explained each step. We used slim tampons very successfully, avoiding mess and odor, and she seemed very comfortable. The only drawback was that it limited our caregiving opportunities. I would not send her to school with a tampon, because I wouldn't want anyone else to change it. But it makes a good alternative when we we're out and about together.

What medications work for menstrual pain?

If she seems uncomfortable, over-the-counter preparations for menstrual pain may be adequate. If these do not work effectively enough, her physician can prescribe a stronger medication to give relief. A hot water bottle on the tummy may help.

Will she get PMS (Pre-Menstrual Syndrome)?

PMS is a predictable pattern of physical and emotional changes that occur just before menstruation. Most women experience these changes from a mild to moderate degree. The symptoms can develop any time after the midpoint of the menstrual cycle, and usually end soon after the period starts each month. PMS may cause bloating, breast tenderness, weight gain, fluid retention, fatigue, nausea, vomiting, diarrhea, constipation, headaches, skin problems or respiratory problems. It may also cause emotional changes that include depression, irritability, anxiety, tension, mood swings, difficulty concentrating or lethargy. If your daughter has a period, you may notice some of these changes taking place. It helps to remember that these changes are predictable and short-lived.

Seizures can become worse prior to onset of periods.

> For her cramps, Dani's doctor suggested Haltran®, an over-the-counter medicine for PMS. It really worked.

What are the options for managing her period?

The birth control pill will reduce her menstrual flow. Other methods to eliminate her period altogether include shots of Depo-Provera®, and surgeries known as endometrial ablation and hysterectomy.

Does the birth control pill help?

Newer low dose oral contraceptives are more effective and have fewer risks. There are dozens of brands on the market today. Your daughter's physician should be consulted about the risks and benefits and the type of pill that is best for her. Possible side effects, which are usually minor, include nausea, breast tenderness, fluid retention, depression and nervousness. A sense of fullness maybe felt in the breasts or pelvis. Weight gain may occur, but in RS, that is usually a plus! Some beneficial side-effects include lighter menstrual flow and fewer cramps, regular and predictable periods, and decreased likelihood to develop breast lumps, iron-deficiency anemia, ovarian cysts, endometrial or ovarian cancer, or rheumatoid arthritis. Birth control pills are usually taken for three continuous weeks and during the fourth week, no pill or an inactive pill is taken. The menstrual flow will then begin. If no menstrual flow is desired, the active pill is continued without interruption.

Will it harm her to take the pill without a break?

It is not harmful to her, and it will help you with hygiene problems by stopping menstruation. While she will not have a regular period, she may have some spotting.

> My daughter takes a birth control pill called LoEstrin®. Its particular value is that it reduces and in some women completely eliminates the monthly period. Angela has no more severe PMS, no cramps and very light periods that never last for more than two days.

> Ashley was placed on birth control pills because of her heavy flow. I can honestly say that her periods are not a problem. I know that before she got on the pills she had cramps but I do not believe that she has them now, at least not to any large degree. I automatically give Ashley Tylenol® the first three days of her period, just to alleviate any possible side effects.

> Heather didn't have her first period until age 18 probably because of low weight. When she started it was with a vengeance – flowing 10 days, stopping for 10 days, etc. Heather was started on Ortho-Novum® and continues to this day. Her periods are generally 1-2 days of flow and the predictability is nice. If she is cranky we don't have to wonder if it's PMS!

What is Depo-Provera®?

Depo-Provera®, given by injection, is a long-acting form of progesterone, which is an ovarian hormone produced in small amounts during the second half of the menstrual cycle. Because it does not contain estrogen, it does not produce many of the side effects of birth control pills. Depo-Provera® suppresses ovulation without completely suppressing production of

estrogen, the other normal ovarian hormone. Depo-Provera® produces changes in the endometrium (lining of the uterus) so that menstruation is less likely to occur. The first shot is given immediately after a menstrual period and every three months thereafter.

What are the side effects of Depo-Provera®?

A frequent side effect of Depo-Provera® is irregular bleeding. After being on "the shot" for six or seven months, most women stop having periods altogether. Some studies have reported weight gain on the medication. Some women have had continued spotting and have discontinued the medication for that reason. Ovulation sometimes does not resume for a year or two after the medication has been discontinued. The American Academy of Pediatrics Committee on Drugs found "no conclusive evidence that Depo-Provera® is harmful to humans but it acknowledges that there is controversy about the potential undesirable long-term effects of its use."

Stacie had a terrible time with Depo-Provera®. It took a couple of rounds of shots before we figured it out. She became very aggressive and irritable. And when we did figure it out, we had to wait months to get it out of her system. I've heard of some girls who do just fine on Depo-Provera®, so it's hard to say how any individual will react.

Becky Sue began Depo-Provera® injections about 3 years ago. She weighed 95 pounds at the time. Within 6 months she had gained 30 pounds and remains stable at 125 pounds. Also she has acne on her forehead, which can be a side effect of the shots. She receives her shots every 12 weeks and we know she is due by the 11th week as she will have mood swings, crying and /or laughing. Her blood pressure is checked bi-weekly. Her doctor said a long term side effect could be sterility. No period and no cramping is the best part and why she began on the shots.

Beth began her period last year. We tried the Depo-Provera® injection throughout the fall and early winter. Beth was extremely depressed. We opted to stop the injection and her smile and wonderfully happy demeanor has returned.

Our daughter received Depo-Provera® injections for several years as a young teen. The periods stopped, but we noticed little change in behavior. The biggest problem for her was weight gain – she ballooned up to 130 pounds, which affected her walking. The weight came off with the discontinuation of the shots. Her periods started again in about eight months.

We tried the Depo-Provera® shot and unfortunately for Courtney, it was a horrible experience. We thought we had gone back in time to our earlier phases of Rett. The poor girl's screams were nearly constant, and she could not sleep. The shot did not totally wear off until approximately 5-6 months went by and we swore we would never consider it again.

Vanessa was on Depo-Provera® for about five years. It took about one year for her periods to slow down, and stop. During that first year, or so, she had spotting, and even real bleeding on and off, without any real pattern. It did not work very well for her, so they had us bring her in every two months instead of every three months for awhile. About 18 months ago, she started having screaming fits. They started out slow, and escalated to the point that I could not even get her out of the house at all. She became violent with everyone around her, and started throwing and breaking everything that she could grab. When we quit the Depo-Provera®, the doctor asked why. I told her about the behavior, and she came right out and said, "It was probably the Depo-Provera® that caused the behavior!"

Rebecca was on Depo-Provera® for about two years with seemingly no side effects.

What is endometrial ablation?

Endometrial ablation is a laser procedure which is done on an In-Out Surgery basis, and is usually performed on women who have an abnormally high degree of bleeding. From one to three months before the procedure, the patient is given a drug to thin the uterus so that the laser can penetrate the endometrium (lining of the uterus). Under general anesthesia, the laser is introduced through the vagina to vaporize the endometrium. The laser has a small camera which projects the image on a screen, and the surgeon follows this image. The procedure requires no incision. Two out of three women have a permanent cessation of bleeding following the surgery. The endometrial ablation has advantages. It does not require hospitalization overnight, there is less pain because it is not an invasive surgery, and it requires less recovery time. Because the endometrium is a tough organ, however, when done in younger women it may grow back, causing the period to return and making it necessary to repeat the surgery.

What are the facts about hysterectomy?

Hysterectomy (removal of the uterus) is the most permanent and certain way to end her period. It requires surgery and removes the possibility of pregnancy, menstrual periods, and eliminates the potential for uterine cancer. Hysterectomy requires hospitalization for several days and a period of recovery is necessary. Each state has different laws and requirements, and most states have some procedural process to protect her rights. Getting permission can be a lengthy process, but hysterectomy is a final solution to menstrual problems.

> The decision to have Megan's uterus removed was the right thing for us. There were many legal obstacles. The most disturbing one was that we would have to have a court appointed guardian for her and it could not be either me or my husband. The only requirement was need for a second opinion. We had it done when she was nine years old and she went right back to school after the holidays. After about a week you would have never known she had the surgery. She is 15 now and the teachers have been especially grateful and appreciative for the procedure. I have talked to other parents in this area and guided them through the process for their daughters. The result is one less humiliation for Megan to suffer at school if she were to have an accident, plus peace of mind for us.

> Amy's procedure was done before she ever had any periods. She came home that night and slept. We never had to give her pain medication and she never showed signs of PMS throughout the years. It's just a non-issue with us now. It's done. I grieved for weeks before the procedure, but felt a great sense of relief the day it was done. It was just one more step to the admission that Amy would always do the very best she could.

> Angie had her uterus removed because of endometriosis, which is not related to RS. She had suffered with it since she was 9 years old and we tried years on Depo (she ballooned up to 130 pounds), birth control pills (she screamed for the 21 days she was on them, and was quiet the week she was off). She screamed the day she ovulated and for two weeks after that she was miserable until she had a period. A laparoscopy was performed two years ago and her fallopian tubes had twisted around behind her uterus and her ovaries were glued with adhesions to the back of the uterus. Ouch. No wonder it hurt to ovulate. The doctor released them and put her on Lupron® for six months, which induced an artificial menopause. She felt pretty good during the next year or so, but the PMS and screaming resumed after that. We tried everything humanly possible to correct the problem without surgery, but in the end her quality of life was more important than any theory about the rights of people with disabilities. All the doctors I consulted felt it imperative to try everything under the sun before doing any surgery. You would have thought I was asking them to put her to sleep forever. She still has her ovaries, but I can see a big change in her overall energy and disposition. Her recovery was uneventful. I wish we had done this years ago.

> I have spoken to several of our doctors and they say if a parent can get the permission by presenting a good case, they would be more than glad to do it. The problem was that they were often sued because some groups felt that handicapped people were being sterilized against their will and had the right to procreate. Well, having children doesn't necessarily make your life complete. If you have normal children and have a normal mind they can drive you crazy also.

SEXUAL MATURITY

Parents often worry about the problems created by sexual maturity. Most are uncomfortable with masturbation. This kind of stimulation is not abnormal. It is a satisfying and natural part of sexual maturity. It can be embarrassing when it happens at inappropriate times, but it will not hurt your daughter. Learning to control the behavior in public places can usually be accomplished through behavior modification techniques.

I am worried that someone will take sexual advantage of her. What can I do?

Most parents share this fear as we look down the road to when our daughters are no longer in home care. As difficult as it is to confront, protecting her against potential abuse is very important. Keep her away from risky situations, watch for the danger signs of molestation that will be seen in her behavior, and trust your instincts.

> I have found our daughter's periods very manageable. I have concerns about the vulnerability to those who might tamper with my daughter's virginity. I made a written request to agency management as well as house management that Mary never be left alone with male staff in her group home. So far, it has been followed.

The author wishes to thank the following professionals for ideas and information which was used to develop this chapter: Sarojini Budden, M.D.; Phyllis Percy, RN, CPNP.

MOTOR PROBLEMS

MOVEMENT

Stereotyped movements include the characteristic hand movements seen in RS, which are not under her control. **Automatic** movements are those that are learned and become a reflex. They include things like lifting her arm to put on her shirt and stepping up a curb. She becomes used to performing these tasks and does not have to think about how to do them once they are learned. **Motivated** movements are those which derive from emotional involvement with the task – whether it is a wish, need, discomfort, necessity or compulsion. These movements arise from emotional excitement and are not consciously controlled by her. She may not be able to perform when given directions, but performs automatically because of her strong motivation. You may ask her to pick up the glass and she cannot. Yet, if she is very thirsty, she may be able to suddenly pick up the glass skillfully and drink it without spilling a drop. She is as surprised as you are, and if you ask her to repeat the action, she is unable. This can happen with speech, when out of the blue she blurts an appropriate word, never to repeat it again. Again, she acted without thinking.

> Leah has under-registration of input and difficulty preparing muscles to initiate an action. This may be contributing to her lack of task initiation. She does have a drive for information to the muscles and joints and it is expressed as teeth grinding. Leah may be doing this to help increase her postural stability.

My daughter never crawled. Is this part of Rett syndrome?

Most infants with RS do not achieve a traditional **reciprocal** crawl (when the left hand and arm move forward, the right leg comes forward, and vice versa). This is due to the difficulty girls have with the kind of motor coordination that is required for crawling. Most girls have different crawling patterns, such as "scooting," "rolling" or "bunny hopping," which do not require coordinated use of the hands. Most girls begin these movements later than usual. Girls who graduate to walking usually discontinue crawling, which is actually more difficult.

Are girls able to sit without support?

Most girls are able to achieve independent sitting, but low muscle tone may interfere with her ability to sit without support. At a later age, the development of severe scoliosis can pose problems with balance when sitting.

Will my daughter learn to walk?

It is difficult to predict which girls will walk and which will not. In general, those with the poorest muscle tone have more difficulty walking. However, girls have been known to walk for the first time as late as 16 years of age. So don't give up easily! Weight bearing exercises, physical therapy with range of motion exercises and practice walking should be done regularly. With proper motivation, support and encouragement, some girls with RS are able to continue to walk independently for decades.

Most girls do not run and almost all have difficulty going up and (especially) down stairs. Their gait is awkward and clumsy, usually with the legs wide apart and stiff. Balance is difficult.

> Megan never walked as a baby, but she did pull up in her bed. Shortly after she accomplished that, the regression started and she never walked. She also never crawled. She gets around on the floor by rolling and scooting on her back. She does love to be on her feet and I have assumed she is too old to learn to walk. But there is a spark inside me motivating me to continue trying to get her to walk. When she stands she doesn't seem to understand how to pick up her feet to take steps most of the time. Then at times she has actually taken more than one or two steps with support.

What are the problems that interfere with walking?

In addition to their motor handicaps, girls with RS have apraxia, sensory and perceptual problems, difficulties shifting from one movement to another and lack of coordination. These combine to make walking a difficult task. As they get older, other problems such as scoliosis, increased muscle tone and decreased tactile perception (feeling) in their cold, swollen feet make walking difficult.

Why is it important to keep her on her feet?

It is of significant importance to her continued health to keep her on her feet and walking as long as possible, even for a short time every day. Once walking is lost, a number of problems can worsen, such as scoliosis, osteoporosis and problems with breathing and digestion. To maintain her body in a standing position, she has to use her hypotonic trunk muscles. Being in a standing position lets her take deeper breaths and bearing weight helps maintain bone density. You may find that if she is an independent walker, she may actually walk better with less assistance. When both hands are held, some girls tend to depend on someone else, leaning instead of walking straight. So, sometimes it is better to use a hand on the shoulder to steady her or to hold only one hand if possible.

Will she be able to use a walker?

"Walkers" come in various types and sizes, according to her needs. Some have seats to "catch" her when she needs to sit down. Others do not have a seat, but rely on her to hold the handles to stay upright. This may be difficult, as it may call for her to maintain grasp for longer than she is capable. If this is the case, creative genius can usually come up with a way to secure her hands to the handles – with gloves, mittens, elastic bandage tape or velcro.

> Kayla used to only walk with push toys but refused to walk alone. One day, her teacher held a broom up and made Kayla hold on to it and walk while she held the top. When Kayla felt safe, she let go of the broom and just started walking holding the broom straight up in the air. After that I thought she might be attached to a broom for life but after about a week she lost the broom and walked alone.

> Allison learned to walk at 6 years after significant intense physical therapy in the home. I turned one of our bedrooms into a "gym" for her P.T., and installed a homemade ladder of 1" dowels that Allie would use to learn her crossing pattern. With her hands on the rungs we would move left hand, right foot, right hand, left foot, and so on. Mom would take the hands and I the feet, or vice versa. We made a game out of it, several times a day. Allie actually enjoyed it once she got used to the game. I don't remember how long it actually took, but in a few months Allie was walking if someone held her hand. She now walks all over the house on her own.

What are hypotonia and hypertonia?

In a healthy nervous system, the muscles are sent messages instructing them to either tighten or relax to a certain degree. This allows us to move freely while at the same time maintaining an upright position against gravity. **Hypotonia** is decreased or "floppy" muscle tone and is the result of a neurological problem, not a lack of exercise. It is difficult for the hypotonic child to move efficiently, as she is generally weak and has poor endurance.

Sometimes, however, the opposite happens and muscles are too tight, or **hypertonic**. These muscles are difficult to stretch or elongate and this makes movement difficult. Hypertonic muscles are frequently referred to as being spastic and in severe cases, can lead to contractures. If the muscles are too "floppy" or too tight, movement can be difficult and abnormal movement patterns emerge. These can be very difficult to correct once they are established.

In many cases, girls with RS start out hypotonic but later become hypertonic during their school years. It is not uncommon to have mixed tone in which some muscles are too tight while some are too loose. This results in structural problems such as scoliosis, which occurs when muscles on one side of the trunk pull harder than the muscles on the other side.

What is spasticity?

Spasticity is muscle tone that is abnormally high and results in muscle tightness that can make normal movements difficult. Spasticity is not usually seen until the school years. It may only be a slight increase in muscle tone which leads to toe-walking, or may be a more severe increase in muscle tone involving the whole body affecting even respiration and swallowing, and leading to scoliosis, or curvature of the spine. It may also lead to **contractures**, irreversible shortening of muscle fibers which cause decreased joint mobility.

What can be done to treat spasticity?

Severe contractures, particularly in the ankle and elbow joints, can develop in spite of regular weekly home and school therapy. Activities which reduce muscle tone and can help temporarily include rotation, weight shift and weight bearing.

What is the vestibular system?

The **vestibular** system is concerned with movement and is responsible for letting us know if we are moving, if we're on something that's moving or if something near us is moving. We then coordinate our body to respond appropriately to that perceived movement. The hallmark of a vestibular dysfunction is motor apraxia. It is also responsible for the fear of imposed movement (moving her) many girls experience.

What is vestibular stimulation?

Vestibular stimulation is used by therapists to help the girl organize her vestibular system so that she can make coordinated and appropriate responses to movement. All adults know that too much vestibular stimulation is not a good thing. Remember the last time you rode the Tilt-A-Whirl? It can wreak havoc on the autonomic nervous system and children with vestibular dysfunctions should receive stimulation cautiously. While rocking back and forth in a chair is both beneficial and enjoyable, spinning on suspended equipment should not be attempted without consulting a therapist.

What is motor apraxia?

Motor apraxia is the body's inability to carry out what the brain signals it to do, i.e. difficulty to perform purposeful movements and actions in spite of normal mobility. Simply put, apraxia is the inability to coordinate thought and movement. It is the most fundamental handicap seen in RS, and involves all body movements, including speech and eye gaze. While the girl with Rett syndrome does not lose the ability to move the body, she loses the ability to tell the body how and when to move. She may have a desire and a will to move, but is incapable of carrying the movement through.

What is the difference between apraxia and dyspraxia?

Apraxia refers to the inability to coordinate thought and movement, while **dyspraxia** is less severe, referring to difficulty coordinating thought and movement. Both terms are applied in describing RS.

How does motor apraxia affect her movements?

In infancy, she may be able to use a pincer grasp (using the thumb and forefinger) to skillfully pick up small pieces of cereal, and she may be able to hold her bottle and play with toys. Over time, she loses the pincer grasp and reverts back to a palmar grasp (using the palm and fingers together in a raking motion) to scoop objects instead. She has difficulty finding the right movement but also in coordinating the strength and speed to carry it out. The apraxia is more evident when she is in unfamiliar situations and becomes even more difficult when she is asked to follow directions. The more she has to think about what to do, the more difficulty she has in performing. She may see something she wants across the room, desire to move toward the object, and end up turning in circles instead. She may want to take a toy from the shelf, but knock it to the floor instead.

Can she overcome the apraxia?

Apraxia is impossible to overcome, but possible to minimize by understanding and putting her movements into perspective. Much of what seems to be aimless or unintentional movement may actually be purposeful action gone wrong. She may stare at an object intently, hyperventilate, rock back and forth and wring her hands — all in getting "geared up" to move. Often, she looks at the object, and then looks away before she reaches or moves. When she does move, she may not be successful in doing what she wanted at all, or she may move in the wrong way. It is most frustrating for both parent and child, but paying careful attention to her body signals is beneficial in helping her to be successful. Look for consistent behaviors and try to interpret her signals. In rare situations, she can momentarily overcome the apraxia, particularly when she is emotionally motivated. This happens when she moves automatically, without thinking about how to move. Examples of this are scratching an itch, reaching out to grab a cookie, or blurting out a word in joy or distress. To help minimize the apraxia, look for activities with emotional incentives that will reward her with success, so that she can "do" before she has to "think."

It really helps Lauren to have a verbal cue. She has a movement therapist who comes to the house and works with movement combined with music. For months she's been trying to get Lauren to imitate her arm movements. Finally last week she told Lauren "Do what I do" and she imitated. Another day Lauren took me to her favorite toy which was partially hidden on a lower shelf and she really wanted to get it out. She stood there holding my hand and moving her other arm and hand back and forth while looking at the toy. Finally I told her "you need to bend over to get it" and she immediately did so. With a little physical help and 3-4 reminders to bend she got her toy. Often I find I must remind her of each movement she needs to take, otherwise she's totally stuck.

Sherry can scratch an itch, or reach out and push my arm away when I'm doing something she doesn't like. The other day she was having a leg cramp in the bath and I wouldn't have known it except that she pinched me pretty hard to get my attention! But when it comes to conscious actions, like when she's staring at an object intently like she wants it, she seems to be unable to translate that desire into action.

Does apraxia affect her intelligence?

Apraxia involves almost all movements and behaviors of those with Rett syndrome. It does not affect intelligence. In fact, it hides intelligence, because it makes it difficult for us to determine what she knows when she cannot use gestures such as pointing or signing to indicate her understanding. Even if she is given extra time to complete a task, the apraxia may prevent her from acting or indicating that she understands.

> I believe Amanda does well with behavioral training because she is apraxic, and apraxic children do better when the focus is one-on-one in environments that are very rewarding and repetitive. We spend as much time with Amanda as we can, but it is difficult after so many years to keep up this pace.

Does RS affect her balance?

Besides an unbalanced gait, she has difficulty with upper body weight bearing. Her **protective responses** (putting out her arms to catch herself in a fall) are usually poor. Backward protective response reactions are often delayed or absent.

How can I help her?

As you learn to read her body signals and her own private language of movement, reward her with praise for her intentions. Explain that you know how hard it is for her to succeed, and praise her for each little step toward the goal. Assume that she understands what you have to say, acknowledging at the same time that she may be incapable of complete success. Use of augmentative communication devices and switches can greatly enhance her ability to communicate and succeed. "Seize the moment" by providing activities that are motivating.

What is spatial disorientation?

Spatial disorientation occurs when she cannot correctly perceive the "upright" position of her body. In order for her to feel that she is upright, she leans forward, backward or to the side. There is less interference with walking if she leans forward, but this may eventually affect her posture and lead to kyphosis. It can lead to loss of ambulation due to an inability to shift weight forward to initiate steps.

What can be done to correct spatial disorientation?

The treatment that has been utilized is an over-correction procedure, taking her into the spaces that frighten her. She should be physically and emotionally supported through this procedure. Start with her lying horizontally on her side, back or stomach for up to 30 minutes and progress to partially upright on a wedge, ball or the therapist's lap. Continue to advance by placing her feet on the floor while leaning into the corrected direction.

What is ataxia?

Ataxia, a disruption of balance, is often the earliest motor problem seen in RS. It leads the joints to become temporarily fixed or locked into a position of stability. This reduces the girl's mobility in changing from one position to another. Due to ataxia, the legs are often far apart both standing and sitting, and weight shift from one leg to another is difficult. Moving her may cause extreme distress at fear of falling, but movements she makes on her own are not upsetting. Her **righting reactions** (ability to return to upright when placed off balance) and equilibrium responses may be slowed and ineffective. Movements in RS are often described as jerky truncal ataxia – the shaky movements that occur when she tries to keep her balance.

What can be done to minimize ataxia?

Weighted vests and belts are used to decrease ataxia. Segmental rolling is used, rolling her over where there is a twisting between her shoulders and hips. This activity helps to stabilize balance. The therapy ball and floor activities can also be used to stimulate the balance system. Repetitive practice of various activities which promote weight shift and rotation in functional movement skills are helpful.

What is meant by transitional movements?

Transitional skills are those movements which allow us to change position, such as rolling, getting to sit, pulling to stand, etc. Sitting and standing when placed are skills which are kept longer. Strong extensor muscle activity in legs and back, spinal rigidity, lack of upper extremity weight bearing, a disturbance in spatial orientation and inability to grade movement are factors that contribute to loss of transitional skills.

What can be done to help with transitional movements?

Transitions are as important as walking. Girls who have retained the ability to walk should have an opportunity to practice transitions daily. Girls who are unable to perform transitions by themselves should be led through the motions with verbal and physical help. This will help maintain mobility and reduce the amount of lifting required by the caretaker. Again, apraxia rears its ugly head, as learning transitional movements is a major motor planning feat.

With the girl seated on a therapy ball, the therapist attempts to elicit righting and equilibrium responses. During this activity, the therapist controls the speed, direction, duration and delivery of the movement to encourage active responses into flexion and rotation. The activity must be carefully geared to the child's level of tolerance. Range of motion, strength and tolerance for these postures are developed.

The therapist should practice functional transition activities while giving verbal direction with reassurance and physical assistance. Getting a child onto all fours is possible even with a girl who has a strong objection to being prone, if she is reassured that the therapist will protect her face in case the hand wringing interferes with her ability to maintain weight bearing on her hands.

When a girl fears falling forward, leaning forward to stand up can be very difficult. When the therapist pushes her forward, she reinforces her pushing backward. To help alleviate this problem, the child can be seated on a bench, which is then tipped back forcing equilibrium reactions to get hip flexion. The child should be assisted to stay flexed as the bench returns to the upright position. This helps her tolerate the forward movement that she fears due to her spatial disorientation. When her tolerance is increased, she will then actively shift forward to pull to standing.

What is proprioception?

Proprioception is the knowledge of where our body is in space. It is one of the senses and originates in the muscles and joint capsules. Proprioception is the sense that allows us to correctly know where our arms and legs are at any given time without having to look. It allows us to make the postural adjustments needed to remain upright in a chair or to bring a cookie to the mouth without missing.

Brittany has a weighted vest and I have seen some positive results as far as calming her by increasing the proprioception. The one for my daughter is constructed with all the weights around the bottom. I am going to make a new one disbursing the weight evenly throughout. The O.T. recommends that you start with no more weight than 5% of the child's total weight, gradually increasing as tolerated to as much as 25% of her body weight without imposing undue restriction on her mobility. Physical conditions should be discussed with her doctor and O.T. The vest should not be left on more than 10-15 minutes. I am in the process of making a weighted blanket. I am using shredded paper for the filler. This has unbelievable weight. Brittany likes to be wrapped up like a "hot dog" in a regular blanket. I know she'll love the weighted blanket.

I made Amanda's weighted vest by taking a fitting jean jacket, cutting off the sleeves, and sewing inside pockets around the bottom for weights. I went to the hardware store and bought different size big washers. I made the internal pockets seal with velcro on one side so I could change the weights. I talked to a couple of therapists before I did this.

The weighted vest provides a sensory experience called proprioception which our girls ordinarily miss out on. Because our girls miss out on so many sensory experiences, we have to give it to them. They also get a little vestibular sensation.

Using weights fatigued Amanda. I would not try it again, but other parents feel weighted vests calm their kids. I think it is a burden to Amanda myself, but before we did it, felt it might help her walk better and stabilize her tremor. It did not. I would not try weights again – I think it pulls her muscles too much, and she structurally can not support added weight.

I like the idea of wraps and joint compression, I think our kids are loose and can not support weight sometimes and that this might help. Putting orthotics in Amanda's shoes definitely helped straighten her feet and helped her walk better – basically took some of the support off her body.

OSTEOPOROSIS

In spite of normal intestinal absorption of calcium and Vitamin D, girls with RS have low bone-mineral content and decreased bone density (**osteoporosis**). Fractures can occur quite easily with minimal trauma. Weight bearing and standing exercises help the bones maintain density and strength. Calcium intake should be encouraged. Because of her abnormal response to pain, it may be impossible to know that a fracture has occurred until there is swelling, bruising or limping.

Michelle fractured her wrist one time; it took us a week to figure out where the pain was coming from. We would have never found the problem had she not had the bruising at the fracture site.

Jocelyn broke her arm and it took us several days to realize it. I noticed on a Monday that she was not putting her hands in her mouth, and I was so elated that she had finally outgrown this that I sent her to school without her arm splints on. I got a note home that day saying that they were concerned that something was wrong and I'll tell you I was so angry that they could not see the positive side! Anyway the next day she winced a bit as I put her arm through her shirt sleeve, but I didn't pay much attention at the time. Had another day of no hands. When I got home from work that night my husband said he thought there was something wrong, because he noticed that she would not crawl when put down on the floor. She just sat back on her heels. That night I noticed her arm was swollen and red. We took her in to have it checked out and she had indeed broken her arm, upper area of her humerus near her shoulder. The doctor felt that it had happened about a 1-1/2 weeks prior due to the healing. We could not recall any falls or injuries, and finally traced it most probably back to her baby brother who had knocked her down from her kneeling stance and began bouncing on her.

Awhile back we had a hand and wrist X-ray done on Lauren for bone age. They also found a healed wrist fracture. Lauren does walk and has had a variety of falls over the years. She tends to be quite a stoic about pain, breathing hard, and getting quiet when in the same situation her brother would have been crying for a long time. We had no idea when it happened.

The author wishes to thank the following professionals for ideas and information which was used to develop this chapter: Susan Hanks, PT; Barbro Lindberg; Linda Reece, OTR/L; Jan Townsley, OTR/L.

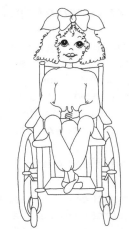

ORTHOPEDICS

THE FEET

What are the most frequent problems seen with the feet?

The feet are often cold, bluish-red and small, due to inadequate circulation. Other foot problems in RS result from muscle imbalance. The most common is **equinus**, a downward pointing of the foot. This is due to tight or overactive heelcords. She she may have **valgus**, when her heels are together and the toes apart, forming a V. Or she may have **varus**, when the toes point toward each other, making an A shape, but this is not as common. She may have **pronation**, walking on flat feet with her ankles appearing to collapse inwardly.

How does toe walking interfere with walking?

She walks on the balls of the feet rather than with the foot flat as normal. This may or may not hinder balance. In some cases it improves balance. It may also make shoe fitting more difficult if severe. In the child who does not walk, contractures may interfere with supported standing in a prone stander.

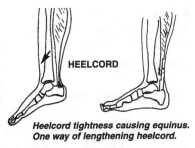

HEELCORD

Heelcord tightness causing equinus. One way of lengthening heelcord.

What can be accomplished with bracing?

If the muscles to the heelcord are overactive, but not truly tight, a plastic ankle foot orthosis (**AFO**) brace may help hold the foot flat. **Short leg braces** and **splints** are often used along with physical therapy to maintain range of motion and to minimize involuntary movements that interfere with functioning. They also prevent contractures, which occur when muscles consistently have increased tone, keeping muscles in a shortened position which can severely limit movement. The brace maintains a specific muscle group in the desired position, which permits optimal use of the joint. If the heelcord is tight and the foot cannot be brought to a flat position, serial casts or heelcord release surgery may be necessary.

How do AFO's work?

The brace consists of a custom-fitted molded plastic splint worn inside the shoe, which extends behind the calf. Decreasing the extension of muscles at the ankle may also help decrease muscle tone in the hips, allowing for sitting in a more stable position. This change of ankle position allows the child to stand with the foot flat, which improves her stability and support. Correction of her abnormal foot posture may also affect the position of her hips and knees when she stands, thus helping her to walk better. Braces and splints are custom-made and need to be changed as the child grows.

What is serial casting?

Serial casting is sometimes done to reduce ankle contractures. The child's feet are fitted with a series of short leg casts which hold the foot in place over several weeks' time. The casts are removed, the feet stretched, and then the casts are reapplied and again removed. The constant stretch of the cast allows tight joints and tendons to relax over time.

How is serial casting done?

Serial casting involves setting the foot, or both feet in a cast for a period of time to help stretch the heelcord and avoid or delay contractions. The first casting is set with the foot in a neutral (90 degree) position if this is possible. If not, the foot is taken to the end of the range and stretched just a little further. The subsequent castings will angle or stretch the foot upward a few degrees each time to achieve the desired outcome, a loose heelcord. Each casting may last from four days to two weeks at a time depending on the recommendation of your therapist, orthotist, podiatrist, or orthopedist.

How does serial casting work neurologically?

Serial casting changes the structure - lengthening muscles. It works because the brain receives the constant feedback of a stretched heelcord and she learns the feeling of walking on corrected feet. The hope is that after the cast is finally removed, the effect may last three to six months, which is long enough for her to benefit from walking or therapeutic activities. If it is successful, you may begin the whole process over again and enjoy the continued benefits.

What are the pros and cons of serial casting?

The positive side of this treatment is that the casts are temporary, the procedure is not surgical, and it leaves the heelcord intact. Casting is also cheaper and safer than surgery. On the down side, serial casting is not a remedy and will not work in every situation. Talk to your doctor or physical therapist. Because of the impaired circulation in her feet and legs, great care must be taken to prevent pressure sores under the casts. Extra padding and frequent cast changes will help.

Will surgery help?

Orthopedic surgery can be useful when severe joint deformities or contractures have developed. A surgical procedure can increase the range of motion through releasing, lengthening or transferring affected muscles. When the heelcord is tight, the child walks on her toes. **Heelcord lengthening** at the ankle may assist walking by giving her a more flat-footed gait. The heelcord is cut in a way that can be lengthened and allowed to heal in a cast. There are many ways to do this. A hamstring release, lengthening or muscle transfer around the knee may also promote better walking.

Careful evaluation should precede surgery, which always has risks and benefits. While surgery may increase mobility and help avoid painful **osteoarthritis** (joint inflammation), there may be complications or the surgical intervention may be less than successful. Discuss the risks and benefits with your child's physician.

How will she recuperate?

She will be discharged either the same day or up to a few days later, depending on how she has done. The feet should be elevated for two days and checked for swelling. She may bear weight according to her own tolerance after one or two weeks. The cast stays on for 6-8 weeks. Extra care must be taken to prevent pressure sores. A brace is then fitted to prevent the contracture from recurring. This periodic immobility should not decrease her ability to walk if she is encouraged to walk within one to two weeks after surgery in her casts.

THE HIPS

What is hip instability?

The hip is a ball-and-socket joint. In some girls and women, due to abnormal muscle pull with growth, the ball is very gradually pulled out of the socket. If this is partial, it is termed **subluxation**; if it is total, **dislocation**. This may cause pain later in life. Hip dislocation may occur from persistent increased hip **adduction** (movement toward midline of the thigh), particularly in the child who does not walk. Release of the hip adductor muscles and removal of the nerve which supplies them can be helpful.

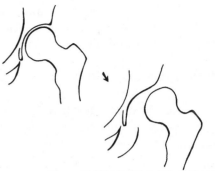

The normal hip (left) is a ball and socket joint. In sublaxation (right) the ball starts to come out of the socket.

How can it be prevented?

Proper positioning in a wheelchair or bed can help if the hip adductors are tight. Stretching and bracing or even muscle lengthening to maintain the hips' ability to **abduct**, or spread apart may be helpful, but is unproven. For all practical purposes, awareness and early detection are the key.

How is hip instability treated?

Early subluxation can be treated by muscle lengthening, a relatively simple procedure. If treated, surgical realignment of the bone, or **osteotomy**, may be necessary later.

THE BACK

Scoliosis is seen often in Rett syndrome. Three-fourths of all girls with RS in three large studies had scoliosis, although some curves remain minor. Why this occurs is one of the mysteries of RS – hopefully to be better understood by research. Scoliosis occurs when the spinal vertebrae rotate from a nearly straight column shape to a shape like a spiral staircase. On X-ray, it appears as a side-to-side curve.

What causes scoliosis?

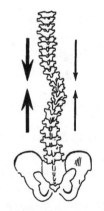

The spine has muscles on both sides. Scoliosis, in general, can be from abnormal muscle tone or balance. The muscle pulls differently on one side of the spine than the other, causing the spine to bend. This abnormal muscle pull probably occurs in response to signals from the brain. Differing muscle pull on two sides may cause scoliosis in Rett syndrome.

Differing muscle pull on two sides may cause scoliosis.

When does scoliosis start?

Usually between nine and twelve years of age, a curve becomes noted if one is to develop. A few girls have developed curves in early childhood although they have not worsened rapidly at that age. Scoliosis should be checked for visually on all girls with RS at any age. This can often be done without x-ray.

How can scoliosis be detected?

Before scoliosis is diagnosed, it can be screened for by observing the shape of the back. If the child is able to stand, it can be done while she bends forward. If not, she should be checked while seated, looking down from above. Normally, the ribs and muscles are the same shape on both sides of the middle of the back. If on one side they stand out much more, an x-ray should be done.

How often should an x-ray be done?

It should be done when a child has an abnormal examination as just described. If a curve is found, follow-up x-rays should be done every year in young girls. With slowly progressive curves, they should be repeated every six months during rapid growth or progression.

How much will the curve increase?

Progression means increase of the curvature. This is extremely variable. In some girls, it rapidly increases, while in others, it does not. This is why all minor curves are not treated from the start. However, the bigger the curve and the closer the child is to the adolescent growth spurt, the more likely the curve is to progress.

> My 31 year old daughter experienced a pronounced increase in the curvature of her spine in her 20's. No treatment was recommended, only observation while she was in her teens. She now needs a lot of prompting to keep her head up when walking and to keep her head out of her plate of food when sitting at the table. She moved through her teens without dramatic scoliosis but in her adulthood both scoliosis and kyphosis are producing dramatic effects on her body.

Vertebra: views from back, side, and top.

What are the effects of scoliosis?

Scoliosis can cause an alteration of sitting balance, which may lead to practical problems with seating. It can also cause compression of the lungs by the twisting of the chest. This becomes significant in curves over about 70 degrees. It is important to prevent this before it happens.

What about prevention and treatment?

Unfortunately, we do not know how to prevent scoliosis altogether, but it can be treated once it starts. For small curves in growing girls, braces are used. In large curves in older girls near the teen years, surgery is used. Physical therapists, orthopedic surgeons and chiropractors don't all agree on how to prevent and treat scoliosis, so it can be confusing. Every child is different and response to treatment varies with each child. Some girls have early signs of scoliosis in spite of aggressive therapy, while others may have minimal curves even as adolescents, even without intensive therapy.

> The orthopedist wanted to brace her. I was devastated. How could she feel my hugs? How would I carry her? She can't walk yet, but crawls, and is not in her wheelchair very much – mostly for long transport and the school bus. I came home and found a private P.T. who stretches her weekly. It doesn't hold all week, but I think she is getting stronger.

When should a brace be used?

A brace should be used when a curve is over 20-25 degrees and the child is still growing. It is not effective if the curve is much over 45 degrees. The brace is a molded, padded and plastic "jacket" designed to apply gentle pressure in the proper areas to straighten the spine. It is worn under clothing. It does not hurt, although it can cause pressure sores if it is started too fast or if the child outgrows it. The brace should be worn for 18-23 hours per day, depending on the doctor's orders. Braces should be checked and changed as necessary and should not interfere with mobility if they have been correctly fit. Ask for an adjustment if there appear to be problems with fit.

How effective is the brace?

The goal of using a brace is to slow the increase of the curve, not to make it straighten permanently. In most cases, the curve will continue to increase, but hopefully, at a slower rate. Thus, the child may have an acceptable curve at the end of growth (less than 40 to 50 degrees). It is usually recommended to postpone surgery until she is nearly finished growing, if possible. In some cases, the brace does not work, or the curve may be too big already, and surgery should be considered.

Plastic body jacket or brace for treating mild scoliosis.

The big argument in favor of braces seems to be buying time. On the other hand, anytime you restrict movement, you automatically restrict the stress the bones require to develop and maintain integrity. When Crystal had her surgery, her surgeon stated that it was refreshing and reassuring to do the surgery on a girl who hadn't been braced. He said he could see that the bones were in good condition and had the stamina to hold the rods.

My daughter Julie started wearing her brace at age 3 when her curve was 18 degrees. She does not walk and at that time did not bear weight. Her jacket opened in the front, putting a lot of pressure on her stomach. She still was able to be placed in a sitting position. She used it about 8 hours a day. I had her jackets adjusted every 3-6 months with new ones made every year. Julie is now 7 and has a 47 degree curve and holding. She had a big jump from 20 degrees to about 40 degrees during ages 5-6. Now she seems to be stabilizing. We know she will need surgery at an early age. The jacket she wears now opens in the back. It's a bear to get on, but it relieves pressure, therefore causing less spit ups.

Angela wore a back brace for many years before her surgery and again for six months after. It slowed the progression of her curve immensely. She had a very minor 5 degree curve at age 5 and we were able to delay surgery until she was 15. Her orthopedist told me that depending on how the doctor measured the curve, it could vary greatly.

Heather's brace was open in the back and we had problems at one point with it being too long. We took it to the brace shop and pointed it out and they cut part of the bottom off so it didn't interfere with her mobility.

We just discovered that Kathryn's legs are different lengths. The orthopedist had her start wearing a ⅝" lift on one shoe. He was hopeful that most of the curve was caused by the tilt of her pelvis which was caused by her different leg lengths. At age 8, her curve has increased to 26 degrees in 10 months. Because of this, the doctor wants her to wear a body brace at night to start. In 4 months, if the curve has maintained or gotten better, we'll continue with the night only bracing, otherwise we'll have to go to the 23 hours per day route. With her brace on, the X-ray showed the correction is very good – the curve is almost gone. (note that this is with brace on.)

Melinda is unable to balance herself with the jacket on and she gave us this big crocodile tear face when we asked how it felt. They trimmed the edges on top and bottom slightly but said any more trimming would make the jacket less effective and outgrown that much quicker.

Angie had scoliosis surgery 10 years ago. She was in a body brace from age 9 to age 15 for 23 hours a day. The brace was a two piece shell, and combined with her AFO's (plastic feet) and experimental plastic hand braces that were supposed to cut down on the stereotypical hand movements, we jokingly called her our Barbie doll. I hated the brace because we lost that nice snuggle contact that is so important – so for that we took it off.

Surgery brought her curve back from 72 degrees to the mid 20s and her health improved so much that we felt like it had saved her life and clearly her ability to walk. The surgeon stated that he doesn't have near the success on those who had previously worn bracing, as their bones lose density.

What does she wear under the brace to protect her skin?

She will need to wear seamless undershirts, which avoid creases that can irritate. These may come with the brace. If not, they can be purchased through department store catalogs or a hospital supply pharmacy.

How do most girls tolerate the brace?

These little RS girls put up with so much and in the long run demonstrate a virtue of resiliency. It may take a bit of adjusting but they do adapt so well. I remember Jenn got so used to her body jacket that she was fearful at first without it! Kids adapt well. It's we parents that go through hell worrying about them!

It has been many years since Heather went into her brace at age 6 but I vividly remember how crushed I was at the loss of her sitting balance and ability to "bunny hop" around the house. In a very short time she regained both skills, brace and all!

Jocelyn was 6 before we had to treat the scoliosis with a back brace. She wore it 24 hours a day and though it seemed hard and cruel at first, she adjusted to it rather quickly. She held steady for several years then she would suddenly increase quite fast. We'd make a new brace and continue to hold for a while. This went on till she was 13. At that time her curve went wild and increased from 55 to 74 in a few months, then she stopped wearing the brace for three months prior to her surgery and the curve jumped to 100. Surgery corrected it to 35 where she has stabilized now for five years.

Angela wore her brace for about four years. She did not wear it to sleep, but we did not take it off if she laid down for a half hour nap. She wore it all the time except at night, when bathing or swimming or if she was sick and in bed. It opened in the front and did make diapers a bit more complicated but otherwise was not a problem. A good fit is important.

How will physical therapy help?

Susan Hanks, Licensed Physical Therapist, has had a lot of experience with girls with RS and has speculated that the scoliosis may start with her abnormal perception of midline, which causes her to lean sideways, thus resulting in the loss of her upright position and the escalation of back curvature. She recommends using over correction positioning. For instance, if a girl falls backwards and to the right, she should be put on a therapy ball, leaning forward to the left and then gradually brought back to an upright position.

What about chiropractic care?

Chiropractors manipulate the vertebrae of the spine and the joints and muscles of the body. This manipulation is felt to improve the flow of nerve impulses to the brain, which increases the body's ability to solve its health problems. Some of the techniques of massage and physical therapy used by chiropractors today are similar to those used by physical therapists.

> I took Laura to a local chiropractor for a whole year 4 days a week. He wasn't able to help the scoliosis from progressing but he was most definitely able to help her in other ways. Through various reflexology techniques he was able to stimulate and strengthen her. She showed dramatic improvements in her seizuring, circulation, digestion, metabolism, balance, strength and well being. It even improved her perception awareness and use of her arms and legs. It was during this time that Laura started to grow from a 34 pound frail girl to now a 124 lb tall young lady. I firmly believe that these treatments served as a sort of tune up for her.

> When she was 5 years old, I used to take Lisa Joy to the chiropractor once a month for her scoliosis. He had helped another older girl with Rett maintain her curve and even improve a degree or so. But the orthopedist insisted the way they sit for their X ray can make the curve look up to 4 degrees different. He wanted to brace her. I have found the best thing for Lisa Joy's scoliosis has been that the P.T. stretches her every week. This has maintained and slightly improved her curve over the last 3½ years.

When should we consider surgery?

This is an individual matter. However, once a curve reaches 40 to 50 degrees, it is likely to keep increasing even after she is finished growing. It might later cause the seating and lung problems mentioned earlier. Thus, a curve of 40-50 degrees should be treated surgically in most cases. In one study, girls who had never walked were approximately three times more likely to undergo scoliosis surgery than those who had walked.

> I think it's always a good idea to get as much information as possible before making any kind of decision regarding a long term thing like a spinal fusion. It was never brought up to us at all that Sara would have a possible problem with arthritis or pain in her future. On the other hand, there was not a choice about whether she would have the surgery or not either, just that it would need to be done sooner or later. Unfortunately, the choice isn't as easy as pain management vs. curvature. I think if having a crooked spine were the only complication of scoliosis we might all think a lot harder about whether or not our daughters would have the surgery. I urge anyone considering this to look at all of the options first and know as much as you can ahead of time. It has been about 7 years since Sara had her first spinal fusion (she later had the fusion lengthened and attached to her pelvis) and we haven't had any problems at all. Sara did stop growing in her torso, but her legs have continued to grow. All things considered, and having gone through numerous pinches and hot sweaty days with a body jacket type brace, I think we could all say we would do it again.

> Heather had an "S" curve which reached 67 degrees before she had a successful spinal fusion which corrected her curvature to 12 degrees, where it has stayed for the past five years. It is important not to wait too long for surgery, because extreme scoliosis crowds the heart and lungs and then it becomes very serious.

> We did everything possible to try to change the progression of her curve in addition to her PT, from chiropractic adjustments to weekly massage therapy. I'm sure all of these interventions helped somewhat but ultimately did not change the fact that surgery was necessary. When the time came we accepted the fact that we did what we could to avoid it but it happened anyway. Her curve was 100 degrees at the time of her surgery, and it was corrected to 35 degrees. She had no complications and was released 8 days after surgery.

How will surgery improve her quality of life?

Surgery will make her straighter, and will markedly decrease her seating difficulty. It may allow her to use a hand which was previously used for supporting herself. Surgery will also prevent the lung compression which may occur with more severe curves. If she is in a wheelchair, it will probably need to be adjusted before she leaves the hospital...she will be taller!

How is scoliosis surgery done?

The spine is straightened using stainless steel or titanium rods. Bone graft is placed along this entire area to cause it to fuse solidly, so that no further curvature will occur. The rods usually become partially covered with bone and can be left in the body forever. They do not cause problems unless the patient is very thin.

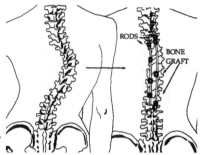

Straightening of the curvature by stainless steel rods

How much can the curve be corrected?

This varies with the size of the curve, age of the child, and stiffness of the spine. Usually, at least 40-60% of correction can be achieved. Anything in this range is acceptable, because, again, the goal is simply to prevent worsening. Straightening the curve too much carries a risk of over stretching the spinal cord. Therefore, the surgeon does not try to straighten the curve completely.   He does not need to do this.

Is anesthesia a problem in the child who has seizures or breathing problems?

Anesthesia is not a problem, because seizures can be controlled under anesthetic. However, the period after surgery may bring problems. Therefore, the seizure disorder should be as well-controlled as possible before surgery. Blood tests for levels of seizure medications should be within the desired range before surgery. In addition, appropriate medicines should be given to her immediately after the operation. It is also important for her to be as well nourished as possible before surgery.

> Heather, 20, had scoliosis surgery about 5 years ago and had rods inserted on both sides of her spine all the way down her back. She had a severe curvature, about 69 degrees. The doctors were quite concerned about her hyperventilation and apnea and how it would affect her breathing. They tried something new with Heather, giving a dose of morphine before giving anesthesia to reduce the amount of anesthesia they had to give. It was so successful with her that they began to use this method on other kids who were at risk.

What can we expect right after the surgery?

She will be drowsy on the first day after surgery, but feeling better by the third or fourth day when she is also eating well. A blood transfusion may be necessary, but this can come from the patient herself by pre-donation or from a relative if desired. The hospital stay is 6-10 days.

Potential complications include infection (1-2% risk), which usually becomes evident within the first two weeks and may require cleansing out of the infection. Rod displacement occurs in up to 5% and may require surgical repositioning. Nerve damage is the most serious risk, but also the least common, occurring in less than one per five hundred patients. This could range from numbness to weakness of one or both legs. If it does happen, it may be partially or fully reversible. **Pseudoarthrosis**, or failure of the bone to fuse at one level, occurs in about 1% of cases, and may require bone graft.

After 10 days in the hospital bed, they put a post-surgical brace on Angie and carefully let her dangle her legs over the side of the bed. Three nurses, a therapist, my closest friend and a deacon from our church were there, too. The medical people said she would be light headed and shouldn't stand yet. Angie grabbed my hands and stood up and took off out of that hospital room (with me hanging on) and right down the hall. She was hot to get out of there! At that time we thought we were observing a miracle.

Angela had a prescription for Tylenol® with codeine when she came home from the hospital but she needed very little of it and did quite well on just regular strength Tylenol®. She was back in school after 4 weeks. It took about six months to be fully recovered from her surgery.

Jocelyn did wonderfully with the surgery. They had her sitting upright the next day and on her feet a couple days later bearing weight, even though she has never walked.

I was trying desperately to delay surgery until Ashley got a little older and grew more. However, her curve grew rapidly from 55-83 during a three month period when she was approximately 13, while wearing a brace 24 hours a day. We were forced into surgery and never regretted it. The surgeon was only able to attain a 50 degree curve after surgery, so we really should have had surgery earlier. Ashley had no problems during or after surgery. Unlike most RS girls, Ashley is very sensitive to pain, so we had to keep her medicated for some time. But otherwise, all went well.

Laura was straightened from an 80 degree curve to a 30 degree curve. No regrets! Here are some suggestions: Decorations for afterwards. Laura likes the colored metallic ribbon with stars and such found in gift wrapping department. I was able to string it from the ceiling. Is there a special pair of pajamas that can be opened or cut all the way down the back? Add pretty ribbon ties. If after the surgery she is uncomfortable and doesn't want to be moved, double diaper her. A smaller one inside a larger one seems to work nicely. Just poke or put holes in the outer protective layer of the inner diaper so when it becomes saturated, it will fill into the outer diaper. Another idea, called a bag bath. Take a clean medium garbage bag in which you have placed several wash cloths. Add enough water to saturate and several drops of antibacterial lotion type soap. Zap in the microwave to warm. You can use them to wash and shampoo, and do not need to rinse off. Bonus is it stays warm until you are ready to use it. Works good on Mom and Dad, too, when you just cannot get out for a shower! Keep a notebook handy. Log doctors' comments and orders. Note all your questions, and such. Sometimes you may be at the beginning of rounds, or vice versa. Doctors will forget what they were supposed to remember!

How soon can she bear weight again?

Bearing weight depends on the quality of the bone and its ability to support the rods. Usually, this is adequate to allow standing within 4-6 days. In some cases, a brace or cast may be necessary, and it is applied at this time. Usually, the energy level is back to normal by 6-8 weeks. It is best for the child to avoid any impact activities or forcible bending for 6 months.

What are the pros and cons to scoliosis surgery?

The drawback of the surgery has been her inability to rotate her spine, which had allowed her to roll over in bed with ease before the surgery. Now, in spite of the fact she can walk, she needs to be turned in bed at night. On the plus side, she is healthy and never had a critical moment in her life – no pneumonia – and her heart and lungs are not compromised by a curved spine. She prefers to hold on to someone's hand when walking, but if there is something she wants to do, such as sitting down, she will let go and walk over to her chair.

Scoliosis surgery is very serious surgery, but if it is needed, it will prevent permanent damage to lungs and heart from crowding and is best done while the patient is strong enough to withstand the surgery. I know it is scary, and I hope Heather never has to go through anything like it again, but I am glad she had it when she did. The surgery was a complete success, with correction to 12 degrees. Heather gained weight after her surgery and also began menstruating, which is common after surgery. For her, it was a good thing.

We had put off surgery because of the pain and the fact Meg had never been through a major surgery. I now wish we had not waited so long. We tried bracing and Meg did not tolerate the brace at all. The brace was hot and uncomfortable and she actually became withdrawn because she was so miserable. She also had P.T. on a regular basis that did not slow the scoliosis. Meg has made a great recovery without complications. The only downfall is she does not walk as well and she is not as flexible, but the scoliosis was interfering with her walking anyway. Everyone and every case is different. Fortunately, Meg is very hearty and healthy so surgery was not as risky for her.

What questions should we ask beforehand?

Deciding whether to do the surgery is probably a very tough decision. The more you know about what will happen, the more prepared and comfortable you will be with your decision. Ask which surgical technique will be used and how it is done. Ask what may be involved in post-operative care, (length of time in bed, when and if post-op brace is fitted, and when weight-bearing can be re-established). Ask for suggestions on techniques to feed her, take her to the toilet and bathe her after the surgery. If the surgeon is not familiar with RS, provide literature on the topic. Talk to other parents who have been through it. It is probably best if someone can stay with her in the hospital, for her comfort and security, and to be able to better interpret her non-verbal messages. Make sure to plan for the post operative period when she comes back home and your own energy level is low. See if you can get help with lifting, bathing and general nursing.

What is kyphosis?

Kyphosis is spinal curvature as seen from the side, often termed "hunch back." A small degree of kyphosis (up to 45 degrees) is normal, present in everyone as part of the normal spine contour. While kyphosis is often seen in RS, it does not usually progress to a serious degree. Kyphosis is not as medically serious as scoliosis. It does not harm the lungs or sitting balance, but it may cause discomfort if severe.

How is kyphosis treated?

Kyphosis is treated by a brace similar to that used for scoliosis. This is indicated if the curve is greater than 50-70 degrees in a growing child. Again, this is not as common as scoliosis in children with RS, and when seen, is usually more of a cosmetic problem than a functional one, as it does not cause lung problems. In curves of 80-90 degrees with discomfort, surgery may be indicated.

Mary is 37 and has a functional kyphosis, meaning that she can be pulled out of it to good posture and lying on the bed it isn't evident. Apparently, she uses it to find her center of gravity when walking. She does sometimes walk with her head down, but with reminders or people around her she lifts it. Sometime back I noticed that her neck was getting stiff and the PT and all staff do exercises with it. She has really shown improvement.

How can therapies assist with orthopedic problems?

Exercises cannot prevent or treat scoliosis or kyphosis. However, she can exercise in the brace. Stretching to decrease hip adduction contractures and hip, knee and ankle contractures may be beneficial. This should be done slowly, over 30-60 seconds each stretch, without sudden force. One study which looked at intervention strategies of over one hundred girls with RS concluded that although physical therapy appeared to be more effective than bracing, none of the various non-invasive methods including physical therapy, bracing, casting and combinations of these appeared to halt the progressive course of scoliosis. Physical therapy can help to maintain the flexibility of the curve so that greater correction can be achieved with less risk of over-stretching the spinal cord. Surgical intervention appeared to be the most effective means to reduce and arrest spinal curvature. It is possible that bracing is less effective due to decreased muscle tone and balance which result from long term use. Therefore, it may be worthwhile to combine an aggressive physical therapy program with use of a brace during periods of inactivity. This study also revealed that girls who had higher motor function had a lower incidence rate of both scoliosis and surgical intervention. While it appears that that non-invasive interventions do not alter the ultimate course of scoliosis, the clear relationship seen between gross motor skills and scoliosis call for an aggressive, ongoing physical therapy program. This program should start at an early age and should be aimed at building, maintaining and retaining gross motor skills.

The author wishes to thank the following professionals for ideas and information which was used to develop this chapter: Susan Hanks, PT; Linda Reece, OTR/L; Paul Sponseller, M.D.; Jan Townsley, OTR/L.

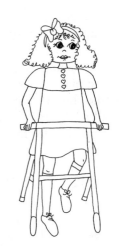

APPROACHES TO TREATMENT

Motor development in RS is almost always delayed, but the extent of the delay can vary considerably. Some girls are never able to achieve independent sitting or standing, while others sit, stand and walk at nearly the expected time. Her gait is often wide-based, unsteady and asymmetrical. Specific motor problems which may need to be addressed are hypotonia, ataxia, motor apraxia, loss of transitional movements, spasticity, scoliosis and/or kyphosis, loss of ambulation, loss of hand function, foot deformities and spatial disorientation. (Oral motor dysfunction with feeding problems will be discussed in the chapter on Nutrition. Speech and communication will be further explored in the chapter on Communication.)

The approach to treatment of motor problems in RS includes many disciplines including physical therapy, occupational therapy, speech therapy, music therapy, hydrotherapy and hippotherapy (horseback.) Each uses a combination of different interventions that are intended to maintain and maximize function in the girl with RS. While these therapies do not cure RS, they can maintain or improve function, prevent deformities, provide positioning and mobility and help keep her in better contact with her environment. It is important to remember that while girls with RS share many similarities, their problems and response to intervention may vary dramatically.

> I long for those days when P.T. meant part-time and O.T. meant overtime, when braces were used to straighten teeth and hand washing was something you did at the sink. It seems that for so long, our lives were consumed with the formality of so many different therapies. There was a constant sense of urgency to find the right combination of stuff that would "fix" her. After a time, we learned that she didn't need to be "fixed" after all. She just needed to be the best she could be. A succession of wonderful therapists have greatly added to her quality of her life over the years.

> The sort of therapy is not the most important; it is the ongoing attention for stimulation and therapy, trying different approaches all aiming for the same goals. There is a natural development in the girls with age, and we have to follow the tide so to speak. Overstimulating will not help. I had to learn over the years to be patient, to accept that changes come slowly. It was a hard lesson for me, for I am one of the world's most impatient persons, always focusing on results in all I do. This child has taught me patience and joy in achievements that count little or nothing in the "normal" world: We are euphoric when she fills her glass at the tap herself for the first time! But still it is often difficult to hold on to all the activities and attempts at teaching her certain things, when she does so often not respond. What keeps me going on is the thought of Karina at the age of 3 and 4 and the completely different girl she is now.

WHAT EVERY THERAPIST SHOULD KNOW

The girl with RS often appears non-compliant or uncooperative and disinterested. Actually, she knows quite well what she wants to do, but she is simply incapable of making it happen because of her severe apraxia. She knows what she wants to say, but cannot say it. Given proper support and encouragement, she can make active choices. Having control over what she does is powerful motivation, which leads to greater cooperation and success.

The therapist must capture her attention and maintain emotional contact with her throughout the therapy session. If she feels too much pressure, she will withdraw and the benefits of therapy will be limited. Verbal input from the therapist is vital and can help her motor planning. Don't talk down to her.

> After being in therapy for about ten out of her eleven years of life, so far, every week of the year, and many days of every week, I certainly understand when Lyndie gives a therapist a hard time. She shows much more patience and perseverance than I know I would in the same situation. Like all of the rest of us, she just appreciates being treated with respect and then tries very hard to cooperate to the best of her abilities.

TREATMENT ASPECTS

Therapists and parents should be realistic about treatment goals, but not hopeless. Too often, goals are based on outdated literature that refers to RS as a degenerative disorder. We have come a long way in realizing that RS is not degenerative, and girls can continue to learn and gain skills throughout their lives. RS is no longer seen as a disorder with a progressively downward turn. Therapies are essential for the development and maintenance of skills.

We know that the greatest handicap for the girl with RS is the enormity of her physical impairments. This often overshadows her ability to prove her knowledge and understanding. The girl with RS understands far more than what meets the eye. She is capable of taking in much more information than she can give out. Until recently, girls and women with RS have been classified as mentally retarded with little or no room for improvement. Intuition has always told us that she understands a lot. Recent scientific studies have illustrated this point.

> Katie's cognitive abilities are pretty good. I cannot get through to therapists and teachers about her need to communicate. They want to start at such a small step with picture communication. I see so many of the girls catch on so fast. I believe a lot of Katie's tantrums would decrease if she had a means of communication.

With many disorders, repetition of the same activities over and over is reinforcing, and in time, will be "learned." However, in RS, no amount of repetition will completely restore hand function. It is not a matter of learning; it is a matter of making the brain connection necessary to carry through the required movement. Providing a variety of activities can lessen boredom and motivate her.

It is important to recognize that girls and women with RS have a severe delay in processing information. Apraxia makes it impossible for her to both think about it and do it as well. She does far better when she acts instinctively, without trying to figure out the movement or action in her head. It will take her longer to respond, so be patient with her efforts.

Finding positive and motivating activities that appeal to her emotions works best. Be patient. Giving verbal directions that call for her to think before she acts, may interfere with her ability to do so.

Since she uses one sensory channel at a time, looking and touching at the same time are as difficult as doing math and calisthenics at the same time. Choosing one impression at a time can greatly enhance her ability to concentrate.

Therapists should know that many of the behaviors seen in RS, particularly hand movements and breathing irregularities, are not under her control. They are happening *to her*, not *by her*. She can no more stop her hand movements, tooth grinding or hyperventilation at will that we can stop our hearts from beating at will. These behaviors increase when she is stressed and under pressure to perform. Instead of making demands, a positive approach with strongly motivating materials can help her temporarily "overcome" the severe apraxia and succeed. This is one reason why she is so successful at picking up pieces of food when she is incapable of picking up other objects, and why she can scratch her nose or rub her eyes when they hurt.

> Katie hyperventilates when she is stressed, and her breathing does get heavier as demands are placed on her. I have felt when a demand is being placed on her, she knows what she is supposed to do, but at that moment, can't get her hand to move, as she knows they are expecting her to "perform."

What is the MOVE program?

The philosophy and attitude of the MOVE program is, "Some things must be believed first before they can be seen," based on the idea that all children can progress in motor skills. The goal of the program is to start intervention early to try to eliminate some of the posture and positioning associated with scoliosis. In this program, every child is upright regardless of disability. The upright position allows the hips and lower body to straighten, the upper body to attain normal positioning, the diaphragm to lower, lungs to expand, and the intestines and all internal organs to remain in place. All of these aspects contribute to greater comfort.

> I believe in the MOVE program because the curriculum is available to all. The beauty is that it does not need to be done by a special education teacher. When our daughter was included for the first time at her neighborhood school, the MOVE program was done by our general education teacher and aides. We had a MOVE mentor come out and help whenever needed. The program is so logical and the curriculum is very concise and easy for anyone to understand. It can be carried out while a child is simultaneously working on a computer, or doing other things on an IEP. For example, we incorporated MOVE while working in the classroom, and we also had Lani sometimes use the walker at recess so that she could play independently with the students, and not require an adult at her side. The kids decided they wanted to teach her football, and they devised their own method of teaching her. She got the MOVE program, peer interaction, occupational therapy (encouraging her to hold the ball), and FUN, all at once! The MOVE staff is so positive in looking at the children's strengths and expanding on them. Although not all children may actually result in being able to walk independently, I firmly believe that all benefit from the program in that at least their health improves significantly as long as they're encouraged to be upright. Our daughter's respiratory problems ceased once we had her upright, and everything just got better after that. Lani did learn to sit, stand, and walk. Folks who saw her six years ago, before we began the MOVE program, are surprised to see how well she looks now. Before MOVE, her body was so atrophied, and she was very sickly, always on antibiotics. Today, her hips and legs have filled in beautifully and her physical stamina is always increasing.

PHYSICAL THERAPY

The goals of physical therapy are to maintain or increase motor skills, develop or maintain transitional skills, prevent or reduce deformities, alleviate discomfort and irritability, and improve independence. The physical therapist may assess and improve walking and sitting patterns, and monitor changes over time. The kind of approach taken will depend on her place in the staging process of RS. A physical therapy program must be individualized for each girl.

Stage 1 is usually overlooked. Many girls experience motor gains before a decline in hand function, play skills and communication emerges. Other girls are delayed in achieving motor milestones. As soon as a problem is detected, it is important to begin treatment in a physical therapy program aimed at independent sitting, standing and walking.

Stage 2 is characterized by a loss of developmental milestones. This may happen over a short period of time, but more often occurs gradually. Gross motor skills continue to be significantly better than fine motor skills. The beginning of physical problems such as toe-walking or scoliosis may be seen. An emphasis should be placed on range of motion and ambulation. If she has severe ankle pronation (turning in), shoe inserts or ankle foot orthoses (AFO's) are recommended. Using assistive devices for walking is sometimes difficult due to her lack of hand control. Sometimes, arm/hand/elbow splints may be helpful to decrease stereotypic movements and increase functional use of the hands for gross motor activities. In this stage, her movements take on an ataxic quality, marked by lack of balance and jerky tremors. She is often very apraxic and fearful of movement that she does not initiate. Great care must be taken to comfort her, telling her how you will move her before doing so. She experiences problems with depth perception and often fears going down stairs or even changing floor textures from tile to carpet. She may always be fearful of movements, but your understanding will go a long way toward making her more at ease. Her constant hand movements interfere with using her hands for support and protection. Give her opportunities to use them.

In **Stage 3**, deformities and contractures may develop. Kyphosis or scoliosis may become more obvious. Seating equipment should be adapted to her needs for postural alignment and comfort. She may continue to walk and remain in Stage 3 for the rest of her life. If she does not walk, effective methods for lifting and transporting are essential.

Stage 4 is defined by loss of mobility. She may be able to continue to participate in a supported transfer (from bed to chair, etc.). Scoliosis and contractures may worsen as she loses mobility. She will most likely have circulatory problems, particularly in the hands and feet, which become cold, bluish and swollen. Feeding problems may increase with difficulty chewing and swallowing. In this stage, therapy should focus on range of motion, transfer skills, positioning and lifting, and evaluation for adapted or custom seating. Some girls with RS do not progress to Stage 4.

AIMS OF PHYSICAL THERAPY

Physical therapy is used to:

- reduce apraxia
- stimulate hand use to assist in mobility
- achieve better balance reactions
- promote better coordination and balance
- reduce ataxia
- improve body awareness
- influence scoliosis
- give better range of motion in the joints
- reduce muscle pain
- maintain and improve mobility
- counteract spasticity
- increase protective responses

The therapist must carefully evaluate her movement patterns to determine any obstacles to her motor function. These patterns can be modified with the use of a therapy ball, facilitation of movement, tone reduction activities and eliciting balancing responses. The girl's tolerance must always be a considered, recognizing that she will probably resist being moved or manipulated.

Scoliosis and kyphosis often begin with tone problems, which are brought on by her inability to judge her own body's place in space (orientation in space). Tone altering activities, active exercise and passive range of movement exercises are helpful. Maintaining spinal alignment is important and can be facilitated by activities designed to provide proprioceptive (position in space), kinesthetic (sensations received from joints and muscles) and tactile (touch) awareness. Kinesthetic awareness combines proprioceptive and tactile input to give information on how the body is moving.

Girls who can walk should be encouraged to walk often. This stimulates the joints and muscles and helps her to better observe the environment. Patience is called for; she walks slowly and often stops or changes directions abruptly. Girls who do not walk should be encouraged to do weight bearing exercises and practice walking.

What IEP goals can be addressed by the physical therapist?

- Improve mobility in a variety of school settings including halls, classroom, playground, etc.
- Improve ability to get on and off the school bus
- Improve ability to access playground equipment
- Improve ability to perform transfers and/or transitional movements in a variety of school settings
- Improve strength and endurance needed for active participation throughout the school day
- The physical therapist can make recommendations for positioning equipment, develop standing programs if appropriate, and serve as a consultant for adaptive physical education.

P.T. HELPFUL HINTS

Encourage her to participate in physical activity so she can learn how her body moves and reacts.

- Use stroking and massage to increase body awareness and relaxation and to decrease hypersensitivity.
- Name the parts of the body as they are being stroked or massaged.
- Tell her what you are about to do, or how you are going to move her.
- Put her joints through full range of motion to prevent contractures and the decline of mobility.
- Provide weight bearing exercises that encourage protective responses in the arms.
- Provide appropriate seating at all times.
- Try to keep her as active as possible.
- Keep her moving with the physical support she needs.
- Use a ball pool, waterbed, or trampoline for her to lie on to provide sensory stimulation if she is immobile.
- Allow adequate time for transition to a different activity or position.
- Provide gross motor activities that involve the entire body.
- Provide vestibular (balancing) movements like swinging, which stimulates other sensory systems.
- Provide strong gross motor stimulating activities, which open her senses.
- Integrate music into the P.T. program to keep her attention for longer periods of time.
- React with sound echoing her sound when she tries to express an emotion.
- Listen for and respond to any words she says appropriately.
- Using elbow splints may free her hands for functional support in gross motor skills such as walking or creeping.
- Foot deformities can be minimized by using exercise and short leg and ankle splints.
- Use a mirror to let her see her movements.

OCCUPATIONAL THERAPY

Occupational therapy provides ways to help her increase use of her body, particularly her hands. The byword of the O.T. is "adapt," whether it is the activity, materials or the environment. The O.T. is very skilled at making an unattainable goal achievable. Since the girl with RS has so much difficulty using her hands, occupational therapy is essential for most of her activities of daily living. Increasing her hand use gives her satisfaction, confidence and great joy.

One important area for O.T. concentration is eating. Some girls do not lose feeding skills altogether, while others do. It may take intensive effort for her to relearn to feed. The most effective approach is giving physical assistance with a long range goal to decrease the level of assistance over time. It is helpful to provide an adapted spoon, cup and dish with plate guard or inner lip plate. There is a wide range of adaptive feeding equipment available that can make at least some independent feeding possible for almost any girl with RS.

> At Molly's private occupational therapy program, the people seemed more in touch with her than anyone else we had ever dealt with. The staff was incredibly tuned in to where she was at when she arrived. They would look at her and decide what she needed that day based on the way she was acting. Of all the people who ever worked with Molly, these were the ones I trusted the most. The people at this program gave me the feeling that the brain could improve, that there was the hope of improvement. This was one of the most positive environments Molly was ever in. No matter what she did, it was wonderful—even when she picked her nose! These people were so positive about everything that Molly did, I thought they were total Pollyannas. Little did I realize then that this would see me through years of public school when so often I was only told what Molly could not do. They gave me the confidence to realize just how together Molly was. They gave me back a perfect child.

> Week after week, the O.T. would have Lyndie do often frustrating fine motor activities, such as trying to put blocks in a bucket or pick up puzzle pieces. This is such a tall order for Lyndie. Sometimes the therapist would put her on the computer, and sometimes she would enjoy it, sometimes not. At times, she would put Lyndie on a bolster swing, much to her delight. Other times the swing made her scream. Needless to say, no one ever knew what kind of a session would be in store for the therapist, or for Lyndie.

> I finally convinced the therapist that Lyndie truly could make some choices, if she only offered them to her. She finally conceded and wrote down a few choices. She used pictures first; it took her a while to believe that she had some reading skills. From the first week when she began offering Lyndie a choice of what activity she wanted to do that day, she was like a new person. She very rarely is uncooperative anymore. She now has been given some control over what she is to do for the day. I can't help but think how very upsetting it would be for me, if I were feeling very dizzy on a given day, hyperventilating to beat the band, and that's the day the therapist decided to rock me back and forth on the platform swing. No wonder she would yell. She loves having a say in it now. She chooses if she wants to be in the gym (if so, which swing does she want to go on?), or if she wants to do the computer (if so, which software?), or if she wants to play a game (if so, chooses the game), or if she wants to do something with her hands (if so, Playdoh, or shaving cream, or lotion, or bubbles). Her YES/NO choices are always available if the therapist is in doubt.

Occupational therapy can also address problems with sensory processing. In RS, the sensory information coming into the brain is not well organized, making it difficult for the girl to respond appropriately to the information she is receiving from her environment. Sensory integrative therapy, using techniques such as brushing, swinging, tactile activities and joint compression can help her organize the information so that she is better able to respond.

> We use a brushing program, with firm strokes, and joint compression every two hours. This is good not only for tactile hypersensitivity (not liking touch) , but also for proprioceptive input (sensory feedback) that the body obviously does not get on its own. Firm pressure and joint compression integrates this natural sensory mechanism.

Occupational therapists are some of the most creative people in the world. Sometimes, it is amazing what they can come up with – a simple solution to a very complicated problem. An attitude of warmth and caring can work wonders.

> A helpful suggestion coming out of an O.T. assessment of Kim's balance and walking was tying bells on her shoes. This was so that she could hear when her feet hit the ground, since she can-

not feel her feet hit the ground. Many people, including teachers, have commented that she walks better with the bells.

We've been very fortunate to have therapists who really enjoying working with special needs children and love them for who they are. I believe this is the key factor in how Kara responds during her sessions. She currently has an O.T. who seems to struggle with her personal feelings. She's harsh, impatient, and rushes her through the session. I strongly believe Kara is able to pick up on this and therefore, doesn't respond to her very well. I've heard repeated stories from her P.T. and classroom teacher whereby the O.T. will ask Kara to do something and she won't do it. The P.T. will then ask her to perform the same task and Kara will respond positively.

Kara's very first O.T. was harsh in her mannerisms but yet was very encouraging and always praised her whenever she did something positive. Kara made great gains. I believe the attitude and approach taken with our girls, coupled with lots of praise, is the passport as to whether we experience positive or delayed results.

When a girl with RS is able to carry through a movement or say something, it comes from her heart, not her head. So, when she does succeed, it is a real cause for celebration. She may say an appropriate phrase, or perform a motor movement that is never repeated again. When this happens, she has broken through the apraxia to give us a rare glimpse of what she is capable of understanding.

What IEP goals can be addressed by the occupational therapist?

- Identify and encourage use of head, elbows, or other body parts over which she may have better control.
- Maximize hand use for functional activities.
- Develop ability to access communication devices.
- Develop ability to access a variety of assistive technology.
- Improve ability to assist with dressing.
- Improve ability to perform independent feeding skills.
- Improve ability to assist with grooming activities.
- Improve ability to tolerate sensory input in school setting.

The occupational therapist can also serve as a consultant, recommending classroom modifications needed to improve the girl's ability to participate in school-related activities and with peers. The O.T. can also monitor the need for adaptive equipment and make recommendations.

O.T. HELPFUL HINTS

- Try to minimize distractions at first, gradually moving the situation closer to reality (less secluded).
- Look for what she intended to do with her hands; not just the end result.
- Provide physical assistance in the amount needed at first. Guide her through the motions with your hand over hers.
- Restrain or hold the non-dominant hand down to increase function in the dominant hand during functional activities.
- Weighted vests can be calming and decrease ataxia in some girls.
- Splints can be used to hold the thumb in a better position for picking up objects.
- During the regression stage, do not place primary importance on fine motor skills. Instead, provide hand activities that give enjoyment, such as splashing water or beating the drum.

- Adapt objects, materials and equipment so they are easier to grasp or maneuver.
- Use utensils with special cuffs or loops; plates with an edge to rest the spoon, and cups with a semi-circle cutout for the nose.
- Use switches for battery-operated toys or devices which can be operated by simple pressure or touch.
- Switches can also be used to achieve independence by activating any electrical appliance, operating computers, turning lights on and off, starting the TV/VCR, running a mixer or blender, etc.
- Place and hold objects of varying weight and texture in her hands.
- Fix objects to her hands with Velcro, masking tape or ace bandage.
- Put her hands in a pan of water, sand, snow, shaving cream, Jell-o, beads, beans, balls...whatever she might like to feel with her fingers.
- Massage her hands with a vibrator or brush.
- Promote arm extension movements by progressively increasing the distance she has to reach for an object.

SPEECH THERAPY

Rett syndrome is known to affect expressive language (communicating with others) far more than it affects receptive language (understanding). Apraxia and more basic motor difficulties which involve chewing and swallowing combine with a lack of words or effective body language to make finding ways a girl can communicate functionally quite challenging. Speech-language therapists sometimes want to work on "speech readiness" skills such as making and imitating different sounds for several years before turning to other methods. In RS, however, these speech readiness skills may be absent and remain so. The girl with RS may demonstrate her potential for communicating in other ways, such as showing her ability to understand language.

In addition, therapists sometimes spend hours preparing the girl to use a communication device by asking her to touch pictures or objects named over and over or to match pictures with objects. She may rebel at this, possibly thinking, "I already showed her I could do that. Why is she asking me again?" Other girls are simply inconsistent in their responses from day to day, so that it is impossible to obtain a goal of 90% accuracy three days in a row, as is sometimes stated in IEP's. Therapists should assume that the concept is understood with a couple of correct responses and be willing to move on. Because her frustration comes much more from her inability to express herself than to understand, therapy should focus on increasing expressive communication. If she does not recognize pictures at first, she will learn the meaning through successes. For example, when using a voice output device, the message for the picture is heard each time, and someone responds in a way that teaches its function and usefulness. When you think you hear her say a word, you did! Respond appropriately.

Speech-language therapists need to work together with other therapists, staff and families to explore potentially successful means of communication, effective positioning and needed vocabulary. When new methods or devices are tried, it may be best to limit their use to specific times of the day or specific activities. It is better to enrich a single activity really well, than to water things down in a way which is never really helpful.

Sessions may best take place in the classroom or throughout the school or home, to practice and make the use of new communication methods both fun and functional. Additional time for developing systems, programming devices and training staff and families may need to be built into a therapist's scheduled time. Sessions might also be combined with those of other therapists so that movement, sequencing and communication all occur together. The girl with RS should be seen regularly, although frequency may vary, for the amount of time she can stay focused. Frequency of sessions may need to increase when a new communication method is introduced and tried until the girl, staff and family are familiar with it and comfortable using it in functional settings.

What IEP goals can be addressed through speech therapy?

- Utilize individualized communication strategy (AAC, FC, Yes/No, etc.)
- Communicate information
- Communicate knowledge
- Make choices
- Increase socialization with peers
- Communicate health feelings
- Increase class participation

MUSIC THERAPY

Music has always had a strong influence on behavior. It provides a powerful means to express emotions, thoughts and experiences. As the famous composer Johann Sebastian Bach said, music has the power to "restore health to our souls." Studies have shown that hearing and making music have a positive effect on the brain, increasing blood circulation, glucose and oxygen. These changes stimulate learning.

Music therapy is the structured use of music or musical activities under the direction of a trained music therapist. These activities influence changes in behavior patterns that lead to specific individual goals that have been set for the child. Music therapy intervention focuses on acquiring non-music skills such as communication, socialization, choice making and motor skills. For girls with RS, music therapy is an excellent supplement to other forms of therapy. Music provides a sense of perception and movement rhythm, and the therapist creates musical "curves of excitement," calling on her to respond to the music with her own actions. She learns to feel and understand time and space, quality and quantity, and cause and effect. Provided in trusting, non-threatening atmosphere, music therapy can yield:

- The stimulation of a variety of musical experiences: texture pitch, mood, pace, intensity, idiom-style.
- Opportunities to enjoy making music spontaneously.
- Experience of movement and playing instruments that can promote body awareness and a more purposeful use of her hands.
- Musically induced relaxation to facilitate freedom of movement and expression.
- Opportunities for communication and self-expression.
- Stimulation for meaningful eye contact.
- Motivation for the extending of attention and concentration span.
- A basis for increased memory/recall.
- A stimulus for decreasing the "delayed response."
- Facilitation in grasping/holding.
- Improvement in self-image and self-esteem.
- Impetus for sensory-motor development.
- Favorable settings for social and emotional growth.
- An increase in vocalization.

How can I convince her school to provide music therapy?

You may want to ask your daughter's physician or neurologist for a recommendation for music therapy. Remember to stress the fact that girls with RS are very motivated by music. It calms them when they are anxious, and allows them to communicate feelings they cannot otherwise express. To have music therapy provided through your daughter's IEP, you may need to be persuasive. Be prepared with written materials supporting the importance of music therapy for girls with RS. You may need to find a registered or certified Music Therapist to do the initial music therapy assessment. You will probably have to pay for it and may be able to be reimbursed by the school system. The assessment will include a recommendation for treatment.

How often should she have Music therapy?

As often as she can! Some music therapists recommend two thirty minute individual sessions a week and once or twice a week group music therapy.

Where can I find a certified Music Therapist?

Locating a good therapist may be a challenge. In some parts of the country, music therapists are more difficult to find. Use contacts in the disability community to find someone who may qualify. Contact the music therapy consultant for the school district, the department of music therapy at a college or university, professionals in other fields who may know of a music therapist. Mental health care facilities may be a source. Contact the American Music Therapy Association, (301) 589-3300.

MUSIC THERAPY HELPFUL HINTS

- The setting for music therapy sessions should be quiet, without distractions. Sessions should be held about the same time of day in the same room.
- It is very important to establish a relationship between therapist and child. Establish contact through eye contact, finger movement, a smile or a look. This may take some time, as she becomes adjusted to the surroundings of the music therapy setting.
- The therapist should nurture contact with the child. It is essential to see her contribution to the session as valuable.
- Each girl has her own taste for music and sound. It is good to use short, repetitive, rhythmical songs when she is young. The repetition makes it familiar, and this provides confidence and security.
- Use music with a strong rhythm. It organizes her inner pulse and rhythm.
- Use movement songs, beginning with hand over hand assistance, then modeling, encouraging her to try and copy your movements.
- Remember her delayed response and always give her plenty of time to respond.
- Make a page or card for each song, and slowly introduce the songs with the card. Fold the card in two parts, one with a picture (symbol) of the song, and the other with a word describing the song. Then let her choose the song she would like to play or hear.
- Sing familiar songs.
- Sing in a high pitch.
- Sing softly close to her ear.
- Make up your own songs with the appropriate text. Use her name and familiar things and people in the song.

What IEP goals can be addressed through music therapy?

Stress that music works on the development of the following skills:
- To enhance purposeful hand use – while playing instruments.
- To develop vocalization – through music.
- To build independence – choosing songs and activities.
- To communicate – in musical activities through picture symbols.
- To increase cognition – by raising the level of focus, attention, anticipation and imitation.
- To improve gross motor movements – through movement songs.
- To increase socialization – through participation.

HYDROTHERAPY

Hydrotherapy (movement in warm water) is essential for the girl with RS. Due to her apraxia, she is unable to plan and carry out movements she would like to make, and walking is always insecure. When other forms of mobility are decreased or lost, movement in water is still possible. Spontaneous movement is much easier in water and hydrotherapy increases range of motion and reduces spasticity. Sensory and perceptual difficulties which she feels on the ground are not present when she is in water, so she is able to achieve better balance without hesitation and fear. Viscosity and pressure provide proprioceptive and tactile stimulation. The water provides support for her limbs, giving her the confidence she needs to bear weight. This helps her to increase muscle bulk, strength and flexibility. The warmth of the water helps to calm the involuntary movements, hand stereotypies and breathing irregularities and increases passive range of motion to a greater degree. Flexibility of the water allows her to move in all planes and allows symmetrical movement which may be difficult on the ground. Buoyance relieves her of her weight, and allows the therapist to provide  treatment with greater and less effort by lifting her into desired positions. It also provides her with support for movement, allowing her to move more easily. Hydrotherapy contributes to the health of muscle and nerve, which her inactivity on ground impairs. It promotes her overall health and well-being, which greatly add to her capacity to learn.

HYDROTHERAPY HELPFUL HINTS

- The water should be warm, from 96 to 100 degrees.
- If she is thin, she may chill easily. Keep her wrapped in a towel before and after she enters the water.
- Keep movements gentle and subtle until she adjusts to the water.

HIPPOTHERAPY

Therapeutic horseback riding (hippotherapy) is enjoyed by many girls. This activity helps promote balance and torso strength, and requires the use of her hands, thus minimizing hand stereotypies and increasing functional hand use. She gains a sense of control, which gives her confidence and satisfaction. Being on the back of a moving horse also helps her experience the rhythm she needs to walk.

> Taylor is very comfortable on the pony and shows excellent balance. Her normal hand mouthing activity is virtually stopped while she is riding. She has a huge smile and lets out periodic bursts of happiness with her voice. Two people work with her at a time. One leads the pony and the other walks along side with an arm around Taylor's backside. She especially likes it when they trot. The instructors occasionally spin her around backwards on the saddle, to stimulate different muscle groupings. She is a little nervous when they are repositioning her, but she is just as happy forward and backward as long as they are moving. Taylor has begun to hold the reins all by herself instead of holding just the saddle knob. The instructors press her legs into the pony when starting from a stop. I'm sure that in time, Taylor will learn the correlation they are patiently teaching her. This is a wonderful activity and something Taylor can enjoy forever.

> Chelsey smiled almost the whole time she was riding. She even held on to the saddle most of the time. They walked her up to a huge mirror in the arena and told her to look at herself and Mr. Snipper, and she looked and smiled. That really surprised me! Chelsey has never been one to look in a mirror.

Karina rides 45 minutes without putting her hand in her mouth! From the beginning, we warned her that she had to stop riding if she did not hold on to the saddle. When she started to take off her protective cap, we did the same. She learned quickly after she had to dismount a couple of times. Now the teacher is teaching her to sit upright, as she tends to let her head hang low.

I can still remember the first day of riding, a month or so before her third birthday. I put my little girl on top of this massive animal and watched them walk away. When she was on the far opposite side of the ring 150 feet away, I realized that was the first time in her life she had ever been that far away from both parents at once. Over the time she has been riding, we have seen Naomi make tremendous strides in her awareness and responsiveness.

Kim has been riding for about 2 years with Riding for the Disabled. She was assessed, and now rides the police horses which are very big – many were once racehorses – but are very well trained and don't frighten easily. They are trained to tolerate people jumping out of trees at them! Once the horse moves her balance is excellent. Her holding on to the saddle is inconsistent unless the path of the horse keeps changing! So they never walk her in a straight line! She cannot manage to hold reins. Sometimes she has to trot, but as she cannot rise up and down she rather goes "plop plop plop" or "flop flop flop" with people on each side holding her on and running along beside her! Kim shrieks with excitement.

LOVE THERAPY

Sometimes it's hard to keep up with therapy appointments. There are never enough hours in the day to do all that we want to. Don't get so busy running from one appointment to another that you forget the most important therapy of all, love therapy. It comes from your heart, your touch, your voice – all the things that say "I love you just the way you are."

Love therapy is the basis for all other therapies — acceptance, protection, patience, tolerance and understanding. All of the expensive and complicated therapies in the world cannot work without it. It starts with recognizing her as an important part of her family, her community, her world, our world. It wraps her up in the warm embrace of our belief that she is valuable and loved, no matter what she may ever achieve. It hears her cries and gives comfort, patiently awaits her sunny smiles with joy and tucks her in gently at twilight. It raises its fists for her when obstacles arise, and cradles her tenderly during long sleepless nights. Love does not give up in the face of adversity. It grows stronger.

The author wishes to thank the following professionals for ideas and information which was used to develop this chapter: Cochavit Elefant, RMT; Cathy Gaines, CCC-SLP, EdS; Susan Hanks, PT; Barbro Lindberg; Meir Lotan, LPT; Linda Reece, OTR/L; Clive Robbins, RMT; Jan Townsley, OTR/L; Marjorie McClure, Ph.D..

FRIENDS AND FUN

CIRCLES OF FRIENDS

Shelly has a great smile. I love her very much. Shelly and I laugh a lot when I sing to her. On Christmas, I help her open her presents and I help her play with them. Shelly makes me feel happy because she always has a smile on her face. She makes me feel better when I'm sad. The kids at school fight over her because everybody likes her.

Ashley Borchardt

Your daughter may be a child with RS, but first and foremost, she is a child. She may need therapies, braces and adapted equipment. Often, she may need medicines and special foods. She may need lots of patience from time to time. Now and then she may need extra attention. But always and forever, she needs friends. And she needs fun! Remember that your daughter is more like other children than unlike them. Fun is good for everyone!

You may think some things are impossible until you try them. Sometimes it's hard to come up with activities that she enjoys. Take a look at what some families and friends have come up with.

On a day to day basis it is very hard to make the time to keep our girls involved. I remember weekends when Jocelyn seemed very bored, and why not? During school she had a 1:1 aide to keep her involved all day. Unfortunately I had many more responsibilities to the whole family to be at Jocelyn's disposal all day just for fun and attention. I would plop her in the middle of the action whatever was going on. Making times for reading, music, watching television together...but it can't happen all day long! We kept busy with other kids' sports as well as their friends. As Jocelyn got a bit older and went to school, she also had friends over. Amazing, they thought of the coolest things to do and didn't even need my help. They played hide and seek, wheelchair races-with one of Jocelyn's old spares, swimming, told stories and jokes, dressed Joce up in different outfits. They sometimes played games including Jocelyn as part of a team member. As they got older, they would all go on trips to the movies, shopping, beach, out to eat, whatever was going on. Non-disabled kids have the same problems of being bored sometimes, but don't need the intense assistance that our girls do. Jocelyn still had some of these days but I didn't feel that it was up to me to keep her constantly entertained and I told her that she'd have to find ways to make her own entertainment at times. Check out the kids in your neighborhood or school. They may be interested in getting to know your daughter and what things she likes. Jocelyn has always had a fairly ready supply of friends willing to help and assist her. (Well, not always but usually they are around if you look and ask – two very key ingredients!) They come and go, but I've found that as some go, others come.

When Rachel is home from school, I am always at a loss how to play with her. I worry that she gets bored. She likes videos, but we try to keep them to a minimum. Her reaction depends on the mood she is in, like any of us. At school they do something called circle time and we imitate this at home with the other children. Rachel also loves interactive songs. Since she cannot use her hands at all, I take her hands or arms and move them to the motions to songs that she likes. She also loves it when her siblings help her to dance or sway to music. She thinks it's great when Papa wrestles with her. I confess that sometimes I don't have a clue what to do. I try to pay attention to what she seems to be interested in and then help her to do it as best we can. I realized it didn't have to be large chunks of time, just little bits here and there throughout the day.

Korie loves to swim. In order to give her total freedom in the pool, she wears a ski belt which we ordered from a sportsmen catalog and water wings on her arms. The water wings can be purchased at any toy, discount, or pool store. With this equipment Korie is completely free and swims all over the pool. Besides the enjoyment she gets from swimming, it's also very therapeutic. The belt and water wings force her to keep her body upright and in order to move in the water, she needs to kick. Swimming is by far, her favorite sport.

On skit night at camp, "Melinda and the Merrills" got on stage and presented "Brush Your Teeth." Mom and Melinda did the Raffi song accompanied by the audience, and then Melinda activated her Big Mac switch which said "No mom, I want to do it a different way!" So Melinda and her siblings put on their baseball caps and shades, and waved their toothbrushes to a rap version of "Brush Your Teeth" - (Rappin' Raffi). The crowd loved it! It was really fun!

Heather doesn't crawl and can only walk with her hands held, but she is a real daredevil. She loves motion! Her favorites are swinging real high, go cart rides, ferris wheels, and lately the umbrella ride at fairs. She also enjoys swimming, horseback riding, music, and of course anything Disney!

Amanda loves to read books and play with and get licked by her black dog, Annie. Annie is the single best investment we made in terms of therapy. Amanda can walk to Annie to get "dog licks." Music is also great, especially with funny or rhyming words and songs. She loves when we are animated.

Get inside gross motor equipment for the younger or ambulatory kids. We have a large swing with a mirror, platform swing, slide and trampoline in our house.

Briana and I fingerpaint and play with a variety of different textured toys and foods. Sometimes playtime is also learning time. I play music, and march her back and forth through the living room, or we march up and down the stairs. We play dress up and sometimes even do baths for fun. In the summer it is hard to get Briana away from her pool, so I make the tub her winter pool and we splash, and play and giggle.

We use interactive CD's for the computer, or just roll around on the floor hugging and kissing. I also do mud pies on the kitchen floor, re-pot plants, smash Jello Jigglers...whatever holds her attention.

Here are Naomi's suggestions for fun:
• Bubbles. A big favorite.
• A small battery powered keyboard. We found one with keys that light up as they play, and invested in a lot of ni-cad batteries to keep it going.
• Picture magazines. Old National Geographics are some of the best; check yard sales.
• Finger painting (Naomi's grasp is not consistent enough for markers or brushes, but art projects are good for all kinds of kids).
• Mylar balloons. Great when fully inflated, even better for fine motor manipulation as they lose pressure.
• Soft balls of various sizes. Foam ones that are easy to grab are some of the best. With many of these, you can experiment and improvise to make up your own. Let your daughter be your guide. Have fun!

Pool balls – round, multicolored, plastic balls like you'd see in kid's sections at amusement parks – are one of Korie's favorite toys at school so we ordered some for home. I bought a large inflatable pool and put the balls in it. It worked out great, until we got a dog. Dog nails and inflatable pools do not go together. However, Grandpa came to the rescue. He went to Toys-R-Us and found a circus tent made for the plastic balls. In addition to the section that holds the balls, the tent sits up off the ground on a trampoline. Korie absolutely loves it. She not only gets to play with the balls, but she gets to bounce around at the same time.

Wondering about gifts? How about a boom box with a switch hooked up to it so she can turn on her own music? Or a beautiful snow globe that plays music? I found gloves with velcro on them so when you throw a ball at her hand it will stick. She thinks that is very funny. We do have a problem getting the ball unstuck sometimes and that is just as funny. We also get books to read to her. Books on tape are another option. Cassette tapes are a standard for us. I just got a catalog in the mail from a company that makes puzzles with big sticks projecting from each piece. Some of the girls may enjoy a Mr. Potato head massager. Some of the older girls may like a regular back or foot massager.

We bought an inflatable moon bounce at Wal-Mart. Then we bought a box of the ball pit balls like they use at McDonald's, and filled the moon bounce thing with them. Shanda loves this. She can play in there by herself or with her little brother and sister.

One of the ski resorts in our area had a program in which they guaranteed they could get anyone skiing. Well this was just to much of a challenge to pass up! We decided to give it a go. The equipment that was selected for Jocelyn was called a bi-ski. Basically it is a seat with rests for the feet mounted on a pair of short skis that are connected to each other. She is strapped in very securely and wears a helmet for additional protection. She is able to go up all the ski lifts, except gondolas, including the chair lifts and can ski on any part of the mountain. The bi-ski is controlled by an instructor specially trained in using this equipment. The instructor skis behind Jocelyn guiding the bi-ski down the slope with two tether straps. On her first time out we all skied all over the mountain, even down a race course. Jocelyn and I raced. I won! I was surprised that not only did skiing with this equipment not slow us down, but with an experienced instructor I actually have to work to keep up with them! Jocelyn likes to go fast and does not like waiting in line at the bottom for the lift at all.

We wanted a bike for Korie, but she can't support herself on a regular bike. We didn't let this stop us. We took 1.5" wide flat stock aluminum and secured it to the base of a tricycle. We then attached a go-cart seat and headrest to the aluminum for a backrest and headrest. We placed 2" wide Velcro to the aluminum and backrest for hip and chest support. To allow Korie to pedal, adjustable roller skates, minus the wheels, were fastened to the foot pedals. A pulley was added to the handle bars with a rope through it and attached to the pedals keep her feet in the correct position. He welded the handle bars to the frame to keep the front wheel straight and also put a long-upright handle in the back for me to push her (we must think about our backs too!). He also used aluminum for added support from the bike to the handle. For that personal touch we put a bike basket on the back support so we can take a drink and snacks with us on our walks. The total cost of the adapted tricycle was $100. In the nice weather, Korie and I take nightly walks when she rides her tricycle. She not only gets exercise, which is important, but she also has a good time, which to me is more important.

We made Korie a platform swing which she likes to swing and bounce on. We started with a 3' x 3' piece of plywood, covered it with foam and plastic upholstery and drilled holes in each corner to put rope through. Three feet above the swing we put a 3' x 3' frame made from PVC pipe, and attached the rope to it. The swing is secured with a heavy-duty spring to a hook in the ceiling. She holds herself upright, which strengthens her torso muscles. This toy provides both enjoyment and therapy.

One day I was thinking that Korie might enjoy a Jolly Jumper being that she enjoys bouncing so much, not to mention the benefits to her leg muscles. I made a pattern for the seat from her walker, cut it out of heavy material and sewed it together. I constructed the square frame from PVC pipe. After we were sure it would fit, we glued the pipe to the elbows and attached the rope and spring. We then hung it from a hook in the ceiling, the same hook we used for the platform swing. We found out that the swing was a great toy for one of our other granddaughters, too.

Mary used her rocking horse until she was 12. She also was a master at jumping on beds and loved the glider swing. She seemed to seek her own vestibular stimulation, though she gave the rest of us heart attacks along the way.

Jocelyn has been on several canoe trips with different youth groups. We usually sit her in a short beach chair in the middle of the canoe. This way she is stable and comfortable. Then at different stops along the river, she can sit in the chair either on the beach or even in the water.

Karina loves music and also shows interest in playing instruments herself. At school they do a lot of singing and playing. She had individual music therapy several times, but there is not enough money for all the kids to have it, so she was left out this year. I asked an acquaintance who gives private piano lessons if he was interested in teaching Karina. Karina sat at the piano with the teacher next to her. She started to play with one finger of her left hand. She touched the keys very well. The teacher played with her, following her rhythm. She then began to use her right hand, to my utter amazement (she never uses that hand) and played with both hands! It was not just hitting, she was deliberately touching, as she listened to her own music. I asked her to play from low keys to high keys. She played a tone ladder as good as you or I would have done. She played with one finger at the time, and then with several fingers at once, imitating chords. When the teacher stopped playing, she stopped too, took his hand and replaced it on the piano to say, "Come on!" We decided that she will have a lesson every two weeks for 45 minutes. The teacher was impressed, and he is making plans for teaching her to play simple songs. Something I would have laughed at just one day ago. I was taken by surprise, and realized once more that it is easy to underestimate my daughter. I tell that to her teachers, and to everyone around her.

Kori's aunt and uncle dropped off a large cardboard barrel which we carpeted, hoping she would crawl through it. While she doesn't crawl through it, she does ride it like a horse. We made an activity box from a 2' x 2' x 2' square wooden box which we covered with carpeting. We placed Velcro on the back of some of her favorite toys and stuck them on the box. If she wants to play with the toys, she has to use her arms or hands to get at or activate the toys.

Fun stuff Katie likes to do includes horseback riding, swimming, playing with bubbles and balls, riding in the car, pestering her brother and sister, swinging on the porch swing, taking baths, and just being around other kids. She likes Barney and dances along to the songs on the videos, and enjoys books. Also, she is always the first one up in the morning. She has made it her official job to go around from bedroom to bedroom and wake everyone up. If they don't cooperate, she crawls in with them, or else gives them a smack on the head. And she loves to eat junk food, especially potato chips!

Does your daughter get a lot of stuffed animals and you don't know what to do with them? We solved that problem with a pole plant hanger. Instead of hanging plants on it, we hang her stuffed animals.

Life with my daughter Jessica is great. We have times when things go wrong, like illnesses and falls. But for the most part, it is a wonderful life. Jessica is so funny at times. We call her our little tom-boy. She would rather be out mowing the yard (she rides on the riding lawnmower) with her daddy than eating (and believe me she loves to eat.) If she is in the house when he starts it up, she goes to the door and stands there and if I don't get the message she comes to me and starts fussing louder and louder, until I finally understand what she wants. When she gets on the mower she looks down to see if any grass is coming out the chute. And you can see her watching it all around the yard. To us, it's funny to see a little girl enjoy stuff like that. She also loves to ride 4-wheelers, but not as much as the lawnmower.

Sometimes, friends are not so much fun after all. There will always be "off" days when things don't go the way we want them to. It's all a part of life.

When I think Sherry's feelings might be hurt, I talk to her about it. After all, everybody gets their feelings hurt sometimes. When somebody insults or teases our "normal" child, don't we acknowledge it and try to explain why people can be that way? Once a little child came over and was playing with a huge ball that Sherry has. He tossed it to everybody in the house, but when it came to Sherry, he wouldn't do it. He would start to, but back off. After he left, I talked to Sherry about it. I said, "it bothered you that he wouldn't play ball with you, didn't it?" I explained I thought he was probably afraid, and he was just a little kid. But I think it would have been wrong to force him. I think that would have done more harm than good. Besides, who wants to play with someone who is forced to play with you? Or interact with you? There are plenty of willing players. At a family gathering a while back, a second cousin that we don't see very often was there. She was tossing the ball to everybody and she very naturally included Sherry in the fun. Sherry had a blast. And so it goes.

Real friends don't care if your socks don't match

EDUCATION AND LEARNING

"A PENNY FOR YOUR THOUGHTS"

COMPREHENSION

We learn something new about Rett syndrome all the time. It doesn't always happen at the molecular level, nor is it always a startling scientific revelation. But every day we hear something more about the capabilities of girls with Rett syndrome. Like our girls, we have a lot to learn. Years ago, when we heard of a child who was making *progress*, we said it certainly couldn't be Rett syndrome. A number of medical articles called RS a form of dementia. One of the first news articles said that girls with Rett syndrome always die in their teens. Most of the medical literature was worse than bleak. Getting the diagnosis of Rett syndrome was nothing short of devastating. The diagnosis and the handicaps are. But not the child within. Her little soul and spirit are there just as they were before, probably stronger and fuller than was ever recognized.

Years ago, we called persons with Down syndrome by the terrible term, "Mongolian idiots." That's what we believed, and that's what they became, because that's what we expected of them. People used to say that kids with Down syndrome were "such happy children" and that's all that was ever expected of them. There was no trust, no faith, little hope for what they could learn or do. Parents were told to institutionalize their kids from birth and "get on with life." Somewhere along the way, someone got daring enough to try and to believe that kids with Down syndrome could learn. Now, some years later, we know of course that kids with Down syndrome can learn an awful lot. That's what we expect of them nowadays. They go to kindergarten and are expected to learn the alphabet, and many of them do. Some even go on to achieve much greater things.

When we're told that our child will be impaired, all of the faith and trust and belief we have are at once shattered. We may fight against it with no less fury than a stampede of wild elephants, but ultimately, most of us accept the inevitable. We do away with expectations. We lose touch with our old dreams because they're out of reach. And sometimes those dreams turn into nightmares as we face the challenges in our new existence in the subculture of *"the handicapped."* Sometimes we're so caught up in it that we forget to make new dreams or to even have the faith that they could exist now that the old ones have been forsaken. We dare not make new dreams because it hurt too much when we lost them before. Instead of remaining our "child," she becomes our *"handicapped* child" and everything takes on new meaning with the new label.

When RS first came to the attention of the American medical community, researchers devised a strict list of diagnostic and supportive criteria and a staging system for describing the natural history. One of the items on the list was "severe mental retardation." However, in 1988, an international team called the RS Diagnostic Criteria Work Group, which was comprised of the foremost authorities in the field, changed the wording to "apparent severe mental retardation," because there was increasing evidence that dementia, an ongoing process, was not accurate. Although all girls with RS *functioned* in the severely retarded range, there was no adequate way of testing their true intelligence. This was the very first hint of a new horizon. It was for the first time accepted that mental retardation in RS was presumed in the absence of a good way to disprove it.

About this time, when parents described higher functions in their daughters, most everyone said, "must not be RS!" *Progress?!* There was nothing in the literature about progress. "Must be someone who doesn't know anything about RS." The "progressive" in RS didn't mean progress. Because we didn't expect progress, we didn't look for it.

Most everyone described bright eyes and a knowing look, the on-again off-again feeling that they were are "in there." Slowly we realized that parents weren't the only ones who were believing. It is not unusual for parents to believe – call it wishful thinking – that their child understands. But it is remarkable for teachers, doctors, therapists, friends and relatives to agree. In RS, they all agree that there is more than meets the eye. She understands far more than we can imagine. Just because she can't show it, doesn't mean she doesn't know it. Finally, after so many years, the medical community has begun to agree that her fundamental handicap is a physical one, one that can be measured. The problem is that we cannot adequately evaluate her mental capabilities.

How is progress measured? Of course, it is easier for the child who can walk to show us that she understands. She can come to the kitchen to show us she is hungry. The child with better preserved hand use can touch the book to tell us she wants a story. But what of the child who can't do either? Does it mean that she understands less? Not necessarily. In fact, keen observers have noted that often it is the girl who is least mobile who is seems to be taking in the most from her surroundings.

When you visit a roomful of severely handicapped kids or adults, it is easy to pick out the girl with RS. Not by looking at her hands, teeth grinding, spinal curvature or hyperventilation. Those are all good clues. But usually, the girl with RS stands out in the classroom among the others because she often is very observant, watching your every move. She seems to be taking a lot in. Her difficulty is getting anything out.

Can girls who have made progress have Rett syndrome? Think about Rett syndrome as a ladder with a bottom and a top and a lot of rungs in between. Since we don't know the basic nature or extent of the brain impairment in RS, why can't there be varied levels of ability? We see it all the time in other disabilities, like Down syndrome and cerebral palsy. Why shouldn't there be kids with RS who have varied abilities?

Some girls with RS got a bigger "dose" than others and will be more severely affected. Some will not make much progress, but some will. It probably has more to do with the "dose" of RS from the beginning. But how do we know? Can other girls do the same if we expect them to? If we believed that they could do it? If we looked for evidence of higher thought?

No one should feel guilty that their child didn't achieve because they didn't try. Many parents have spent most of the daylight hours working with their girls to try to get them to demonstrate knowledge. We would all die trying. Some families have patterned their girls for years without dramatic success. But maybe that is the key – what if they can't demonstrate it – does it mean that we should believe in them any less? Could it be that we just haven't devised a way to help them demonstrate their knowledge? Think about the number of times your daughter said something you thought was appropriate or acted like she understood.

"Typical" children are self-fulfilling prophecies. When we constantly tell them they are bad, or stupid, they know no other way to act. When we praise them for the good things they do and recognize their strengths, they live up to our expectations. If we give up at the outset and determine that our girls with RS will never achieve, for sure they will never achieve. Belief and praise won't strengthen muscles or stop seizures, nor can they miraculously conjure up ability that is not there. But belief helps us to recognize strength. Trust helps us to have confidence in our own ability to judge. And as the mothers and fathers of these girls, we are more equipped than anyone to be able to "read" them and to intuitively know when they're with us. We shouldn't be afraid to say so.

Imagine how it opens their world for our girls just to be able to communicate "yes" and "no!" And imagine how much they can tell us about what they know with these two little words – the two most powerful words in existence. We have to continue to find ways to reach our girls and teach them. But most of all we have to believe in them – because all of the modern technology in the world, all the switches and computers, all the bells and whistles, will not work if we do not believe and trust and expect it to happen. We are pioneers on the frontier of this new wave of thought. The new horizon is before us. It's before our reach. All we have to do is believe.

> *There is something much more scarce, something rarer than ability. It is the ability to recognize ability.*   ***Robert Half***

There are several important factors to take into consideration when trying to determine how much the girl with RS comprehends. The most important aspect is her delayed responses. It may take her some time to react to what she has been asked. Sometimes we make a request and then move on to make another request before she has had time to act on the first. She doesn't concentrate in a conventional way, so it may appear that she is not listening, distracted or bored. Her lack of eye-hand coordination and apraxia combine to make it difficult for her to give you the correct signals that she understands – whether it is by talking, acting or following directions. Add to this the fact she does one thing at a time. This is significant for intake and output issues (listen and do), but also important when  she is asked to do two things at once, such as walk toward an object and pick it up. For her, listening and reacting or walking and grasping are as confusing as trying to type and do math at the same time. She often uses one sensory channel at a time and becomes absorbed in it, tuning out the other senses to lessen her confusion. Asking her to follow verbal directions only makes it harder, because she has to think about how to do it. We wish she could follow the Nike philosophy and "Just do it", but she must have emotional motivation first so that she can act without thinking. All of these handicaps prevent her from fully participating in her world, which allows her to gain the necessary experience to reach her full potential. When you put it all together, you can understand that it is a difficult problem for her to show us how much she knows. We are left to rely on our interpretation and intuition, which may not always be correct. It is important to take into consideration all of her difficulties along with her own motivation and interests before judging her abilities. It is also helpful to recognize the difference between her "intellectual level" and her "functional" level. They are not the same.

> What matters is that I take Lauren from where she is now to as high as she can go in learning about her world. I do, however feel that for too many years I bought into the idea that Lauren could learn very little, and allowed her to be placed in classrooms where she learned almost nothing, and except for what we did with her, was not exposed to normal learning situations. As a result, she has very minimal understanding of many aspects of the world around her. As I have changed in my attitude, asked her what she understands and what she doesn't, and started really exposing her and explaining things to her, I'm amazed at the smiles I get when giving her much more advanced information.

> I think all the girls have a reasonable intelligence. Some are better able to show it, because they have less intrinsic motor problems and/or have learned to use communication tools. Girls who say an appropriate complete sentence once every five years or even once in a lifetime, don't become suddenly intelligent for one minute and then dumb again. They just have a rare moment when they can express themselves because they do it reflexively. On the other hand, its nice to know our girls have language even when they don't have speech.

Most experts who spend some quality time with RS girls agree; the girl with RS understands far more than she can tell us. Since it is easier for her to take information in than it is to interpret and act on it, she always takes in more than she gives out. She may seem disinterested or unresponsive, when in fact she is concentrating very hard on what is being said. Parents have many stories about how their daughters have shown what they understand. It is through these confirmations, and not through judging their outward appearance or their performance on standardized tests, that we come to understand how clever they really are.

> We are proud of her and have always known there is more substance to her than she is given credit for. All you have to do is spend some time with her and you realize she understands and will respond in her own way to everything that is said to her and even conversations that aren't directed to her.

> When Molly was considered to have autism, her disability was explained to me as difficulty processing information – both coming in and going out – like the wires were shorted. This always made sense to me, even when the diagnosis changed to RS. I don't think she decoded language very well or consistently – I think she was more together visually than auditorily – like maybe we should have screamed all the time because she really liked it when we screamed (we are a rather intense family). In my heart of hearts, I feel she was brilliant because who knows how it felt to be her and still get through the day and laugh and smile and connect with us? But convincing anyone else of her cognitive abilities was a mind-boggling challenge.

GOOD DAYS, BAD DAYS

> When Taylor has "good" days, she's happy, energetic, vocal, more open to change, very responsive and her cognitive level is high. When we play learning games on these days, she is usually correct in her responses 100 percent of the time. When Taylor has what I call "autistic" days, she's lethargic, inattentive, indifferent and either doesn't participate in the learning games or responds incorrectly. I can't link these changes in Taylor to medications, sleeping patterns, stress or diet.

> One problem is that sometimes our girls are "with it," and sometimes they are, as I put it with Sherry, "zoned out." So sometimes people see "evidence" of Sherry's comprehension, and sometimes she is unable to respond. I have explained to Sherry that each time she reaches somebody it is something important, and when she does, sometimes I will turn and whisper in her ear, "you are convincing them, aren't you?" or "you showed them you understand," and we smile over the victory. The results have been especially wonderful lately with some family members who always loved Sherry but didn't really understand her and who wanted to believe she could understand but hadn't had enough personal interaction with her to be sure about it. They get so excited! It's been a joy.

> I went to a school supply store and bought a package of 8x10 alphabet cards with the letter and a big picture on each card and a package of 2" sponge letters. I got some sticky tack and hung up the A, B & C at eye level for Chelsey. I showed her the A, B & C sponge letters and told her what each one of them were. I took her across the room and showed her the "C" first and told her to go pick out the "C" on the wall. It took her a few minutes but she went right to it. We were excited! We worked on A-B-C for about 15 minutes and she got them right 80% of the time.

> The other day the school told me that they had begun to show Shanda two different flash cards with letters on them and ask her to eye point to a certain one and low and behold she got all 26 letters right! I have been telling them that she could read for months now. If you ask me I think the labels they give our girls could sometimes be given to the very people that label them. Thank God for the professionals out there that at least try to see our point of view on our girls!

We have witnessed time and again that Beth, 15, makes a dramatic and memorable response when something is very important to her. And even though we think we know her well, we can't always predict what's most meaningful to her in life. Most recently, she was watching my son and I shoot basketball outside. She had been working on her basketball skills at school preparing for Special Olympics, but I didn't really know the specific skills she was working on. Fifteen minutes into our game, I saw Beth toss her soft book, which is her complete and total obsession, and I knew something important was about to occur. So I approached her with the ball and offered it to her on the side of her wheelchair. She patted down on it to dribble so we dribbled a few times. Then she scooped the ball up and held it real high and turned toward the basket, as if she wanted to launch a 3-pointer. She repeated this several times. She was very involved, and it was very meaningful. It really wowed my son and me!

Megan can identify all her colors by color and word. She can also match objects to words and pick out her name from a group of words. She knows all the days of the week and most of the alphabet. She touches the card or object with her hand, rather than eye gazing. For example, if we lay out four squares of construction paper in various colors and ask her to touch the blue one, she does. She can do the same with a group of words such as blue, red, green and yellow.

I'm no expert on early reading programs, but Rebecca could read and had good comprehension. We didn't do anything special. We just read to her a lot as a child and then when she started school she did the regular reading program and homework (simple books). We read them together. She also used to watch TV which often has words written and pronounced at the same time. We taped Sesame Street off the TV and let her watch these. Rebecca could read but never had anyone explain the concepts to her. We didn't think she could understand, so the reading was a huge surprise. She had a good general knowledge but had strange gaps—she didn't know about traffic lights for example, but from her seat in the back of the car she wouldn't have had a good view and of course couldn't ask why we stopped and started.

We made some alphabet shapes out of cardboard and thick sandpaper. Emily loves the feel of this. We also made some letters out of fur fabric. We try to spend 20 minutes at home in the morning before school just feeling and talking about the letters. Emily put the C next to a picture of the cat. We have made some large flash cards with pictures of words beginning with ABC. We made the flash cards 8x5 inches so they are nice and clear and easy to touch. They are laminated so they are durable.

ALL KIDS CAN LEARN

We are still learning how to teach, the most effective ways to teach...it is an ongoing process. What we do know is that all children can learn, and it should be based on that child's ability. We need to remember to challenge our kids, not to keep them pacified. Learning is thrilling and exciting and all children should share in this.

You may wonder if anything is getting through, but it is better to give something to think about and take the chance that you are not wasting your time, than the reverse. And education, once begun, can go on forever through books, cassettes, videos, etc.

Girls with Rett syndrome learn by looking and listening. They are very responsive to what goes on around them. They understand cause and effect and object permanence. They react to tone of voice and seem to understand verbal messages. They seem to understand the sequence of events when situations are repeated. They are able to make associations between what they see, hear or feel and something else they experience in a given situation. Although most are non-verbal, it is not uncommon for girls with RS to utter a sudden word or phrase when highly motivated. Parents give many convincing examples of how they know and understand their world. New scientific studies have shown that at least some girls with RS can recognize colors, shapes and letters of the alphabet. Their level of understanding seems to be greater than what traditional tests can demonstrate. Contrary to earlier theories, it appears that girls with RS continue to learn following the regression period. Studies are now under way to determine factors which influence learning in Rett syndrome. We have much to learn.

> Megan, like many girls with RS, does speak occasionally. When she does, it is very clear. A word seems to come from nowhere at odd times when we least expect it. She is fairly consistent with saying "Mama," especially when she is agitated. If this is evidence of higher thought processes, we are delighted.

TESTING METHODS

Classic developmental testing methods require use of the hands or verbal communication, both of which are difficult for the girl with RS. Methods for assessing their cognitive development are not adapted to their specific problems, such as delayed responses, sensory confusion, dyspraxia, slow visual and auditory processing and fluctuations in consistency. These problems pose a risk for underestimating their intelligence. On the basis of these tests alone, it is assumed that girls with RS function very low. However, parents and professionals who work with these girls recall example after example of associations they make, indicating that their level of understanding is higher than test results reveal. Traditional tests tend to reveal more about what they cannot do than what they can do. It is therefore, not appropriate to use one test or scale to make assumptions about their cognitive level.

> IQ's are just measurements of the ability to take IQ tests. At some point with the schools, I just refused their stupid assessments. Instead, the assessors wrote down their individual statements of what Molly could do and what she needed to do. I long ago refused to participate in the "dig three raisins out of the cup" test, because Molly knew that was really dumb and if she flung the cup just right, she could booger up the wall with raisin squish. Molly was not about taking tests and being smart and quantifying stuff. She was about getting up in the morning and having a good time. She had more spunk and personality than any of the so-called experts who constantly judged her abilities, or lack of them. She really taught me that who you are is much more important than what you can do.

> Last spring I took a graduate special education assessment course. The measures they use for our girls are simply not appropriate. I know, because I know what they are using to test our girls and gave one of them to Heather as part of the course. Most of the questions were not applicable to Heather's situation. She scored very low on it, but it was because of the way the questions are worded and what is asked. There is no standard of measure appropriate for girls with RS available to use. There is no test for kids with RS which has been specifically designed to measure what they can or cannot do in a fair and unbiased way.

> Ro knows not only her numbers, letters and colors, but everything that is said and heard by her! This is not a new revelation to us. Very early on we felt Ro's intense eye gaze, alert face and smiling reactions meant much more comprehension than psychologists were giving her credit for. At 4, she took a timed psychological test. They asked her to ring the bell when a block and bell were placed on a briefcase. Ro looked intensely at the bell, but after one minute of repeated directions while Ro continued to wring her hands, the tester began taking away the block. Then very subtly, Ro began to strike the briefcase with both fists again and again. Suddenly, I said, "Look, she's making the bell ring with each hit!" The tester acknowledged that this was an atypical response and in his opinion, did not master the task. We have since demanded that all psychological evaluations be done by observation and parent/teacher interviews and not a test where 90-95% of the responses need to be typical fine and gross motor responses.

Alyssa was tested before we had the Rett diagnosis when she was 2. At the time they wanted her to stack blocks and grasp objects. Of course they determined that she had the cognitive level of a 3 month old. This simply blew me away because at the time our son was 3 months old and I understood and communicated with Alyssa a heck of lot better than Tommy. It bothered me that they had never met her and ignored both me and her caseworker who told them she can't use her hands, but they just used standardized testing on her which, of course, she didn't do well with. I hate that letter that they wrote back because if you read it, it depicted no help for her. I don't want the testing to limit her in the eyes of the school.

Pre-Requisites For A Testing Situation:

1) The tester should be someone with whom she is familiar and comfortable.
2) She should be positioned comfortably and a P.T. or O.T. should be present to give input. This is helpful because the therapist/s can evaluate while helping the main tester do her job.
3) Testing should be done in a setting which is familiar and comfortable for her. It is most helpful if she can be evaluated in various settings—at school during meaningful activities, and at home one-on-one with a parent or caregiver.
4) Part of the testing should be informal "behavioral observations," taken in a natural setting, where skills not found on the tests can be observed.
5) Tests which measure receptive language or reading skills should be adapted to her motor needs. While the school may argue that the test is invalid unless delivered in a standardized format, you may argue back that the test is invalid for her to begin with if it is not adapted to her needs.
6) Don't try to do too much at once. If she gets tired, stop and begin again on another day.

Remember that you are always free to disagree with the school's evaluation, and get another evaluation done by a professional of your choice. The school also has to allow you to provide supportive documentation such as medical reports which must be included with her evaluation.

Methods Of Adapting Tests (If Testing Is Necessary):

Before testing her receptive language, it is important to determine if she knows the words/pictures used and the concept of yes/no. The test should be given over a number of days so as not to get a "down" day and make a wrong conclusion.

A) Use the Peabody Picture Vocabulary Test, in which a child points to named pictures. This test is felt to measure intelligence accurately. The pictures can be copied, pages cut up or pictures enlarged, then placed on an eye gaze frame or placed further apart for easier pointing if necessary.
B) Use similar tests which have parts that can be adapted. You will get a non-standardized score, which more accurately reflects her abilities. This may not work in all cases, but may help some.
C) Use a "Yes/No" response as the tester points to the pictures asking, "is this a ____?", using word cards she can touch or look at for "Yes/No". This is a higher receptive skill than asking her to point to the ____.

Lauren was tested using facilitated communication in 6th grade on this test, and came out at least at the 5 year level, where previous testing had her at the 10 month level. As technology improves, we will develop better testing methods, and need to team up with groups where children have other severe motor limitations to develop adaptive methods.

I have often wondered why every time Kelsey has been evaluated for intelligence the professionals have refused to test her abilities while she is doing her therapy program at the table. She knows hundreds of labels, categories of objects, attributes, prepositions, numbers, counting, can

match categories of things, knows many action cards, and even abstract ones. Ex: I put three picture cards of people doing different things on the table. One of them is two people hugging. I say,
"When you love you _____." She touches the people hugging. I think that is pretty smart. I put
out several numbers and ask how old Kelsey is and she touches the number 4. No one has ever
tested her while she is doing her structured therapy program. They just want to put her in a room
with blocks, which she hates, and toys that don't make sounds when the only ones she will pay
attention to are the ones that talk to her or make music. She ends up doing nothing, and they end
up with a diagnosis of severe delay. It makes me a little angry, and I am baffled by it.

What she learns is enhanced by her level of motivation, interest in the information, and the structure
and repetition of the situation. She may be disinterested because she is bored or frustrated, not because
she does not understand. Her capacity for learning is increased by the number of experiences she has.
One day, you may be impressed that she seems to know everything there is to know, and the next day,
you can easily be convinced that she knows very little. She may be calm and peaceful at breakfast and
agitated and irritable at lunch. Solemn and detached in the afternoon, alert and interested at bedtime.
She may react to the same music in different ways on different days. She may start out crying and end
up laughing. It can be difficult for her, but also for parents, who try everything that should work, but feel
powerless. Many families report that their daughter is the emotional thermometer of the family.

It helps to recognize that these fluctuations are not under her control. Again, they are happening to
her. Whether you call them irregular impulses, short-circuits or system overload, something physiological is happening to her. It is not her fault because it happens and it is not your fault because you can't
control it.

We have had to accept that she will not give us consistency. Some days are better than others, but
even on the best days she will do well for a while and then not so well. Some of it is motivation,
much of it is overload and the demands responding put on her, and some — who knows?

The girl with RS does not have a good understanding of time. When she hears the pots and pans rat-
tling, she is ready to eat. She may become very angry or sad if her food is not served immediately.
Routines and schedules are helpful in everyday situations. Gradually, she learns that her food will be
served in due time. But it can make things more difficult when the routine must be changed, for instance,
to eat out. Having handy a few morsels of finger foods, i.e. raisins, grapes, or crackers may save the day.
When she approaches the toilet, she urinates. Be ready!

LEVELS OF MOBILITY

Those who come in regular contact with RS girls often comment that she is aware, but difficult to reach.
Many issues are at play, not to mention how complicated the girls are themselves. They share many common characteristics but may vary widely in motor performance. Her level of mobility does not affect how
much she understands, but does affect how she is able to respond.

The girl with higher mobility often began with a preliminary diagnosis of autism. She has a higher
activity level and often has more pronounced hyperventilation. She may attempt more purposeful hand
movements, but also has more intense hand stereotypies. Her attention span may reach dramatic shifts
in a short time and she may be more prone to emotional outbursts. She is more physically active and
seems to have a higher psychic tempo overall. Her mobility allows her to demonstrate her needs (she can
walk to the faucet for a drink), while at the same time, causes her frustration (she has to figure out how
to get there).

The girl with lesser mobility often began with a preliminary diagnosis of cerebral palsy or global delay.
She is less active and her hand stereotypies are more calm. Her psychic tempo is slower and during
delayed responses, she often appears to be in deep thought. She does not experience the mood swings as
dramatically and appears to be more emotionally stable. Her motor coordination is slower and she is better able to regulate incoming sensory stimuli and responses. While her lack of mobility gets in the way of

demonstrating her wants and needs, she develops a good eye-gaze response.

Some girls will be a mixture of both groups, or will change groups over time. All in all, the degree of her physical impairment does not correspond with her intellectual ability. If she has less mobility, it does not mean she has less comprehension. Because she is able to walk does not suggest that she is smarter. However, different therapeutic approaches may be more or less successful in a given group.

THE TEACHING PROGRAM

For every girl, a good teaching program begins with a secure emotional environment, which contributes to her potential for learning. When she feels safe, she is more reachable and teachable.

The program should revolve around her own abilities, wants and needs, taking each of these into account in addition to her stage of RS. For instance, in Stage 2, the regression period, it may be wiser to delay concentration on fine or gross motor development, choosing instead to provide security at a time when she is feeling emotionally unbalanced. When she feels more secure, she will be more capable of using her body.

> We've also done some alternative things. Auditory training did not help. Sensory integration did not help that I know of, although the tasks are enjoyable to us and to her. Play therapy helped with communication, but no other skill building. Cranio-sacral therapy seemed to help with walking issues initially but does not seem to help now. Prism glasses seemed to help initially, but we do not continue their use since Amanda is hyperventilating and very resistant to the glasses. Allergy testing and treatment with drops did not seem to make a difference, but it was hard to tell.

What is the Lovaas method of teaching?

The modern version of Lovaas therapy is very time intensive, taking from 20-30 hours each week. Only positive reinforcement is used. The child is asked to do a task, such as clapping, making a specific sound or touching something, and given a reward, which is usually food and praise, when she succeeds. At first the responses are prompted by the adult moving her through the motions. The adult fades assistance over time, and the child is expected to do the task with responses that are close. In time, help is reduced completely. When the task has a high rate of correct responses, another task is selected which builds on the previous tasks.

> We tried Lovaas for Leah, starting when she was about 3, and quickly modified it. We gave far fewer hours, since Leah needs rest and gets overload. We accepted a lower percent of correct responses, since Leah can't always comply, even when she wants to and knows the answer (and Rett girls can take a while to comply). Also, we found that she became easily bored. Once she shows us she knows something, she doesn't see the point to constantly showing us. Her percent of correct responses increase while she is interested and then rapidly decrease as she becomes bored. We did, however, find benefit to Leah – the repetition and reward helped her in learning motor tasks such as pushing herself up from sitting and isolating her pointer finger. It has also been of benefit to us since it showed us how much she knows. She showed us she can identify different colors and letters, pick between big and small, and put an item into a category, such as food versus clothing. It convinced us that we do not have a severely mentally retarded child and to expect more from her.

> The first thing I did with Mary was read a lot to her. Then, we did matching cards with the words printed on them, opposites, pictures of action to get verbs in, combine pictures of familiar words with verbs. Then we added modifiers to the now familiar sentences. And we played games with absurd sentences so that she'd have to find the right word to have the sentence make sense. We used words that sound similar and had her discriminate between the two. By this time, she was reading books on her own. She seemed to devour them. You don't know how shocked I was when recently she chose adventure books to read. I'd never have thought of it. Our girls are so full of surprises!

My daughter is 3 and will be entering school soon. Where do we begin?

Before the first meeting, make a list of your daughter's classroom options. Check out every setting from the regular neighborhood school to the early childhood classroom to the special needs classroom. If your school district does not have all of these programs available, they are required to provide transportation if an out-of-district program is the most appropriate for your child. Visit each of these programs and take lots of notes. Visit once when the children are present and re-visit with the teacher when you can talk alone.

MAKE A LIST OF QUESTIONS TO ASK. YOU WILL WANT TO KNOW:

- Do they have experience with RS? Children with communication problems?
- How many months a year does the school run?
- Are summer programs available?
- How many days do the children attend class?
- What are school hours?
- What professionals are in the classroom?
- Will she have a personal aide?
- How many children will be in the class?
- What is the ratio of adult to child in the classroom?
- How far is the restroom? Are there provisions for privacy?
- How many hours of therapy would be available for your child?
- How many room transitions must be made each day?
- Is there a provision for inclusion with typical students?
- What kind of therapies will be provided?
- Does the school have good adaptive equipment?
- What is a typical school day schedule?
- What is the curriculum? Do they do art and music?
- Will they take field trips?
- Are parents encouraged to participate?

Before you get started, do your homework. Know the law. Call your State Department of Education and request copies of all the laws, programs and school (public and private) listings that you can get. Get a copy of the Parents Rights from the school and read it ahead of time. Fight for what you believe in. As the best experts on their child, parents have enormous power. Don't be intimidated by professionals. You are your child's best advocate and the most important person involved in planning for her.

Make sure to discuss your child's history, her needs, and potential placement in that order. It is illegal for the school to tell you what they have first and then try to fit your daughter into it. Her needs come first, and then placement according to those needs.

The key words to use are "**appropriate**" and "**inappropriate**" when discussing her school program. Always talk in terms of your child's needs and provide written documentation for what helps her and what does not.

Her program must be based on her needs, not the staff needs; what she needs, not what the budget can afford. There is no standard RS teaching approach, just as there is no standard CP teaching approach. It must be tailored to her specific needs. If you do disagree with their suggested approach, request to go to mediation and due process. Explain why you do not agree that the program they are suggesting is appropriate to your daughter's needs. Stay calm and stick to your guns.

Plan to drop in for a short, friendly, informal meeting with the principal, school psychologist, therapists and nurse before the formal meeting. They won't be able to discuss her placement outside of the formal meeting, but you can get valuable information about the program and insight about the school's philosophy and a feel for the school's atmosphere.

If you want your daughter to have a full time aide, make sure to get a doctor's note. The school is protected by law from the delivery of medical services, so they may tell you they don't provide medical care.

Make sure the doctor's note is worded from the perspective of your daughter's need to be successful in school.

When it comes to therapies, make them apply to her need to be successful in school. If she needs to have physical assistance to move from one place to another during the school day, it can be used to justify the need for physical therapy. If she needs to be able to sit and attend to be able to learn, they may have to work on balance and focus, etc. Phrase things according to what needs to be done in a school setting, long and short term, and then what supports need to be in place to meet those requirements.

Make sure you have some academic requirements set up before you walk in the door, in the form of cognition, self help, fine motor, gross motor, and speech and social psychology. Base the requirements on things they do in school for kids your daughter's age. That's why it helps to walk around the school. You'll get better ideas.

If this is her first time in school, try to schedule the meeting well ahead of your daughter's third birthday in case you have to go to mediation. Delivery of services must begin with a designated time after everyone agrees on the services.

Take good notes, and put all of your requests to them in writing with a copy to the school's superintendent if you think it is necessary.

What if we don't agree on the delivery of services?

Ask the therapists what they recommend and why. Get as much information as you can before a review meeting. Keep a "Let's see what we can do to help my daughter" attitude. Ask how getting less services helps your daughter. Provide written documentation of her need for therapies. If the excuse is used that she is "not making progress" in therapy, use the argument that in RS, where loss of mobility is likely, "maintaining" is progress.

What if we don't agree on placement?

If you go to mediation or due process, the law states that the school has to keep your daughter in her current program until the dispute is settled.

How do we decide which program will suit her best?

It is possible that more than one placement would fit her needs. You may want to consider a combination program. For instance, she may benefit from being in the early childhood classroom twice a week and a "regular" preschool twice a week. Or, she may do well in the special needs classroom three times a week and the early childhood classroom twice a week. It is important to take everything into consideration after asking the right questions and discussing the issue with her therapists. Sometimes they can be your best advocates!

What is the IEP?

IEP stands for **Individualized Educational Program**. It is a written plan for the special education and related services specifically designed to meet the unique educational needs of a student with a disability. IEP meetings are held to develop the program by a committee that includes a school administrator, the student's teacher, the parents, and the student when appropriate.

Can others be included in developing the IEP?

Yes. A school administrator or representative must be present at all IEP meetings along with all other required personnel. Additional participants in the IEP meeting may include regular or vocational teachers, therapists, guidance counselors, rehabilitation counselors, pupil personnel staff and others at the discretion of the school and/or parent. You may bring along an experienced parent as your advocate.

What does the IEP include?

The IEP is an outline for the child's special education, a commitment in writing of the resources the school agrees to provide. It specifies goals and objectives based upon the student's present level of educational performance, which are outlined by those involved in planning and providing services. The IEP also designates the educational placement or setting, and the related services necessary to reach these goals and objectives. It must include the date when services will begin, how long they will last, and the way in which the student's progress will be evaluated.

How is the IEP used?

The IEP is a good tool to identify the student's needs and specify how they will be provided for. It is an opportunity for parents and educators to work together as equal participants. The IEP is revised as the needs of the student change, and is reviewed periodically as an evaluation of the student's progress toward meeting the educational goals and objectives. Finally, the IEP serves as the focal point for clarifying issues and cooperative decision-making by parents, the student and school personnel in the best interest of the student.

What should be included in an IEP?

The IEP should:
- be comprehensive, covering all areas of need, including communication, behavior, socialization, self-help, academics, perceptual-motor and gross-motor skills, vocational skills, and transition services, related services, and needed accommodations in both general (regular and vocational) and special education.
- have goals and objectives that are stated in measurable, observable behaviors.
- be based on a developmental or functional sequence of skills.
- fit the student's student's current level of functioning and expected growth rate.
- be written in language that is easily understood by both parents and professionals.
- be developed as a partnership of parents, the student, and school personnel.

How can we make sure she gets therapies on the IEP?

Teachers and therapists are there to assist her in any area she cannot accomplish alone. If she can't hold a spoon, brush her teeth, use the toilet or turn pages, occupational therapy would be appropriate. If she needs help with learning to walk or range of motion, physical therapy would be needed. Each of these is necessary to help her get the best of an education. Knowledge and persistence pay off. Sometimes it's all in the way you word it in the IEP. The more creative you can get to make the goal "appropriate" for school, the better your chances of getting the goal approved. If it assists her learning, it should be on the IEP.

When is the IEP done?

By law, the IEP must be developed within thirty calendar days after eligibility for special education is determined. The IEP must be completed before actual placement and before the start of special education and related services. Unless requested more frequently, all IEPs must be reviewed at least annually by the IEP committee.

> We approached the IEP with a list of things we wanted to see included in her program, but by the time the teacher and the assistant principal were through reviewing their proposed goals, most everything we'd planned to bring up had already been covered. Many of the activities are written to include peer participation as a source of motivation. They are looking for ways to incorporate a music therapist, at least for an assessment, but everyone who works with her told us how responsive to music Naomi is. And we didn't have to tell them! Things often take longer than we would like, but the attitude from the top down has been respectful and cooperative. And the classroom environment is wonderfully positive and inclusive.

How will I know about the IEP meeting?

You will be notified in writing with a notice that must include the purpose, date, time and location and a list of who will be in attendance. The meeting must be scheduled at a mutually acceptable time and place.

Can the IEP be changed?

An IEP committee must meet, with prior notice to the parent/legal guardian or surrogate parent. If the revised IEP results in the partial termination of special education and related services, written parental consent must be given before the termination of services.

What are Direct Services?

Direct services are specialized instructional services provided directly to the student in the general education classroom, the special education classroom, community or other appropriate settings.

What are Indirect Services?

Indirect services include consultation services by other service providers (e.g., school psychologist, vocational counselor, guidance counselor) to assist them in developing programs appropriate for the student. The special educator may monitor the student. The general education teacher(s) of all mainstreamed students should be provided consultation services as needed.

What are Related Services?

Related services consist of transportation and any other developmental, corrective and other supportive services, such as ordering and setting up equipment. This may include speech therapy, physical and occupational therapy, recreation, including therapeutic recreation, social work services, counseling services, including rehabilitation counseling, and medical services (for diagnostic and evaluation purposes only) as may be required to assist a child with a disability to benefit from education.

What are Transition Services?

Before a student turns 14, the IEP must include an annual statement of needed **transitional services** to postschool activities. This includes a statement from **agencies** responsible for services after graduation before the student leaves the school setting.

What are Assistive Technology Services?

Assistive Technology Services are those that help an individual with a disability to select, acquire or use an assistive technology device. Services include a functional evaluation in the person's customary environment; and the selection, design, fitting, customizing, adapting, applying, maintaining, training, repairing, purchasing, leasing, or otherwise providing for the acquisition of assistive technology devices.

How is placement determined?

Once the IEP is developed and the annual goals and short-term objectives have been agreed to, placement must be determined according to these goals and objectives. The student must be placed in the least restrictive environment (LRE) appropriate for her.

Considerations for least restrictive environment include:
  • The opportunity, to the maximum extent appropriate, to participate with nondisabled age appropri-

ate students in academic, nonacademic, and extracurricular activities.
* A setting as close as possible to which the student would be assigned if she did not have a disability.
* Consideration for the amount of time and the distance she must be transported from her home
* Removal from the regular educational environment only when the nature and severity of the disability is such that education in regular classes with the use of supplementary aids and services cannot be achieved.
* Consideration for any harmful effects the placement may have on the student.
* Provision of the quality of services the student requires.
* Program and services as specified in the student's IEP must be appropriate to meet her needs.
* The same type of placement may not be appropriate at every stage of her life. The Admissions and Release Committee (ARD) should decide together what best meets the student's needs at the time, and as a group develop the IEP. Once the IEP is developed, the committee decides where it can be best implemented. Be sure this isn't the other way around. Placement is determined by the committee usually once a year, but more often if needed.

> Sometimes the answer is inclusion, other times it is a quiet self-contained classroom. Sometimes it is half a day in each. Sometimes it is home schooling. So on and so on...

What are options for placement in the public schools?

Option 1: Direct instruction and/or consultative services within regular/vocational education
Option 2: Direct instruction and/or consultative services within regular/vocation education with content instruction in a resource room
Option 3: Direct instruction and/or consultative services within regular/vocational education with content instruction in a more special education classes
Option 4: Self-contained in a special education classroom with integration as appropriate
Option 5: Self-contained in a special education classroom with no integration in regular public school
Option 6: Separate public day school for students with disabilities
Option 7: Separate private day school for students with disabilities
Option 8: Public and/or private residential facilities
Option 9: Homebound
Option 10: Hospital

> We should be out there trying to get the funding, education and support we need in caring for our daughters. But we need to do it in a way that informs, educates, and wins minds over, not demands and threatens, though there is a time and place for that when all else fails. I don't want my School Board to help us because they "have to." I want them to help because they see and understand the need. Otherwise all that happens is the squeaky wheel gets oiled, but never changed, and the next person in line has to go through all the hassles we did.

> While I think it is beneficial to get attention to Rett syndrome and the plight of our girls, and not to sugar coat anything, the last thing I'd want to see is a gloom and doom presentation that convinces educators there is no point in wasting resources on a Rett girl who is helpless and hopeless. We should point out the problems of a capable mind being stuck in a body that won't respond to it, but also point out her capabilities and the need for resources to be allocated and developed to enable her to reach her full potential.

> We use a communication notebook, but the staff wouldn't always fill in all we needed to know. I decided to make it easier on them and in turn provide us with all the information every day. I developed a form on the computer so they would only have to circle responses, like:
> * Alyssa ate Breakfast? All Some None
> * Alyssa ate Lunch? All Some None
> * Alyssa ate PM snack? All Some None

- Had B.M.? Yes No
- Took Nap? Yes No

Then, I left a blank section at bottom for notes. This has proven quite successful as it allows teachers time to write special things about her day and also provide us with the information we need to know every day.

I have found on several occasions that goals are set, and then not met. The reasons given are that she refuses, or shows no interest. I recently helped another RS mom set up goals for her daughter's IEP. They wanted to cut down her therapy time, because she wasn't making the goals. They were not motivating her to do what they wanted. Trying to get her into a four point stance (hands and knees) was modified to attempt to make her crawl to a toy. Getting her to take steps was modified by putting M & M's around the room that she could have if she walked there. Make the goals realistic, but give her the incentive to want to do it! Stick to your guns. This mom called me after the IEP meeting, and was excited to report that they ended up giving her more time, rather than cutting it! She even got an extra snack time added to Maria's day by writing the goal: Maria will increase fine motor activities with a pincer grasp on small food items for 15 minutes each day. She gets the direct O.T., and the extra calories!

At Amanda's IEP review, the therapists listened when I told them just how much she does understand and what she can do. We are working on reading and are developing a much larger communication system for her. Her IEP reflects HER abilities and strengths, and recognizes her potential. Lately I have greeted her at school saying things like, "Guess what we are going to try today?" She giggles and gives me that knowing look.

EDUCATION HELPFUL HINTS

- Assume that she understands you.
- She may need a security symbol, such as a blanket or doll.
- Show consideration for her fears and hesitancies.
- Limit outside stimuli to those that are necessary.
- Explain everything to her before you do it.
- Make situations meaningful.
- Choose activities that appeal to her emotions and her senses.
- Make sure activities are age-appropriate.
- Structure activities in a fixed sequence.
- Give her one task at a time.
- Schedule her activities with tangible reminders (bag by the door) (bib before lunch).
- Choose signals that she understands (words, signs, pictures).
- Combine several signals so that she gets more than one cue.
- Don't say it…sing it.
- Allow her to move about her environment; she learns from taking it in.
- Provide different sights, sounds.
- Allow ample time and opportunity for new experiences.
- Provide repetition of activities, but not to boredom.
- Motivate her by creating anticipation for continuation or completion of a process or action…pause for her response.
- Give her the chance to participate at her own physical level.
- Make sure she is physically comfortable and well supported.
- Record activities in a daily communication book to share between school and home.
- Instead of asking her to give a response, such as "say hello," just give her a "hello."
- When trying to get her act, don't ask her to act. Make comments on the activity or the object. Instead of saying "pick up the candy," you could say, "you like candy." Instead of "come sit at the table," try

saying "cookies are on the table." Here you encourage her to act incidentally, instead of having to plan her actions.
- Give her enough time to respond.
- Look for her body language to respond to you.
- When she gets "started," don't interrupt her by commenting on what she is doing. Her focus will shift to how she's doing it and she'll likely stop.
- Look for activities that are motivating. Most girls with RS like: cuddling, "roughhousing" play, music, books, television, swinging, riding in a car, bathing and swimming, outdoors, food, photos of familiar people and places, babies and small children (particularly voices), and men!

A NOTE TO THE TEACHER

It must be difficult for teachers to understand parents. We can be wily creatures! We can be demanding and critical, and even downright cranky sometimes. We can expect too much of you, and we can expect you to have all of the answers. We can insist on having you do it our way when you know that you learned differently in school. We can probably test your limits. We sometimes expect you to spend all day 1:1 with our daughters, even though we know you have many other students. Sometimes we are very sure we have the only right answers. Sometimes we can't have enough of your time or attention. We can be unsufferingly demanding. You can understand that better when you realize that everything we do is born of love for our children. There is no more formal education than by experience. We are the best experts on our child.

We give our children up to you. It's up to you. We look to you for wisdom, knowledge and expertise. We trust you with our most precious possessions. We appreciate the time and love it takes to make the best for our children. Let's work together.

INCLUSION

A rapidly increasing number of girls with Rett syndrome attend regular classrooms in their own neighborhood schools, from pre-school and kindergarten through high school. Through successful parent-teacher collaboration and good school staff support, this has been a very positive trend.

We all want our children to have friends and to be accepted. The other children and the staff are constantly acknowledging our kids when they see them. It does my heart good! I think we do need to teach children and adults alike that we all have feelings and although we are all very different, we are all very much the same.

What does "inclusion" mean for the girl with RS?

The potential learning ability of girls with Rett syndrome has been overshadowed by their enormous physical deficits, which eliminate their ability to communicate in traditional ways. Receptive language, however, is thought to be much higher than has been routinely accepted. Exposure to age-appropriate academic material has proven to be stimulating and challenging, with great rewards in self-awareness and self-satisfaction for the student with RS. Friendships and social relationships are encouraged through this inclusion process, which no doubt increase her exposure and value in the community.

Full inclusion is about anybody and everybody being there. You don't have to have a certain score or cross some line to have it. Just being a person is enough. Sometimes administrators forget or perhaps never thought about it, but special education is a support service, not a place. Girls with RS do not have to earn a place in a regular classroom – they are entitled to it.

From the time she was 10 years old, Molly attended regular schools. I don't think anyone really could prove or disprove just how smart she was. For our family, inclusion was the dignity of being as full a player as she could be. It was about having a group of girls to eat lunch with and then go out on the playground with, with adults available if assistance was needed, but not hovering. It was the opportunity to be a part of the real world. It was about where we wanted Molly to be as an adult – in the regular world and what she needed to learn about it by being there.

Is inclusion meant only for girls who are higher functioning?

Inclusion means that everyone is invited and everyone is included. Some girls with the most serious handicaps are successfully included in regular programs.

She wasn't in regular classes to learn 8th grade social studies or 10th grade earth science, although she might have. Who really knows? She was there because she was a student in our community and this is where she learned how people interact with each other and how to behave and get along. Along the way she occasionally made a friend who truly cared about her and spent time with her because she or he liked her, not because it was their job, and they were being paid to be with her. I sometimes made the argument that because her needs were so great, she needed the supports of a regular environment even more.

How will attending school with typical peers help her?

Inclusion with non-handicapped peers increases her motivation. Parents report that some girls are able to achieve a greater attention span and develop the ability to sit and to concentrate for longer periods of time, and their negative behaviors are decreased.

The other students learned consideration, responsibility, tolerance and confidence, and we are experiencing a much happier, content and alert little girl at home. We are having a wonderful year for a change.

Kayleigh has a better quality of life and a chance to be a flower girl, have birthday parties with buddies from the our neighborhood school, share secrets with her older sister and quick kisses from her brother. Last year a few of the girls in Kayleigh's class at school really "took a shine" to her. Two of them even invited Kayleigh to their birthday parties, a very big first for her. We decided to take the next logical step and have a "kid" birthday party this year for Kayleigh. We invited three of the friends from school, a neighbor girl and another girl from a neighboring suburb who also has RS. They all accepted the invitation! What a great start. We planned three of Kayleigh's favorite things; swimming, eating pizza, and eating birthday cookie. It all went wonderfully and I don't know when I've ever seen Kayleigh so happy and excited as when all her friends arrived at the front door! The whole party was a great success. The "typical" friends were fascinated to see another girl with RS and realized that Kayleigh isn't totally unique. Their acceptance of both girls with RS is an incredible boost for our family morale. We can do anything now! She is in a classroom with children who adore her and pay lots of attention to her and a teacher who is fun, stimulating and includes her in everything. She goes to an after school program where the leaders treat her like a "normal" child, talking to her and expecting her to participate completely. We take her with us everywhere we go as a family and to places she loves as well. I am so encouraged as I reflect on her progress.

Is inclusion a choice for everyone?

Inclusion, just as the word implies, means that it is available to everyone. However, some areas do not offer inclusive programs and some parents do not choose inclusive settings, preferring instead a more sheltered environment. There are no situations that work for everyone. Each family must decide what is best for their daughter. True inclusion takes a lot of commitment, teamwork and cooperation. Poor inclusion is worse than no inclusion at all.

> Children on both sides benefit from being allowed to spend lots of time together and some of our "special" children do very well in "regular" classrooms all day. But, to say that full inclusion works for everyone, I must disagree. We need choices for appropriate classes for each individual child.

> Kimberly is in a "special" class and has P.E., library, music and art with 4th and 5th graders. I would not want her placed in "regular" classes all day. I think it would be very stressful on her and at times distracting to the other children in the class. Kimberly was placed in an all inclusive school for one year. We were told by the teacher and the classroom aides that she was getting her stretching exercises everyday, like her IEP requested. We asked this question very often and were always told that she was getting stretched and massaged every day. When summer school started that year, the summer school teachers and therapist were astonished at how much Kimberly's physical condition had deteriorated. I requested that Kimberly be moved back to her old class, where she will stay until next year. We feel she gets the appropriate amount of therapy, interaction, inclusion and education "for her" in this class.

> We tried a full inclusion approach for Amanda with emphasis on communication for 2 years. At the end, she was no better off. Her gross motor skills were worse (I think from depth perception), fine motor skills were the same, communication was a little better when in a quiet isolated environment, noise sensitivities were about the same, and her social emotional ability seemed about the same. During that two year period she had some ups and downs in almost all areas, but overall never got much better. Then we put her in an at home behavioral training environment, 20 hours per week. It really helped decrease aggression, taught her some cognition skills like "give me," matching, and noun and verb recognition – things we had tried to work on as part of therapy for years with inconsistent results. Her fine motor skills got better and she could do four piece puzzles with positional prompting. Gross motor stayed about the same, and expressive speech and imitation got a little better. Her noise sensitivities seemed to come and go, but did not affect her learning since she was learning in quiet, isolated environments. She could not do her drills if the blinds were open or she could hear noise outside her room. This fall, we put her in a school placement for about 15 hours a week. She also has O.T., P.T., S.T. and some social time. She still cannot eat with other kids. She's too scared or too unfocused – either way she doesn't eat well with other kids. She does go to another classroom about one hour a day in the afternoon to be with other kids. When I pick her up now she is quite happy, likes being at school, seems able to be social and is doing well. Bringing her to school is still pretty difficult. She hyperventilates during the transition a lot, may pass out, and is scared to death of the other kids in the morning. The behavioral approach, exposure and support do not seem to help with transition issues consistently. The bottom line is we now take a mixed approach with a lot of protection and she seems okay with this. Altogether, I prefer this mixed program. I do find if we emphasize the social stuff too much, it does not work for skill building. Amanda needs quiet, one-on-one to build skills. But I don't want her isolated all day – everyone needs a buddy. It was only this year that she seemed to be consistently happy in a classroom situation.

How can we find a good pre-school that will include our daughter fully?

Finding quality day care is a challenge for all families. The special needs of girls with RS may make a day care setting reluctant to include her. While you want to "get her in," you really want to "get her in" where she is welcome and appreciated. Is the day care director supportive of having your child there? Reluctance is not a good beginning sign, but don't give up. Other families have reported this unwillingness at the start. If it persists, it's probably best to look elsewhere. Ask about staff turnover. This is a good indicator of the day care atmosphere. If staff are coming and leaving all the time, it is not good for your daughter. She needs consistent care, and staff that changes often will be disruptive and interfere with the good care she needs. Visit the room where your daughter will be spending the day. Is the staff excited about having her attend? Does the staff interact with kids at a kid level? Is the classroom well run? Is it structured and organized? Or are the kids just running around out of control? The facility does not have to be brand new and modern. It is not the school site that creates excellence, but the people who work in the setting who make a difference. Look for a setting where the people who will care for her are warm, understanding and willing to adjust, and who believe in her as a positive addition to the program. This is true from day care through high school.

> The best day care placements we had for Stefanie were those where the staff loved her devotedly. They weren't special education preschool teachers, just day care staff who loved kids, and had a special place in their heart for Stefanie.

> Really good schools do a good job with students with all kinds of needs and conversely, not-so-good schools tend to be less than thrilling for many students. There is very little that can be done for a student in a self-contained classroom that can't be done in a regular classroom, if all the team players are very creative.

How have parents reported their daughter's experience with inclusion?

When everyone is prepared, the program is well supported and the child's needs are met, parents report success. Experience is the best teacher.

> Nothing prepared me for the evening when my daughter's neighborhood school spoke of the possibility of including her there the following year. My mouth must have dropped a million miles. I couldn't speak. I stuttered and then, lapsed into a stunned silence. Oh, I was certain this speech and language pathologist thought Laura Leigh came by all her problems naturally. Never had I been so dumbfounded! That eve was the dawn of a miracle. Through blurry eyes, I watched the construction crew renovate the existing ramp and add another ramp onto the school. Handicapped parking places were designated in bold, bright colors. The principal assured me that the law stated that public buildings should be accessible. There were parents with disabilities who could utilize these ramps also. That part may have been true. However, I knew that parents would not be using the polished changing table, the stander, the bean bag and stadium chairs, the computer, or the light board with the sticky figures Laura Leigh enjoyed. No, all these things were added for the love of a child. I will never forget Laura Leigh's first day of school when five adults hovered over her like guardian angels. Then came the phone call from the communication specialist that she had fallen in love with my daughter. Laura Leigh's regular education instructor wanted to retain Laura Leigh another year because she was an asset to the classroom. The music teacher actually taped songs for Laura Leigh that she appeared to enjoy during class. Laura Leigh had already been incorporated into the neighborhood Brownie troop, and she was loved and accepted there. Children were coming to the door to play with her, and there were invitations to birthday parties. I am a fortunate mom. It's not something I take for granted. Once I was a victim of shattered dreams. Now, I am living a miracle, the miracle of life!

Syleana's school programs since we moved three years ago have been less than impressive, but this year has been different. These children weren't afraid of her and she learned quickly that if she wanted to be with them, she needed to control her behavior. We went with our instincts and pushed for integrated time for Syleana, but it was a complete struggle. We found that we had to police her activities and even do some detective work. We finally resolved that things would not change and began searching for other programs. Her special education teacher jokingly told me last week that she hardly ever sees Syleana anymore. She is mainstreamed into other regular education classrooms for art and music and a regular physical education class, in addition to her adaptive physical education class. This fall, Syleana started at a new school. When I first told her teacher of our plans for mainstreaming, I thought I noticed a look of surprise and possibly hurt come across her face, but she was confident enough to say "let's give it a try." Our goal over the next two years is to continue to increase Syleana's "mainstreamed time" and to decrease the amount of time that the aide must accompany her, by having her classmates shoulder responsibility for her. It is also our hope to help her establish some relationships for her big move into junior high.

Kim must have spent 10-15 years in various "special school" settings, where special education teachers tried to teach her "living skills." These consisted entirely of motor actions that she was unable to perform because of her severe dyspraxia (i.e., inability to perform the action while nevertheless understanding the nature of the task). The terrible boredom of being "taught" to brush your hair, brush your teeth, etc when the actions just cannot happen is enough to make anyone scream and bang their head – I know I would! Putting RS girls who cannot talk in a class with a bunch of others who cannot talk doesn't make for really interesting discussion. And it doesn't allow them to make friends. How do you make friends if you cannot communicate? What can you possibly do? Learning to read, and hence receive a real education, is giving them a lifelong ability to be interested.

How do teachers react to having girls with RS in the regular classroom?

The program is only as good as the people who believe in it. As a new wave in education, inclusion is not readily accepted by all teachers. Some feel they are unprepared for teaching students with special needs. However once they experienced a child with RS in the classroom, many teachers who were reluctant to participate in inclusive settings became their best advocates.

Crystal was in a special education classroom in a public elementary school for the past four years. Previously she was in a special education school. I would never put her back into that situation. Now we have the best of both worlds! She has an excellent teacher who always goes beyond the call of duty in and out of the classroom, which is definitely the key to having others be accepting.

Lauren in almost total inclusion for the first time this year, but the staff has very little knowledge of how to modify things for her. I'd expected her to have more of her own curriculum in those classes. It's a mixed blessing though, since it forces us to work with more high school subject matter. Who knows what she'll learn this year? To me, the most important thing in exposing Lauren to new material is observing her reaction and interest level, and checking to see if she seems to be understanding it. If she isn't interested in a book I'm reading, she is able to reach over and close it. I think most of our girls can give us pretty clear messages about interest.

When should inclusion begin?

It's never too late to start, but it is best to start early. Kids are much more open and accepting at the elementary level. By the time you reach junior high school, if you don't part your hair on the right side, you're teased. When typical kids go to school with differently-abled kids right from the start, it becomes typical.

I think that parents who decide that inclusion is the way to go should start this process from the beginning. In our case, we were "not up on" inclusion when Ashley first started to school, so we placed her in special education. Years later, when she was in the 6th grade we decided to give it a try. We had just moved, so Ashley had to adjust to a move plus a new school, plus inclusion. Her primary teacher was opposed to inclusion so we did not have any help from her. Ashley became so stressed out that year, and began grinding her teeth again and also had some crying episodes. Ashley was the first student that year to have inclusion, so the district itself did not really know what to do, we did not know what to do and so therefore, did not have much support. Of course, now it is done all the time here.

But, we struggled along. I can say that Ashley made two very good friends that year. The next year, Ashley moved on to junior high where she was one of two students in her class. Because she had one-on-one, which we had already requested the year before, we decided that she would just have history, band and lunch with "normal peers," and would work on her own goals in her classroom. The next year she was moved to the high school because she would have been the only student in her junior high class, and they could not afford a teacher for one student. Because Ashley was so behind by then in regular classes, we felt that we really had no choice but to put her in special education. For the last three years in high school she has been in a special class and goes to band, dance and regular lunch. Ashley is the only student in her class who cannot talk, so she is around speaking children all day long. Once a week, "Pals" (normal peers) come to her class and share activities with the special education students. We are fairly happy with our choices, as we do not know what would have happened had we had inclusion all along. Ashley has a lot of fun in school, she goes on field trips, sees movies, has birthday parties, has her "Pal" days, goes to dance, band, and lunch with normal peers. And, she has one-on-one with her personal IEP goals. These goals include computer activities, reading, math, and physical activity. There are four assistants in her class, and they alternate and each have Ashley one week per month, one-on-one, all day long. And, they absolutely adore her. I feel that even though Ashley does not have full inclusion, she has a pretty good educational thing going. Special education can be okay, but you have to make it what you want it to be.

Molly was better cared for and pampered in regular classrooms because there was a whole roomful of people there for her. When it was necessary, she had the one-to-one support of special education staff. She also had some regular teachers who made her so welcome in their classrooms that it was a higher level of pampering than any special education staff could provide. It wasn't about special training or medical training – it was about using a lot of common sense about what kids need. The same regular teachers who were outstanding teachers with her three siblings, did a great job with Molly.

How do kids react to having a child with disabilities in the classroom?

Most kids do not see the social stigma that is often attached to kids with disabilities. Once the situation is explained clearly, they regard each other as just kids. However, preparation is the key word for success in an inclusive classroom – for teachers, students and other parents alike.

We have always been very protective of Crystal and at first didn't know if public school was really a "safe" place for her with other children whispering, making fun and all of those mean things that some kids do to those less fortunate. What really helped us to feel comfortable about it was the sensitivity training the teacher did with some of the grades that would be integrated with our kids. The results were wonderful! It gave the kids a chance to meet our kids, ask questions and to understand a little about everyone having some type of "special needs" and that they have a lot of the same likes and dislikes that they do. No longer are they afraid of our kids and they know now that it's okay to say "hi" or to play at recess with them.

The author wishes to thank the following professionals for ideas and information which was used to develop this chapter: Cathy Gaines, CCC-SLP, EdS; Barbro Lindberg; Linda Reece, OTR/L; Jan Townsley, OTR/L.

COMMUNICATION

Ability is not only that which can be measured by external achievements—ability is everything that exists within, whether it can be expressed or not.
Barbro Lindberg

LOVE SPOKEN HERE

Girls with RS vary widely in their communication methods and abilities. Some girls retain speech to varying degrees. This speech may pop out when least expected or when her need or emotional level is so strong it seems as if an electrical connection suddenly is made, then lost again. Some girls use their eyes and eye gaze to communicate, while others may be able to use their hands to point or give a picture to another person. Some can produce sentences through typing with a pointer or by touching a series of pictures on a communication device. Communication may start with a single message on a switch, and over time develop into much more complex language, or it may never become clear and functional. Body language is an important element of communication, though it is sometimes subtle and difficult for other observers to interpret. Sorting through all of the possibilities for methods of communication may seem mind-boggling at first for families, educational staff and even speech-language therapists.

Parents consistently report that their daughters understand far more than they are able to communicate. They see their girls laugh appropriately at jokes or things which happen to other family members. They see her eyes briefly turn toward something being discussed or a movement in response to a question. It is important to stimulate her receptive language in order to enrich her life, develop a base for emerging communication and develop academic concepts.

> I talk to her, just as if she would understand everything, because maybe she does. She does! I tell her everything that will be happening, in great detail. I explain things to her about the wind blowing today or the sun is hiding behind clouds today and that makes it cooler. Anything and everything. Many times she will "talk" back to me with sounds or her eyes. I always listen to every utterance she makes.

> They told me that because Maria made no attempt to talk, she didn't need speech therapy. We started Maria at a private speech therapist, and low and behold, she was able to identify pictures on command. We started her with two simple pictures, like a duck and a ball. We asked her which one was the duck, and she would touch the picture. Sometimes it took her awhile to respond, of course.

> It is a good feeling when you speak with the teachers, aides and therapists at school and they are blown away by her ability to communicate. It finally makes you feel less alone in knowing how much your daughter truly understands!

The girl with RS often appears to know what she wants to say, but cannot plan out the movements needed to say it, due to verbal apraxia. In addition, she may have underlying oral motor problems which affect speech, as well as chewing and swallowing. Her ability to communicate in sign language, gestures and other body language is hindered by her lack of purposeful hand use and her apraxia. Though she knows what she wants to do, it may be difficult for her to use computers, switches and other devices because they require too much eye-hand coordination. Even her eye gaze is affected by apraxia, so that eye-pointing can be difficult. Understandably, this can be very frustrating for her, so motivation is very important. If she believes she can get what she wants without communicating, she probably won't work up the effort, because it is so very difficult for her. She will take the easier approach and just wait for others to provide what she wants or needs. Communication is a very basic human need, and the lack of it can lead to complacency, frustration, social withdrawal or severe behavior problems.

> By using signing, both visual and tactile, along with the spoken word and object association, Ann seems to really tune into her world. Tactile signs are presented to the listener in the palms of her hands. Ann loves this and will stand still when we offer her this input.

> I know this is a tremendous oversimplification, but sometimes it seems that communication with Sherry is like trying to talk on a cell phone with someone in bad weather, heavy traffic and unfavorable terrain all at the same time. I listen hard and try to figure out the garbled transmission, through the "fuzz" and interference. Which is the communication and which is the interference?

> When Rebecca was four we pretty much believed that she would never communicate with us. We'd figured out that she was smart in some areas. For example, she laughed at the jokes on The Muppet Show, had a distinct preference for Caramel Dairy Food, grizzled when she was thirsty, etc., so we'd got past the articles' theory that she was a vegetable. But we didn't think she would be able to read and write. I went to a conference and heard someone talking about Facilitated Communication (FC). I asked about Rett Syndrome and couldn't believe it when she said they were working with people with RS. I went straight home and told Rebecca about it, and that I knew she understood every word I said—Rebecca didn't stop smiling for days!

> At times someone will ask a question about what Sherry likes or thinks. Much more often now I say, "Well, let's ask her" rather than answering for her, even if I think I know the answer. Also, I am making a point of talking directly to Sherry when in a group in such a way that people can be "educated" about her ability to respond, and see firsthand how she does this. Now a lot of people are feeling much more comfortable interacting with her, and they get very tickled when they see the responses. This has carried over to when I'm not standing right there with her.

Where do you begin? There are a number of ways of teaching communication strategies, depending on what she can do and how she does it. The first step is to take time to observe the strategies she is already using. They may be subtle and not very effective, but all children find ways to communicate. Does she fuss or smack her lips when she is hungry, rub her eyes when sleepy, lay her head down to show boredom? To show you what she wants, she may move toward it, or gaze at it with her eyes. She may reach out and touch or "swat" at it or stare at it with her eyes to draw your attention toward it. She has very expressive eyes, and she may talk with them. Her ability to eye-point increases with age. She may increase her overall level of activity or hand stereotypies to express herself.

By acknowledging and putting words and actions to those messages, even if they don't seem to be directed toward anyone or really purposeful, you can show her you know she is telling you something, and her actions will become more purposeful. For all of us, communication occurs in many ways, and you will find that different strategies work best in different situations. By combining methods you will find that she becomes a more effective communicator. It is very important to start with items or actions which are very meaningful and motivating to her, and gradually increase their number.

> I found that she is a very complex young woman, and that she has lots of things to communicate but only a few ways in which to do this. Her vocalizations/cries/screams/tears can mean different things in different situations. She may make the same sound to go to the bathroom, get someone's attention, show us that she does not want to leave the hockey game, wants to go faster down the mountain when skiing, or stop an activity altogether. I try to ask her what she's trying to say by

giving her different choices and trying to narrow it down. She will usually stop "vocalizing" when I have hit the right choice. Usually by then she gives me a smile of relief that I finally got it! I know how she communicates and that she will tell me. It's best to watch her body language with your eyes and listen with your heart, and it helps to put yourself in her position and think of what you might be trying to say.

Ideally, parents, teachers, therapists and care givers can get together to work out common goals and a plan for action. The plan needs to have small steps and instructions that are practical and specific so that everyone can incorporate them into the daily routine. A consistent approach is vital. When planning a communication program, consider expectations for each setting carefully. Communication programs must start with an assessment of her own interests, along with what and how she is already successfully communicating. You need to build on her successes, not replace them with other methods. For example, if she takes your hand and drags you to the garage door at home when she wants a ride, she will probably not be motivated to point to car on a communication device elsewhere in the house.

AUGMENTATIVE AND ALTERNATIVE COMMUNICATION

Most girls will benefit from Augmentative and Alternative Communication (AAC), which includes any methods used in place of speech. Everyone uses AAC through written language, body language and facial expression. These avenues may be difficult for the girl with RS, so she may need to use eyegaze, head pointing, communication boards, switches and voice output communication devices. Methods for AAC could be divided into three levels of technology complexity. "No Tech" methods would include signing, using pictures and objects without voice output, facial and body language, and eye gaze. "Low Tech" methods would include devices with voice output, but only one choice or one page recorded on them. "Higher Tech" devices are capable of using a number of pages and a larger vocabulary can be stored. The "Highest Tech" devices are like computers, allowing for the greatest number of options.

It takes Leah a long time to even become interested, much less become good at new skills. We had been exposing her to communication boards for over a year before she began using it on her own. It took probably 18 months for her to use it routinely and now she is showing constant improvements. Likewise with computers, at first she ignored them, then became a little interested and then finally began to interact with them. I believe it is important to be patient and keep working with our girls. The seeds we plant may take longer to sprout than we are used to, but the ground is still fertile.

DEVELOPING CHOICE-MAKING SKILLS

The opportunity to make active choices can mean the difference between becoming a passive or active participant within her world. If she is not given enough opportunity to interact as independently as possible, she may just sit back and watch the world go by, depending completely on others to decide for her. If she has a reasonable means to communicate, she will be reinforced by the communication itself and will be more willing to keep on trying.

Following are some ways to assist her in choice-making:

- Make sure the choices involve objects, people, or activities that are motivating and desirable to her, and that are available when the choice is made. Determine the method of making the choice which requires the least effort and time on her part. You want her energy to go into communicating, not improving her motor skills. Always give her plenty of time to respond, and be aware that she may need to gear her body up with other movements to get started.

- When beginning, offer her only two choices at a time. As her clarity and skills improve you can increase the number of choices to as many as she can handle at a time, usually 3-4. Make sure to show her you understood her choice by naming it and providing it immediately. For example, "Oh, you want the music. Here it is!" Each successful communication will lead to more motivation to communicate again.

- You can start by offering her only choices of things you expect her to want. If her choice making seems random, you can try pairing something she really likes with something neutral, such as a Barney tape with a pair of pants. Remember, she gets what she chooses, so she will learn quickly to choose her favorite.

- Determine whether she can recognize pictures, and how realistic they need to be, starting with familiar photos as most concrete, and moving to line drawings as most abstract. If pictures are difficult for her, use real objects, miniatures, or parts of objects, such as a rope to signify her swing. You can then pair the picture with the object and eventually fade out use of the object.

- She may require some extra cues at first. For example, you can hold or point to the choice on the left while naming it, then do the same with the one on the right. You can cue visually by shining a flashlight on each picture or moving your finger toward it to help her eyes track and to draw her attention. You can use auditory signals such as tapping each picture or snapping your fingers to remind her to look. Physical cues include hand-over-hand assistance to help her touch a desired choice, nudging her elbow toward a choice, or gently touching her face to help her turn toward a choice.

- You may be able to fade out cues, then need to increase them again when introducing new concepts. Having pictures available during ongoing activities may help to introduce her to them before she must make active choices.

- If she will not make a choice, try changing to something else which may be more motivating. If you are pretty sure she wants one of the choices, try making it clear that she must communicate first. For example, "First show me which you want, then you can have the coke or cookie." Remember that if she is not used to making choices it can be very tiring for her at first. She may also wonder why you suddenly cannot anticipate her needs. She may also take the choices a step further than you expect.

> We found that when Lauren had the choices of "hi" and "bye" she would typically point to "bye" when she wanted to leave a situation, and she would point ONLY to "hi" with her best friend, hoping she would stay.

Choosing vocabulary is important. It may help to make a schedule of daily activities, such as eating, tooth brushing, dressing, group activities, free time, television. Determine possibilities for choice-making within each activity. For example, choosing which article of clothing to take off next at night. Remember to include fun actions and social comments, not just objects. Many people start with "yes" and "no" for the first choices. For some girls this works well, but for others, use of more concrete choices is better. Think of typical toddlers and their first words. "No" comes pretty early, but it follows other social words and requests.

USING YES/NO

Parents have discovered many creative ways to make "yes/no" work for their daughters. They also suggest a third option of "maybe" or "I don't know" because sometimes the answer is not "yes" or "no." Make sure your questions are clear and concrete at first. Sometimes it helps to tell her both possibilities first, for example, "Do you want to stay home or go in the car?," then ask each separately to allow her to answer, and be ready to honor her choice. Generally it is best to keep the "yes" and "no" consistently in the same positions, rather than switching them, though some parents have found switching helpful in clarifying answers.

> We have recently started working with Shanda on "yes" and "no." We took a 5x8 three ring binder and put a green piece of construction paper with "yes" and a smiley face on it, and a red piece with "no" written across it and a sad face. She does really well with eye pointing her choices. We are now requiring her to actually touch her choice. It is a little harder for her to get those hands going, but she can do it with enough time.

We have begun offering her "yes/no" choice cards on her tray (with big red and green dots on them as well as the word "yes" and "no" in large black and white letters). Using this requires her to marshall a hand movement, which takes awhile, but works some of the time when she is not too tired.

Lauren used a "yes/no" necklace, which was simply a narrow, elongated piece of cardboard covered with clear contact paper and hung on a string, with symbols and the words "yes/no" on one side and "hi/bye" on the other side. We held the necklace for her and steadied her hand to point.

Angela uses "yes/no" cards and is very consistent with them if the question is simple. When she had her scoliosis surgery, she was too weak and confined to effectively point, so we purchased two mylar balloons and used a magic marker to write on them so they would approximate her cards. We tied one on each side of the bottom of her hospital bed and she could make choices by looking at the appropriate balloon.

When we use the "yes/no" cards, I let her know I just want to make sure I understand her answer, switch the positions of the cards to make sure her answers are consistent and repeat the question. I have found that when the answer is "no," it takes her longer to respond. Be patient! I let Maria know that if she refuses to answer me, I take it as a "no" until she answers. So if I'm trying to determine whether or not she wants something, if she doesn't answer, she gets nothing. It has prompted her to respond rather than ignore me.

I took a paper plate, and cut out the center circle. I wrote "yes" in green marker on one, and "no" in red marker on the other one. I show them to Maria, telling her which one is which, and ask my question. She uses an eye gaze at the appropriate response.

Maria did the "yes/no" cards for the first time in speech therapy. The therapist was surprised—Maria answered 21 out of 21 questions appropriately!

One thing I often do for a check is to reverse the question. "Do you want your bath now?" can reverse to "Would you rather have it later?" I always let her know that it is her receiving I am checking, not her ability to answer!

Lapel pins work, too. Stick "yes" on your right shoulder and "no" on your left shoulder. The caregiver can easily determine which one she is looking at.

BODY LANGUAGE

In many respects, we share her handicap. We may find it more difficult to understand her than for her to understand us! When we speak to her, we can change our pitch or tone of voice to aid our expression. But, we may not know how to interpret her behavior, emotional expressions, body language and facial expressions.

Whenever Jenn puts her hand on our faces, we call those "Jenny's kisses." If I ask for a kiss she can respond so sweetly by placing her hand on my face. It is one of the most delightful, exhilarating experiences ever! It is definitely a cherished moment of great magnitude.

Sherry makes a fist, slightly held up, similar to the sign language "yes." She must have picked this up from other kids at school who were using sign language, because we never taught it to her or suggested it. We simply saw that she was doing it as a definite gesture and discovered she was using it for "yes."

Stacie can nod her head for "no" when she is very motivated, and particularly when she has had enough to eat or drink. It happens spontaneously, and she actually surprises herself!

FACILITATED COMMUNICATION (FC)

The DEAL Clinic run by Rosemary Crossley in Australia trains people with a variety of disabilities to use facilitated communication. They have defined it as: "to facilitate is to make easier. In facilitated communication, the task of using a communication aid is made easier for a person with severe communication impairment. The degree of facilitation needed varies from person to person, ranging from an encouraging hand on the student's shoulder to boost confidence, to full support and shaping of a student's hand to enable isolation and extension of the index finger for pointing." The goal is to allow communication to flow as easily as possible, but also to gradually decrease support when able, so that the individual is doing more on her own. Facilitation also can be used to support other body parts, such as the head when a head pointer is used. It is very important to let the person being facilitated clearly control the direction and end point of the movement, to decrease facilitator interference as much as possible. If you need to show her how to find a picture or spell something, make it clear by telling her you will be moving her hand and make your movement clear and in control. Let her know when it is her turn to take over again.

Angela uses Facilitated Communication to speak with her family and teachers. She uses a combination of methods to communicate, such as "yes/no" cards, a language board and a keyboard. Although she uses the language board and the yes/no cards with her family and at school, Angela doesn't type for everyone. Typing isn't easy for Angela since it requires concentration and a steady hand. To type, she isolates one finger and rests her hand on another person's hand or arm. The facilitator doesn't guide Angela's hand to different letters, but merely helps to steady the hand by providing resistance.

We have been working on Facilitated Communication for several years. I am convinced that Chantel appreciates being able to have some control in her life. She has surprised me more than once with her answers. She has a little communicator computer or used the alphabet board, but mostly a "yes/no" board at home. Our 12 year old son doesn't bother with any of that, he just puts up his hands says "right is yes, and left is no" and expects her to answer him. She always does.

Lauren uses FC also in a variety of ways. One "no tech" method that's successful, especially for doing school work when we need new words, is an erasable board. I help her first by placing her finger on each word as I read them, then use FC to let her choose the answer she wants. With a large enough board, eye gaze might work, and its very quick and easy.

The use of FC has been controversial. It is important when this method is used to be sure that the girl, and not the facilitator, is making choices.

EYE POINTING

Eye gaze or eye pointing can be a very good way to communicate, but is sometimes difficult for the girl with RS. It may help to space things far apart or to place them in an up-and-down plane instead of side-to-side. There are a variety of ways to hold or place pictures or objects for eye gaze. Positioning of both the girl and the objects or pictures is important. Make sure she is positioned for maximum stability of her trunk and head so that her gaze can be accurate. Observe the direction she watches the best, down on a table, on a slanting board, up at eye level, mostly to the left, etc., and use this information for placement. If possible, teach her to look around at all the items until she sees what she wants, stares at it, then looks at your face to make it clear she has made a choice.

There are a variety of homemade and commercially made holders for eye gaze pictures or objects. An E-tran is large clear plexiglass board with a hole in the center or made in an open three sided shape for the other person to watch through. Items are attached around the outside, usually by using Velcro. A similar, but more easily portable holder can be homemade out of PVC pipe and velcro. It can be placed on a table or held, and tilted in the best direction. An eye gaze vest is worn by the receiver person, and can have velcro or pockets on the front to contain items. (Description will follow)

> I try to give her as many choices as possible in her life. A couple of examples are: I show her two boxes of cereal and ask her which one she wants today. She will "eye point" to the one she prefers. The same goes with watching a video. I show her two and ask which one she wants to watch. She will eye point to the one she prefers.

> Lyndsay communicates well with her eye gaze. We give her a selection of 4-6 pictures depending on the situation. Her vocabulary has increased tremendously, as her cognitive development grows. We started out using eye gaze and touch. We soon realized Lyndsay could move much quicker just using her eyes. She was getting very frustrated waiting for her own hands.

> Lyndsay has a backpack that her aide carries with her everywhere, with all of her folders labeled appropriately (Wants and Needs, Academics, Social, Holidays and Themes). Inside the folders are laminated pictures with velcro on them. They pull out the appropriate ones that apply to the activity that they are doing and put them on a board for Lyndsay to choose from. This is working out very well. We have a bag at home and one at school. As soon as she arrives at school they start giving her questions or just letting her talk with her pictures and she does this the entire day. She is very happy that she is able to express herself.

> Becky Sue uses eye pointing when she is eating. I separate the foods on her plate and she looks at the one she wants next. It takes a while to develop the skill to understand what she is wanting but it is worth it in the long run and it gives her the chance to make some choices in her life.

EYE BLINKS

Parents are very creative in finding ways to use their daughter's most available movement for communication. In addition, there are some new computer systems which use a camera to track eye movements and eye blinks to control programs. A few girls have been successful in operating these systems.

> We just happened upon the eye blink as a fluke—one day my husband just asked Sherry if she could blink once for "yes," and twice for "no," and she immediately blinked. She's gotten better and better at the one blink for "yes," and although she doesn't do the "two blinks for no." Just having a reasonably dependable "yes" response has allowed her to have at least some control over her life and to make some choices. We know more about what she likes than we ever would if we couldn't ask questions and get a response. We now know that she likes sci-fi and action/adventure movies, Elvis, the color blue, beads and lots of other stuff. She is more recently interested in the music group, Hanson, wearing regular nylons instead of tights, wearing (just a little, occasionally) face make-up, and getting her ears pierced.

Communication Boards

Communication boards can be a very functional and portable way to provide access to choices. They can be made out of anything from a manila folder covered with contact paper, to a foam board with a velcro strip along its length, to a large piece of cardboard, to the front of your refrigerator. They can hold objects velcroed on or placed in pockets, pictures, words, or any combination. They can be set up so that she can take pictures off and hand them to a receiver, or point with her finger or even her nose, a head pointer or light. They can be stationed anywhere in a classroom and geared to specific activities in that area, placed on a lapboard to go with her, or placed in strategic locations around your house. She can point to them by herself or with someone steadying her arm or head (Facilitated Communication).

Generally communication boards should be used expressively. A goal is to get her to initiate use of the board without always just responding to questions. A board can also be used to show academic knowledge, holding colors, letters, or words for her to identify when named. Remember that pointing to named pictures or academic information can be a good teaching tactic, but it may quickly become boring for your daughter. She has a great need to express herself, and that should be the main purpose of the boards. Remember to place social language, information about favorite people, etc. on boards whenever possible. When boards are made for specific activities, they should contain conversational words such as "Wow," "Cool," "Uh Oh," or "My turn."

> Amanda is very noise sensitive, nervous of other children and cannot focus or concentrate with other kids present, so her therapy is 1:1 in an isolated room usually. We also use a communication board system. Individual pictures are available for her to choose and give to her teacher. They are up on the wall in her classroom. She has about 20 to choose from.

> We have one set of picture cards at home, and one at school. School uses a lapboard with velcro on the board and on the cards. At home we use a desk easel. Rachel makes choices from two or three items – food, toys or activities. It's been great. She came home from school with a note from the teacher yesterday saying that she knows all her colors but brown. Not bad for 3 1/2!

> She uses her boards most successfully when they are hung on walls as the walking seems to help her with her motor planning for pointing. She initiates communication on her own by walking to the boards herself or coming up to an adult and looking them straight in the eye until someone takes her there. Many times she points independently but often needs a physical prompt under her arm. She's even able to use a menu board which tells us which board she wants to use. We are currently offering vibration to her arms and hands and she will reach for it, apply vibration and then push it away. She likes it so much that we will add that as an option on her boards. It's been a thrill to watch her communication grow. She's a happier girl!

Calendar boards or boxes are similar to communication boards, but are generally used receptively. They contain pictures or objects which show the activities of the day. One might start with circle time, include therapies which occur that day (maybe a picture of the therapist), lunch, art, bus, etc. Her teacher can use a piece of cardboard with a velcro strip, and each morning velcro pictures or words depicting the schedule on the board. This can be discussed with her at the beginning of the day and before each change of activity. When an activity is finished, its picture or name can be placed in an envelope at the end of the board. Calendar boxes can be lined up in a row, with each holding an object which is taken out during the activity and picture symbolizing an activity. Then, when the activity is completed and the object is returned, the box is closed. Daily calendars can be extremely helpful with girls who are upset by changes and transition, since they can anticipate what comes next. They can also help teach sequencing skills.

HEAD POINTERS

A head pointer can be a light attached to a visor or headband. Or an actual pointer can be connected to head straps made to fit firmly on her forehead or chin and angled so that she can touch pictures, words, letters, or a communication device as accurately as possible. When using a laser light pointer, care must be taken to keep the beam out of others' eyes, as it may be harmful. Some small flashlights and lasers also heat up and care must be taken to protect skin. A pointer can be very effective for a girl who has relatively accurate head movement, but little hand use. It may be much quicker and easier than gearing up a hand and arm for a controlled movement. Make sure when using a pointer that the communication device is not held too close for her to see it accurately. It is also important to make sure the laser or pointer is lined up with her eye gaze or the result can be very confusing.

> My husband bought a little laser pointer which looks like a penlight. These are usually used for teaching purposes as a pointer as they can be used close-up or fairly far away. He made a hole with a hot skewer in the front of a cheap rigid plastic sun visor we already had, inserted a rubber band through the hole, and attached the laser pointer to the front of the visor by hooking the rubber band loops around each end of the pointer. He also made holes in the back of the visor to put elastic through, so the visor would fit snugly. Then he used a small pinch-clip (like the kind that attaches a pad of paper to a clipboard, but very small) to the pointer to hold the button "on" and voilá! The whole process took about half an hour. Sherry loves the pointer. She loves to look at lights anyway so she had a blast playing with the light and making squiggles on herself and around the room. But she also spent time focusing on a book placed in front of her, on the Speak and Spell letter board, and her yes/no board. After just two sessions, she was able to hold the light steady on the "yes" and "no" instead of just passing the light over them. She is very motivated to "play" with the pointer and I got a lot of eye blinking for "yes" when I asked questions like "would you like to do one more practice and then just play with the pointer?" Hopefully, as she gets used to pointing with the laser pointer, which seems to be really easy for her, she'll be able to work into the more complicated task of pointing and pressing with a regular head pointer. One thing I really like about the idea of using the laser pointer is that it appears Sherry will be able to control it independently, without facilitation, so while her communication will still be somewhat subject to the interpretation of others, it will be more obvious that it is really her own communication.

> At school, they have been using a laser pointer that fits on a headband so Lyndsay's choices have been able to increase with the laser. She is getting very accurate with the light beam. She also uses it to pick out things in books. With her eyegaze, we still encourage her to use her hand to reach to give her the practice and to keep that skill.

Sometimes facilitated communication and head pointers can work together:

> We sit side by side. as I gently rest my hand on her head to give her some proprioceptive feedback about where her head is in space. To prevent her hands from coming together during a session I sit on the side of her dominant hand (left) and put it between. I then hold the Canon (communicator) so that the (small) keyboard lies in the plane of movement of the tip of Kim's head pointer, so that the tip starts in the center of the top row of characters. Then I wait for her to move to the desired letter and depress the key. The keyboard has a guard over it with holes over each character a little larger than the rubber tip of the head pointer.

Sometimes girls and women with RS show a higher level of communicative abilities. It is important to be aware of the range, because too often assumptions are made that the possibilities are very limited.

USING SWITCHES

Through the use of cause and effect she learns, sometimes accidentally, that "If I do this, something predictable will happen." At first, use the switch to activate something she already enjoys such as a tape recorder with music she loves or a VCR with her favorite movie. When using the switch is rewarding, she will be more willing to do it. She may need help to steady her hand or press harder. To connect a switch to an electrical, rather than a battery run device, you will need an extra piece of equipment to change the current. Explore different switches to see which works best, looking at pressure needed for activation, size, pressing versus swatting, etc.

Single switch talkers come in various sizes and shapes. They can be used alone or in multiples, spread out to get the best accuracy. Pictures or even objects can be velcroed or taped onto switches to show a message which you can record and change as often as needed. Some communication devices come with jacks set up to plug in multiple regular switches, which can be used in place of single switch talkers. The device is then programmed rather than each switch, but pictures can still be placed on then. Switches can be placed at strategic locations at home or in the classroom, so she can indicate bathroom, food, music or whatever she chooses. Some examples of switch talker use at school are; during circle time she can say "I'm here" or she can be the child who asks what the weather is today. She can take messages to another teacher down the hall, going with a friend. She can say "How's it goin'?" to a cute boy. She can even say the Pledge of Allegiance. Having verbal output is very rewarding itself both to a girl and to recipients of the message.

Switches can be used to operate computers and communication devices, both for simple cause and effect programs and for more complex programs which require scanning. This can be a difficult concept, because a girl must follow a light or box as it moves across a line of pictures and be able to press a switch to stop it as soon as it reaches her choice. Some simple communication scanners called clock scanners can contain several pictures, and a switch is hit to start and stop a dial as it moves around the set of pictures.

POSITIONING AND SWITCH PLACEMENT

Positioning her for maximum hand use and accuracy is important. Her feet should be flat on the floor or on some other supporting surface. To get her to use her hand to activate a switch, place her non-dominant hand in her lap or hold it down gently. This will help break up the hand movements which interfere. Try placing her dominant forearm on a table or desk for support and stability needed to activate a switch. She may need instead to have room to "wind-up" and use her arm to swat at the switch. You can use any part of her body which works to activate switches, including cheek, chin, foot, knee, or elbow. Look for where she has the most functional movement.

BEGINNING USE OF A SWITCH

To start with her hand, try placing the switch just to the inside (thumb side) of her dominant hand. It should be positioned so that it is as easy as possible to activate. In the beginning, she may press the switch accidentally. Soon she will begin to understand the connection and learn to press it on purpose. If she doesn't attempt to press the switch herself, you can tell her to "press the switch" and wait a few seconds. Then, if needed, help her move her hand onto the switch by gently lifting her arm just under her wrist, telling her again to "press the switch." As she gets better, gently tap under her wrist to "cue" her to move her hand along with your verbal cue. Gradually, as she improves, tap or touch further back on her arm to "cue" her. Your goal is to fade out both the physical and the verbal cues so that she is initiating switch use herself. This should not be a problem if you have found a movement she can use voluntarily and a resulting action or activity she really likes. Remember that she will probably become bored quickly unless you change the activity frequently, though many girls have certain favorites which they can repeat infinitely.

We use Ablenet buttons for "yes" and "no," a green one and a red one. I put the picture symbols on top of the buttons and Rachel can make choices this way.

Christina is unable to use verbal communication to express herself, however she is able to communicate with facial expressions and eye gaze. Our assistive technology team developed a scanning device which allows Christina to, with the help of a light cue and verbal feedback, scan pictures and objects to enable her to make choices. Christina is prompted and with physical assistance hits a vertical blue switch mounted on her tray to move the light. She also uses this switch to interact with adaptive toys and interact with computer software. Each day is different for Christina. My approach to therapy has to be flexible due to my dependence on how Christina is feeling that particular day. Her ability to hit her switch varies from day to day, however I can always get Christina to smile! My frustrations lie within the fact that her responses are so inconsistent and something that I see one day I may not see for another week. I never give up hope that Christina will be effective with communicating and using this system. She has taught me to be patient and to never give up. She'll show me through her beautiful smile and laugh that there is a little girl who has so much to say and give to others.

Sherry's speech pathologist is getting ready to order a clock communicator, which uses a switch to stop the hands on a clock-style face when they are pointing to a desired selection. Sherry's been using a three-station switchboard with flash cards, so we'll see if she can do the clock communicator. The speech pathologist says it may be difficult for her because it requires anticipation and the ability to activate the switch at just the right moment to choose the desired selection.

VOICE OUTPUT DEVICES

Use of a voice output device (more easily referred to as a "talker") is attractive for a number of reasons. It gives her a voice, which changes the way people look at her and what they expect from her. People are more likely to speak to her if they realize she can speak back. It also allows a message to be broadcast across the room, when no one is with her. Voice output devices are considered assistive technology equipment, thus they are covered by education regulations.

At home we found the talker to be helpful in Lauren's communication with her brother. To get her turn she could press the "I want to swing" message when he was swinging, which was much clearer than longingly watching him swing. Having a real voice works! The voice and its potential are motivating to us as well as to Lauren.

A variety of talkers are available, ranging from very simple, with just a few message squares, to very complex, computer-like devices with almost infinite vocabulary available. They can be used by touching the message squares (direct selection), attaching switches for messages, or using a switch for scanning. Each device has advantages and disadvantages including memory time, pressure of touch required, size of message squares, ease of changing pages or message screens, and ease of programming. Size and weight of a device may be important for a girl who is ambulatory, while ease of access may be more important for a girl who uses a wheelchair and has less movement.

Some devices have digitized speech which allows you to record your own messages or have a child of similar age record them. Others have synthesized speech, which sounds slightly robotic, but generally allows a variety of voices, and uses less memory per message, which is important in complex devices with many messages. Some devices change from one level or overlay to another, allowing you to place a different topic on each one. The more computer-like devices have a touch screen and the set of messages can be changed at the touch of a programmed symbol or icon. All devices allow you to choose your own messages, how they are displayed, and how many are available at one time. New or improved devices are constantly coming on the market. They are lighter and easier to program, with more options and more flexibility. For our music lovers, you can even record or synthetically program music on devices.

When choosing a device, try to find a speech-language therapist who is trained in AAC and familiar with a variety of devices, their advantages and disadvantages, and can train people to use them. It is best to try out several different devices to see her reaction, and ability to activate messages, and to explore the complexities of their programming. When doing a trial, allow for plenty of time for her to adjust to and learn the system. Try to obtain a device which she can use effectively now, but which also provides room to grow as her skills improve. It may take awhile for her to realize its usefulness or she may quickly figure it out and use it functionally. It may take a long time before she initiates its use. Many devices are expensive, but you may have insurance coverage that will help. Medicaid pays for devices in almost every state, and schools are required to fund appropriate devices which are needed to work on IEP goals. The law also says that if a student needs assistive technology equipment to complete homework so that she can benefit from her educational program, the device must be available at home. Communication in all settings including home is necessary in order to learn how to communicate at school, so using her talker can be considered her homework.

It is unbelievable how well Laura did with the Alpha Talker. It is easy to use, high quality speech and uses anyone's voice. The Alpha Talker can be configured with either 4-8 or 32 locations. It can be accessed by the keyboard, head pointer or by scanning. It has a lightweight, sleek design and a carrying case is available. It can interface with a computer to save work to disc, and to perform limited computer stuff. It can also can also be used to load commands to operate environmental controls as well as plug in for a Jelly Bean switch. A remote switch adapter is available to permit up to 8 single switches to be connected to the Alpha Talker.

Lyndie makes independent choices of three words on the Dynavox. We also have a letter board programmed into it, to look very similar to the manual board she used for a long time. She wears an adaptive pointer splint to help her point to the letters, and also uses facilitated communication when using this board.

Mary uses an IntroTalker with 8 cells containing digital messages. We started out with switches on two, "hungry" and "thirsty," and when she achieved them, moved to "yes" and "no." From there we prioritized her needs. The IntroTalker has become Mary's voice. The switches are so easily activated that movement across the room would set one off. Once, Mary's teacher told her "Oh, shut up; you're talking too much," which sent Mary into laughter.

Leah uses Cheap Talk, a device with eight buttons covered by pictures, for which we record a "command" - "I want to eat," "I want to drink," " I need to go potty," "more." Leah touches the picture and the device says the recorded command. In the morning when I feed her, help her eat, give her a drink, etc. she typically won't use her device since I don't make it necessary. The other morning I started reading the paper and immediately I heard "More," "I want to eat" coming from the Cheap Talk. The week before we got busy and forgot she was still sitting at the table after dinner and sure enough after a while she used the device. So while I find it difficult to ignore my little darling, sometimes it works.

What I like most about the DynaVox 2C is that it easily changes from level to level so, in other words, you could ask Dani what she wanted for dessert, "ice cream" or "cookies," and if she chooses ice cream, you can have another page linked to that page and the screen would immediately change to give her a choice of say vanilla or chocolate. It's quite impressive but it comes with a big price tag.

I was amazed at Lauren's ability to use the DynaVox 2C compared with simpler devices which limited her vocabulary and options too much. In six weeks at an intensive AAC clinic she learned how to link together words to form phrases and could move from screen to screen when asked. We use facilitated communication methods to steady her hand, but everyone who has worked with her feels she is making clear choices about what she wants to say. It's time consuming to program, but school staff can do some for specific topics that come up, and I can do the rest.

CHOOSING VOCABULARY

Choosing appropriate vocabulary can sometimes seem more difficult than choosing a communication method. She will not be interested in using the device or method unless it contains vocabulary which is motivating and functional for her, and which she cannot communicate more easily in another manner. Stay away from using only words like "lunch," "bathroom" and "music." Make sure that anything available for her to choose can be acquired immediately. For example, placing "bus" on her device, which is only available at the end of the day is useless at any other time. However, if going for a short walk is an option throughout the day, it might be more useful. It is best to start with specific activities, especially if the number of messages are limited. Sometimes simple talkers or communication boards can be set up in several places around the classroom or house, to be available for different activities. There is no reason she must be limited to having only a single talker available.

Pictures can be photos, magazine cut-outs, flash cards, or labels from favorite foods or music. In addition, there are computer programs such as Boardmaker, which can be used to generate pictures or icons. These days you can also scan in pictures to print off your computer.

Often teachers and therapists limit the number of choices based on how many pictures can be grouped together for a girl to identify one receptively. Just because she can deal with only two or three pictures at a time during an activity does not mean it's the maximum she should have on her communication system. When using the pictures is motivating she may be able to deal with a larger grouping for expressing herself. Generally, use of a system starts with pictures or icons (symbols) which contain complete messages, for example, "Blow more bubbles" and a picture of the bubbles jar. Later, depending on her coordination and abilities, it may be possible to separate out words so that she can build her own sentences. This works well on the more complex computer-like devices. She may also be able to go from screen to screen changing themes herself on these devices. You may have certain messages, such as "yes/no" or "I'm done" which go in the same place on every page or screen. Here are some examples of vocabulary for talkers, communication boards, and eye gaze boards:

During therapy time: "Pick me up," "Swing me around," "Bounce me on the big ball," "Rub my feet"

For the VCR: pictures of 2 choices of tapes, "Put it in the VCR," "Turn it on," "That's my favorite," "I don't like that one"

What hurts: place pictures of any parts of the body which tend to hurt her, maybe starting with head, stomach and feet, then using "yes/no" to get more specific as you touch parts in the area she chooses and ask if each hurts

Circle time: "I'm here!," "Its raining today," "My turn," "Let's sing favorite song"

Social: "Hi my name's _____, what's yours?" "How's it goin'?", "Come talk to me," "Have a good one, "See ya later," "He's cute."

USING WORDS

She may make mouth movements and try very hard to talk. At times she may say a correct word in the middle of a string of babble. Most often, her words come at random, when she is not concentrating on speaking. She may call out "mama" when she is in distress or feels frightened. She may blurt out an appropriate word when you least expect it, and then be unable to repeat it ever again. This is usually limited to a few words; most girls with RS do not achieve considerable spoken language. Sometimes, in a highly motivating situation, she will utter words or phrases.

Maggie never had words before she started regressing at 15 months. Now she is 5 years old and she can say some words with a lot of prompting. She can say "all done," "yeah," "no," and "mom."

Sometimes she says a word out of the blue and we are all amazed. Our other daughter Rachel is always trying to get Maggie to say words and will quite often succeed. Maggie thinks this is very funny to have her little sister prompting her to speak. I love to watch the two of them interact and see the bond. They both end up giggling!

Much of what seems to be babbling or "Rett rap" is, I think, attempts at speech. Good speech requires exquisite fine motor control and coordination, which of course is tough for our girls unless they speak reflexively. My experience in listening to deaf students and those with with fine motor difficulties gives me some help in understanding Leah. "Mah," for example can be "Ma" (for mommy), "Milk," "More" and probably other things as well that are obvious in the correct context but not very obvious otherwise. I think "Mmm" is a kiss.

One time when I was picking her up, she said "Ma." Lord knows what she meant, and I reacted by saying "What do you mean "Ma," you should be saying "Daddy." You're hurting my feelings." She immediately said "MaMa" and started giggling. For a while afterwards she would say "Ma" when she saw me and start laughing.

The last time Gina said something was about 5 years ago. She was sitting on the toilet and I went in the other room, so she could do her thing and she yelled "I done." My husband was sitting in the room and he said I think Gina is done. It is funny, when she did say something, it was out of the blue and clear and never to be said again.

Angela is 18 still says an occasional word or two. "MaMa" is consistent. She says "no," "all wet," "ready" and a few others sporadically. Occasionally she will say someone's name. Sometimes she just comes up with a word or phrase out of the blue and we never hear it again. She always speaks more when stressed, particularly when she has a fever.

Sherry says an occasional verbal "yes" or "esssss." It seems to us that she uses whichever of these "yes" responses she can manage to produce at the given moment. The only thing close to a "no" we get is an occasional definite shaking of the head, also hard to distinguish from her frequent "head-swinging" side-to-side.

Although Amanda has some spontaneous words, they are few and far between. To say something when we ask her to is almost impossible, but with the apraxic approach we are getting about 30 sounds/words out of her when we ask, and attempting to imitate even if she doesn't do it right for other sounds and words. This has taken about a year to get this far. Anyway, one of the words we worked on is "more." She'll say it when I ask when she wants more of something, although sometimes she'll just say "mo" or "mmmm." Yesterday, I bought her a cheeseburger at McDonald's and I was eating a hot fudge sundae. She pointed to the sundae, and I gave her a few bites. Then I was sitting there daydreaming about who knows what, and I heard her saying "mmm" "mmmm" but didn't really pay attention and then she said, slowly and very articulately "mmoorrreee" with the "r" and everything. That was a real breakthrough.

Heather does not not say much. Actually, people can know her for months without hearing her say a recognizable word. On day, her speech therapist asked her a question with her "yes/no" cards, but instead of looking at her cards she said "yes," plain as day. The speech therapist jumped back several feet in shock. The best part is the therapist had a video camera taping the session.

My family went to an amusement park. Usually I'm too scared for the rides, but there was a little balloon ride for smaller kids that went up in the air and around. l asked Rosie if she wanted to go on (cause I thought I could handle that) and she popped right out of her chair and walked up to the ride, so we went on. It went faster then I thought and I had my eyes closed almost the whole time, bent over and scared, cause I hate going around in circles. Rosie, on the other hand, was sitting up straight not scared at all. My husband even had the person stop ride early so I could get off. I told Rosie that ride really scared me and asked her if she was scared and she said "no" and started laughing. Mom's a wimp and Rosie's a daredevil!

A Communication Success Story

The other day, I was working on the computer in one of my classrooms when I heard a recorded voice say, "Hi, my name's Sherry." Sherry, one of my students, recently got a voice output augmentative device. I assumed she had just activated her greeting message. I turned around to greet her. She was nowhere to be seen. Instead, standing next to Sherry's device, was Mary, who has Rett Syndrome. She is 9 years old and full of vinegar. She coyly glanced at me to make sure the message had gotten through and impishly galloped off to another corner of the room. I chuckled and then shook my head in amazement. I thought back on a scene four years ago when I first met a very different Mary. She came to us as a kindergarten student enrolled in our primary classroom for the developmentally impaired. She was aloof and frequently unhappy. Mary's communication skills consisted primarily of idiosyncratic behaviors that needed to be carefully interpreted by those close to her. During the previous year, a good deal of effort had been put into validating her communication attempts. This was done by consistently responding to specific behaviors in a predictable manner. Mary was beginning to understand that she had some positive control of her world by repeating certain behaviors. She also had been introduced to some very concrete symbols. A spoon represented eating and a roll of toilet paper represented a trip to the bathroom. These symbols were used primarily to aid Mary in transitions. By showing her these items, she began to anticipate meal time and a trip to the bathroom.

In her first year with us, we built on this foundation by associating more symbols to routine occurrences throughout the day. We also provided Mary with frequent choices between different food items and leisure activities. Initially, we simply held up two items in our hands, verbally requested a response, and waited for her either to look or reach for one. We then began to provide choices using something that represented the item. A piece of a cereal box represented cereal or an album cover represented music. We were even able to use some photographs to which Mary would point, to represent choices and activities. Mary made impressive progress during that first year with us. This progress was, in large part, due to the driving force and commitment provided by her family and her dedicated classroom aide. It also became obvious that Mary was very motivated to communicate with us.

I began my second year with Mary ready to introduce more small steps to expand her ability to communicate. I was comfortably nestled into this plan until I got a pivotal phone call from Mary's mom. She began by telling me that some girls with Rett syndrome had benefited from the use of voice-output augmentative devices. These devices can range from being quite simple, using recorded speech or primitive computer speech with very limited message storage, to extremely sophisticated systems. She then asked if I thought we should consider one for Mary.

I was caught totally off guard. I am conservative when it comes to recommending these expensive technological wonders. I had always thought that voice-output systems for people at Mary's communication level merely provided bells and whistles and did little to encourage communication growth. I recognized that they simplified the listener's job of understanding the message. However, I felt that all of us in Mary's sheltered world were so invested in her that we didn't need the help of such a device. But then there was her mother, waiting for a response. She is extremely knowledgeable about Rett syndrome and I had never known her to push for Mary in the wrong direction. I found myself agreeing to look into some devices.

We have the advantage of having a special education technology center in our state. They have several different augmentative systems that can be checked out for three week periods. With their advice, we began to try out some devices. Luckily, Mary could activate these devices by touching a picture, rather than using a more complicated access method. We soon found out that Mary did not respond well to using a device with artificial sounding computer voices. However, she was quite interested in activating devices with recorded speech. We finally selected the Digivox from Sentinent. It is similar to other low-end augmentative devices on the market but it seemed particularly suited to Mary's needs. It has several levels. These levels can be thought of as pages in a book. You can program each page to reflect different communication needs. For example, Mary has one level that is very specific to home and another that has some general school vocabulary. Each level can be programmed to provide from one to 48 different messages. The multiple level feature and the flexible number of message areas have proven to be indispensable. Additionally, the use of recorded speech enabled us to use familiar voices on the device.

Mary's parents pursued funding for the device through their insurance. This was justified because Mary had no clear method of showing when she was sick and, with little voluntary control over vocalization, she could not reliably even gain attention to get help. We had been warned that this process could take up to one year. It did, in fact, take ten months from the time we selected the device until it was delivered. While we were waiting for the device, we resorted to my "small step" plan. Mary gradually could use some line drawings, rather than more concrete photographs, to relay her messages. This skill helped us keep up with her growing expressive vocabulary. We kept several of her pictures in a communication notebook. We also posted pictures on the fronts of cupboards, doors, walls, and the refrigerator at school. Mary's family did the same at home.

We received the Digivox at the beginning of Mary's 2nd grade year. She had been in a regular first grade class for portions of the day during the previous year. Mary began second grade as a member of a regular 2nd grade class, with support being provided by an instructional aide in the classroom. She was also "pulled-out" of the classroom for some specific skill training. When the device arrived, Mary's family took primary responsibility for programming and maintaining it. Mary's aide supervised its use during the school hours and her classroom teacher made suggestions for content. I would make suggestions for the vocabulary, help in developing overlays (the "pages" for the levels), and generally troubleshoot. This team approach resulted in an augmentative device that, eventually, proved to be relevant and motivating to Mary. We did not necessarily see an overnight miracle. Mary needed to be prompted or reminded frequently to use her device.

At first, her peers viewed the device as an oddity. In an attempt to make the device more tempting to Mary and less strange to her peers, we made a "friends" level. We reduced individual pictures of the students so we had everyone in the class represented on the board. Then Mary's mother had each student record a message to Mary. Each student's message was activated when Mary touched the respective picture. Activating these messages instantly became one of Mary's favorite activities (especially, I was told, in the wee hours of the morning). Additionally, her friends were thrilled to be part of Mary's device. This really became the turning point for Mary's communication.

I am enthusiastic about Mary's growth in communication. She is very intentional in her communication attempts, whether they are initiated using the Digivox, body gestures, or facial expressions. It is hard not to attribute much of this growth to the voice-output device. Interestingly enough, though, I don't think that the device directly triggered her growth. Rather, because her "listeners" could understand her more easily when she used the Digivox, we began to view her as a more legitimate communicator. We responded to all of her attempts more consistently, no matter the method she used. Thus, Mary communicates with us more frequently because her attempts pay off for her.

Mary is nearing the end of 3rd grade. Her use of the Digivox has continued to grow. She is using the device more spontaneously as time goes on. She sometimes combines symbols to express herself. For example, she activated "I'm sick," and "home," last year to send us a very clear message. This skill is synergistic—it allows her to come up with novel phrases that we had not necessarily anticipated when developing the "single thought" vocabulary. She is also beginning to use "yes," and "no," in response to questions. And now—as she showed me the other day—she is using it to express humor.

by Mia Emerson, CCC-SLP

COMPUTERS

Full-sized computers are a great vehicle for learning and play in the classroom, although they are not very portable. While laptops are more portable, their screens are small and their keyboards cannot be moved out of the way if alternative access methods are used. While touch sensitive screens are available, they are harder to find and more expensive on laptops. When used with communications software meant for a communication device, computers respond much more slowly. However, they are very good for cognitive development and interactive games. Computer programs and games can be very motivating, especially those with sound and action. Sound cards, external adaptive devices and software can be easily added to your computer to provide needed input and output methods.

Some external adaptive devices include:

Touch Window: This is a clear plexiglass cover, attached to a full sized computer monitor and it responds to light touch. It can also sometimes be removed from the computer screen and used as a large switch for some cause/effect programs. Manufactured by Edmark.

Intellikeys keyboard: This is a large, flat board which comes with various alphabet and number overlays which are large and easy to access. Software is available from the company, including Intellipics and Overlay maker which can easily be used to create your own overlays. These can be used for learning and some communication. Some software from Intellitools and other companies comes with overlays designed for use with it. Keyguards can be purchased for any of the overlays which come with Intellikeys, and for some other standardized overlays.

Discover Switch, Switch Activated Mouse, Switch Interfaces: The Discover switch is a way to use scanning setups with a student. Scanning can have a high cognitive load for many girls, and requires precise timing of the switch press to coordinate with the screen. The other switch interfaces are generally used more for cause/effect and simpler, but fun software. Several companies put out software which can be activated with a switch. A switch can be activated with any part of the body and any switch will work with any of the interfaces. A switch activated mouse or other interface is needed to connect any switch to the computer.

Eye Tech Digital Systems: Along with several other manufacturers, Digital makes an eyegaze setup for a computer which uses a video camera focused on the user's eyes watching for pupil movement and eye blinks. It requires rather precise eye control, but some girls are able to use it.

New adapted access comes on the market constantly, and adaptations other than those mentioned here may fit a specific girl's needs better, so that it is important to explore several possibilities. She may find that different access methods work best for different purposes.

> Laura presently has an Intellikeys that works in conjunction with her lap top computer that she uses at home. It takes a lot of preparation and foresight to prepare the overlays (like a placemat that has pictures or words you must design with a program like Anthelices overlay maker). Each time you change the overlay you must also make a change the computer program. The Anthelices works with the computer, but not separately. It isn't a portable set up.

> I got some very simple, but bright software with good sound that's just cause-effect off AOL. One of them was called Baby Smash and another, even better one, was Baby Power. Both were for Macs, but probably similar stuff is there for IBM's. They were both set up so that a child could touch any key on the keyboard and make something happen. They'd work with a touch window on or off the computer screen.

> You can adapt a keyboard by making a cardboard cover with pieces that stick out underneath to hit keys you designate, so that she can depress a key by hitting anywhere on the cover.

IEP OBJECTIVES FOR COMMUNICATION

1) Marsha will say "Hi, how ya doin'?" to at least one other student each morning using her single switch communication device.
2) Sally will use eye gaze to answer yes/no and "none of them" questions about what she wants to do next using cards containing icons plus words, which will be placed on her eye gaze frame during choice time, at least 3 times per week.
3) Laura will use her 8 message talker to have a conversation during at least one classroom activity

per day. Examples of messages: During therapy: "yes," "no," "that's fun," "I'm finished," "let's do more," "bounce me on the ball again," "twirl me around," "rub lotion on me." Birthday Party: "first line of Happy Birthday, " "blow out the candles, " "How old are you?," "I want some cake," "I want some ice cream," "juice please," "this is yummy!," "I don't like that."

4) During circle time Danielle will use 3 switches with pictures and words attached, and connected to her talker to say "I'm here," "Let's sing 'If You're Happy and You Know It', " and/or "Let's sing Old MacDonald" at least 3 times weekly.

5) Mary will use eye-gaze to match 4 colors placed on the eye gaze frame to colors on pictures held up by her teacher, at least twice in a row.

6) Lauren will point to 3-4 icons on a screen of her talker to make a phrase used to describe something she has just done or wants to do, with a helper steadying her hand and arm during group time.

7) Sherry will use a headpointer to spell out words at the second grade level, to provide information to others using a small letter board, at least 3 times daily.

8) Cara will hand a picture to another student when given 3 pictures as choices for what she wants to eat or do next at least once per day.

9) Lauren will present a short verbal report in at least one class each grading period using her communication device with an adult steadying her hand and arm.

10) Lindy will imitate one syllable words when asked to tell what she is doing, using any of 5 familiar activities at least twice per day.

11) Carol will tell what part of her body hurts with 4 choices, or how she is feeling (5 choices) on the same page, using icons plus words as needed.

12) Lilly will look at the photo of what her mom should put on her next when dressing her, placed on a large communication board on the wall next to her bed.

How To Pay For This Stuff

By law, the school must pay for any equipment required for your daughter to receive an appropriate education as defined by her IEP. Medicaid also pays for AAC devices in most states, and some insurance companies will pay for devices. With Medicaid and insurance companies be sure to emphasize the medical, not educational need.

Typical costs at this writing:

BIGmack, One Step Communicator: Single switch talkers made by Ablenet: $80 each

Cheap Talk (4 or 8 messages), **Twin Talk** (2 messages): Simple single level talkers. Made by Enabling Devices Toys for Special Children: $70-$160 each

Hawk: Simple 9 message device with recorded voice with a tough case for rough children. Made by ADAMLAB: $250

Wolf: Older version which can have several pages in same case as the Hawk, but with robotic sounding synthesized speech, and difficult to program. Made by ADAMLAB: $400

Voice Pal: A small device which can be accessed in several ways including switches called taction pads, which can stick on an object or picture and are activated by very light touch. Made by Adaptivation: $350

Attainment Talkers: Small, portable devices with 5 or 15 messages which can be used with a carrying case and attached to the belt: $225(for 5 message device)

MACAW: A more complex device which can have multiple pages and 1-32 recorded messages per page which comes with various levels of memory and thus available pages and messages. Made by Zygo: $2,000

Alpha Talker: A device which can have multiple pages and 4-32 recorded messages per page or level, and can be activated by a special optical headpointer. Made by Prentke Romich: $1,600

Digivox: Another similar device which has multiple recorded messages and pages which can be activated with light touch made by Sentient Systems: $1,600

Super Hawk: Also has multiple recorded messages (up to 124), from 2-72 per page, and multiple pages and can be activated with light touch. Made by ADAMLAB: $850

Dynavox: A computer like device, with touch screen type activation, which can have almost infinite messages and screens using linking icons to move from screen to screen. Takes some time to program if using many messages and uses any of 10 synthesized voices: $6,500

Liberator: Uses a single screen with many icons which take on meaning when linked together to form words. Modules for early learning of language and play using their system can also be purchased. Made by Prentke Romich: $7,350

COMMUNICATION CATALOGS

Ablenet	1-800-322-0956	BIGmack, other switches
ADAMLAB	1-313-467-1610	Wolf, Hawk, Super Hawk
Adaptivation, Inc.	1-800-723-2783	VoicePal
Attainment Co.	1-800-327-4269	Talkers, Pre-Vocational Pictures
Creative Communicating	1-801-645-7737	Light Activated Switch Software
Don Johnston	1-800-999-4660	Discover, Speaking Dynamically
Intellitools	1-800-899-6687	Intellikeys software
Laureate	1-800-562-6801	Software for Language, Learning
Mayer-Johnson Co.	1-619-550-0084	Boardmaker, Picture Symbols
Prentke Romich Co.	1-800-262-1990	Alpha Talker, Delta Talker, Liberator
R.J.Cooper	1-714-240-4853	Biggy, computer software, switch activated mouse
Sentinent Systems	1-800-344-1778	DynaVox, Digivox
Technology for Education	1-800-370-0047	Special equipment, Software
Toys for Special Children	1-800-832-8697	Cheap Talk, switches, toys
Words+, Inc.	1-800-869-8521	Message Mate
Zygo Industries	1-800-234-6006	MACAW

Following is a summary one mother put together about her daughter's non-verbal communication skills. It is very helpful for caregivers, teachers, therapists and friends.

Laura's Communication Digest
by Janine Battistone

Very Important: Once it has been determined that Laura has been attempting to communicate something by any of these means, she often will confirm her response with another of her many assorted body languages, or with her Yes/No/Maybe/I don't know board.

When I do this:	It means:

Facial

Looking away:	This the most misinterpreted body language gesture Laura has. She does this in order to temporarily redirect her energies. It allows Laura to regroup her movement to properly address an item or task requiring her attention (Not to be interpreted as lack of attentiveness).
Smile:	"I am happy," or "I am glad to see you."
Opens mouth:	Has something to say.
Opens mouth when eating:	Anticipation of accepting more food.
Look at something intently:	"I would like that." (Be careful not to misinterpret this look for a temporary redirection of her energies to focus on another task.)

Closes her eyes temporarily:	In order to temporarily regroup.
Smacking lips:	Giving kisses
Grinding teeth:	Temporary episodes of teeth grinding. Laura is stressing a point or issue. Or if grinding for longer periods, she is really mulling over something.
Head nods:	Usually a method she uses to confirm her input.
Turns head away and snubs:	Miffed! Ticked off!
Winks:	"Yes, I agree." Or flirting with some fellow.
Opens and closes eyes:	Confirmation

Vocalizations

Giggles:	Pleased to see someone. Finds something humorous.
Moan:	Attempting to say something. Not necessarily a negative behavior.
Cry:	Sometimes a happy cry out of gladness. Sometimes cries as a result of sadness/disappointment, like being left out. Rarely cries as a result of pain. (Laura has an abnormal pain intolerance). Emotional hurt.
Laughs:	When she finds something humorous! Or when another child is verbally reprimanded.
Body Wiggles:	Confirmation. Usually uses in combination with another form of input.
Pelvis rocks:	Confirmation. Usually uses in combination with another form of input.

Hands: Laura has different hand patterns, with different meanings.

Hands individually poised:	Attempting to purposefully use her hands. Perhaps something she wants to touch or pick up.
Fingers partially in mouth:	Trying to tell you she has something to say. Rarely uses this to indicate that she wants to be fed.
Back of hands to her mouth:	Signal that she has something to say, or has an opinion regarding subject being discussed.
Wrestling with her hands:	Attempting to gain purposeful control of her dominant hand.
Squeezing another persons hand:	If someone is holding Laura's hand while they are feeding her, she will squeeze their hand when she wants more food. OR hand squeezes to indicate she has some thing to express. Will also use hand squeezes to confirm something said in her presence, or something she has expressed.

Breathing

These attempts need to be acknowledged. Laura invests her energies whatever way she can to enable herself to communicate. Her altered breathing either over, or under exaggerated should be acknowledged as ways she uses to empower herself to communicate a need or express herself.

Flaring of nostrils:	Laura has something she is trying to say. Requires us to encourage her efforts, while we figure it out. After all, she knows what she wants to say; we need to decipher.
Altered or exaggerated breathing:	

Communication Devices

Ringing bells on shoes/ stomping feet:	Confirmation. "I agree" with something someone said in her presence. Or "I have something to say. Please come here. "Or, "I want or need something."
Double foot stomp:	Same as stomping her feet, and ringing the bells on her shoes, except, "This is more important! I definitely have something to say. That is really important to me!"

COMMUNICATION HELPFUL HINTS

- Remember that she has not lost the will to speak and act, just the way to speak and act.
- Be alert to her subtle cues, particularly visual ones and body language
- Modify signs that are easier, in her repertoire of movement, and suit her needs
- Increase her self-confidence by improving her self-awareness; use mirrors, photos, slides, videos
- Allow ample time for her to respond
- Make the reinforcement fit the message, and find vocabulary which can be used frequently or during specific daily activities
- Minimize distractions
- Be sure that she is seated comfortably and positioned correctly for maximum control and movement.
- Some girls cannot communicate when they hurt. When she is well, ask her what was troubling her before.
- If she is uncomfortable or agitated, make a list of likely problems and ask her those, using "Yes/No." It's best to include "Something else?" on the list.
- Start small, but do not underestimate her language level or potential.
- If she seems bored and does not respond, things may be too simple, not too difficult.

Use any method that works, and uses the least time and physical effort to communicate, including:

- eye pointing or use of a head pointer or light, or even nose pointing
- use of a pointer attached to any part of her body which works the best
- use of yes/no cards or switches of various sizes and shapes, hand operated, chin operated
- use of a voice output communication device

MAKING THE EYE GAZE FRAME

Materials
- 8-10' of 2" diameter PVC pipe
- 4 caps
- 4 T-shaped connectors
- 6 elbow shaped connectors
- saw or pipe cutters
- PVC pipe cleaner
- PVC glue
- strip of self stick velcro-at least 24"

DIRECTIONS

1) Cut pieces of PVC pipe using a saw or pipe cutters to the lengths shown in the diagram. Note: feel free to make dimensions smaller or different to fit your child's needs.
2) Put pieces together as shown in the diagram using connectors and using caps on ends of the "feet" of the frame.
3) Clean ends where connected using the pipe cleaning liquid, then glue together (optional).
4) Stick on strips of the fuzzy side of the Velcro on the top, sides, and bottom of the frame, so that pictures or objects can be attached.
5) Use small pieces of the hook side of the Velcro on whatever you want to attach.

MAKING THE EYE GAZE VEST

Materials

- Plain, lightweight material
- Lining material if desired
- 1 yard of clear plastic (found at sewing stores)
- Sew-on Velcro

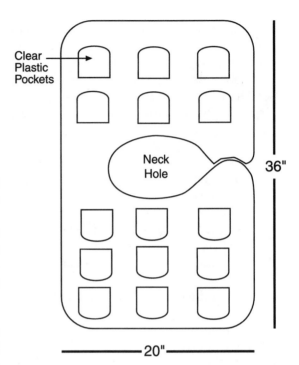

Directions

1) Cut out and sew vest to the dimensions shown in the diagram, making a hole for the neck and opening on one side of the neck.
2) Cut out and sew on plastic pockets, making each about 3.5" square, and spreading them apart evenly. Pockets are placed on both the front and back to allow the wearer to have two sets of pictures and simply turn the vest around to change topics.
3) Sew on Velcro to make an easy neck closure.
4) (Optional) On the inside you can sew Velcro strips so that you can make the vest reversible and attach small toys or other objects and allow a child to reach for them or use eyegaze while your hands are free.

The author wishes to thank the following professionals for ideas and information which was used to develop this chapter: Cathy Gaines, CCC-SLP, EdS.

NUTRITION AND FEEDING

"Nutrition represents one of the most important aspects of treatment in RS. It is the cornerstone by which all other forms of therapies are made possible."
Marylynne Rice Asaro, Registered Dietician

Most girls with RS present a challenge when it comes to providing enough nutrition. Even those with healthy appetites are usually quite thin and short, and many meet the definition for protein-energy malnutrition. Malnutrition results when dietary intake is insufficient to meet the body's energy needs, and it has many causes. Studies have shown that the majority of girls with RS syndrome have lower energy (dietary) intake than healthy girls the same size or age. The result of insufficient dietary intake is thinness, loss of muscle tissue, and decreased resistance to infection. Nutrition and feeding are very important to improve their quality of life and make other therapies possible.

Every girl has her own unique food likes and dislikes. While she may have different tastes and nutritional needs, she shares a number of characteristics with the typical girl with RS. She has a good appetite, enjoys food and has strong food preferences. She can eat a wide range of foods but may need longer time at meals. She has limited self-feeding skills. She does not need a special diet, but may have problems chewing, swallowing and eating different food textures. Constipation is a common problem which occurs in part due to delayed movement of food through the intestinal tract.

Adequate intake of food does not guarantee good nutrition. The gastrointestinal tract must be able to perform mechanical movements in three major functions: the controlled movement of food from the mouth to the anus, the digestion of food and the absorption of nutrients.

The girl with RS may have problems sucking, chewing or swallowing. She has poor tongue mobility, which makes it difficult for her to take in and move food around as she needs to. Food does not clear the esophagus as it should. When she swallows, solids and liquids pass into the larynx. The churning movements (peristaltic waves) needed to propel food through the intestinal tract may be reduced, and there may be delayed emptying of the stomach. All of these factors add up to the potential for nutritional problems.

Many of the characteristics of Rett syndrome add to problems with feeding and nutrition, and different stages may present unique challenges. Following is a list of the clinical features commonly seen in RS and the effects which they have on the girl's nutritional status.

Clinical Features	Nutritional Results
Failure to thrive	Stage 1: Lack of weight gain
Growth retardation	Stage 2: Weight loss
	Stage 3: Poor linear growth (height); Weight stabilization
	Stage 4: Weight Loss ; Linear growth arrest
Decreased Energy/Nutrient	Weight loss
Intakes	Poor linear growth
Loss of Hand Use	Loss of self feeding skills; Increased caretaker time; Increased feeding time
Impaired chewing/swallowing	Increased risk of aspiration

Clinical Features	Nutritional Results cont'd
Increased Salivation	Increased risk for dehydration; Increased fluid needs
Seizures	Drug/nutrient interaction; Altered vitamin/mineral needs; Ketogenic diet for seizure control
Scoliosis	Distorted gastrointestinal anatomy

Does the abnormal breathing contribute to her poor weight gain?

One study showed an association between poor nutritional status and breathing disturbances, suggesting that hyperventilation and hypoventilation interfere with breathing. However, hyperventilation does not increase total daily energy expenditure.

My daughter seems to eat constantly, yet she remains very thin. Why?

Weight gain is poor in more than 85% of girls with RS, although most parents believe their daughters have average to enormous appetites. Parents often describe their daughter's intake of food as surprisingly large considering her age and size. An early theory suggested that girls with RS may burn more energy while engaged in their constant stereotypic hand movements. However, studies have now shown that even though girls with RS spend a lot of time in motion with their repetitive hand movements, they actually burn less energy, have lower energy intake and sleeping metabolic rates than their age-matched peers, and may use their body's energy less efficiently. These factors combine to provide an imbalance over the long run which contributes to the growth failure so common in RS. Many girls actually meet the criteria for moderate to severe malnutrition. Girls with RS usually require more energy than other girls their age to reverse their poor weight gain and growth arrest.

If we give her high energy supplemental feedings, will she gain weight and strength?

Increasing her caloric intake will increase her weight, but it does not replenish completely her muscle mass. For some reason, when she gains weight, body fat is increased, but muscle wasting still persists. Preliminary studies suggest that abnormalities in body protein metabolism and the hormones which regulate it have some role in this process. An increase in body protein catabolism leads to body protein insufficiency and subsequent muscle wasting and growth failure. It is possible that decreased lean body muscle mass may be due to increased rates of amino acid ("building block" of protein) oxidation despite increased rates of urea nitrogen (constituent of protein) recycling. Studies are now underway to seek better understanding of this muscle wasting problem. We are hopeful that treatment strategies will be developed soon to reverse the problems of growth failure and muscle wasting in girls with RS.

What considerations are important in planning a feeding program?

A nutritional assessment will help to determine if it is necessary to supplement or change her current feeding program. Her feeding plan should be aimed at improving nutrition, promoting weight gain and linear growth, developing and enhancing feeding skills, reducing feeding time and minimizing constipation.

For women with little appetite and serious feeding difficulties, this checklist is helpful:

A score of 0 (no problem), 1 (problem), or 2 (major problem) is given by the chief caregiver on the following items in so far as they affect feeding:

- shape or posture of head and neck;
- ability to keep the lips closed on food;
- defective chewing, defective swallowing;

- choking; involuntary or obstructing movements;
- vomiting or regurgitation; excessive secretions;
- poor appetite; and dependence in feeding.

When the total score is around 10, expert help is needed and a period of alternative feeding may be necessary until the nutritional state improves.

Alison Kerr, FRCP, FRCP & CH
RS Association UK Newsletter

What are some options for improving her nutritional status?

The options for nutritional rehabilitation depend upon the degree of malnutrition, the degree of chewing and swallowing difficulties, the risk of aspiration, and your preference. Regular meals can be supplemented with extra snacks or meals. When this approach is inadequate to meet her nutritional needs or if she has significant swallowing problems and risk of aspiration, other methods of feeding are often necessary. Nasogastric (NG) tube feedings may be recommended. With this method, a tube is passed through the nose and esophagus into the stomach, so that food is taken directly to the stomach. NG tubes generally are recommended as a temporary measure. Or, your physician may recommend a gastrostomy button (G button), a device which requires a surgical procedure under general anesthesia to create an opening through the skin into the stomach. The "button," which resembles a mushroom on a stalk, is placed in this opening (stoma), giving a direct route for feeding to the stomach.

Does she need to take vitamins?

Vitamins and minerals are essential for her health as they contribute to growth and development. A healthy child who eats well will receive a good amount of nutrients in her diet and does not need vitamin supplements. However, if she has allergies, is tube fed with a homemade blenderized formula or is extremely underweight, vitamins may be helpful. Giving too many supplements can be dangerous. Always consult with her doctor before giving vitamin and mineral supplements.

- All vitamins and minerals are important for children, but they do not increase weight. Only energy will increase weight. Key vitamins/minerals include folate, vitamin D, calcium, iron and zinc.
- Amounts should be based on weight, dietary intake, exposure to sunlight and drugs. Excessive dietary intake of vitamins and minerals can be just as harmful as insufficient dietary intake.

How can we supplement her energy intake?

Increasing her dietary energy intake will increase her weight and linear growth and improve her alertness and interaction. A high-energy, high-fat and high carbohydrate diet has been shown to improve weight gain as well as to achieve better seizure control. You can increase energy by adding margarine, butter, cream sauces, and syrups to vegetables, fruits, and cereal. A mid-morning, mid-afternoon, and bedtime snack can be given in addition to three regular meals. Carnation Instant Breakfast, milkshakes, and Ensure or Pediasure are high energy supplements which can be given between meals in liquid form. Small frequent meals during the day with added carbohydrates and/or fats help increase weight and also may decrease irritability and agitation.

> Our daughter takes Scandishake, which is a high calorie supplement—600 calories in 8 ounces. It comes in a powder that you mix with milk or lactose free product in vanilla, chocolate and strawberry. It does actually taste good. Kate started taking it and she has gained 5 pounds. She had not gained in 3 years.

> Christina drinks "Deliver" which has more energy, vitamin D, and MCT oil which we're told is good for her. Its very thick and tastes great! She drinks it out of a bottle, too.

What are some kinds of food that are high in fat and energy content?

Each time you serve a meal or snack, ask how you can sneak in some more energy. Try adding extra of the following:

Avocado	French Fries	Peanut Butter	Bacon
Fried Foods	Processed Cheese	Banana	Butter/Margarine
Gravy	Processed Meats	Half and Half	Cheese/Cheese Spread
Salad Dressing	Chips	Ham	Sausage
Cottage Cheese	Hot Dogs	Sour Cream	Cream
Ice Cream	Instant Breakfast	Steak	Cream Cheese
Mayonnaise	Whole Milk Yogurt	Custard	Whipped Cream
Fish Packed in Oil	Oils	Nuts	

Nutritious foods are often low in fat. How can I increase their fat content?

Fruit: top with whipped cream, yogurt or nuts
Pasta: bread, potatoes and vegetables—use liquid squirt butter or margarine or add gravy.
    Fry or saute vegetables, potatoes or bread crumbs.
Vegetables: top with cheese
Dairy products: add Instant Breakfast, flavorings, Ovaltine or non-fat dry milk, ice cream,
    milkshakes, eggnog
Crackers or bread: spread peanut butter or cream cheese

What are some other ways to promote weight gain?

Increase Energy Intake:
- Increase the number of meals daily
- Increase amount of food at each meal
- Provide high energy liquid supplements
- Give high-energy snacks
- Increase fat and sugar content of foods
- Limit mealtime fluids
- Limit high fiber foods (which are filling)

Increase Fat and Carbohydrates:
- Fry foods
- Add oil, gravy, butter to foods
- Use syrups and table sugar
- Increase intake of fruits and juices
- Add fat to carbohydrate foods

What is carnitine?

Carnitine is a natural substance which is necessary for energy metabolism. It is produced in the body and is also found in the diet, particularly in red meats and dairy products. Carnitine transports fats into the mitochondria, the cellular furnace, where these fats are converted into an energy source.

Why is carnitine important?

The heart and skeletal muscle tissue rely on the utilization of fat as their major source of energy. Without carnitine, the use of fatty acids as an energy source for all tissues is reduced.

What causes carnitine deficiency?

Deficiency can be due to a decreased natural synthesis of carnitine in the body, or an altered transport of carnitine across the muscle cellular membrane, where carnitine is known to be active. If the diet lacks carnitine or the body over utilizes or loses carnitine, deficiency can result. Young children with neurological disorders who take multiple anti-convulsant drugs are at the highest risk for carnitine deficiency. The use of valproate (Depakote®) may be associated with carnitine deficiency.

What are the symptoms of carnitine deficiency?

Clinical symptoms include muscle weakness, lethargy, hypotonia, encephalopathy (altered mental status), neurologic disturbances and impaired growth and development.

How is carnitine deficiency detected?

Examination of muscle tissue is the most accurate way to measure carnitine. However, blood level determinations are preferred since they are not invasive.

> Amanda's carnitine levels were fine. But since we had read about carnitine deficiencies and Depakote®, we decided to try it anyway. On carnitine, she definitely had more energy and needed less sleep. Without the carnitine, she slept 4 to 5 more hours a day.

How is carnitine deficiency treated?

Levocarnitine, the synthetic form of carnitine, is the only treatment approved by the Food and Drug Administration for the treatment of carnitine deficiency. The brand name is L-Carnitor, and it must be given by prescription. Your doctor may suggest carnitine supplements, which can be purchased at health food stores under various brand names. However, the regulatory requirements for health food supplements are not equal to those of prescription drug products. Insist on a prescription.

> Nicole's overall disposition and mood have improved and she seems to be less fussy. Her appetite has increased and she has gained two pounds. Her bowel movements come almost every day and are less hard than before. We had a hard time convincing our last pediatrician to write a prescription because her test came back negative for a deficiency. We ended up going to Nicole's neurologist for a prescription. The doctor's feeling was that there was no real risk in trying and if we didn't see improvement we would discontinue use. In Nicole's case it has been well worth the trial.

> The evidence we saw of improvement was increased alertness, better attention span, more initiation on her part with her peers and teachers. Her teachers would testify to this also.

What are the side effects of Carnitor?

Mild gastrointestinal complaints may occur, including nausea and vomiting, abdominal cramps and diarrhea. These usually disappear when the dose is decreased. A "fishy" body odor may appear, and also disappears when the dose is reduced.

What are some problems that might occur with feeding?

Problems related to feeding and nutritional needs are frequent concerns, as girls with RS seldom develop mature patterns of chewing and oral motor function. Swallowing may be difficult, especially with liquids. It may be difficult for her to bite hard enough at the right time to eat a sandwich. Abnormal tongue movements, low or high tongue tone, scoliosis, increasing shoulder girdle tightness, and neurological problems may contribute to feeding difficulties. Many girls develop gastroesophageal reflux (GER), which occurs when acid from the stomach backs up into the esophagus, causing burning, pain and irritation.

CHEWING

Dysfunction of chewing and swallowing is common in girls with RS. These may begin early in life. The cues which trigger normal chewing of solids or semi-solid foods seem to be lost. Many girls with RS have abnormal movements such as **tongue-thrusting** and waves of **involuntary tongue movements** that get in the way of effective chewing. When younger, the oral motor tone of her cheeks, lips and tongue is abnormally low, but as she gets older the tone increases to abnormally high. These changes in tone and tongue movements interfere with chewing.

> When Rae was 2, we noticed that she had poor chewing, although it never stopped her from eating much. But she did have problems eating certain foods—peanut butter, or mushy foods. They suggested stimulating her mouth with a nuk trainer. It's like a toothbrush, but with "nubs" instead of bristles. It also stopped the grinding a little. We do not give her things that she absolutely cannot deal with, but we do give her foods to make her chew, to help strengthen the tone in her mouth.

> Gina has trouble chewing different textures. Food must be put in her mouth on either the left or right sides of her back teeth in order for her to be able to chew it. Her therapist says she has trouble lateralizing her tongue to maintain proper chewing. She has difficulty with many foods so for the most part her meals go in the food processor. Usually when I try something new, she winds up gagging, which leads to vomiting. Her speech therapist does a lot of feeding therapy and is basically teaching her how to chew correctly.

How can chewing and swallowing difficulties be minimized?

A careful evaluation of chewing and swallowing should be obtained to determine the best intervention strategy. Correct positioning and therapy will decrease rigidity and may be all that is necessary to minimize the problem. Frequently, the use of thermal stimulation (ice slush or popsicles) helps the girl who "forgets" the food is still in her mouth. This technique heightens the sensory awareness in her tongue and cheeks and allows her to better chew and swallow. If she hyperventilates during eating, caution should be taken to make sure she has swallowed before offering her another bite. One sip of liquid should be given at a time to avoid swallows that could cause choking or aspiration.

SWALLOWING

The cues which trigger the swallowing of liquids, particularly thin liquids like water or juices are often impaired in the girl with RS. Swallowing requires coordinated muscle contractions to move the food or liquid from the back of the tongue to the pharynx and then down the esophagus. It is necessary to close the mouth to swallow, which can be difficult for the girl with RS. Thin foods and liquids are more difficult to swallow. To make it easier, food can be mashed, chopped or pureed and thin foods and liquids can be thickened with commercial thickening agents.

Positioning is important to enhance swallowing during mealtimes. The closer you can get her in the normal upright position, the better. Her head should not be tilted back. This is not only uncomfortable but dangerous, as well. Her chin should not be touching her chest—it is very difficult to swallow in this position. She should not eat or drink while lying down—this increases the chance of inhaling a small amount of food or liquid into the lungs. Her bottom should be firmly seated in the chair to avoid fatigue and her feet should have a proper footrest.

Oral motor activities should begin with the use of a dry towel first, and then progress to a wet towel. If she resists the towel, the hands can be used. Stroke the face muscles from ears to mouth, and then from eyes to mouth, following the edge of the nose. Then, stroke from the center of the top lip to the right side of the mouth and repeat on the other side. Stimulate the teeth and gums in a circular motion from the center of the mouth toward the back and then toward the center.

To swallow effectively, the food must be organized into a bolus (clump). Thin liquids are harder to swallow than solids or thickened liquids. Also, raw carrots are difficult to swallow because the pieces tend to scatter in the mouth and don't clump together to swallow. So, what might appear to be a "touch" thing may really be a "swallowing" thing.

> Amanda started to have problems swallowing when she was 6 years old. Her weight dropped to 24 pounds. After a swallow study, we were told she was at a high risk for aspiration, so they suggested that we have a feeding tube put in. First we tried a nasogastric tube for a month to see if she would tolerate tube feedings. She could and we had the permanent gastrostomy button put in two weeks later.

> I attach aquarium tubing to a plastic water bottle (thermos with a short flip-up spout). The bottle can rest in a bag on the belt of Dani's wheelchair and she can still drink from it from the long tube without assistance from anyone.

> We went to a beauty supply store and bought a bottle used for applying hair color or perms with a pointed tip, very pliable and "squeeze sensitive." We cut a comfortable length of fish tubing to run from the very bottom to several inches above the tip. We snipped the point of the bottle to fit the tubing snugly and threaded it thru. This takes very little pressure to send the liquid upward. It is also clear, which facilitates allowing only enough liquid into her mouth as is comfortable or to get her sucking.

> Crystal uses a sports bottle. It must be an air-tight bottle. At first we had to squeeze it a little to get the "juices" going. Since she closed her mouth around the straw, when she swallowed, a siphon would automatically be started. She caught on and the process is easily initiated by her except on "down days." On those days, we sometimes need to help her get started. The sports bottle is nearly spill-proof and age-appropriate. She reaches out for it.

> We use a squeezable plastic glass with a straw in it. As she drinks we slowly squeeze a little fluid up so that the fluid goes up the straw and so that she can drink freely, but has to suck to get it out. Then we gradually squeeze less fluid until she gets the hang of it, and has to suck on her own.

> We use a Pat Saunders drinking straw, which has a one-way valve. After removing the lips from the straw it stays almost full. There is also a clip on the side of the straw to hook onto the side of small glasses or cups. The clip prevents the straw from falling out of the cup. Only clear liquids can pass through the valve.

What are some commercial products that can be used to thicken liquids?

> No More Lumps is an all purpose thickener. No pre-mixing is necessary and it can be stirred directly into foods (hot or cold). It has no taste to it, or detectable texture when used. It is distributed by The Dial Corp, Food Division, Phoenix, AZ 85077. Phone # 1-800-528-0849 for questions or comments. A 6 ounce container sells for about $2.

> Thicken Up is available from TAD Enterprises, 9356 Pleasant, Tinley Park, Illinois 60477, 1-800-438-6153. An 8 ounce can is $3.50; Individual packets are 24 cents or 75 for $18.00. I buy a case so I only pay for shipping once every 4-5 months.

How can we measure her swallowing?

A video fluoroscopic study can be done during swallowing if **oral-pharyngeal** (swallowing) **dysfunction** is suspected. Minor problems can be handled by changing the diet to include foods that are easier to swallow. If there are serious swallowing problems, a gastrostomy button often is recommended to avoid problems of aspiration or pneumonia and to decrease the long and difficult process of oral food intake.

> Clare had no problems with the video fluoroscopy, although she wasn't awfully keen on the taste of the barium, which was mixed with her favorite breakfast cereal. We found the video fluoroscopy very helpful in explaining many of Clare's difficulties in eating and drinking. Until we saw the video we did not know, for example that the reason for her delay in swallowing was due to her acquired habit of "tongue blocking" to prevent aspiration.

What causes gastroesophageal reflux (GER)?

After a meal, food and acid from the stomach surges back up into the esophagus. GER occurs when the muscular part of the lower esophagus that normally prevents food and acid from the stomach backing up into the esophagus malfunctions. It can cause vomiting or inflammation of the esophagus, called **esophagitis** and inhalation of food or liquid to the lungs, called **aspiration**.

What are the symptoms of GER?

Gastroesophageal reflux is common and for most people it does not interfere with health. GER is suspected when there is weight loss, irritability after meals, vomiting after eating or continued upper airway congestion. Heartburn is a specific symptom for reflux and conservative treatment can begin without further diagnostic studies. However, heartburn cannot be seen, so it is sometimes difficult to detect in girls with RS. Other early symptoms include clusters of coughing, frequently increasing at mealtimes, and increased swallowing. Stomach contents can reflux all the way into the throat or nose (regurgitation) causing coughing, choking and difficulty breathing. She may regurgitate at night, and you may notice only nighttime coughing or wheezing. You may find evidence by the presence of fluid or blood on her pillow. She may have recurrent pulmonary infections that are brought on by regurgitation with aspiration.

> Heather began having sporadic episodes of forceful belching, "dry heaves," and gagging for no apparent reason. Her appetite decreased to outright refusal to eat or drink.

> Lauren didn't have the typical regression, but the screaming and not sleeping started around the time she was eating more solids. During the next several years she cried for hours, slept very little (except heavily during the day when on phenobarbital), vomited blood, vomited yeasty smelling stuff that fermented in her esophagus because it was refluxed up and stuck there. My pediatrician would say "that's interesting," and "she's neurologically irritable." Finally another pediatrician saw her, put things together and started her on Reglan and an acid reducer-MIRACLE! Sleeping improved, screaming almost totally stopped most of the time. During a month trial off Reglan, he couldn't even bear to read my daily diary it was so bad. This didn't happen until she was 5-6 years old. I wish we'd been able to get beyond the "it's just…" earlier.

What can we do to minimize the GER?

Symptoms may be provoked or aggravated by lying down or bending over after meals, wearing tight-fitting clothes, straining for bowel movements, eating the wrong foods at the wrong time or exercises such as physical therapy soon after eating. Some medications may make GER worse.

How can she be tested for GER?

Gastric acid reflux can be diagnosed by using specific tests. A barium swallow study is not sufficient. The doctor may order an upper gastrointestinal series (UGI). She is given a food or drink mixture of barium and a series of subsequent x-rays follow the path of ingestion. If the series study does not reveal GER but it is still suspected, it is important to do an overnight pH probe study, which is the most definitive test for GER. In this test, a wire probe is placed near the esophageal sphincter muscle. The acid reflux is measured while she goes about normal activities. The doctor may also decide to do an endoscopy to look into the esophagus with a camera. Biopsies are taken to confirm the presence of inflammation. If inflammation is found, the doctor may order a gastric emptying scan to rule out delayed emptying of the stomach as a cause of the reflux. Manometry is a test that may be used to look for malfunction of the gastroesophageal sphincter, but this test is not practical in girls with RS.

> Stacie's biopsy showed severe esophagitis and reflux. She was not symptomatic except for periodic crying which had recently accelerated after breakfast and during the night. For anyone whose child is repeatedly crying with no apparent reason, get her checked for reflux. And know that the UGI series only confirms reflux in 50% of the cases, so it is not at all conclusive. If your child has symptoms of reflux, even though the UGI series is negative, get an endoscopy. The endoscopy inspection has only a 30% correlation with the biopsy, so the final results rest on the biopsy. The photographs of Stacie's insides look normal to the naked eye, but the biopsy confirmed severe problems.

How serious is GER?

GER can be very painful. Some adults who have this problem mistake it for a heart attack. The most serious consequence of reflux is food being drawn into the lungs, resulting in aspiration pneumonia or lung abscess. In addition to causing great distress and discomfort, reflux may lead to cessation of breathing or other respiratory problems, poor weight gain and esophagitis.

How is GER treated?

Initial treatment involves an anti-reflux diet which restricts spicy, acidic, and greasy foods as well as coffee, tea, cola, alcohol, peppermint and chocolate. The quantity of food eaten at one sitting should be limited. Weight should be kept within the normal range. Elevating the head of the bed 6 inches for sleeping or resting is very important. Putting blocks under the legs of the bed or a wedge under the mattress is more beneficial than pillow-bolstering. Use of pillows may actually make symptoms worse for some people. Chewing gum or sucking candy may relieve symptoms because the release of a lot of saliva can soothe an irritated esophagus. Feeding solutions can be thickened with commercial thickening products to decrease swallowing and choking difficulties.

> Heather is not happy about giving up her spicy foods. She loves Italian dishes! (Getting her to give up her cigarettes and margaritas wasn't difficult!) We keep Heather sitting up in her wheelchair for a minimum of 20 minutes following meals. If she needs to get out of her wheelchair, we maintain an elevated head position. She sleeps in an electric hospital bed for easier positioning. Heather can neither chew gum nor suck a candy, but I did notice an increase in her drooling during the period of symptoms. I associated it with reluctance to swallow when in fact, her body may have been working to soothe itself.

What drugs are used?

Antacid medications such as Maalox or Mylanta may be helpful. **Do not initiate antacid use without a doctor's direction,** as antacids interfere with the absorption of many other medicines and are to be completely avoided with some medicines. If symptoms persist, drug therapy is begun. Drug therapy is aimed at either changing the sphincter pressure or decreasing gastric acid production. Different drugs affect different sphincter muscles. In some cases, it is desirable to increase esophageal sphincter pressure but decrease pyloric sphincter pressure. Acid blockers include drugs such as ranitidine (Zantac®) or famotidine (Pepcid®). Lansoprazole (Prevasid®) or omeprazole (Prilosec®) are used when the symptoms are severe.

> Heather's reflux is being comfortably controlled by a combination of Zantac® which inhibits gastric acid secretion and by Reglan® which accelerates gastric emptying. The medications however, have increased her problem with constipation.

> I use papaya tablets with for Megan's reflux. Since we started using them she almost never has a reflux problem and only needs them occasionally now.

Are there medications which should be avoided in girls with RS?

Propulsid® (cissipride) is sometimes prescribed to increase esophogeal and gastric motility. **However, it should not be used in girls with RS,** as it increases the potential for heart wave abnormalities (prolonged Q-T syndrome) which are often found in RS.

What is the goal of treatment of GER?

The aim in most cases is to achieve symptomatic relief with medical therapy while watching for complications. In addition to esophagitis, complications can include ulcers and strictures in the esophagus, aspiration pneumonia and other chronic pulmonary diseases, gastrointestinal bleeding and failure to thrive. If symptoms persist or complications develop, surgery may be necessary.

How does surgery help GER?

A surgical procedure called a fundoplication may be done in which the opening from the esophagus to the stomach is made smaller, thus preventing reflux. When fundoplication is done for the purpose of treating GER, it does not interfere with taking food by mouth.

> Lauren had reflux which has been so severe for her entire life that she now has some permanent cellular changes in spots on her esophagus called Barrett's Esophagus. Fundoplication really helped greatly, but some damage was already done. We did have her on acid blockers and Reglan since she was five, but the last few years it wasn't enough.

My daughter just won't drink liquids. How much does she need to drink each day?

Water is essential for life. The girl with RS may have difficulty sucking and swallowing fluids, which puts her at risk for dehydration and constipation. Drooling may add to her fluid loss. The following fluid requirements may be helpful:

Age in Years	Weight in Pounds	Cups of Fluid
1-3	29	6¾
4-6	44	8¾
7-10	62	10
11-14	101	10½

Meeting fluid requirements can be a real challenge. You'll have to be creative and persistent. Here are some helpful tips:

• Distribute fluid intake evenly throughout the day.

- Request her school to give fluids in a minimum amount daily.
- Thicken fluids to make drinking easier (with pureed fruit, instant oat cereal, unprocessed bran, dehydrated infant foods).
- Use a variety of foods which count as fluid when they become liquid at room temperature (popsicles, ice cream, jello).
- Slushies" or other "icy" drinks are a good source of fluid.
- Include lots of vegetables and fruits in her diet. They contain the highest amounts of water of all solid foods.
- Decrease natural loss of water by putting a humidifier in her bedroom or keeping her indoors when it is very hot.
- Avoid highly sweetened fruit juices as they can actually increase her need for fluids.

> Rebecca found drinking a challenge. She couldn't hold the cup and had trouble closing her lips. Our technique was to hold a cloth under her chin to give her lower jaw to give some support, and to catch the drips. We used a tilted or cut out cup so we could see how far to tip it.

> We taught Jocelyn to use a straw by giving her juice boxes. You can squeeze it gently and force the juice up thru the little straw. Once it gets started you can almost continue the sucking action just by swallowing the juice in your mouth. Kind of like priming the pump. Once she gets going, it's close to an automatic action and she doesn't have to think to much about what she is doing. I just squeeze again if she needs help to get going. Jocelyn now will drink from any straw, any length, without help to initiate.

How can we tell if she is dehydrated?

If you are not sure if she is getting ample fluid, look for these signs:

- decreased amount of urine (check number and wetness of diapers)
- dry lips
- sunken eyes, dark circles under the eyes
- dry skin (press on skin to see if skin bounces back)
- extra thirst
- headache, fatigue, dizziness
- weight loss

What should we do if she shows signs of dehydration?

Call her doctor immediately. Dehydration can be serious.

When is a gastrostomy (G-button) placed?

If she cannot suck, swallow or chew well enough to get enough nourishment or if she has recurrent bouts of aspiration pneumonia, when food surges up from the stomach after a meal and causes vomiting into the lungs, a gastrostomy should be considered.

> Jenny experienced recurring pneumonia and bronchitis for several years. Approximately every six weeks she would be on antibiotics and we made numerous trips to the hospital. She almost died about two years ago from a severe case of pneumonia. This prompted a major push to determine the cause. Swallowing studies indicated that Jenny was aspirating everything from liquids to solids. The doctors recommended a gastrostomy button. After viewing the fluoroscopic video of Jenny's swallowing compared to a normal swallowing, we were convinced that Jenny could not continue to thrive without the gastrostomy button. The doctors all said she would not survive if we continued to feed her by mouth. Jenny did not have a problem with weight, only aspiration. After she recovered from the illness we took her to the hospital for placement of the button.

Our daughter vomited easily and even when she didn't actually vomit she had a great deal of reflux which caused ulcers in her esophagus. Her reflux had been controlled pretty well with Zantac® and Reglan® until the last couple of years. We recently had fundoplication and a gastrostomy button for her reflux, and her esophagus has healed completely. She still eats by mouth, but we supplement it with G-button feedings. Her only problem is that she cannot eat as much because her stomach was made smaller by the fundoplication and it is hard to get enough energy into her.

Shelby constantly sputtered on any liquid we gave her, and the result was she was lethargic and weak. She also never chewed, and I calculated that we were spending approximately 5 to 6 hours a day just trying to get nutrients in her. Major frustration for both child and caregiver. She was also starting to aspirate. Finally, we never knew if she was getting all her medicine, since it always seemed like half of it would come rolling down her chin. Or, she would pocket it in her cheek somewhere like a squirrel, and it would come out later. Shelby has had her gastrostomy button for 15 months now, and it has saved her life, literally. Medicines are no longer a problem and can be given even if she's asleep. She now weighs 50 pounds. It was the best decision for us, and Shelby agrees, because she has no interest in struggling with food anymore. That's sad, but I prefer it to the way it was pre-gastrostomy button.

How does the gastrostomy button work?

A small opening is made surgically in the abdominal and stomach walls, and a small, plastic, pliable device (the button) is placed through the opening into the stomach. This is minor surgery, but generally requires anesthesia. Through the button, the child is fed either blenderized feedings or commercially prepared formulas. Before she leaves the hospital, you will be taught how to care for the tube. A one-way valve prevents stomach contents from leaking out of the stomach. For feedings, the plug is removed and tubing is inserted. Another procedure for creating an opening for a tube feeding into the stomach is called a **percutaneous endoscopic gastrostomy tube** or **PEG**. This procedure may not require general anesthesia and can generally be done with local anesthesia and intravenous sedation. If she is at risk for aspiration, a **fundoplication** may be done as well. The surgeon makes the opening from the esophagus into the stomach smaller, which prevents regurgitation (vomiting) and reflux.

How can we take such a drastic step?

The idea of using alternative feeding methods is often upsetting for parents. It is hard to consider letting go of traditional feeding methods for a way that seems "unnatural." Some parents feel that they have failed or look at it as yet another skill that she will have to lose. These are all normal reactions. However, the best way to cope with change is knowledge and information. One big consolation is that afterwards, families are always glad they made the decision. The most often repeated comment is, "Wish we had done it sooner." The child gets the nutrition she needs and is more alert, healthier and more comfortable. There is no more second guessing about how much medication was swallowed. Adequate fluids are easy to provide. To top off the list, parents no longer have to spend hours each day struggling to get her to eat.

What kind of formula is used?

Commercially prepared nutritionally complete formulas are designed specifically for children, and home-prepared formulas are acceptable substitutes. However, you should consult your physician and dietitian for assistance in the preparation of blenderized formula to ensure that your child receives adequate energy, protein, vitamins and minerals. Supplemental vitamins are not needed if she is taking a commercially prepared formula.

How often are the feedings done?

Formulas may be given as either a continuous drip, an intermittent bolus feeding, or a combination of the two techniques. Continuous drip feedings, as the name implies, are given by continuous drip over a 10-12 hour period or more. Bolus feedings consist of several ounces of formula given over a 10-20 minute period. The total amount of formula given and the rate of administration varies on the basis of energy needs and the tolerance level of your child. A combination of these techniques allows greater flexibility in feeding and can be adjusted to fit the family schedule.

What problems can we expect?

If the formula is given too rapidly, nausea, vomiting, bloating, abdominal cramping and diarrhea may occur. Constipation may be encountered, not as a result of the formula, but due to the increased volume. This can be remedied by giving additional free water, formula with fiber or a bowel stimulant such as Milk of Magnesia, lactulose or a Senakot preparation. Problems associated with the button include tissue build-up or granulation around the gastrostomy button, a blocked tube, and leaking around the button. These problems are easily remedied. Rarely, infection or an allergic response occurs and may necessitate removal of the button.

How much does the formula cost?

The cost of tube feeding will vary depending on the quantity of formula used. The costs include formula, syringes, bags—if milk is given by continuous drip tubing, and a pump. Many insurance companies or Medicaid will cover the cost of all or a portion of these supplies. Check with your physician's office. Sometimes a letter of necessity is helpful in getting these costs covered by the insurance company.

What are the results of supplemental oral or gastrostomy button feedings?

The results of supplemental oral or G-button feedings are positive. Girls who have been supplemented with adequate amounts of formula gained weight and grew taller. Parents and teachers also reported improvements in attention span, eye gaze, disposition and stamina.

> Shelby is able to swallow fairly well, but she never has been able to chew. At age 6, she had been stuck at 30 pounds for three whole years, and was painfully skinny. We also noticed that she was getting very weak. It turned out that she was expending more energy in the effort to eat than we could actually get her to ingest, resulting in a deficit in energy intake with each meal! I was spending about five hours every day just trying to shove nutrients into her. It was exhausting and frustrating for BOTH of us. Only the dog enjoyed all the stuff that was rolling down her mouth and onto the floor. Hence, she became a model candidate for a G-button. Now we know that Shelby is now getting all of her medications. Before, when giving it to her orally, she would spit some out, or it would run down her cheek, or she would sneeze. Now, she also grins widely when she sees me setting up a feeding.

Can she still eat food by mouth?

Unless there are reasons such as poor oral motor dysfunction leading to the risk of aspiration of food into the lungs, children with gastrostomy buttons can continue to eat food by mouth. At this time we are unable to predict the length of time gastrostomy feedings may be necessary. However, if supplemental feedings are no longer needed, the gastrostomy button can be removed. Neither the button nor the hole is permanent, but a scar will remain. Even if the button is not used for feedings, it is often used to "vent" air from the stomach when air swallowing and bloating are a concern.

How do girls with RS respond to placement of the G-button?

We found there is an adjustment phase after a G-button is placed. Jenn had sporadic vomiting the first couple of months after the surgery. But once we settled on an appropriate schedule and her body adjusted and we learned not to move her immediately after a feeding or allow her to bend forward after a feeding the vomiting subsided. Finding a feeding schedule tailored to Jenn's nutritional needs yet allowed time for water feedings as well without overloading her was a challenge initially. But once set, it runs smoothly. And it's easily adaptable if we get off-schedule. With the timed feedings, giving water, toileting, and medicine, we live by the clock!

Michelle is 10 and had the G-button placed about three years ago. Before Michelle's G-button was placed we spent 30 to 90 minutes feeding her each meal. The food had to be pureed and it got to a point where Michelle was throwing up as soon as the hot or salty food was given. When we started with the dessert like smashed Jell-O or yogurt, she threw up. I can tell you from my own experience that this procedure was the best thing I ever did for my daughter. Her quality of life improved in every aspect; she had more strength, endurance, alertness, better eye contact and best of all she gained weight. It was a global improvement.

Shelby had aspiration pneumonia four times last year, and I can tell you for sure that the G-button literally saved her life. She now gets all nutrition through her G-button. I don't blame her though. I remember well how she struggled so much to get just a little food down without choking and gagging. Meal time was truly an awful time for her, because she knew that it was the only thing that would make the hunger pangs in her belly go away, but it took hours every day to do.

We almost lost Jenn because of poor swallowing and aspiration problems. Recurring bouts of pneumonia within a nine month period and a second swallow study confirmed that Jenn was at high risk for aspiration. G-button time. Jenn's button was placed 2 years ago. She feels better, is more alert, is rarely sick anymore, and doesn't cough, choke and sputter at mealtime anymore. Her appetite is satisfied and she even giggles in anticipation of feeding time. I will be honest here though. Jenn still does cough, sputter and choke even though she no longer takes any food or drink by mouth. Her swallowing skills have deteriorated to the point that her own saliva is her enemy. We just constantly coax her to cough to clear her throat and swallow. Some days it's not so good, but we're making it.

Kayleigh had not gained any weight in 3 years. The gastroenterologist told us that nutritional supplements were needed and possibly a G-button. We were upset. I thought I could fatten my girl up. I am a farmer's wife and I had fattened the rest of us up. So I came home ready to cook up a storm and fatten my girl up. For two years with the help of specialists and nutritionists we tried, but Kayleigh only got worse. So, 18 months ago my daughter had G-button surgery, and today she has a Mic-key button. She is 70 pounds, not 38 pounds. She is on the growth chart! She is using her hands, stronger, advancing in skills, and she has a better quality of life. She was failing to thrive before surgery. She bounces back from seizures better today. She still eats foods she likes, but she gets her supplement at night.

How will increased nourishment affect her general health?

Last year at this time she was about 29 pounds and looked like she was starving. Today she is a beautiful, round-cheeked 44 pounds, and much healthier. For us, the G-button was the only way to go, and we have not regretted it for one moment. Shelby actually grins from ear to ear when she sees me coming towards her with the feeding stuff. She knows that she can be satisfied without that awful struggle. She has so much more strength and energy. She's actually trying to stand for the first time. She hardly naps anymore. She is more "there," and laughs and laughs. Her eye contact is three times better than a month ago. I also have an extra four hours a day to play and snuggle with her instead of trying to pry open her mouth or trying to make her swallow something, anything! I *know* her medicines are in her system, not in the rug or my hair. And I get an added bonus: less laundry!

The results have been amazing. Up until only recently Jenny had no illnesses at all, no bronchitis, pneumonia, not even a cold. The G-button has made caretaking much easier for us and her teachers at school. Her vomiting is greatly reduced, but still occurs on occasion. Since we feed her totally through the G-button, we were much concerned with her loss of enjoyment in eating. My wife and I went on a diet of canned liquid formula to see what it would be like. We would gulp down the formula as fast as we could to avoid any taste or eating enjoyment. After 48 hours we got used to it. I don't think it is too bad and feeding through the G-button is much better than vomiting, being sick, and in the hospital all the time. In our experience the G-button was a major improvement in Jenny's life.

Naomi has the G-button without the fundoplication. She still has occasional reflux. We are very pleased with the way the tube works for her. She doesn't swallow at all, so we had very little choice. At four and a half, she is now almost 40 inches and 48 pounds.

Will she always be thin?

Unless aggressive nutritional rehabilitation is undertaken, she may always be thin. However, for reasons we don't understand, a small number of girls gain too much weight and become obese after their teen years.

Ashley weighs 115 lbs and is 18. She went through a chubby period around 5 years old. I will tell you, though, that she went through a skinny period around 10. I would suggest that you keep the fats down to a minimum when possible. This extra weight may come in handy later on just do not stuff her too much, as extra weight is tough later on that I can tell you, for sure. Ashley needs to lose about 15 pounds. I know that some parents cannot believe this, but it is true.

The author wishes to thank the following professionals for ideas and information which was used to develop this chapter: Marilyn Rice Asaro, RD; Merry Meek, CCC, MS; Kathleen J. Motil, M.D., PhD.

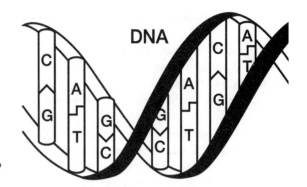

DNA

GENETICS

Are genetic *and* inherited *the same thing?*

No. Literally, the word *genetic* means "of a gene." Therefore, a genetic disorder is one that involves a faulty gene. *Inherited* means a gene that is passed from one generation to the next. It is possible to have a genetic disorder caused by a new mutation to a gene that is not inherited from the previous generation. However, once the person with the mutation reproduces, there is a chance the faulty gene will be passed on, or inherited.

What are genes and chromosomes?

Human beings have 46 chromosomes in a set of 23 pairs. The chromosomes are different sizes and shapes, and they contain the genes that act as a "blueprint" for how a person develops. The genes are all scrambled up on the chromosomes such that a gene for making hemoglobin in blood may be right next to a gene that influences hair color or brain development. Each cell in the body contains all 46 chromosomes with the exception of the eggs and sperm, which are special. They have gone through a special kind of cell division to get only one copy of each chromosome in each cell. This is so that when they meet and join together to make a baby, they don't increase the number of chromosomes in the child. (You want to end up with 23+23=46). So you end up with one copy of each chromosome, and therefore, one copy of each gene, from each of your parents. Because the genes are separated onto the different chromosomes, they can sort themselves differently into each egg and sperm so that all your kids don't look just alike but resemble each other and you.

What are the X and Y chromosomes?

The special pair of chromosomes which determine sex are called X and Y. To get a girl, the sperm and the egg both carried the X chromosome (so that girls have two XX's). For a boy, the sperm carried a Y and the egg an X (so that boys have an XY). X chromosomes are very different from Y chromosomes. They are big and contain thousands of genes. Y chromosomes are very tiny and only carry a few genes. So that females don't end up with two "active" copies of all those genes on the X (which appears to have severe developmental effects on the embryo), something curious happens shortly after fertilization of the egg. It begins to divide to make new cells. While there are still just a thousand or so cells, each cell "decides" to turn off one copy of the X. In most cases, this is a random event meaning that in one cell the X from Mom is turned off or inactivated, while in the next cell the X from the dad is turned off. When these cells divide, they keep the same X active from there on out, so that a cell which contains an active X from Mom gives rise only to cells with Mom's X active. They don't turn on or activate the other copy again.

When you see a tortoiseshell or calico cat, you know that they have inherited genes for different color coats from each of their parents." The mixed up pattern of colors is indicative of the randomness of inactivation in the whole body.

In most females, the pattern is essentially random throughout the body. Because the process happens so early in development, sometimes one tissue happens to get made up mostly of cells which inactivated the same X each time, which is called skewing. And sometimes, if one of the X chromosomes contains a gene that has a mutation or change that interferes with the normal division of cells with that X active, we see that the other X chromosome is always active in each cell. About 10% of women have non-random inactivation (keeping the same copy of the X active). So it can happen without a mutation which influences survival and division of cell just by luck.

What do dominant and recessive mean?

The X and Y chromosomes are referred to as sex chromosomes. All other chromosomes are called **auto-somal**. **Dominant** means that if there is a mutation in one of the two copies of the gene, you get symptoms. For **recessive** diseases, both copies of the gene involved have to have mutations before there are symptoms. So for dominant diseases, if a parent carries the mutation, we can generally see it because it affects the parent's development just like the child. For recessive diseases, the parents are silent carriers because just one normal copy of the gene is enough to get by without symptoms. For disorders caused by genes on the X chromosome, it gets more complicated. Dominant and recessive are determined by whether a woman who carries a mutation in the gene (on one copy of the X) has symptoms (dominant) or not (recessive). A key feature of the two is that X-linked recessive disorders tend to lead to more males being affected than females, while X-linked dominant disorders are seen more often in girls.

What are "fortunate" and "unfortunate" X-inactivation?

These are terms used to describe X-chromosome inactivation patterns in females carrying mutations in genes on the X-chromosome. If a woman is carrying an X-linked recessive mutation, then she usually does not have symptoms of the disease. The exception to this happens if she happened to have inactivated the normal copy of the gene in most of the cells in her body, i.e. **"unfortunate inactivation."** The opposite event is **"fortunate inactivation"** and generally is noted in X-linked dominant disorders where a carrier of a mutation is expected to have symptoms but does not. In the case of fortunate inactivation, they have fortuitously inactivated the X-chromosome carrying the mutation and left the normal copy to function.

So, is Rett syndrome considered a genetic disorder?

There has been a long debate about whether or not RS is a genetic disorder. Early theories about the cause of RS considered viral infections and post vaccination injuries. The rare families with more than one case of Rett syndrome have led to the current belief that RS does represent a genetic disorder. It is felt to be an X-linked dominant disorder which is caused by a new mutation in the causative gene 99% of the time. This means that the gene was normal in all the cells in the parent, except that in the egg or sperm that went on to make that child, there was a mistake made when the gene was copied in that particular cell. We know that mutations occur more frequently in sperm than in eggs, probably because there are a lot more cell divisions taking place to make males with more chance for error. Females have all the eggs they are going to have by the time they are born. So if the mutation in the RS gene is occurring more frequently in sperm and the gene is on the X chromosome, we will see a lot more affected girls than boys. Researchers are now studying these families in order to narrow the search for the responsible gene. Hopefully, this research will soon lead to a scientific test that will be used to diagnose and predict RS.

Is Rett syndrome inherited?

Because RS is thought to be a new mutation 99% of the time, it is usually not inherited. The genetics of RS are complicated and confusing, and experts do not yet agree on inheritance patterns which may be involved. If RS is usually caused by new mutations in the gene in one egg or sperm, most families would not expect to have any recurrences - male or female.

How common are X-linked dominant disorders?

X-linked dominant disorders are pretty rare. If this theory is correct, Rett syndrome is probably the most common of them. In other X-linked dominant disorders, the mutation is lethal in males. In some of these disorders, severely affected male fetuses have been seen as miscarriages. Since none of the genes that cause these diseases have been found yet, we can only guess why this occurs. The thought is that the product of the gene is absolutely required for early development, so that if a male has only the faulty copy, he cannot develop normally and is miscarried. Girls will have some cells with an active normal copy and some cells with an active mutant copy (because they have two X's).

Why don't we see more cases in one family?

If having a mutation in the gene means that the child will have RS, then we are not likely to see it run in families, since women with RS don't usually have children. In only one case do we know of a woman with RS who had a daughter with RS. She had a 50% chance that the X chromosome in that egg would be the one with the mutation, so a 50% chance that if she had a daughter, she would also have RS.

To understand the familial recurrences, there is also a phenomenon called **germline** or **gonadal mosaicism** that is likely to be involved. This is an unusual situation that occurs when a mutation in a gene happens not in the egg or the sperm, but in a cell in the developing baby. Depending on when during the development the mutation occurs, it could end up in a lot of the tissues in the body or just a few, depending on the fate of the original cell in which the mutation occurred. A person who had this happen in the RS gene during their development may be asymptomatic, because the mutation is not in the cells of the brain. They may, however, make eggs or sperm carrying the faulty copy of the gene and thus transmit the disorder more than once. This may account for the recurrence of RS in sisters. Germline mosaicism has been seen in some autosomal dominant and X-linked dominant disorders and can occur in males and females.

Why haven't there been males with RS?

There have been a few sporadic cases of males with Rett syndrome-like symptoms reported; but none of them were classical cases, making it impossible to know whether they really have the same thing or some other disorder that looks similar. One thought is that males carrying a mutation in the RS gene never develop normally and miscarry early, maybe so early that there is never a recognized pregnancy. Another possibility is that the symptoms look entirely different in males. Maybe they have problems that would actually be considered exclusion criteria for RS. There have been at least two male children who had problems beginning shortly after birth that were born into families with more than one affected female. We do not know if these males were carrying mutations in the RS gene, but are suspicious that they may be. If they are, then the symptoms are so different, we would not recognize it as related to RS.

There has been some speculation that males can carry RS silently, meaning that they carry the mutation in the gene but it does not affect them. We don't think this is happening because of another X-linked disorder called Juberg Heilman syndrome (JHS). In JHS, females are affected; males are unaffected but transmit the disorder to all their daughters (who receive their only X chromosome) and none of their sons (who get their Y chromosome). This is a really rare disorder with only two known families. In these families, the disorder is present in multiple generations and blossoms down the family tree, with more and more affected females. It is unlikely that RS mutations are silent in males since there are a lot of families with RS, and we have never seen a family that has had this pattern.

What is the risk of having another child with RS?

There are only a small number of family recurrences (less than 1% of the reported cases), and these are mostly sisters or twins. There are some families who have RS in two generations (aunt-niece). In one of these families, we have evidence of fortunate inactivation in the normal female carrier who transmitted the disorder. In this case, the sister of a girl with RS gave birth to a daughter with RS.

> Mary was our first child. She now has five other siblings. I know I'm biased in this regard because I love children so much and believe they are a gift from God, but I would certainly encourage you to have more children. Not only will it be good for you, but your daughter will be truly blessed as well. Mary's greatest advocates are her sisters and brothers. They'll be her future caregivers (whether it's in a supervisory role or directly). Having other children helped us to appreciate and understand Mary so much more. Just like Mary has taught us to appreciate and understand the other children.

It would be nice for one sibling to have another "typical" sibling to relate to. Someone that he can share his thoughts and feelings with and someone that he sees is treated like him instead of only being able to compare himself to his sister, who gets "special" care. Not that all those things don't work out to the good, just that we can see the benefits. Sure, there's always a gamble, there always was, we just weren't aware of it before it happened to us. I can't say whether it's "right" for you, but I can say it has been a real blessing for us. I've often thought that in Heaven you won't hear too many people say "I wish we hadn't had so many children," but I can imagine them saying they wish they had more.

As we came to terms with RS and saw beyond the disorder to the daughter that we loved and treasured I realized that if it happened again it would be OK, and at least we'd hit the ground running second time around. We decided that whatever we had we'd welcome it into our family and love it.

When it is inherited and not sporadic, does RS pass through the mother or father?

We have to be very careful about how we interpret the family trees when we are looking at a disorder with a high number of new errors in the gene. Recurrences in families may not result from passage of the same faulty copy of the gene from one generation to the next, but may be the chance occurrence of two new errors in the same family. But for close relatives, like sisters, it is more likely that they inherited the same faulty copy from one of their parents who is carrying it silently. We believe that for affected sisters, it may come from either parent, through germline mosaicism in the father or either germline mosaicism or fortunate X-inactivation in the mother. We have identified a few families where RS occurred in two generations and was transmitted through a mother who carried the faulty RS gene silently through fortunate X-chromosome inactivation. We do not believe that a male can inherit a faulty copy of the gene and carry it silently.

What are the chances of having another girl with RS?

If you have a daughter with RS and no other affected relatives, the recurrence risk is less than 1% for your family (you and your children). In families with more than one child with RS, the situation is different and would need to be addressed through a professional genetics counselor.

What is the hope of genetics research?

Geneticists are looking at families with only one case of RS to try to find out what is different in the child that neither parent has. They are also studying families with more than one case of RS, enabling them to narrow in on the culprit gene which is responsible for the disorder. This should help them to develop a test to offer you one day to ease your minds about your other kids and grandkids. When we learn more about what is not working, we can target our treatments earlier, and even stop or alter the progression of RS in affected kids.

These girls are my daughters and I love them more than anything in the world. Maybe I'm not the person you want to hear from when deciding whether or not to have another child. We are the less than 1%. It happened to us and when we first found out we were devastated. But I'm getting really good at this RS thing. It gets easier. You will probably not have another child with Rett syndrome. Your chances are very low. And please don't let my situation freak you out, having more than one RS child is not a common thing. But if it does happen again, you can survive it. My family is doing very well. We live life just like every other family, with a few accommodations. We go to movies and to Barney concerts and horse-back riding. We go out for ice cream and McDonald's. We tell everyone who's interested about Rett syndrome and how they can help. I don't plan on having a third child until the gene is found, and if that miracle is meant to be, it will happen. Until then, we just live day by day and try to find the joy in living.

How close are we to finding the gene?

There has been a surge in progress in the research over the last couple of years. We have narrowed the search to about 0. 6% of the genome. We believe that the gene lies in Xq28, which is the band at the end of the long arm of the X-chromosome. This is an exceptionally gene-rich region where there may be more than a thousand genes. There are numerous diseases that are caused by genes in this region, thus the Human Genome Project has targeted it for sequencing and gene searching. We hope that these resources will help speed up our search. It is impossible to say, though, how fast we will find it. It could be tomorrow, but it may take a few years to sort through all those genes and find the one that is not working right in RS.

When we know the gene, what can we do?

We hope that we will be able to develop a test for diagnosing RS. This will be helpful both for making the diagnosis promptly when a child begins to develop symptoms. Right now, we have to wait on the child to go through the regression before we can know that RS is the problem. If we could identify RS before the child lost skills, there is a potential for earlier and more specific treatment. This test could potentially be used as a prenatal test or to check for silent RS carriers.

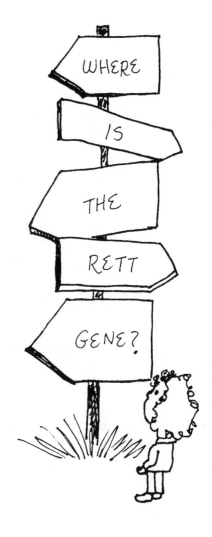

The author wishes to thank the following professionals for ideas and information which was used to develop this chapter: Carolyn Schanen, MD.

WHEN THE SCHOOL BUS DOESN'T COME ANYMORE

There are advantages for the woman with Rett Syndrome. Her mental state is essentially stable and she continues to learn; her motivation and skill for hand use may increase; her potential for walking continues in spite of the tendency to develop deformities; and her ability to communicate improves. We can help this communication by protecting her long term relationships with the people who matter most to her, by making time for undemanding face to face interaction, and by learning to use nonspeech vocalization and music as a personal means of communication.

Dr. Alison Kerr, FRCP, FRCP & CH
The Future for Rett Girls, invited lecture 1991, revised 1994

When the school bus doesn't come anymore, the woman with RS needs an appropriate adult program that meets her own special needs. A number of different programs may be found in the community, which should be explored for the one best suited to her. Often, these programs are a carry-over of the developmental approach used in the public schools. However, while the structure of the program is important, the most crucial aspect is finding caregivers who understand her and are knowledgeable about RS. They will make the biggest difference in her life. She needs to continue therapies that will help her remain as mobile as possible, and a communication system that allows her to relate her wants and needs and to make choices. She should have good medical care by professionals who are aware of the changes which take place as she advances in age and stage of RS. She should have opportunities to participate in community activities and experiences that enrich her social life. Her parents are getting older, too, and may not be able to continue to provide the same quantity and quality of care as in earlier years. It is wise to seek help so that she is allowed the continuity of good care.

Many families tell us that in many ways, the older girl and woman with RS is more settled and mellow, better than she has been her whole life. She makes better eye contact, is less irritable and has fewer panic attacks, seizures and breathing problems. She may sleep better. The sweeping mood changes that characterized her early years are gone and she enjoys activities that once frustrated or angered her. Her hand movements may become less complicated and intense.

It seems the older Mary gets, the better she has been doing. Lately, we've noticed that when she reads a book she is turning the pages on her own, which is a skill lost years ago. She is hooked on the television game show, Wheel of Fortune and becomes agitated when a contestant chooses a wrong letter or guesses wrong. Many of her physical skills have improved.

Heather did not learn to walk independently until she was 18. She now often crawls into the living room from her room, pulls up on the couch, turns around and walks back into her room. She will repeat this several times, and I'm certain it is just something she's enjoying doing because she's discovered she can. She has also made small progress in other things. She actually watches TV now, when she used to never be interested in it at all, and loves classical and semi-classical music programs like the Boston Pops on TV. She's always liked classical music, but is clearer in

> her preferences now. She is more assertive, more demonstrative about what she does and does not like than when she was younger. All in all, she is becoming more observant and seems more "with it" than she was when she was younger.

She may continue to walk well into adulthood, but as she gets older she may face other problems. Her muscle tone may increase, causing contractures of her joints that limit mobility. Girls with RS who have the least muscle tone (hypotonia) as children become the most rigid or spastic (hypertonic) in adulthood. When tight muscles pull her joints into abnormal positions, she may develop foot deformities which make it more difficult to walk and even to find shoes that fit. Dystonia may begin with the foot turning in and over time, may advance and worsen with movement. She may have increased kyphosis or scoliosis and intermittent muscle spasms. All of these factors can lead to decreased mobility.

To minimize deformities:

- Promote good standing and sitting posture
- Encourage active movement through walking and exercise
- Use hydrotherapy
- Do passive range of motion exercises
- Use hand, elbow and/or foot splints
- Treat rapidly progressing scoliosis with bracing or surgery
- Correct foot deformities before they cause discomfort

Many women gain sufficient weight in early adulthood, and some even become overweight. However, if she weighs well below what she should for her height, measures should be taken to increase her weight. If this cannot be accomplished by adding calories through extra meals and snacks in her diet, inserting a G-button may be necessary.

Seizures often come less frequently or even disappear in adulthood. In women who continue to have seizures, they are usually well-controlled with medication. If she has not had seizures for a considerable period of time, it may be possible to reduce or gradually stop anti-seizure medications. **This should always be done very slowly, and only with a doctor's permission.**

As she gets older, the disorganized breathing patterns which she had as a child may decrease. Hyperventilation usually decreases, although she may continue to have breath holding episodes. While sometimes difficult to watch, these episodes do not seem to cause pain or distress. They may occur rarely at night, but they do not seem to contribute to a drop in blood oxygen supply. If you notice long breath holding at night or breath holding that produces a color change, it may be important to see an Ear, Nose and Throat specialist to rule out a simple obstruction caused by enlarged tonsils and/or adenoids. In rare cases, surgery is necessary and helpful.

While we do not understand why, some women return to the crying and irritability which characterized their early years. This is frustrating for everyone concerned. Sometimes the source can be traced to a toothache, constipation, heartburn, headache, menstrual pain or muscle aches. Sometimes it can be identified as anger, frustration or boredom. Unfortunately, at other times these crying spells cannot be understood. It is very important to rule out obvious physical causes for pain, such as mentioned above. Some of the remedies which worked in childhood may work again. If not, sometimes giving her comforting words and some quiet space to recover is what she needs most.

While sudden death in sleep does occur, most women with RS can continue to live well into their 40's and 50's with good medical care, nutrition and therapy.

> I feel so blessed that my daughter has lived 33 years. She grows more precious and beautiful as the years go by and with each additional day I feel blessed with her presence.

What kind of programs are available when her school years are over?

In most cases, education in the public schools can continue until age 21. After this time, the availability of programs varies vastly from one area to another. Programs range from respite and in-home care to sheltered workshops and day centers. Residential programs present another option. More recently, some girls with RS have been able to attend college classes with assistance or work at community jobs with a job coach.

HOME AWAY FROM HOME

Sometimes a family feels they can no longer care for their daughter at home full-time. Parents may be getting older or have health problems that limit their ability to provide the quality care their daughter needs. The physical and emotional strain on the family may be too much to cope with, especially for the single parent. There may not be adequate support or respite care from the extended family or through the community. In some cases, the family feels that she will do better in a residential setting which can provide 24 hour care. Whatever the reason, making a decision to find an alternative living arrangement can be painful and difficult. Finding the right home is often hard, and sometimes impossible. The family must choose to either remain in their situation and feel drained, or place their daughter somewhere else and feel guilty. There is often no choice that is good for everyone. Parents may face criticism and judgement from others, and they will probably always feel some sadness.

Dawn is in a group home. She also was in what you would call an "institution" for years when she was younger. I am not going to defend myself or my family on this as I have done it a million times. I never bring this up much because many people have very harshly judged my family on this decision. That is not right. No one has ever walked in another's shoes. Even each Rett family/circumstance is very different than the next. We need to be supportive of all situations. I know many have their girls at home with them, but for many reasons, some of us cannot.

It is easy to be quick to judge when we couldn't possibly know all the circumstances. Our adult daughter has been placed out of our home since she was five. At that time, around 1970, service providers and services were limited except perhaps in major population centers. The trend was to centrally locate the individuals with special needs and gather the "resources" and provide the services. Families believed that by institutionalizing their child, they were obtaining the best services available for their disabled child (remember that there was limited information on disabilities then). Although Missy has lived apart from us for 20 plus years, we continue to love her dearly and to be heavily involved in her care. She lives four miles away in a small group home. I serve on the Board of Directors of the home and we remain her legal guardians. Ironically, I feel that I would never have been this close to my only daughter through the years if she had not had Rett syndrome.

Mary was placed in an institution, then later moved to a group home. As a single parent, I had to rely on babysitters, and Mary's behavior had become so bad that I could not keep a sitter and she was kicked out of every school, including the one that took the worst of the worst. My guilt sent me into therapy until I accepted that none of us can be everything to our children. Mary moved into a group home and I have never been out of her life. I go to every treatment planning session. I fight all the battles all of us do, and bring Mary home for weekends. She never lost me. She just has me in a more loving capacity because I am not doing the hard work of training her. We can enjoy each other much more. Mary is 37 and I'd say I've done a darn good job of hanging in there with her.

How easy it is to judge others. I think we are trained to be cautious and are primed to defend our situations and our daughters. When the majority of us hear the word "institution" we envision the cold, heartless, horrible places of years past. Every family is different and I feel does the best they can and makes the right choices for their individual situation. I can see it from both sides of that fence as I am the parent of a girl with RS and the foster parent of a young lady with cerebral palsy. She was "placed" with me when she was six. People always ask me that nasty question, "why?" I answer them with the truth. The parents knew that to allow her to live with my family and me was the best for Melissa. It broke their hearts to let her go and to not be a part of her everyday life. But they did it purely out of love for their daughter and her needs.

How do we find out of home placement?

It is probably best to contact your state Developmental Disabilities Administration (DDA). Today, children are not placed into state facilities (institutions). All of the agencies participate in a review of each case. If she is over 18, she automatically qualifies for Medicaid, which provides assistance in the home at crucial hours, foster care in a family especially trained to deal with her problems or a group home.

"Out-of-home placement" were once words that terrified me. However, my child, Deborah, was only four years old and exhibited severely disruptive and aggressive behaviors toward her seven and six year-old sisters, as well as anyone else who got in her way. We considered out-of home placement for more than a year before actually making what was the hardest decision of our lives. Fortunately, we found a wonderful small family care home for Deborah and everyone has benefited as a result. Deborah has improved socially and communicatively but of course remains severely handicapped. Her sisters love to have her home for visits, but are also happy to not be living with the turmoil and disruption of Deborah's daily life. We retain legal guardianship and are very involved in her life. Since having a good experience with out-of-home placement, I am no longer scared of those words. I am grateful that there are such good care providers and homelike facilities available.

The process for placement is different from state to state but a cry definitely needs to go out to the social worker or caseworker. If I were looking for care for a loved one I would talk to other parents who are in your area. The local Association For Retarded Citizens (ARC) is a good starting point. People should not discount foster care when they are looking for placements. I know the feeling is sometimes that "if our family can't do it anymore then how can another family?" Well, the other family hasn't been doing it all these years. They also may have different family situations than your family that may make providing care a possibility for them. I've met some pretty amazing foster families that have done marvelous things for some people with some severe disabilities. Every situation is different, just as every person is an individual.

When should we think about residential placement?

Some families keep their daughters at home for all of their lives. If sufficient resources allow for good support and respite services, this can work well. However, the life expectancy of women with RS is well into her 40's. When parents are in their 60's and 70's, it is difficult for them to maintain the level of physical care and attention she requires. They also must face the fact that their daughter may survive them. Parents should plan ahead for when they can no longer care for her at home.

What options do we have for residential care for her?

Large institutional settings are no longer an option for people with disabilities. Small group homes are a least restrictive alternative, providing a home-like atmosphere in the community. Some families prefer to combine resources and benefits to provide her own house or apartment close by with full-time caregivers.

> My idea is that she find two friends that would like to share an apartment with her. I would see if she may be eligible for any kind of subsidized housing or something, and offer her roommates free or greatly reduced rent in exchange for care and support. The whole idea of having two is so that it is more fun and also as backup for each other. I would also be available as backup and would still do lots of things with Jocelyn so we could all still be flexible. I would want Jocelyn to live nearby, probably in the same town. Jocelyn does need 24 hour support and care. Her room-mates could still hold jobs and she could have an assistant to support her during the day.

> Amy is in a group home and has been for eight years. She went there when she was 19. I share her care. Amy gets tremendous support and love at her other home. It was the best decision we ever made. It took us two years to make the decision and when an opening came up we had to compete with the state because they are downsizing and closing the state home for the mentally retarded and sending those clients to community group homes. There is very little money available for this project and these clients get placed before our children that we have kept at home and cared for years. You have to protect your family unit, and marriage and learn to let go at some point and trust that all of this is somewhere in God's plan. I remain Amy 's guardian and she is home every weekend and holiday. I attend all doctors appointments and take her to the Rett Clinic in every year for evaluation.

> We have a Contingency Intervention program and Carla was "placed" at a nearby regional center this summer. I was told in March that there was a vacancy and Carla had a number one priority because I was a single parent and not getting any younger! If I said "no," there was no guarantee of placement in the near future. Furthermore, since this was her last year at school, there was no guarantee that there would be a day program available if she were still living at home. So after many restless nights, I decided to give it a try, especially since I was told I could change my mind at any time during the transition. I made my list of pros and cons. The pros included the follow-ing: it was a small facility with six beds to a unit and four units to a building designed with two units on each level; it was two miles from home—a big plus; the staff were warm and caring peo-ple who had worked there several years; and another girl with RS who was 25 years old would be Carla's roommate. All the cons were "Mom related:" I didn't want her to go; I wasn't ready; and maybe I should do this next year. I spoke to family, friends, Carla's teachers, therapists, and cler-gy. I had to do it! So the transition began. For May and June I would bring Carla to the center after school for visits. The visits got easier and then we had our first overnight. I stayed until she was asleep and then cried all the way home and most of the night. I was there when she woke up the next morning. She seemed a little confused, but happy. The overnights became more frequent, but not easier—for me, anyway. Then in July, she moved in. I tried to think of it as going to camp. She spent Monday through Thursday nights there, attended summer school at her regular school, and was home from 2-7 p.m every day. August 1 she was officially admitted. I was devastated. I heard myself talking at the meeting, but what I said was not what I felt. I knew what had to do, but it wasn't what I wanted to do. I had to believe it was best for Carla, but I wasn't convinced. I felt I was giving her away. I had never experienced such pain even though I had gone through a divorce and lost a parent. Those events didn't even come close to the pain I experienced that day. I was awake and up all that night. I cried and cried and cried, a full-box-of-tissue cry. Morning arrived and zombie like, I went about my chores. Carla was fine, though, and I got one of her "Don't bother me" looks when I visited her. That same day, I was involved in an auto accident. When they say that God works in mysterious ways, I believe it. I had been praying for guidance

and this accident was an answer to my doubts in a way. It made me realize that if I had been seriously injured or killed, there was a place for Carla with people she knew and with those who knew how to care for her. For the first time in four months, I felt okay with the decision. I had mourned my loss and now it was time to celebrate Carla's new life. If I said everything was wonderful now, I'd be lying. It still hurts bringing her there Sunday nights. It's wonderful bringing her home weekends. We share only quality time together now. I'm beginning to enjoy my new freedom. For the first time in 21 years I can do things like making appointments without making arrangements for a sitter or like working my daily events around Carla. I visit her daily, they asked if I wanted a part-time job since I spend so much time there. She enjoys the constant activity and attention. It's really fun to watch her and Cheryl, the other girl with RS. Some real bonding has taken place. However, they do not like to share chocolate chip cookies! And look out if one is getting more attention than the other!

What is my advice to parents who might be in this stage? Do it! Do it while your daughter is still in her regular school program, if possible. It's easier for you, and for her, too. Don't let her see that you're upset. Be happy for her and her new "independence." Don't get upset with friends who say its just as if she were away at college. They could never understand the pain of letting go of a child who is still so dependent on you. Kids choose to go to college and choose the college as well. They can tell you what's happening. In our case, we're making all the decisions and hoping and praying that they are the right ones. Carla has a new family now, and I have, too. I keep thinking that if I won the lottery, I'd bring Carla home, and have live-in help. But would Carla like that arrangement? Finally, pat yourself on the back for being such super parents. You've won all the awards for best parents and now it's time to enjoy life. Let others do the daily caregiving. Be there to love her, have fun with her, and keep an eye out for her. There's no place like home, but your daughter can have two homes. Try to view the new setting through your daughter's eyes. She is blind to situations that may not be pleasing to you. Isn't it better to be the one in charge of finding your daughter a new home and family than waiting until it's too late and letting strangers make the decisions?

Our experience looking for permanent placement for Nina has been a roller coaster. Our social worker did not help us locate any group homes. In fact, permanent placement was never discussed even once. Our social worker wanted to avoid that subject altogether. We had to do all the detective work on our own. We toured a few facilities and found the perfect group nursing home for Nina. As luck would have it, it was only five blocks from our house... We put in our application and waited five long years until they had an opening. During the five year wait, we placed Nina in foster care when she entered kindergarten. The foster parents were like the grandparents Nina never had. After two years of caring for Nina, the couple began having trouble lifting her. We had to find another home for her. Unfortunately, our county did not have any other placement. Nina was placed in a neighboring county in another foster home on a temporary basis. We were not very happy, but luckily it lasted less than eighteen months. Later, Nina was able to move in to the group home. It is the perfect facility. Thirty-two children and young adults live in the facility. Nina was the first girl with RS to live there. The staff was excited and had read all the literature available before Nina even arrived. After Nina's first week there, the staff called and asked us to come and look at an older girl who had been living there for the last eleven years. We will always remember that day when we immediately spotted a 21-year-old woman with "busy" hands swinging on the glider. The doctors never knew what happened to this young woman who had been a perfectly normal baby until she was two years old. Our concerns about the staff not knowing how to deal with a girl with Rett syndrome had completely vanished when we all realized the home had been caring for one for the last eleven years. Nina's group home is part of a large non-profit organization that deals with handicapped individuals on all levels. This home has a dietary staff; Nina gained 25 pounds and grew five inches in her first year living there. They have a therapy staff, a recreation staff, loving care givers, abundant volunteers, an indoor whirlpool, a large activity room, a separate family room for family sleep-overs, and a laundry and housekeeping staff. A family can be as involved with their child as they want. Besides seeing Nina on a daily basis, I personally decorate her room and do her laundry. Nina's attitude changed dramatically when she moved into the group home. She calmed down and is hardly screaming anymore. We found that if she is surrounded by peers who have limited physical capabilities like herself, she isn't nervous about someone running into her. Even though we see Nina daily, she has made strong attachments to certain staff members, even showing a little jealousy if they talk to another child. They have since nicknamed Nina, "princess." It is a perfect arrangement for our family. We are able to give attention to Nina and still have time for giving attention to our other children and our marriage. We also now have that important commodity, time to ourselves.

What kind of adjustment will we have when she moves away?

It is an individual family decision whether she lives away from home or not or not. Since Kristas is adopted, in some ways it is easier to say that when the time comes we may institutionalize her. We have no intention to do this, but since she has three other siblings with needs too, there may come a time when we can no longer provide for her in our home. At this time, we are able to take care of her, as well as participate in activities with our other kids. Families need to make choices that best fit their needs, and the needs of their child with RS. Sometimes emotionally or financially, people are not able to care for their daughter with RS. It should always be a decision that best fits the family's needs. Parents should not feel guilty about their decision, and should not have to make excuses or explanations. I think we all need to give ourselves a pat on the back for just being the parent of a disabled child!

How can we evaluate a residential setting?

Despite the best reviews by state case managers, you will never "trust" the quality of the residential setting without making a personal visit and speaking with the staff. There is no other way. And probably the bottom line will be an instinct, a gut feeling, that this is a good place. Certainly, ask the tough questions such as: Are your staff trained? Is the facility licensed? How often is it inspected by government agencies? Can I see your last report? Would it be okay for my family or my daughter's advocate to visit her and take her out occasionally? And, of course, the big questions; how much and what do we receive for this amount?

How do we pay for residential care?

In Minnesota we are obligated to be financially responsible for Nina until she is 18 years old. The state had a sliding pay scale. The more you make the more you pay. It also takes in to consideration your family size. The fee is relatively small. For example, a family of five making $40,000 annually would pay $83 a month. When the child turns 18, she does not move. The state then makes up the difference.

Whether she lives at home or away from home, those who care for her must be given adequate support and respite in order to meet her many needs. Caregivers need regular time off and some holidays without responsibility for the woman with RS. Caregivers should be provided with ample information about the woman with RS, and any problems, aids or adaptations that are necessary for her success. If she lives away from home, the caregiver should be contacted regularly by family members, who will always be her foremost guardians and advocates.

What is guardianship?

Guardianship is a legally recognized relationship between a competent adult and an adult with a disability (ward) who is incapable as determined by a court of law managing her affairs. In this relationship, the guardian has the duty and right to act on her behalf to make decisions which affect her life and to promote and protect her well-being.

When is guardianship necessary?

According to law, guardianship for those with developmental disabilities "shall only be ordered to the extent necessitated by the person's actual mental and adaptive limitations." After she turns 18, it is important to consider guardianship because of her unique needs. If she is capable of making her own decisions, then no formal guardianship is required. If the family feels that she will need guidance in making decisions or she is incapable of making them, guardianship should be considered. It is a very difficult decision, because her rights are taken away. However, the family has to ask the very simple question, "If she cannot make decisions, who will?" While you may trust your local or state case manager, do you trust them enough to carry out this heavy responsibility? When you consider the fact that there is a high turnover in this case management area and your favorite social worker may leave, you may want to provide that personal support yourself.

Who should the guardian be?

Parents can be guardians once the child turns 18. In fact, many parents carry out this role without the formal legal guardianship by the simple fact that the person continues to live at home and most agencies respect the parents' informal position as advocate (someone who assists the person without the legal authority to make decisions). It is only when someone or an agency refuses to recognize the parent's decision that things can get complicated. For example, your daughter may need surgery and the hospital will only accept her signature for consent. The hospital attorneys may simply refuse to accept her signature because they do not believe she can give "informed consent," so everyone is stuck in limbo. Legal guardianship can avoid this problem because the parents can act on her behalf. While we usually speak about the parents acting in this role, any sibling or relative can do so. Even good friends can serve as guardians.

Is the guardian responsible for the ward's care?

Yes, the guardian is responsible. The courts or an appointed social service agency will/should check on the person on a regular basis. This is not always done, however. If the case manager suspects any abuse or neglect, he must report it. The guardian could lose custody. There are laws in place to protect the person. However, the bureaucracy doesn't always keep up. Therefore, it is essential for families to recommend people they trust.

Is the guardian financially responsible for the cost of the ward's care?

No. Generally, the guardian does not assume financial liability for his charge. Therefore, it is essential that you set up a trust or other account so there will always be funds available for your daughter.

The guardian is not legally responsible for any debts incurred by the person. However, if the guardian incurs the debts, he or she is responsible. If the person charges a TV on a credit card, the guardian does not have to pay. If the guardian charges a TV for the person, then the guardian must pay. Without this safeguard, few people would take on guardianship. They would be sued for things the person did.

How do we go about establishing guardianship?

Depending on your state, the process can be easy or extremely difficult. The first thing you must do is consult an experienced attorney. Find someone who does guardianships on a regular basis. The attorney will file a motion with the local court. The court will appoint an attorney who will act on behalf of your daughter. Generally, the court will send an investigator to meet with you. In some states, the local or state agency will also conduct an investigation. Everyone goes to court on the appointed day, at which time the judge will review the reports and ask questions. Again, it depends on the state, but many of these guardianship hearings are held in smaller courts or even in the personal chambers of the judge.

Are there different types of guardianship?

The types of guardianship which should be considered are:

- Full - All rights are taken away and given to the guardian.
- Limited - no rights are taken away; however, the courts may give certain responsibilities to the guardian, i.e., sign contracts, handle finances, make housing decisions, etc. Approximately 30 states recognize limited guardianship.
- Co-guardians and back-ups. It is always a good idea to obtain a co-guardian or a back-up. For instance, the court may appoint the mother as the primary guardian. The father would be appointed as the co-guardian to act with the mother or as a back up if anything happened to the mother, such as illness or death. Many states permit the guardianship papers to include successor guardians. In a situation where an elderly mother is the guardian and she has to go into a nursing home, the court could approve the siblings as successor guardians at the same time they approve the mother's guardianship. In this way, the minute the mother goes into a nursing home or dies, the siblings have legal authority to take over.

How can we make sure she is cared for if we die?

Guardianship is important, but it does not replace a good, well-written life plan and letter of intent. Parents need to put in writing what they would like for the future. This document, which is not legally binding, is called a letter of intent. It gives future caregivers insight into how your daughter should be provided for in the future. Unlike a detached analytical report written by a case worker, the letter of intent is a warm personal document which gives information on how to provide the best possible care. This letter of intent combined with a life plan or strategy for providing guardians, advocates, housing, etc. will be the difference between basic care in an institutional setting and a warm, loving lifestyle. Comprehensive planning will assure that adequate funds will be in place if you die first.

Who can handle these matters?

The team should include an estate planner, an attorney and a CPA. Look for an estate planning team that is experienced with special needs families. They should have a good working knowledge of government benefit programs and the service delivery system for the disabled from birth to death. The team must take the necessary time and feel comfortable working with special needs families. The National Institute on Life Planning, dedicated to serving the needs of disabled persons, recommends the following approach to developing a Life Plan:

- Decide what you and your loved one wants - the person with the disability is the key member in the decision making process. It is her life. Look at all areas - housing, employment, medical care, etc.
- Put your desires in writing. Prepare a Letter of Intent which will let future care providers know what you want for the future.
- Decide on an Advocate or Guardian - someone who will look after, fight for and be a friend.
- Determine the cost of your Life Plan and find the resources.
- Do the necessary legal work which might include Last Wills and Testaments, Special Needs Trusts, Durable Powers of Attorney, etc. - Consult a qualified attorney for this specialized work.
- Develop a good record keeping system to keep all of your materials in one place. When there is an emergency (like your death or nursing care), people need to find this information quickly. Let others know where you keep your records.
- Review and update your Life Plan at least once a year. Keep it current.

> I have made a plan in my will for money to be set aside for Amy's extras. Leaving money to Amy directly will upset her SSI. I do not want her sister or brother to feel that they are responsible for her but they will look after her and continue to be her advocate.

One way to provide for the long-term needs of our kids without putting their SSI resources at risk is to establish a "special needs trust." Any assets of the child and any gifts or bequests they might receive need to be redirected into the trust, which then "owns" them instead of the child. The trustees of the trust make the decisions about how and when to spend any of the money, but it does not get in the way of any of the governmental services the child is entitled to. Trust money can be used for clothing, outings, vacations, etc. at the discretion of the trustee(s). The trust will get its own tax ID number, and will have to file a separate return with the IRS each year. This is a fairly specialized type of trust and you might want to seek out someone who has specific knowledge about special needs trusts to guide you in setting one up. One potential hazard is inheritances that the benefactor leaves to the child, rather than the trust. The planner we worked with calls this the "rogue grandmother" problem. We have had one drawn up for Naomi, but I just learned this morning that it's income is taxed at a pretty steep rate, so we are now working on a strategy to deal with that. Because the trusts are set up to dovetail with the federal SSI regulations, I think that there is not a whole lot of variation from state to state.

First we talked to as many people as we could. Not surprisingly most other parent's hadn't made any provision. We talked to three separate lawyers and two Trust companies before settling on the Public Trustee. We were looking for stability with similar families, and also, secondary consideration, their fee structure for on-going administration. Some have an hourly rate, and some take a percentage for every year. We purchased a second house and rented it out so that the rent helped pay off the mortgage. We had mortgage repayment insurance so that if we died prematurely Rebecca would have had steady income. This kept us poor! You could probably get the same effect from some good life insurance but there were tax benefits for us to buy a house, and also we rather hoped that it would provide some retirement income. We wrote into our wills our desired standard of care -heaters, tv in her room, holiday every year, most comprehensive medical insurance, nice haircuts, trendy clothes, maintain activities. We also said we would prefer she lived in our family home with caregivers, preferably a family if she was younger, or with able-bodied roommates if she was older. We left all our assets to a discretionary trust to be created on our deaths. Because it was "discretionary" it did not affect any social security benefits Rebecca's would have been entitled to, because it did not belong to her and she could not depend on any regular income from it. The trust was to be administered by the Public Trustee which is an organization that manages people's estates and they would pay all her bills, in return for an hourly rate. They have a number of clients with disabilities.

Our objectives were:
• Financial independence for Rebecca
• Good life-style (not hand to mouth on social security) with all the niceties of life
• Experienced advocate to oversee her care and provide a 'parental' figure for her
• Experienced administrators to do all the bill paying etc. so that family were not burdened by it
• Ongoing life in the community—same one she grew up in, familiar house
• Ongoing family involvement, without them being required to spend hours on administration
• Power over Rebecca spread over three different groups -the family is not able to conserve her estate in anticipation that they would inherit more

SUPPLEMENTAL SECURITY INCOME

When your daughter reaches her 18th birthday, she becomes eligible for Supplemental Security Income (SSI) automatically. There is no financial formula, and the parents' income is not counted.

She can probably qualify for the highest amount of benefits. It is best to apply a month or so before she turns 18 so that her benefits will not have to be retroactive. If you do not apply, she does not receive the benefits. These funds are to be used to pay for her lodging, food, clothing, recreation and other needs. The Social Security Administration uses a mathematical formula to calculate her benefits. If she lives at home, you should assign an amount for her to pay "rent" to access the higher benefits. If she lives away from home, her SSI check is sent to her residential placement to help pay for her needs.

You should expect a 6 month wait for the bureaucracy to get all the paperwork approved. They will still backdate payments.

> Jocelyn just purchased her first accessible van. She is able to pay for this with money from her SSI check that she became eligible for at age 18. So she and friends have transportation to get where they need to go. Hopefully by the time she needs to worry about paying for housing, her van will be all paid up!

What can she do in the community?

> Community Supported Living Arrangements (CSLA) is a program that takes over when the school system quits, around age 21. This is when they find workshops or whatever they have for the disabled. Lynn took part in this for a number of years, but nobody told me that I could have the money to do her program myself. Basically, it is the sum of money that's given to the placement for her education/placement at a day facility. So, after finding out, I got the sum of money myself (thru a payroll) and I administer her day activities myself. I hire aides to do it with her at $10 dollars an hour, 6 hours a day, 5 days a week, which comes out of the sum allotted for her for the year. That way she does what she can do, instead of the day center taking all the money and giving her what they got, which in my experience has not met Lynn's needs. It was a struggle at first trying to arrange activities and plan her day, but now three years later, it runs quite smoothly. I have no problem finding help. It is a good alternative to what is available in Adult Workshops/Day centers.

> Money is available to your daughter for programs when she is over 21. All you have to do is submit a plan for the program. Workshops facilities have persons who will write up a plan for you (but beware it comes with a cost, which comes out of her total money for the year and quite frankly you can do quite easily yourself.

> Jocelyn (and Meloney) deliver the mail to two offices on the same floor 4 days a week. They go to the office, pick up the mailbox key, go back down to the mail room then bring the mail upstairs. They separate it and bring it to individuals or to central areas. One office also is finding other little jobs that they can try. I told Mel to let me know if and when she thinks they are ready for more, then I will contact a few more offices in that building to try and expand their job. This is a volunteer job but one office had a problem with that and is looking for a mechanism to pay her a stipend. Mel and Jocelyn have really enjoyed the experience and feel very welcome and appreciated.

> Another job that I've been working on developing for Joce is working with junior high age kids in an alternative school placement. These kids are "troublemakers" in school so are in a different environment, working on skills they need to develop to succeed in life. Hopefully she will "work" with them on projects one afternoon a week. She will work with them by giving them opportunities to think of ways of helping her to help them. Problem solving skills, positive attitudes, compassion and understanding. I think these are things she can help to teach them very effectively. Jocelyn already has some of the support needed to make this happen, is in the community meeting new people and making more friends, and already has a few close friends that could potentially meet the need and could be interested. Currently she has 25 hours per week of support service. Possibly by then we could increase this service. Her caregiver assists her with taking a college class, including reading the material. She will be taking her to a therapy pool at the local rehabilitation hospital to walk laps and get some exercise several times a week, and to her jobs that we've set up in the community.

The author wishes to thank the following professionals for ideas and information which was used to develop this chapter: Richard Fee, EdS.

LAUGHTER...THE BEST MEDICINE

Life is not a laughing matter—but can you imagine having to live without laughing?
Leonid Sukhorukov

Seven Reasons Why I Love My Daughter:
by Mike Juhasz

Reason #7: She still fits on my lap.

Reason #6: She likes to take naps on my lap.

Reason #5: All the smiles we get at church.

Reason #4: She laughs at my jokes.

Reason #3: The great parking spots we get at the mall when we take her shopping and use the handicapped card.

Reason #2: When we take her to an amusement park we can buck line and ride the ride several times in a row.

Reason #1: The love and light and sweetness she brings into my life.

Life is too serious to be taken too seriously. Some days, if we didn't laugh, we'd surely cry. We need a little laughter every day to stay healthy.

We are all major players in the soap opera of life called Rett syndrome. We can fully identify with titles like Days of our Lives, Another World, All My Children and As the World Turns. Most of us could write our own scripts for General Hospital and probably win an Emmy award for Best Drama. Our girls are the Young and the Restless and we all wish we were the Bold and the Beautiful. There are days when we all wish we could walk off to start our own new show, The Tired and the Aggravated.

Can't you just hear the cast call now? Actors wanted. Real life drama. Must be available 24 hours a day, 7 days a week, years on end. Must be able to speak medicalese and special education jargon. Need the patience of Job, the wisdom of Ghandi, and the sense of humor of Jerry Seinfeld. Must know VCR repair and be willing to negotiate with a cranky bus driver on short notice. Helpful to have shares in Scott Paper Towel company. Must be able to do everything while singing the Barney theme song. Must be able to discuss constipation at dinner, over and over. No insurance. No time off. Self-centered actors need not apply.

And the commercial? Come join our Tired and Ticked Off family. Will they give IN before they give OUT? Will she get music therapy on the IEP? Tune in for another exciting episode of the Rett Rats at Home...

In real life, we finally get used to people asking, "WHAT syndrome?" right after we say, "Rett syndrome." Take a typical day at the park. The casual conversation might go this way:

Q: "Rett syndrome. Isn't that what you get from taking too much aspirin?"
A: "No, you're thinking of Reye syndrome. In RS, parents can't get enough aspirin."
Q: "You must mean Tourette syndrome?"
A: "No, they're two retts and we're one."
Q: "So what's the difference between Rett and Tourette?"
A: "Tourette patients cuss a lot. In RS, the parents cuss a lot."

Q: "Rhett syndrome, is it named for Rhett Butler?"
A: "No, Rhett syndrome is what you get from watching too many reruns of 'Gone With The Wind.' Not to be confused with Scarlet Fever..."
Q: "What's WRONG with her?"
A: "She asked too many questions."

> Alyssa's brother is almost 3 years old. Tommy really has been noticing that Alyssa can't feed herself or walk and always wants to know "why." I used to be able to say that Alyssa's arms don't work like yours do, or that she doesn't have muscles like you do for walking. Well, like every good two year old, he still wants to know "why?" At lunch he looked at me as I was feeding Alyssa and said, "Mommy, 'Lyssa can't feed herself because she has "Rett Cinderella." Of course, we all laughed, but the best part was the look that Alyssa gave to Tommy. Her eyes said, "I have WHAT?"

Each day, we encounter more than our share of side glances and straight on stares. Parents have come up with some really creative comebacks for insensitive people.

> We were visiting the zoo—all six of us. Molly must have been about 12 or 13 and since there was a lot of walking involved we had her in her MacLaren stroller (my unscientific experience is that you get significantly more stares when your daughter is riding in something rather than walking). Anyhow, all of a sudden, I notice that there is a monorail riding above us with about twenty people staring, gawking, and laughing at us. My first gut-level reaction was to get really mad. Then I realized they were all looking at my husband and teen-age son, who were doing very dramatic ape imitations—I guess we all can become animals at the zoo, if we want to.

> You know those days when you wonder what and why this is happening to our daughters. Humor helps! I told a friend about these days and he shared this story about his nephew who was physically and mentally disabled. His nephew loves ice-cream and they took him to a local ice-cream parlor, and the stares began. No problems with the stares, he said, but then came a remark from a adult male. "What happened to him?" Looking around at all the people eating their ice cream and anticipating the answer, our friend replied, "You know it was the darndedest thing. Contaminated ice-cream!" he said. All those folks dropped their spoons. They had no further comments !

Sometimes, people just don't get it.

> The phone rang the other night at dinner, and I should have guessed that it was some telemarketing scheme. I was caught off guard when the voice at the other end asked in a somewhat authoritative tone to speak to my daughter. I asked who was calling and he gave the name of some banking company. I smiled a toothy grin with the answer we should give all telemarketers, "She does not speak." There was a long silence while I patted myself on the back for the ultimate comeback. Then, the voice said with confidence, "Ma'am, are *you* over 18?"

Kids will be kids, and they can come up with some doozies. Like the kids who put a 5 cent sticker on their sister's head at a yard sale when she was acting up, or 4 year old Jonathan, who announced with great jubilation on Christmas morning that his sister was going to be okay. He just figured it out she only needed new batteries. Or the kid who told his new friends his sister really was a big baby and his buddies came running in amazement to see the new neighborhood giant. One parent told a story about her daughter, Ashley, who was standing on the sidewalk rocking from side to side, wringing her hands and breathing very hard. A new kid in the neighborhood walked up and after studying her carefully from all angles, he said, "Is she an *American*?"

When folks realize that our girls are more like them than they are unlike them, they are able to enjoy our daughters more.

Lauren's classmates gathered around around her to look at her communication device and, of course, find our if it could pronounce the most important four letter words in their vocabulary. I was thrilled when it could, as it was Lauren who kept pressing it. One student even asked if she was planning to go to college. A far cry from what she gets when associated with her special education class!

Molly had the good fortune of being fully included at our middle school. A significant portion of the special education staff's energy was used to support the regular education staff and students so that Molly could function as independently as possible at school. When she was in the 8th grade, there was a Friday night sleep over at school consisting of a roller skating party at the rink, a movie back at school, the sleep over itself, and donuts for breakfast for about 150 students. The plan was for me to come by the school around 10:00 p.m. to help Molly get ready for the night (we were able to pull this whole thing off with just regular staff and parent volunteers.) When I caught up with Molly and two of her friends, they had just returned from the roller skating rink. The first thing I noticed was that Molly's lips were blue – a bit more blue even than with a seizure, and the first thing I found myself thinking was that she must have had or was having some type of seizure. Her friend, Jessica, must have realized I was concerned about something and volunteered: "Molly really liked the blue cotton candy."

We've all had our embarrassing moments...

The nice thing about the brace was that when she swallowed air, it had nowhere to go, since her stomach couldn't expand. What didn't go through her came back in the form of burps that could be heard in the next county, and what did go through accelerated enough to lift her off the church pew when she tooted. Before the brace we said, "Angie fluffed." After the brace, her toots sounded more like a machine gun. Once, when my brother was watching Angie try to pick up something that was out of her reach, he was startled to hear her toot. When she was all done, he said, "That's right, Angie, if you can't reach it, shoot it."

Becky seems to always be thirsty so I was constantly holding the cup for her to drink. We started a program on teaching her to suck out of a straw and after a year and a half she learned to do it! I'll never forget that day! The school secretary called me and told me she had just made an announcement over the school loudspeaker to the entire student body, "Becky Sue can suck!"

One day at her program, Mary had a very good looking male aide working with her at lunch. Well, he felt she had had enough to eat so he started cleaning up. Mary hit the hungry switch, so he started to give her more to eat. Every time he thought she had to be full, she'd hit the switch again. After 5 times, he said "enough" and went back to cleaning up. Mary hit the drink switch and he started giving her more to drink. It took him a while to figure out she was just trying to keep his attention on her. I happened to attend her conference that day when he told me about lunch. I told him that Mary's not dead, she knows a good looking man when she sees one. These girls are GREAT!

This is a true story about Becky Sue and an 8 week old kitten. Becky Sue is learning to feed herself and this can create a very messy situation! When she is eating. one of the kittens loves to sit under her chair and grab up whatever comes his way. Mealtime for Becky is also medication time. One morning he wasn't under her chair for breakfast so I went looking for him. I found him lying under a table on his side, quivering, glassy eyed and unable to hold his head up. I picked him up and he was limp. Respirations were extremely slow and he was unresponsive. I searched the house to find what he could have gotten into but found nothing. We nursed him through the day, holding him with his little legs hanging over my arm and head cradled in the palm of my hand. We gave him water with an eye dropper. At one point I knew his bodily functions were working as my shirt became warm and wet! But we were still puzzled as to what could have happened to him. At dinner time, I went to put Becky in her chair and noticed something on the floor. There was about one quarter of a 200mg Tegretol under her chair. It was obvious that it had been chewed by tiny little teeth! Then it dawned on us! Becky Sue must have spit out that pill during dinner the night before and this little kitten had chewed it up! By that evening he was back to normal.

Every year our family loved to camp in the Wilderness in the Sequoia National Forest. There were 8 of us who would go for two weeks during the summer. We slept in a stock trailer and cooked in a tent trailer. We hauled our water in and dug our pit for the toilet. As the kids got older and involved in a local 4H Club, they raised livestock (sheep, pigs, goats and a steer) for the Annual Fair. Since these animals were the Club member's responsibility only, the kids had to feed, exercise, groom and clean up after them. They could not be left for someone else to care for them for two weeks at a time. The only solution was to bring them with us. And since we had numerous baby goats during the summer who were bottle fed, they went with us also. So our list of things to bring became a little larger. Grain and alfalfa for the Fair animals, goat meal and bottles for the baby goats (warmed up 4 or 5 times a day for their feedings), rakes, shovels and pens to keep them safe from the coyotes at night. A couple of years we brought the 3 horses just for fun! We enjoyed romping in the meadows with the baby goats and sheep. Becky Sue and Melissa loved to watch them jumping on the rocks in our camping spot. I never was brave enough to bring the pigs (as they tend to tunnel out under their pens), and the steer could have lost weight during the long drive there. For many years this was our idea of a relaxing summer vacation!

We were at church and it was my turn at children's church so my husband was watching Lisa. He came to get me saying something was wrong with Lisa; she was turning blue. I went out to find her a blue-gray around the mouth and her fingers up to her hands. This really scared me because her fingernails had been turning blue when she held her breath, but this was the bluest I had seen her. We had a nurse present and she was concerned too, so the nurse and I rushed her to the emergency room. They checked everything and could find nothing unusual. This was getting very strange—everything normal, Lisa sitting there laughing. Then, it dawned on me what the problem was! Lisa was wearing a new dress I had made her. It was a very pretty blue-gray with pink flowers. She had been rubbing her hands on it and then to her mouth. I told the E.R. people what I thought it was but they didn't believe me until they got a washcloth and the blue came right off! I didn't feel too stupid because she had them fooled, too.

Ashley did lots of vomiting when she was young. However, this did not stop our family from frequenting restaurants. One day as we were leaving one of the local cafeterias, Ashley decided she had had too much to eat and proceeded to throw up in the flowerbed. An attractive couple passed by us on their way in and observed the "goings on." Just as they passed, Cliff replied, "Do not eat the broccoli." Even after all these years, whenever we go to this cafeteria, Cliff never fails to comment on how well the flowers are growing.

The other day we went to Bri's school for her Birthday party, and she was in the pool. Her sister, Erica and I got down and splashed with her from the sides. I had hold of Erica's dress, and before I knew what happened the dress went limp and I heard a splash – in goes Erica! My immediate response was, of course, to jump in behind her, and I did! Before it was all over, we had two teachers and three aides in a pool trying to save a 2-year-old who, by the way, can swim and float. I choked half to death, to my daughter's utter amusement.

Ashley used to do this little thing with her hands when she would come up behind someone's back, it was kind of a little massage action. One day as we were leaving a restaurant and waiting in line to pay, Ashley and I walked up behind this rather tall, good-looking gentleman and before I could stop her, Ashley began her little massage. Well, because this man was rather tall, her little fingers came about to his "rear end." Watching this but being unable to stop her I just stood there. Shortly, the man turned around with raised eyebrows, and I simply said, "She did it," pointing to Ashley.

Once at a mall, my husband and I were walking with Amanda. My husband was drinking coke from a soda can. As we rounded a corner, Amanda let out a huge, loud, rather belching burp. A young teenage girl gave my husband the dirtiest look. We laughed and she just walked away, even more disgusted.

Shortly after receiving Ashley's evaluation of RS and having just familiarized ourselves with all the grim predictions, Ashley, her grandmother, Kathryn and I were at the hospital. Ashley had just undergone a series of tests and evaluations. As we were preparing to leave the building I took Ashley to the potty. When we came out and as we began walking, we suddenly discovered that Ashley could no longer walk. Kathryn and I became puzzled and alarmed, as Ashley would not take any steps, and would refuse to walk. Finally after a few moments, Kathryn hesitantly uttered the unspeakable, "Could this possibly be the loss of walking regression that we had read about?" After pondering this idea for a moment I commented that this could not possibly happen so quickly, as she had just been walking a moment ago. I quickly began inspecting her legs by pulling up her dress. I shortly discovered that when pulling up her lace panties, which I so modestly covered over her diapers, I had erroneously put both of her legs into one panty leg. We soon realized the cause of Ashley's inability to walk, and were able to laugh with joy and delight.

We went to Branson, Missouri with the grandparents last winter for a weekend at Silver Dollar City and to enjoy the holiday atmosphere. Needless to say it was very cold. Most days we dressed in at least three layers of clothing because temperatures did not get above freezing. All you could see of Anca was her face on occasion. Everything had gone well, and we had a very good time, until the last day. The temperature outside was a chilly 16 degrees. We were loading up for departure in Papa's two-door pick-up truck. The luggage was put in the bed of the truck and we were just about ready to tie the tarp over it. Mama was in the condo making sure we had not forgotten anything. Anca and Judy made their way to the truck after it had been started and had warmed some. Barbie, the diligent person she is, put everyone's purses and her coat into the truck. Judy got out of the truck, it was okay to leave Anca alone, someone was always by the truck – yeah right! Anca was doing her usual "hitting" on whatever she could to make a noise. Well, Anca leaned on the back of the seat and while pounding on things, she hit the automatic locks, *locking everyone out!* The keys were in the ignition keeping the truck warm – the other set of keys was in the purse on the front seat Papa said, "can you get her to hit on the door again?" – yeah right! And, to top it off, it was early Sunday morning. After some maneuvering with a wire hanger, banging on condo doors, and calling security, a locksmith finally came to our rescue. In the meantime, Anca was quite at ease lounging in the back seat sucking her thumb and having a heyday. This spring, Papa said to Anca, "I have something just for you" – he pulled his wallet out of his back pocket, reached in, and pulled out a spare key.

When Molly was in 5th grade, she went to school with another girl with RS, Susan, who was in the 6th grade of a full inclusion program. All sixth graders in the district spent a couple days at a facility owned by the district as part of the environmental education program. Along with the parent permission forms that all 8th grade parents got, Susan's parents received a letter about how this was an isolated location where medical help wasn't readily available, and that if Susan should have a seizure it might be upsetting to other students and staff. This letter was rather strange, if for no other reason than Susan doesn't have seizures. The principal of the school was a fortyish man who had a heart attack and had been out on medical leave but had returned. Susan's mother sent him a letter saying that she hoped that if he had another heart attack, he didn't have it in front of Susan, because it might be upsetting to her. She got an apology.

I took Mary to the bathroom and pushed her stroller into the wheelchair accessible stall. Just as I was getting ready to put her on the toilet she had a seizure, falling with her head into the next stall,which was occupied by some poor unknowing woman who was hysterical. I kept trying to reassure her that Mary would come out of the seizure. Meanwhile, I was fighting laughter as I pictured this stricken faced woman trying to use a toilet with a head at her feet with eyes rolled back. If we don't laugh at these embarrassing moments, we only feel bad. The lady exited before Mary recovered.

Pain is inevitable,

but misery is optional.

PEARLS OF WISDOM

"There are only two ways to live your life. One is as though nothing is a miracle.
The other is as though everything is a miracle."
Greg Anderson

Snowflakes are one of nature's most fragile things. But just look what they can do when they stick together.

Once I saw a man who was dying of cancer being interviewed on television. The reporter asked him if he ever felt angry that he would not get to watch his four-year-old son grow up. "No," he replied. "There are worse things that can happen, like having a retarded child."

It's my personal experience, not just a feeling, that there are also worse things than having a child with RS. With each child we are given a bag of joy and a bag of pain. Angie's bag of pain is larger than most, but her bag of joy is filled with extremely high-quality stuff!

I wish you could see her smile. When she smiles, sometimes her eyes twinkle so brightly I fancy I see her soul fairly bursting to get out. Ever see a baby smile all over? Doesn't it make you happy, too? Well, that's how Angie smiles. She makes me happy. Here's a child who should be a freshman in high school this year, worrying about algebra and boys. Instead, she loves to be held tightly across my lap and dipped suddenly backwards to the tune of Rock-A-Bye-Baby; she loves to have me hold her hand up in front of my mouth and kiss each soft, barely-used fingertip, while she watches with intensity, momentarily stopping her repetitive hand-wringing. She often grins when I pull her pajama top over her head and say "peek-a-boo!"

I am always impressed with her patience with me when I try to imprison those compulsive hands to keep them out of her mouth, or try to read in her eyes just what her needs are. Small things to some perhaps, but we communicate, she and I. When we look into each other's eyes, there is no wounded relationship between us to mend. Our souls speak and I feel intense joy and swelling and love in my heart, no different in intensity than I feel for my other children when I am extremely proud of their deeds. But Angie doesn't have to do. She is. That's all that is required of her. Oh, certainly we try to teach her—we will never give up, yet my love for her is not dependent on her performance. I am learning to value others the same way. I am now a retired perfectionist. I suppose every parent hopes for a miracle and I'm no different. I've seen enough to know they exist. I've ordered one, and I suppose I'm on some sort of waiting list. Barring that, perhaps it will be a miracle enough when Angie passes from my hands to God's and sheds Rett syndrome just like a butterfly sheds its cocoon. She'll be free then. She'll soar higher than you or I ever will here on this earth.

Reading what I have written is sort of like opening that bag of pain again. I don't want to paint too rosy of a picture because certainly there are struggles. Yes, I'm tired of diapers. Yes, my back aches every evening. Yes, I still cry, although not as often and not as bitterly.

The sense of isolation has lessened considerably since I've been receiving phone calls and letters from other parents with children having Rett syndrome. I told one caller, "This is costing you an arm and a leg." She said, "Who cares? I've waited ten years to talk to someone who understands." Other parents feel the same way. They are all as excited as I was about finally getting a specific diagnosis. We are no longer fighting an invisible enemy.

Claudia Weisz

The best advice that was given to me was from a doctor who said, "Whatever you do, no matter what, always keep that smile on Jenna's face."

In the development of group homes, as in special education, health care, recreation programs, community acceptance, and civil rights, parents have always been a vital force. They have dreamt dreams and worked to make those dreams reality. As parents, we must recognize our vital role as motivators, innovators, monitors, change agents, supporters, and above all, as the experts who know our children and their needs better than anyone else. The price of freedom is eternal vigilance!

As Rebecca's mother, I was forced to take two separate and, I believe, conflicting approaches. The positive: In order to give her my best, get the best for her, and to preserve my sunny disposition and sanity, I looked at all the things she could do, the joy she brought us, how clever she was, the important lessons she taught me. Sometimes this was hard—we all know the challenges we face daily. The negative: In order to get every tiny bit of support I was forced to catalog her "defects" great long lists of everything she couldn't do, minute detail about how hard life was and how it was wearing me out. This was also hard – it felt like a betrayal of her to speak of her so negatively. After a session of negative behavior, it would take me several days of hard work to get back to positive. It would have been much easier to live in the negative but that would have handicapped the whole family. I'm sure this is the same for every family, and I'm convinced that it is really unhealthy and unhelpful for us and our daughters. It is ironic that the very services that are meant to support us have this very unfortunate side-effect.

Some of our girls seem so much more fragile than others. So often our options for helping them force us to choose from a list of things, none of which we like. Don't get hung up on making the PERFECT choice—it often doesn't exist. Just learn all you can and make the best choice you can. Even deciding to wait is a choice. But please remember that most of our girls are hearty little fighters, strong of spirit with lots of soul.

Certainly having an angel for a daughter has been a blessing! I love my daughter more than anything on this earth. She is the easiest child to love. She is pure beauty and innocence. She has a smile and a laugh that could melt even the coldest heart. But she endures so much. If they are here to teach us, I would just like to say for the record that I understand...*enough* already!

Once I was a victim of shattered dreams. My heart was broken, never to mend. My daughter, Laura Leigh, had just been tentatively diagnosed as having Rett syndrome. I struggled against acquiring, perhaps, the greatest handicap of all times. I could not see past my own pain, and a seed of bitterness sprouted within my aching soul. Yes, time had a gentle way of healing; I learned how to love my little girl when there was no progress. I learned the value of treasuring the simple things in life. I had no choice but to live one day at a time. Today is all we have — today!

I am especially touched by the strength, fortitude, perseverance, positive attitudes, love and friendship woven in the sharings amongst all of us. And although we don't always feel like it, we continue to move on and find the silver linings in these dark clouds of Rett syndrome. I am hoping that you feel that joy and peace that comes from such a realization. We are really doing a great job of handling RS! I am reminded that our girls have a real purpose here on this earth. I strongly believe that it is to "touch us" and to teach us about the world of those with special needs. RS girls are so cute and beautiful and personable and can complete their task so easily. Our purpose is to assist them in fulfilling their purpose.

My daughter is one who has been severely affected physically by Rett. Since she has been so sick, I got so lost in the physical aspect that I lost sight of her inner beauty, wisdom, patience and forgiveness. I am in awe of her majesty, her strength, her spirit. Dani is still very weak physically, but is even stronger spiritually.

Mark and I have long since come to the same conclusion regarding those who do not understand why we can't fit into their plans. After Stefanie's development stopped and she got further and further behind the other kids her age (a whole group of us at work had babies the same year), most of my co-workers stopped talking to me, period, and those who did talk to me never mentioned Stefanie. It was very painful. I finally decided that those who were so insensitive probably didn't have much to offer me in the way of friendship anyway, so I basically have a different circle of friends than I used to. Many of my friends coincidentally also have a child with a disability, (we have more in common) but there are others who don't, who accept Stefanie as is and we go on with the friendship.

I think another reason some people avoid those of us with special needs children is that they feel embarrassed that their children are normal and they did not suffer as we are and their children don't suffer as many of our girls do. They feel there is nothing they can do or say to help and they feel very awkward. I wish they would know that they are wrong. Kind words, no matter how fumbling, are helpful, I've found. And of course, simply providing friendship to us keeps us from feeling so disconnected from the world.

Don't look at what your daughter can't do—look at what she can do. Don't spend more time on Rett syndrome than you spend on your daughter. Treat her like she's really smart, because she is.

The Gift

From God's arms to ours she came,
A gift of wealth untold;
Not of money or of things,
But richness of the soul.

A little girl like many others,
But different in her way;
All the things that she would give
We did not know that day.

A gift of love each day received
From kisses, hugs and smiles;
A gift it's been to share with her
Her young life with its trials.

A gift of joy to watch her grow,
To want for her the best;
A gift of pride that she is ours,
To God we leave the rest.

The gift of strength she gives to us
When to our hand she clings;
And when we have her near to us
The gift of hope she brings.

That she has given all these gifts
She's much too young to know;
Our little angel unaware
We'll always love her so.

Iatwah, Inc.

I had Josie at a time when seemingly half the people in my little company were having babies. What a joyful time. Everyone else's baby of course kept developing normally. I know they were devastated when they found out about Josie, but they all handled it differently. Admittedly, one friend who had developed a habit of inviting Josie and me to the zoo every other Sunday or so with him and his young son suddenly stopped calling. I still talk to this friend, but he never ever asks about Josie! He has since had yet another baby, and I ask about his children all the time. Then others ask about Josie on a regular basis. I think they find that once they ask and get their feet wet, it's not so scary to talk about.

My symphony is Dani. Each day I have with her is more precious in my memory. The other day I was holding her and she snuggled into my breast and looked up at me with those eyes of hers and I just melted. I heard a cacophony of music in my head and we both fell fast asleep. What a treasure this woman/child of mine is and how I yearn for more time with her. She helps me to live simply, to appreciate the little things in life, and to put everything in perspective. She is my peace. She is the music in my life.

Appreciate all your daughter has and don't cry over what she has lost. She is a very lovable child who loves to do everything any other child does with a little help or adaptation.

Since I adopted Mary, I always have felt that we were fated to meet. We've been through some very tough times, but I can honestly say I would not change my decision given the chance. I have learned unconditional love, I see the world differently, my values have changed to embrace the gift of a smile, and it has made me much more tolerant of others. I no longer chase the almighty dollar, but live comfortably in each moment. That is a lesson Mary taught very well. Mary came bearing gifts.

Get as much help as you can from someone or some group, then move on.

If a therapy approach is otherwise innocuous and may help your daughter, try it.

Go out with your spouse one or two times a week, and do not discuss your daughter. This single handedly got us through the year of the diagnosis.

Get a hobby or outside activity that takes you away from the family once a week if possible. Get government benefits as soon as possible (title 19, school therapies, social service programs.) Get your income waived for these programs, base your applications on severity of medical need.

Talk as much to your daughter as possible. Ours understands much much more than she can communicate.

Protect your daughter. If you are not sure something is right, don't do it. If you are not sure your doctor knows what he/she is doing, get a new one. If the school wants your daughter in a program that they already have, make sure it's appropriate for your daughter. If she seems in pain or duress, remove her from the situation.

Don't strong arm her. Her problems are not primarily behavioral in nature.

Get a Rett specialist involved. Most doctors, even at leading hospitals, are not up to date on current therapies and medicines, and your child may suffer at their hands due to ignorance.

Love your daughter with all your heart. Don't change your hopes and dreams you had for her before RS. Change the path, not the destination.

Keep your sense of humor, for it will help you in the hard times. Keep your faith in God, for it will help you in the even harder times.

We truly believe we have been blessed with Mary. We believe Mary is a gift from God and that when we accept her for the gift she is, we have a peace and joy that lasts, even if we can't explain it. Not the peace and joy that commercials try to sell us with their "perfect" one daughter, one son families. Mary has a special gift of bringing out the best in our family. So often we think, "poor Mary, she can't do this, or that." Then she gives us this look like, "What! Are you kidding me? I'm not the one trying to obtain and be things I'll never be…you're the crazy ones, chasing after all these things you think will satisfy you or make you happy… worrying about things you have no control over." Mary is content being who she is. She loves life. She loves her family (even when we act like idiots.) Mary has taught us so much about what is important in life. She is peaceful, content, funny, and loves to tease. She notices everything. I truly believe her brain powers are 5 times that of mine (though that might not be saying much.) Mary just plain loves life. Would we ever think for a 100th of a second of trading her for a baby Einstein? Never! We love Mary for who she is, not WHAT she can or can't do. Is caring for Mary physically and emotionally tough? YES! Does Mary get frustrated at our lack of ability to understand her? YES! Do we want Mary to have Rett Syndrome? Of course not! But I often wonder: Who's happier? Who's more content? Who really enjoys life more? We always conclude it's Mary.

When I was new to RS, I was forever whining about "the child I had lost." I spent every conference I went to wanting to talk about the grief, the agony and the unfairness. Little by little, I began to realize that the little girl I have is so sweet and beautiful and giving and loving and selfless. As my other children have grown into adolescents, oh, the headaches they have given me, (and yes, joy, but you know what I mean). Amy has never given me a moment of trouble, never whines, never asks for anything. Her love is so unconditional. So now, instead of focusing on what she will never be, I think about the negative things she will never go through, how she will always be in this cocoon of love and security her family will provide. The disillusionment of RS is just how we look at our "normal babies" when they are small and wish them nothing but love and happiness. That is what we can give our little girls with RS. That's all they need.

I guess my best words of wisdom to parents would be these, yes, your daughter has Rett Syndrome. Yes, she may require extra attention, and yes, she may get on your nerves with her screaming and other behaviors. Just always be sure to take time out for yourself and your spouse often. Take advantage of respite care and the offers of friends for babysitting. You will find that these breaks rejuvenate you and make another day bearable. Also, don't forget to make special time for the typical siblings in your family. They are affected by RS, too. Your daughter will be a blessing to you and give you all sorts of reasons to smile, sometimes you may have to look a little harder than others. Just give her lots of love and hugs, and she will give it back to you tenfold.

Even though our girls all share the common bond of Rett Syndrome and they have a lot of symptoms that are alike, each of them is still an individual person, and will do things in her own way. She will learn in her own way at her own pace. What works for one, may not necessarily work for another girl. A communication program that sounds like a miracle for one, may not be just right for another. One will excel at hand skills while another may not, but she may excel in communication.

While going through Corinne's newborn clothes to find a few summer things for a friend's new baby girl, I started thinking about her and when we first had her. I remembered how much we loved her right from the start, even before she was born. It didn't matter that she cried, or that she constantly threw up all over us. I think that remembering the love we had for her, even before we really "knew" her helps me realize that, Rett or not, she is the same beautiful perfect baby that I brought home from the hospital. All children take lots of effort and hard work, many (maybe most) have big problems along the way—maybe medical, maybe social, emotional or behavioral.

Our girls just have different problems. They, and we as parents, will also be spared some problems along the way from our Rett angels. When I first read about RS, before diagnosis, I was devastated. I knew she had it, I didn't need a doctor to look at the same diagnostic criteria and look at her history to tell me the same thing. That took three months. I cried for about 10 straight days, for the loss of my "perfect" baby. Then I got over it and started to act. My crying wasn't helping her any. She now gets 5 times the amount of therapy she did before the diagnosis and is starting in a wonderful school program soon. If I kept crying, these things would not be happening. She would not be the happy little girl that she is. I know that there will always be times when I will feel sorry for her and for myself. I know I will be angry at Rett and the world. It will be difficult to watch her new sister reach milestones that Corinne has not. At these times I know I will feel pain. As long as I don't dwell on these feelings, I will still be able to see the milestones that Corinne reaches, the small steps that result from mountains of effort. I will be able to appreciate those milestones as much as the ones that we usually take for granted. By Corinne's first birthday, when she was miles away from being able to stand, much less walk, I promised her that we would have a party when she learned how to walk. We are getting closer to that prospect. Maybe we will modify it to when she can walk independent in her walker, but we will have that party.

It was just months ago when we got the diagnosis of RS for our Briana, and there are still times that I find myself looking at my beautiful little girl and asking God what I did wrong. Was there anything I could have done to stop this disease? Something I could have done early on to prevent the regression? Then I grab reality once again, and know that there is nothing I could have done then, but there is so much I can do now. My dreams for Briana have not stopped, but have changed course, so to speak. Her smile brightens our house, her laughter fills our hearts. Each day she teaches me to cherish the simple pleasures in life like the tickle a sneeze brings, or the completely satisfying pleasures of the birds singing. Briana is the pure essence of love. She is quick with a smile or a giggle, her arms are perfect for hugs, and her

It's not what you have in your life,
but who you have in your life
that counts.

kisses can brighten anyone's day. Her determination to conquer the impossible is contagious, and her love of discovery is something I look forward to each day. For anyone who has to travel this road, I would only be able to tell them that the hard times are numerous, but the rewards are plenty. To dwell on the impossible is a waste of time, but to see what these girls can do is blessed. This summer Briana has crossed many of the bridges we were told she would never pass. She is now walking with the use of dual canes, she has picked up three more words that she uses consistently, and she can now feed herself some foods. All of these things bring her great pleasure, and the smiles warm us through to the soul. If there is one thing that Rett Syndrome has taught me, it is to never dwell in the negative...so much more can happen with positive thoughts and actions. I may not be able to change what has already happened to my daughter, but I can make sure that she is allowed to live life to its fullest potential. I would not trade my Briana for anything, and I love her deeply for who she is, not what she has...RS is not Briana.

In the overwhelming whirlwind of fighting insurance companies, attending disastrous IEPs, the masses of therapies, and just caring for your daughter on a daily basis, it is easy to dwell on the burden of the handicap and to overlook the blessing of the child. Rett Syndrome, itself, is a miserable, tragic, and crippling disorder; enough to tear the human heart into shreds of bitterness. But look into your daughter's eyes and capture the warmth of her love and innocence. The beauty of the child quickly chases away the weight of her handicap and heals the human heart!

WHERE TO GO FOR HELP

The best place to begin is within your state and local community. Laws are in place to help you get the supports and services your child needs. It is important that you understand your rights and responsibilities under the law.

Public Law 94-142 is the primary federal legislative act involving the education of children who have educational disabilities. Called the Education for All Handicapped Act of 1975, this law aims to assure the availability of a "free appropriate public education" for every eligible child. It sets forth a range of school and parental responsibilities as well as procedural safeguards to ensure the due process of law.

The **Individuals With Disabilities Act (IDEA)** is a law which guarantees a free appropriate public education to all eligible children with disabilities. A child cannot become eligible for special education and services until an evaluation has been done. This evaluation must be provided by your state and local school district, but you may have to request it.

If your daughter is under 3 years of age, she is eligible for **Early Intervention Services,** which include any supports an infant or toddler may need to help her development. These programs differ from state to state. After the age of 3, your daughter is eligible for a free appropriate public education.

The IDEA provides support for special education and related services in many different settings, including child care, preschool, kindergarten, and elementary, junior high and high schools. The philosophy of IDEA is to provide a way for children to be educated as much as possible with children who do not have disabilities.

Section 504 of the Rehabilitation Act of 1973 is a law which prohibits discrimination against individuals with disabilities. The law applies to all programs and activities which receive federal funds, including local school districts and Head Start programs. Any program which gets federal funds must provide a free public education to children with disabilities. Section 504 provides legal rights for children with disabilities. Some states also provide mediation services, which are useful in settling disputes about eligibility and the kind of services your child should get.

The Americans with Disabilities Act (ADA) is an important law for people with disabilities. It prohibits discrimination in employment, public transportation, services provided by state and local governments, services and accommodations offered by private businesses and telecommunications. The ADA is intended to remove barriers that prevent individuals with disabilities from getting an equal opportunity to share in and contribute to American life, such as in restaurants, theaters, child care centers and other community resources.

Parent Training and Information (PTI) Centers are located in each state. These centers are run by parents to provide education and training to all parents on their rights under the law.

GETTING HELP

Medicaid Waivers are home and community-based waiver programs which are targeted to individuals with mental retardation or developmental disabilities, the elderly or disabled. A number of states also have programs specifically directed at other populations such as those who are medically fragile or technology dependent. Many of these programs do not count parental income or resources in determining eligibility. The Medicaid waiver is generally what people are referring to when they talk about the **"Katie Beckett Waiver."** The guidelines require the child to need an "institutional level" of care, such as hospital, nursing facility, or intermediate care facility, because the waiver program is an alternative to institutional care. If your daughter is under 18 years, one option for resources is getting this waiver. It is intended to offer what is needed to keep the child at home, recognizing that many individuals at risk of being placed in a medical facility can be cared for in their homes and communities, preserving their independence and ties to family and friends at a cost no higher than that of institutional care. It may provide assistance in the home at crucial hours, foster care in a family especially trained to deal with her problems or a group home. Information on the home and community-based waiver program can be found on the World Wide Web at: **http://www.hcfa.gov/Medicaid/ltchomep.htm.** Here you can find a complete a complete listing of all approved home and community based services waivers along with a brief description. You will also find a link to a listing of State Medicaid Directors which you can go to for more information on a particular state's waiver program. Individual states have the flexibility to design each waiver program and select the mix of waiver services that best meets the needs of the population they wish to serve.

Eligibility for the Katie Beckett waiver is determined by the child's degree of disability, in that one would require 24 hour care, (which RS does!), but it does not require that you have a 24 hour nurse available. The hours of assistance you are eligible for can vary according to the need of the family.

There are seven services which may be provided in Home and Community Based Service waiver programs:
- case management
- homemaker services
- home health aide services
- personal care services
- adult day health
- habilitation
- respite care

Other services, requested by the state because they are needed by waiver participants to avoid being placed in a medical facility (such as transportation, in-home support services, meal services, special communication services, minor home modifications, and adult day care) may also be provided, subject to approval.

Where do we apply for the Medicaid waiver?

Contact your local Social Security office or Medicaid agency in your state to see whether there is a Home and Community-Based Service (HCBS) waiver program which would meet the needs of your daughter. In most states, when you apply and receive Supplemental Security Income (SSI) for your daughter, she automatically qualifies for Medicaid. However, if your daughter is under 18 years of age, your income is considered in the determination, so she may not get SSI. Your local Social Security case worker may not know about this special waiver. Mention it during your appointment, and like all dealings with the social security office, be persistent. You have a great chance of winning your appeals.

> Our first application was denied because of income. The second time around we had our tri-county representative send a letter detailing Nicole's condition and we were approved. The program pays for Nicole's prescriptions and doctor visits that our insurance won't cover. We also get diapers delivered to the house each month free of charge.

> I contacted a Home Health Agency who came to our home and did an assessment then told us to go to the Department of Human Resources for the medical card portion of the Waiver. We were first turned down because Ann wasn't disabled enough. I asked them if you had to be dead! I appealed and we got through that stage. Then the papers went to the Medicaid office who also denied it, saying that Ann did not qualify. I told them that was unacceptable and took it to a hearing. The hearing officer ruled in our favor because a state office or clerical staff cannot override the medical professionals who had already made a level of care determination. It has been wonderful for us. Currently we have the attendant care portion of the Waiver and have a caregiver 45 hours a week as well as diapers and the medical card to pay for medical care not covered by our insurance.

Kristas has been on the Waiver for the past nine years. At the time we applied for the waiver, we were denied because we were seen as "foster parents." However, with a couple of years of fighting, threatening institutionalization, and then a great lawyer who previously worked for Medicaid, we got it. Shelly would have qualified three years prior if someone had told me something that made any sense. Here's a round-up of what we are now receiving as a result:

1. 16 hours a day skilled nursing care in the home. 8 hours of this must be at night, in case she goes into distress in her sleep.
2. Wheelchair modifications.
3. Car seat (Gorilla) that holds up to 105 lbs.
4. Medical care that our HMO doesn't cover.
5. A hospital bed, IV pole, Kangaroo pump, and suction machine.
6. Free diapers delivered to the door every month.

Every Monday I called and said we couldn't survive any weekend without help. I told them we had no energy left, we couldn't continue to care for Amanda and have any family left. I know I looked pretty tired. Of course you couldn't separate Amanda from my hands while I'm still breathing, but they didn't need to know that. I just told them how tired we were, how we were running out of money, how it was so consuming. I didn't whine or repeat myself, I just kept it to the difficult things. They don't need to know about the positives. Anyway, we qualified in one day after I finished all the paper work based on need and not income.

We also have a Supported Living Grant, which is funding we use to keep and pay a qualified person with her while we work. She goes with us on vacations so we can participate with our son in things she just cannot do.

COMMUNITY RESOURCES

FREE NATIONAL PARK ACCESS

The Golden Access Passport is a free lifetime entrance pass to National Parks, available to citizens or permanent residents of the United States regardless of age who have been determined to be permanently disabled. You may obtain a Golden Access Passport at any entrance fee area by showing proof of medically determined disability and eligibility for receiving benefits under federal law. The pass admits the pass holder and any accompanying passengers in a private vehicle. Where entry is not by private vehicle, the passport admits the pass holder, spouse, parents and children. The passport also provides 50% discount on federal use fees charged for facilities and services such as fees for camping, swimming, parking, boat launching or cave tours. For information, contact the **Department of the Interior, (202) 208-3100.**

RONALD MCDONALD HOUSE

Ronald McDonald Houses are publicly supported lodges built to meet the needs of families during a child's hospitalization. Families can stay overnight for a nominal daily charge. Transportation is often provided between the hospital and the Ronald McDonald House. The houses have facilities for storing food and cooking. For information, call **(630) 623-7048**.

We were eligible to use the Ronald McDonald House, across the street from the hospital. It made all the difference in the world. Randy and the boys would come down on weekends, and could then spend time with Heather. It made the entire month-long stay much more bearable (the only time I've ever been away from the boys). At that time, the cost was only $3 per night! A few meals were even brought in for us while we were there. A very great resource.

BRASS RING SOCIETY

The Brass Ring Society is a tax-exempt non-profit organization whose mission is to reach out to children with life threatening illnesses. They have asked to be the "official" wish granting organization for all girls with RS in the USA. They have determined that all children with RS automatically qualify for a dream come true. For information and application forms, call them at **1-800-666-WISH**.

FREE MEDICAL TRAVEL

American Airlines has a program called **"Miles for Kids in Need,"** which offers free round trip airfare for eligible children and their parents for air travel related to medical reasons. You must submit two letters. The first letter, from a charitable organization, must include an explanation of the need and verification of need for financial assistance with airfare. The second letter must come from a physician and must include the name of the parents, place of residence, type of illness and necessity for treatment at the requested destination, age of the child, proof that the child is medically stable to fly, dates of travel and place and origin of destination. These letters must be sent by mail to **American Airlines, Frequent Travelers Special Programs, MD 1394, P.O. Box 61916, Dallas-Fort Worth Airport, TX 75261-9616** or sent by fax to **(817) 931-6890**.

CATALOGS

Making Life Better is a catalog of catalogs, a one-stop access to low-tech assistive equipment for people with disabilities. Published by Easter Seals, the catalog features 48 of the top suppliers of assistive and adaptive equipment in sections geared specifically to the needs of children and sections devoted to increased mobility, medical supply services and more. Send a check or money order for $5.00 to **Making Life Better, National Easter Seals Society, P.O. Box 06440, Chicago, IL 60606-0440**.

CHOOSING EQUIPMENT

Purchasing rehabilitation and adaptive equipment can tap a variety of feelings. The first purchase of a special needs stroller was the toughest. With Jenny still at the initial stages of what we later found out to be RS, my emotions were still often expressed in tears. My heart ached already. Did we have to purchase this huge adaptive stroller for our sweet little girl? It not only stood out in the crowd like a sore thumb but like a bleeding one at that! What bothered me was that this stroller was a very obvious reminder that our daughter is "specially different." Denial? You bet! Eventually, I worked through my feelings and put a priority on Jenny's needs. The stroller provided her with proper positioning. She became more alert, more receptive, and more responsive to her environment. Also, the durability of the stroller with its large tricycle-like tires allowed us to take Jenny to a variety of places not so easily accessible to a standard stroller. We were now able to enjoy hikes in the woods and walks along wet beaches. It was definitely a good purchase.

How do we know what kind of equipment to purchase?

The initial evaluation is very important and should be done by your child's local physician, physical or occupational therapist, or a local medical center, who may consult with vendors (equipment supply stores) to find the right piece of equipment for your daughter. It is good to do your own research. Call or compose a form letter requesting catalogs from a variety of rehabilitation equipment vendors. Browsing through the catalogs will educate you as you comparison shop for styles, features, models, colors and prices, all in the comfort of your own home. Some vendors will bring the equipment to your home or will allow you to keep it on a short trial basis. It is helpful to talk to other families of girls with RS syndrome and ask how they feel about their daughters' equipment. Just remember that the piece of equipment should be suited to her individual needs. When you meet with the equipment representative, ask questions about items that otherwise might not have been explained. Vendors often have their favorite pieces of equipment and companies with whom they deal. Once you are an informed consumer, you will be an active participant in the evaluation process.

FUNDING EQUIPMENT

INSURANCE

How do we get insurance to pay for it?

Contact your insurance company and check out your policy thoroughly. Follow any required procedures to the letter. Any deviation could result in a reduction of benefits. You may need pre-approval. If so, take care of it right away. After you purchase the equipment, it may be too late. If you need a prescription for the equipment, get the forms you need from the insurance company and take them to your physician to complete. After an evaluation, the physician will write a prescription describing the equipment which is recommended, along with a letter of justification. Here is what to include in the letter of justification:

- Name, age, sex and diagnosis of RS. Include a brief and simply worded explanation of the diagnosis with symptoms and prognosis. For example: Susie Q., 6 years, female with Rett syndrome - a neurological disorder which leads to loss of speech, gross and fine motor skills and muscle weakness, seizures and breathing irregularities.
- Add a description of her functional skills. For example, Susie is non-ambulatory, nonverbal, incontinent and dependent for feeding, bathing, and dressing.
- Describe the durable equipment she already has and explain why the new equipment is needed.
- Describe the piece of equipment which is being prescribed now and why it has been requested. For example:

  "Susie needs a light weight manual wheelchair because she can't walk. She must have a properly supported seating system to prevent scoliosis and avoid pressure sores. "

  "Susie needs a stroller because she can't walk long distances. She tires easily over long distances and runs greater risks of falling. She does not have purposeful hand use and cannot self-propel a wheelchair. She does not need the complex positioning support system of a wheelchair at this time."

  "Susie needs a toilet chair because she can't sit independently on the toilet. She cannot be toilet trained without appropriate equipment for her to be successful. Toilet training reduces long term damage to her skin and relieves the cost of diapers."

  "Susie needs a bath chair because she can't sit or stand independently for bathing or showering. She has an increased risk of serious injury if an accident occurs while bathing without appropriate equipment."

- Include the name and phone number of someone the funding agency can call if they have questions. Signatures should include the person writing the letter and the prescribing physician if possible.

How is the equipment funded through insurance?

The vendor (equipment supply company) provides a quotation of cost. The vendor sends it along with the doctor's prescription and letter of justification to the funding agency or insurance company. Insurance and governmental agencies generally pay the vendor directly. If a family chooses to deal directly with the funding source, it becomes their responsibility to work closely and communicate with the vendor regarding funding approvals or denials.

How long will it take?

You should start early, especially for large or custom items. It may take 4 to 6 months to get a new wheelchair. If your request is denied, follow up with an appeal. You may have to make some phone calls and get more documentation. You may have to get a second medical opinion, but the extra work often pays off.

What are some other ways to fund devices and services?

There are a number of funding sources for devices and services and it is important to go through them in proper order. First, try insurance or Medicaid, schools or the Vocational Rehabilitation Agency. Each source has its own procedures and policies. Do your homework first; check to find out what has worked for others.

- **Insurance/Medicaid:** A claim of medical necessity is a must. Denial is not the end of the story. Make it clear you will appeal.

- **Schools:** Schools may purchase communication devices to enable the student to participate in a normal academic setting. However, the device belongs to the school, not the student.

- **Vocational Rehabilitation Programs:** Vocational Rehabilitation Programs may fund equipment if the lack of it is the main obstacle to employment. Eligibility requirements vary from state to state. Look in the white pages of your local telephone book.

- **Private Corporations:** Businesses can take a tax write-off for a charitable contribution and will get good public relations benefits at the same time.

- **Trust Funds:** Check with trust division of banks in your area to see if a trust fund exists for the purpose of helping people with disabilities. Banks don't often advertise this availability.

- **Service Clubs:** Local civic organizations such as the **Lions Clubs, Kiwanis** and **Rotary** often contribute to the purchase of equipment.

- **Fundraisers:** Churches and other organizations are often helpful in putting on a fundraiser in your community, such as a car wash, bake sale, dinner or raffle.

- **"Wishmakers":** These organizations grant wishes to people with specific needs. Contact the **Sunshine Foundation** at **4010 Lefick Street, Philadelphia, PA 19135** or call the **Make a Wish Foundation** at **1-800-722-9474**, or the **Brass Ring Society** at **1-800-666-WISH**.

- **Public Appeals**: Contact local media to help get the word out in the community.

BOOKS AND MAGAZINES

Exceptional Parent Magazine
Call 1-877-372-7368

Enable, official magazine of the **American Association of People with Disabilities (AAPD)** You can receive a complimentary copy by calling 1-800-436-2253

Anderson, Winifred
Negotiating the Special Education Maze: A Guide for Parents and Teachers
Rockville: Woodbine House, 1990
269 pages, $12.95

Bernstein, Jane
Loving Rachel: A Family's Journey from Grief
Boston: Little, Brown, 1988
279 pages, $17.95

Bratt, Berneen
No Time for Jello: One Family's Experience with the Doman-Delacato Patterning Program
Cambridge: Brookline Books, 1989
210 pages, $17.95

Crossley, Rosemary
Annie's Coming Out
New York: Penguin, 1980
256 pages, $6.95

Crump, Iris
Nutrition and Feeding of the Handicapped Child
Boston: Little, Brown, 1987
163 pages, $22.50

deVinck, Christopher
The Power of the Powerless
New York: Doubleday, 1988
153 pages, $14.95

Dickman, Irving
One Miracle at a Time: How to Get Help for Your Disabled Child – From the Experience of Other Parents
New York: Simon & Schuster, 1985
351 pages, $17.95

Featherstone, Helen
A Difference in the Family: Life with a Disabled Child
New York: Penguin, 1982
288 pages, $6.95

Freeman, John
Seizures and Epilepsy in Childhood: A Guide for Parents
Baltimore: Johns Hopkins University Press, 1990
287 pages, $16.95 softback

Goldfarb, Lori
Meeting the Challenge of Disability or Chronic Illness: A Family Guide
Baltimore: Paul H. Brookes, 1986
181 pages, $16.00

Hagberg, Bengt
Rett Syndrome: Clinical and Biological Aspects
London: Cambridge University Press, 1993
120 pages, $49.95, IRSA

Hunter, Kathy
Bridges: A Book of Hope and Inspiration for Families
Clinton, MD: IRSA, 1992
104 pages, $10 members, $15 non-members, IRSA

Hunter, Kathy
The Parent Idea Book
Clinton, MD: IRSA, 1990
55 pages, $4 members, $5 non-members, IRSA
(in Japanese) Cherry Blossom Club: 1992
IRSA Library

Hunter, Kathy
Educational and Therapeutic Intervention in RS
Clinton, MD: IRSA, 1991
122 pages, $5 members, $10 non-members, IRSA

Jones, Monica
Home Care for the Chronically Ill or Disabled Child: A Manual and Sourcebook for Parents and Professionals
New York: Harper & Row, 1985
306 pages, $12.95

Kupfer, Fern
Before and After Zachariah
Chicago: Academy Chicago Publishers, 1988
241 pages, $7.95

l'Association Francaise du Syndrome de Rett
Le Syndrome de Rett
41, Rue Roger Bodineau
37270 Larcay, France
155 pages, IRSA library

Levin, Jackie
**Breaking Barriers: How Children and Adults
with Severe Handicaps Can Access the World
Through Simple Technology**
Minneapolis: Ablenet, 1986
66 pages, $13.95

Lewis, Jackie and Wilson, Debbie
Pathways to Learning in Rett Syndrome
London: David Fulton Publishers, 1998
133 pages, $25.00, IRSA

LINC Associates
**The Specialware Directory, 2nd Edition:
A Guide to Software for Special Education**
Columbus: LINC Associates, 1986
160 pages, $22.50

Lindberg, Barbro
Understanding Rett Syndrome
Toronto: Hogrefe & Huber, 1991
172 pages, $29.00, IRSA

Mantle, Margaret
**Some Just Clap Their Hands: Raising a
Handicapped Child**
New York: Adams Books, 1985
263 pages, $16.95

Nordic Committee on Disability
**The More We Do Together: Adapting the
Environment for Children with Disabilities**
New York: World Rehabilitation Fund, 1985
84 pages, $5.00

Nordoff, Paul; Robbins, Clive
Therapy in Music for Handicapped Children
London: Gollancz; distributed by
David & Charles, 1985
191 pages, $13.95

Ohio State University Research Foundation Staff
Toilet Training: Help for the Delayed Learner
New York: McGraw-Hill, 1978
106 pages, $17.60

Pages, Xiomara
**Mi Cruz Ilene de Rosas: Cartas a Sandra Mi
Hija Enferma (My Cross of Roses: Letters to
Sandra, My Sick Child)**
Spanish only Miami: Editorial Universal, 1996
83 pages, $9.95
E-mail: XJP10@aol.com

Perske, Robert
Circles of Friends
Nashville: Abingdon Press, 1988
94 pages, $9.95

Perske, Robert
**Hope for the Families: New Directions for
Parents of Persons with Retardation or
Other Disabilities**
Nashville: Abingdon Press, 1981
96 pages, $9.95

Perske, Robert
Mealtimes for Persons with Severe Handicaps
Baltimore: Paul H. Brookes, 1986
136 pages, $17.50

Powell, Thomas H
**Brothers and Sisters—A Special Part of
Exceptional Families**
Baltimore: Paul H. Brookes, 1985
226 pages, $16.95

Pueshel, Siegfried
**The Special Child: A Source Book for Parents
of Children with Developmental Disabilities**
Baltimore: Paul H. Brookes, 1988
368 pages, $22.00

Rose, Harriet Wallace
Something's Wrong with My Child!
Springfield: Charles C. Thomas, 1987
196 pages, $26.75

Russell, Grant, Joseph, Fee
Planning for the Future
Evanston: American Publishing Company, 1993
420 pages, $24.95
1-800-247-6553

Russell, Mark and Grant, Arnold
The Life Planning Workbook
Evanston: American Publishing Company, 1995
272 pages, $24.95
1-800-247-6553

Schleifer, Maxwell
The Disabled Child & the Family: An Exceptional Parent Reader
Boston: The Exceptional Parent Press, 1985
183 pages, $15.95

Shore, Kenneth
The Special Education Handbook: A Comprehensive Guide for Parents and Educators
New York: Teachers College Press, 1986
224 pages, $14.95

Sienkiewicz-Mercer, Ruth
I Raise My Eyes to Say Yes: A Memoir
Boston: Houghton Mifflin, 1989
225 pages, $17.95

Simons, Robin
After the Tears: Parents Talk About Raising a Child With a Disability
Orlando: Harcourt Brace Jovanovich, 1987
89 pages, $4.95

Verlicchi, Angela and Ambrosetto
La Sindrome di Rett
Trento: New Magvazine Edizioni, 1992
108 pages, IRSA library

Witt Engerstrom, Ingegerd
Rett Syndrome in Sweden
Goteborg: 1990
114 pages, $16.00, IRSA

Zimmermann, Susan
Grief Dancers
Golden, CO: Nemo Press, 1996
243 pages, member $14.95, $20 non-member IRSA

BOOKS FOR CHILDREN

Brown, Tricia
Someone Special, Just Like You
New York: Henry Holt, 1984
64 pages, $14.95
(Ages 3-6, on multiple disabilities in the classroom)

Cohen, Floreva
My Special Friend
New York: Board of Jewish Education, 1986
$5.95 (Ages 5-8, on friendship)

Cohen, Miriam
See You Tomorrow, Charles
New York: Greenwillow Books, 1983
$2.95 (Ages 4-7, on blindness)

Emmert, Michelle
I'm the Big Sister Now
Niles, IL: Albert Whitman, 1989
$12.95 (Ages 7- 10, on being the "bigger" little sister)

Exley, Helen
What It's Like to Be Me
New York: Friendship Press, 1984
127 pages, $10.95 (Ages 9-12, on thoughts and feelings of children and teenagers with disabilities)

Meyer, Donald
Living With a Brother or Sister with Special Needs: A Book for Sibs
Seattle: University of Washington Press, 1985
110 pages, $4.95 (Ages 6-11, on sibling feelings and experiences)

Moss, Deborah
Lee, the Rabbit With Epilepsy
Rockville: Woodbine House, 1989
$12.95 (Ages 3-7)

Muldoon, Kathleen
Princess Pooh
Niles, IL: Albert Whitman, 1989
$12.95 (Ages 7-10, on learning what it's like to be disabled)

Prall, Jo
My Sister's Special
Chicago: Children's Press, 1985
31 pages, $4.95 (Ages 4-8, on being an important part of the family)

Quinsey, Mary Beth
Why Does That Man Have Such a Big Nose?
Seattle: Parenting Press, 1986
26 pages, $4.95 (Ages 4-7, on fostering positive attitudes)

Rosenberg, Maxine
Finding a Way: Living with Exceptional Brothers and Sisters
New York: Lothrop, Lee & Shepard, 1988
48 pages, $11.95 (on the special nature of sibling relationships)

Rosenberg, Maxine
My Friend Leslie: The Story of a Handicapped Child
New York: Lothrop, Lee & Shepard, 1983
$13.00 (Ages 5-8, on kindergarten experiences)

Schwier, Karin
Keith Edward's Different Day
Downsview, Ontario: G.Allan Roeher Institute, 1988
28 pages, $4.95 (Ages 4-7, on learning that different isn't bad)

Shalom, Debra
Special Kids Make Special Friends
Bellmore, NY.: Association for Children with Down Syndrome, 1984
43 pages, $5.00 (Ages 3-6, on similarities instead of differences)

Stein, Sara
About Handicaps: An Open Family Book for Parents and Children Together
New York: Walker, 1974
47 pages, $6.95 (Ages 4-8, preparation for realities)

Wolf, Bernard
Don't Feel Sorry for Paul
New York: Harper & Row, Harper Junior, 1974
96 pages, $18.50 (Ages 5-8, on physical differences)

Wright, Betty
My Sister is Different
Milwaukee: Raintree, 1981
31 pages, $15.35 (Ages 5-8, on feelings)

CATALOGS AND DIRECTORIES

Directory of National Information Sources on Handicapping Conditions and Related Services
US Government Printing Office, Superintendent of Documents
Washington, DC 20402, $17.00

Directory of Organizations Interested in the Handicapped
People to People Committee for the Handicapped
1111 20th Street, NW, Suite 660
Washington, DC 20036

Directory of Private Schools for Exceptional Children
Nat'l Association of Private Schools for Exceptional Children
1625 Eye Street, NW, Suite 50C
Washington, DC 20006
Free.

The Illustrated Directory of Handicapped Products
497 Cameron Way
Buffalo Grove, IL 60089
$12.95

Services for Women and Girls with Disabilities: A National Directory
Educational Equity Concepts
114 East 32nd Street
New York, NY 10016
$12.00

Directory of Residential Centers for Adults with Developmental Disabilities
Oryx Press, 2214 North Central at Encanto
Phoenix, AZ 85004
$75.00

The Early Intervention Dictionary: A Multidisciplinary Guide to Terminology
Woodbine House Publishers
5615 Fishers Lane
Rockville, MD 20852, (1-800-843-7323)
300 pages, $16.95

Travel for the Disabled: A Handbook of Travel Resources and 500 Worldwide Access Guides
Twin Peaks Press
P.O. Box 129
Vancouver, WA 98666
185 pages, $11.95

PUBLICATIONS, NEWSLETTERS AND PERIODICALS

Accent on Living Magazine
P.O. Box 700, Gillum Road and High Drive
Bloomington, IL 61702
$8.00. Quarterly publication with information on products, medical updates, family issues and other topics of interest.

Augmentative Communication News
Sunset Enterprises, One Surf Way, #215
Monterey, CA 93940
$24.00. Six issues a year

The Bridge, Parent Resources on Disabilities (PROD)
P.O. Box 14391
Portland, OR
$10.00. Quarterly publication with information on resources and support services.

Closing the Gap
P.O. Box 68
Henderson, MN 56044
$26.00. Six issues a year with information on the practical use of technology in special education and rehabilitation.

Computer-Disability News
National Easter Seal Society
70 East Lake Street
Chicago, IL 60601
$15.00. Quarterly newsletter with information on computers and computer aids for disabled persons.

Especially Grandparents
ARC of King County
2230 Eighth Avenue
Seattle, WA 98121
$10.00. Quarterly newsletter for grandparents of children with disabilities.

The Exceptional Parent
605 Commonwealth Avenue
Boston, MA, 02215
Toll Free: 1-877-372-7368
$16.00. Eight publications a year with information on every aspect of the care for children with special needs.

Focus on Exceptional Children
Love Publishing Company
1777 South Bellaire Street
Denver, CO 80222
$24.00. Nine issues a year with information on special education.

Focus on Fathers
Fathers Outreach Project
Experimental Education Unit WJ-10
University of WA
Seattle, WA 98195
Free. Quarterly newsletter for fathers of special needs children.

Growing Child
22 N. 2nd Street, P.O. Box 620
Lafayette, IN 47902
Monthly newsletter for parents of children with disabilities from birth to 5 years. Also publishes Growing Parent specifically for parents of children with disabilities.

JASH: The Journal of the Association for Persons with Severe Handicaps
TASH, 7010 Roosevelt Way NE
Seattle, WA 98116
$30.00 or with membership

New Ways
P.O. Box 5072
Evanston, IL 60204
$23.95. Quarterly publication with information on current trends and thinking in the field of disability.

Special Parent, Special Child
Lindell Press
P.O. Box 462
South Salem, NY 10590
$18.00. Six issues a year with information to help young children learn developmental skills.

FREE MATERIALS

The Chronically Ill Child and Family in the Community
ACCH, 3615 Wisconsin Avenue, NW.
Washington, DC 20016

Families and Disability Newsletter
Beach Center on Families and Disability
University of Kansas, Bureau of Child Research
4138 Haworth Hall, Lawrence, KS 66045

The Family Resource Coalition Report
Family Resource Coalition
230 North Michigan Avenue #1625
Chicago, IL 60601

A New Way of Thinking
The Governor's Planning Council on
Developmental Disabilities
State Planning Agency
201 Capitol Square Building, 550 Cedar Street
St. Paul, MN 55101

HEATH Resource Directory
HEATH Resource Center, American Council on
Education
One Dupont Circle, NW
Washington, DC 20036

The National Easter Seal Communicator
National Easter Seal Society
70 East Lake Street
Chicago, IL 60601

**NARIC Quarterly: A Newsletter of Disability
and Rehabilitation Research and Resources**
NARIC
8455 Colesville Road, Suite 935
Silver Spring, MD 20910

Speak Out
PEAK Parent Center
6055 Lehman Drive, Suite 101
Colorado Springs, CO 80918

Family Support Bulletin
UCP Community Services Division
1522 K Street, NW
Washington, DC 20005

**Pocket Guide to Federal Help for Individuals
with Disabilities**
**A Summary of Existing Legislation Affecting
Persons with Disabilities**
**Selected Federal Publications Relating to
Disability**
U.S. Department of Education, OSERS
Room 3132, 330 C Street, SW
Washington, DC 20202

**Epilepsy: Breaking Down the Walls of
Misunderstanding**
Abbott Laboratories, Public Affairs
Abbott Park, IL 60064

Epilepsy
National Institutes of Health
Office of Clinical Center Communications
WGMCC
Building 10, Room 1C-255
Bethesda, MD 20892

**Fact Sheets, Article Reprints, Resource
Information, Specialized Packets,
Bibliographies and Disability-Related
Groups on a National, State and Local Level**
NICHY, P.O.Box 1492
Washington, DC 20013

SAFE (Schools are for Everyone)
SAFE, P.O. Box 583
Syracuse, NY 13210

News Digest on Siblings
NICHY, P.O. Box 1492
Washington, DC 20013

ASSOCIATIONS

**The ARC (formerly the Association for
Retarded Citizens)**
500 E. Border Street, Suite 300, P.O. Box 1047
Arlington, TX 76010
1-800-433-5255 or (817) 261-6003
e-mail:thearc@metronet.com

**Association for the Care of Children's Health
(ACCH)**
7910 Woodmont Avenue, Suite 300
Bethesda, MD 20814
(301) 654-6549
Fax: 301-986-4553
e-mail:acch@clark.net
URL: http://www.acch.org

**Association for Persons with Severe
Handicaps (TASH)**
29 W. Susquehanna Avenue, Suite 210
Baltimore, MD 21204
1-800-482-8274 or (410) 828-8274
e-mail:tashbalt@aol.com

Council for Exceptional Children
1920 Association Drive
Reston, VA 20191
(703) 620-3660

Federation of Families for Children's Mental Health
1021 Prince Street
Alexandria, VA 22314-2971
(703) 684-7710

National Association of Developmental Disabilities Councils
1234 Massachusetts Avenue, NW, Suite 103
Washington, DC 20005
(202) 347-1234
e-mail:naddc@igc.apc.org
URL: http://www.igc.opc.org/NADDC

National Association of State Directors of Special Education (NASDE)
1800 Diagonal Road Suite 320
Alexandria, VA 22314
(703) 519-3800
TDD: (703) 519-7008

National Center for Learning Disabilities
1401 New York Avenue, NW, Suite 900
Washington, DC 20005
(202) 879-5767
Fax: (202)879-5773

National Easter Seal Society
230 W. Monroe, Suite 1800
Chicago, IL 60606
1-800-221-6827
(312) 726-6200
URL: http://www.seals.com

National Parent Network on Disabilities (NPND)
1727 King Street, Suite 305
Alexandria, VA 22314
(703) 684-6763 Voice/TTY
e-mail:npnd@cs.com

United Cerebral Palsy Associations, Inc.
1660 L Street, NW, Suite 700
Washington, DC 20036-5602
1-800-872-5827
e-mail:ucnatl@ucpa.org

GOVERNMENT AGENCIES

Administration on Developmental Disabilities
U.S. Department of Health and Human Services
Hubert Humphrey Building, Room 3290
200 Independence Avenue, SW
Washington, DC 20201
(202) 690-6590

Clearinghouse on Disability Information
Office of Special Education and Rehabilitative Services
U.S. Department of Education
Switzer Building, Room 3132
330 C Street SW
Washington, DC 20202-2524
(202) 205-8241

National Council on Disability
1331 F Street, NW, Suite 1050
Washington, DC 20004-1107
(202) 272-2004

National Institute of Child Health and Human Development
P.O. Box 29111
Washington, DC 20040
(301) 496-5133

National Institute on Disability and Rehabilitation Research
Office of Special Education and Rehabilitative Services
U.S. Department of Education
Switzer Building, Room 3060
600 Independence Avenue, SW
Washington, DC 20202-2572
(202) 205-8134
TTY: (202) 205-8198

National Library Service for the Blind and Physically Handicapped
Library of Congress
1291 Taylor Street, NW
Washington, DC 20542
(202) 707-5100
TTY: (202) 707-0744

Office of Special Education Programs
U.S. Department of Education
MES Building, Room 3086
600 Independence Avenue, SW
Washington, DC 20202-4611
(202) 205-5507

Social Security Administration Headquarters
6401 Security Boulevard
Baltimore, MD 21235
1-800-772-1213 or 1-800-325-0778

GOVERNMENT SUPPORTED ORGANIZATIONS

Abledata: The National Database of Assistive Technology
8455 Colesville Road, Suite 935
Silver Spring, MD 20910-3319
1-800-227-0216 or (301) 608-8998

Beach Center on Families and Disabilities
Haworth Hall
University of Kansas, Lawrence, KS 66045
(913) 864-7600
e-mail:Beach@dole.isi.ukans.edu

ERIC Clearinghouse on Disabilities and Gifted Education
Council for Exceptional Children
1920 Association Drive, Reston, VA 22091-1589
1-800-LET-ERIC or (703) 264-9474
(703) 264-9449
e-mail:ericec@inet.ed.gov

Institute on Community Integration
University of Minnesota
102 Pattee Hall, 150 Pillsbury Drive, SE
Minneapolis, MN 55455
(612) 624-6300
e-mail:ici@mail.ici.coled.umn.edu.
URL: http://www. ici.coled.umn.edu/ici/

National Clearinghouse on Family Support and Children's Mental Health
Portland State University
P.O. Box 751
Portland, OR 97207-0751
1-800-628-1696 or (503) 725-4063

National Information Center for Children and Youth with Disabilities (NICHCY)
P.O. Box 1492
Washington, DC 20013-1492
1-800-695-0285 or (202) 884-8200
e-mail:nichcy@aed.org

National Parent to Parent Support and Information System
P.O. Box 907
Blue Ridge, GA 30513
1-800-651-1151 or (706) 632-8822

National Rehabilitation Information Center (NARIC)
8455 Colesville Road, Suite 935
Silver Spring, MD 20910-3319
1-800-346-2742 or (301) 588-9284 or
(301) 495-5626

World Institute on Disability
510 Sixteenth Street, Suite 100
Oakland, CA 94612-1502
(510) 763-4100 or (510) 208-9493
e-mail:wid@wid.org
URL: http://www.wid.org/wid

HOTLINES AND INFORMATION LINES

Americans with Disabilities (ADA) Information Line:
1-800-514-0301

International Rett Syndrome Association:
1-800-818-RETT

National Health Information Clearinghouse:
1-800-336-4797

National Information Center for Children and Youth with Disabilities (NICHY):
1-800-999-5999

National Organization for Rare Disorders (NORD):
1-800-999-NORD

National Rehabilitation Information Center (NARIC):
1-800-346-2742

Parent/Family Information and Support:
1-800-922-9234, ext. 301

United Cerebral Palsy Association:
1-800-USA-1UCP

U.S. Department of Education Information Resource Center:
1-800-USA-LEARN

INTERNET SITES

Our Kids (parenting resource site)
URL: http://wonder.mit.edu/ok/

Parents Place
URL: http://www. parentsplace.com/index.htm

Special Child
URL:http://www.specialchild.com

National Fathers Network
URL:http://www.fathersnetwork.org/easy/easy.htm

PARENT TRAINING AND INFORMATION CENTERS
(1-800 numbers are in state only)

ALABAMA
Special Education Action Committee, Inc. (SEAC)
1-800-222-7322

ALASKA
Alaska PARENTS, Inc.
1-800-478-7678

ARIZONA
Pilot Parent Partnerships
1-800-237-3007

ARKANSAS
Arkansas Parent Support and Information Network
1-800-223-1330

CALIFORNIA
Northern California Coalition for Parent Training and Information
Region I
(510) 644-2555 (TDD available)
Fax: (510) 841-8645

Region II
(415)499-3877

Region III
(408) 727-5775

Region IV
(209) 229-2000

Parents Helping Parents-San Francisco
(415) 564-0722

Team of Advocates for Special Kids, Inc. (TASK)
(714) 533-8275

COLORADO
PEAK Parent Center, Inc.
1-800-284-0251

CONNECTICUT
Connecticut Parent Advocacy Center. Inc. (CPAC)
1-800-445-2722

DELAWARE
Parent Information Center of Delaware, Inc.
(302) 366-0152

DISTRICT OF COLUMBIA
COPE Parent Training and Information Center
1-800-515-COPE

FLORIDA
Parent Education Network (PEN)
1-800-285-5736

GEORGIA
Parents Educating Parents (PEP)
(707) 732-1122

HAWAII
Assisting with Appropriate Rights in Education (AWARE)
(808) 536-2280

IDAHO
Idaho Parents Unlimited, Inc.
1-800-242-4785

ILLINOIS
Family Resource Center on Disabilities (FRCD)
(312) 939-3513

Designs for Change
(312) 857-9292

INDIANA
Indiana Resource Center for Families with Special Needs (INSOURCE)
1-800-332-4433

IOWA
Iowa Pilot Parents
1-800-952-4777

KANSAS
Families Together, Inc.
1-800-264-6343

KENTUCKY
Kentucky Special Parent Involvement
Network (KY-SPIN)
1-800-525-7746

LOUISIANA
Project PROMPT
1-800-766-7736

MAINE
Special-Needs Parent Information Network
(SPIN)
1-800-870-7746

MARYLAND
The Parents' Place of Maryland, Inc.
(410) 712-0900

MASSACHUSETTS
Federation for Children with Special Needs
1-800-331-0688

MICHIGAN
Citizens Alliance to Uphold Special
Education (CAUSE)
1-800-221-9105

Parents Are Experts/Parents Training
Parents Project
(810) 557-5070

MINNESOTA
PACER Center, Inc.
1-800-53PACER

MISSISSIPPI
Parent Partners
(601) 366-5707

MISSOURI
Missouri Parents Act (MPACT)
1-800-743-7634

MONTANA
Parents Let's Unite for Kids
1-800-222-7585

NEBRASKA
Nebraska Parents' Center
1-800-284-8520

NEVADA
Nevada Parents Encouraging Parents (PEP)
1-800-216-5188

NEW HAMPSHIRE
Parent Information Center
(603) 224-6299

NEW JERSEY
Statewide Parent Advocacy Network, Inc.
(201) 642-8100

NEW MEXICO
Education for Parents of Indian Children
with Special Needs
1-800-765-7320

Parents Reaching Out Project
1-800-524-5176

NEW YORK
Advocates for Children of New York, Inc.
(718) 624-8450

Parent Network Center (PNC)
1-800-724-7408

Resources for Children with Special Needs
(212) 677-4650

NORTH CAROLINA
Exceptional Children's Assistance Center
(ECAC)
1-800-962-6817

PARENTS Project
(704) 433-2662

NORTH DAKOTA
Pathfinder Family Center
(701) 852-9426

OHIO
Child Advocacy Center
(513) 821-2400

Ohio Coalition for the Education of Children
with Disabilities (OCECD)
(614) 431-1307

OKLAHOMA
Parents Reaching Out in Oklahoma
1-800-PL94-142

OREGON
Oregon COPE Project, Inc.
(503) 373-7477

PENNSYLVANIA
Mentor Parent Program
1-800-447-1431

Parent Education Network
1-800-522-5827

Parents Union for Public Schools
in Philadelphia
(215) 546-1166

PUERTO RICO
Asociacion de Padres Pro Bienestar de Nines
con Impedimentos de P.R., Inc.
(809) 763-4665

RHODE ISLAND
Rhode Island Parent Information Network,
Inc. (RIPIN)
1-800-464-3399

SOUTH CAROLINA
Parents Reaching Out to Parents of South
Carolina, Inc. (PRO-Parents)
1-800-759-4776

SOUTH DAKOTA
South Dakota Parent Connection
1-800-640-4553

TENNESSEE
Support and Training for Exceptional
Parents
1-800-280-5TEP

TEXAS
Path Project Partners Resource Network, Inc.
1-800-866-4726

Project P.O.D.E.R.
1-800-682-9747

Special Kids, Inc.
(713) 643-9576

UTAH
UTAH Parent Center
1-800-468-1160

VERMONT
Vermont Parent Information Center
1-800-639-7170

VIRGINIA
Parent Educational Advocacy
Training Center (PEATC)
1-800-869-6782

WASHINGTON
Washington PAVE (Parents Are Vital in
Education)
1-800-572-7368

Specialized Training of Military Parents
(STOMP)
1-800-298-3543

Touchstones-More Alike than Different
Parent Advocacy and Access Project
(206) 721-0867

WEST VIRGINIA
West Virginia Parent Training and
Information
(304) 624-1436

WISCONSIN
Parent Education Project of Wisconsin, Inc.
(414) 328-5520

WYOMING
Parent Information Center
1-800-660-WPIC (9742)

STATE SPECIAL EDUCATION DEPARTMENTS

ALABAMA
Alabama Department of Education
Division of Special Education Services
P.O. Box 302101
Montgomery, AL 36130-2101
Contact: Bill East (334) 242-8114

ALASKA
Alaska Department of Education
Office of Special and Supplemental Services
801 Tenth Street, Suite 200
Juneau, AK 99801-1894
Contact: Myra Howe (907) 465-2971

ARIZONA
Arizona Department of Education
1535 W. Jefferson Street
Phoenix, AZ 85007-3280
Contact: Kathryn A. Lund (602) 542-3084

The Disabilities Help Line of Arizona
The Annex, 1515 E. Osborn
Phoenix, AZ 85014
1-800-352-3792 or (602) 263-8856

ARKANSAS
Arkansas Department of Education
4 State Capitol Mall, Room 105-C
Little Rock, AR 72201-1071
Contact: Diane Sydoriak (501) 682-4221

CALIFORNIA
California Department of Education
515 L Street, Suite 270
Sacramento, CA 95814
Contact: Leo Sandoval (916) 445-4602

COLORADO
Colorado Department of Education
Special Education Services Unit
201 E. Colfax Avenue
Denver, CO 80203
Contact: Fred Smokoski (303) 866-6695

CONNECTICUT
Connecticut Department of Education
Bureau of Special Education and Pupil
Personnel Services
25 Industrial Park Road
Middletown, CT 06457
Contact: Tom Gillung (860) 638-4265

DELAWARE
Department of Public Instruction
Division for Exceptional Children
P.O. Box 1402
Dover, DE 19903-1402
Contact: Martha Brooks (302) 739-5471

DISTRICT OF COLUMBIA
State Office of Special Education
Goding School
10th and F Street, NE
Washington, DC 20002
Contact: Garnett Pinkney (202) 724-4800

FLORIDA
Florida Education Center Bureau of Student
Services/Exceptional Education
325 W. Gaines Street, Suite 614
Tallahassee, FL 32399-0400
Contact: Bettye Weir (904) 488-1570

GEORGIA
Georgia Department of Education
Division of Exceptional Students
1952 Twin Towers E, 205 Butler Street
Atlanta, GA 30334-5040
Contact: Paulette Bragg (404) 656-3963

HAWAII
Hawaii Department of Education
Special Education Section
3430 Leahi Avenue
Honolulu, HI 96815
Contact: Robert Campbell (808) 733-4990

IDAHO
Idaho State Department of Education
Special Education Section
P.O. Box 83720
Boise, ID 83720-0027
Contact: Nolene Weaver (208) 334-3940

ILLINOIS
Illinois State Board of Education
Center on Policy, Planning and Resource
100 N. First Street, Mail Code E-216
Springfield, IL 62777-001
Contact: Gail Lieberman (217) 782-6601

INDIANA
Indiana Department of Education
Division of Special Education
State House, Room 229
Indianapolis, IN 46204-2798
Contact: Robert Marra (317) 232-0570

IOWA
Bureau of Special Education
Grimes State Office Building
Des Moines, IA 50319-0146
Contact: Jeananne Hagen (515) 281-3176

KANSAS
Kansas State Board of Education
Student Support Services
120 SE 10th Avenue
Topeka, KS 66612-1182
Contact: Mike Remus (913) 296-0946

KENTUCKY
Kentucky Department of Education
Division of Exceptional Children Services
500 Metro Street, Room 805
Frankfort, KY 40601
Contact: Hal Hayden (502) 564-4970

LOUISIANA
Louisiana Department of Education
Office of Special Education
P.O. Box 94064, 9th Floor
Baton Rouge, LA 70804-9064
Contact: T.L. Borne (504) 342-3633

MAINE
Maine Department of Education
Division of Special Services
23 State House Station
Augusta, ME 04333
Contact: David Stockford (207) 287-5950

MARYLAND
Maryland Department of Education
Division of Special Education
200 W. Baltimore Street
Baltimore, MD 21201-2595
Contact: Richard Steinke (410) 767-0238

Governor's Office of Children, Youth, and Families
Maryland Infants and Toddlers Program
301 W. Preston Street, Suite 1502
Baltimore, MD 21201
(410) 767-4160

MASSACHUSETTS
Massachusetts Department of Education
Program Quality Assurance
350 Main Street
Maiden, MA 02148-5023
Contact. Marty Mittnacht (617) 388-3300

MICHIGAN
Michigan Department of Education
Special Education Services
P.O. Box 30008
Lansing, MI 48909-7508
Contact: Richard Baldwin (517) 373-9433

MINNESOTA
Department of Children, Families and Learning
550 Cedar Street
St. Paul, MN 55101
Contact: Wayne Erickson (612) 296-1793

MISSISSIPPI
Mississippi State Department of Education
Office of Special Education
P.O. Box 771
Jackson, MS 39205-0771
Contact: Carolyn Black (601) 359-3498

MISSOURI
Department of Elementary and Secondary Education Special Education Programs
P.O. Box 480
Jefferson City, MO 65102-0480
Contact: Melodie Friedebach (314) 751-2965

MONTANA
Office of Public Instruction
Division of Special Education State Capitol
P.O. Box 202051
Helena, MT 59620-2501
Contact: Robert Runkel (406) 444-4429

NEBRASKA
Nebraska Department of Education
301 Centennial Mall South,
P.O. Box 94987
Lincoln, NE 68509-4987
Contact: Gary M. Sherman (402) 471-2471

NEVADA
Nevada Department of Education
Special Education Branch
440 W. King, Capitol Complex
Carson City, NV 89710-0004
Contact: Gloria Dopf (702) 687-3140

NEW HAMPSHIRE
New Hampshire Department of Education
Bureau of Special Education
101 Pleasant Street
Concord, NH 03301-3860
Contact: Nate Norris (603) 271-6693

NEW JERSEY
New Jersey Department of Education
Office of Special Education
CN 500
Trenton, NJ 08625-0050
Contact: Barbara Gantwerk (609) 633-6833

NEW MEXICO
New Mexico State Department of Education
300 Don Gaspar Avenue
Santa Fe, NM 87501-2786
Contact: Diego Gallegos (505) 827-6541

NEW YORK
New York State Education Department
Office for Special Education
One Commerce Plaza, Room 1624
Albany, NY 12234-0001
Contact: Tom Neveldine (518) 474-5548

NORTH CAROLINA
North Caroline Department of Public
Instruction
Division of Exceptional Children's Services
301 N. Wilmington Street
Raleigh, NC 27601-2825
Contact: Lowell Harris (919) 715-1565

NORTH DAKOTA
Department of Public Instruction
Special Education
600 E. Boulevard
Bismarck, ND 58505-0440
Contact: Carl Gronberg (701) 328-2277

OHIO
Ohio Department of Education
Division of Special Education
933 High Street
Worthington, OH 43085-4087
Contact: John Herner (614) 466-2650

OKLAHOMA
Oklahoma State Department of Education
Division of Special Education
2500 North Lincoln Boulevard
Oklahoma City, OK 73105-4599
Contact: Darla Griffin or John Corpolongo
(405) 521-4859

OREGON
Oregon Department of Education
Special Education and Student Services
Division
700 Pringle Parkway, SE
Portland, OR 97310-0290
Contact: Petrea Hagen-Gilden (503) 378-3598

PENNSYLVANIA
Pennsylvania Department of Education
Bureau of Special Education
333 Market Street
Harrisburg, PA 17126-0333
Contact: William Penn (717) 783-6913

RHODE ISLAND
Rhode Island Department of Education
22 Hayes Street
Providence, RI 02908-5025
Contact: Robert M. Pryhoda (401) 227-3505

SOUTH CAROLINA
South Carolina State Department of Education
Office of Programs for Exceptional Children
1429 Senate
Columbia, SC 29201
Contact: Ora Spann (803) 734-8806

SOUTH DAKOTA
Department of Education and Cultural Affairs
Office of Special Education
700 Governors Drive
Pierre, SD 57501-2291
Contact: Deborah Barnett (605) 773-3678

TENNESSEE
Tennessee Department of Education
Division of Special Education
710 James Robertson Parkway
Nashville, TN 37243-0380
Contact: Joseph Fisher (615) 741-2851

TEXAS
Texas Education Agency
Special Education Unit
1701 N. Congress Avenue
Austin, TX 78701-2486
Contact: Jill Gray (512) 463-9414

UTAH
Utah State Office of Education Special
Education Services
Unit 250 East 500 S
Salt Lake City, UT 84111-3204
Contact: Steve Kukic (801) 538-7587

VERMONT
Vermont Department Of Education
Division of Special Education
120 State Street
Montpelier, VT 05602-3403
Contact: Dennis Kane (802) 828-3141

VIRGINIA
Virginia Department Of Education
P.O. Box 2120
Richmond, VA 23216-2120
Contact: Douglas Cox (804) 225-2402

WASHINGTON
Superintendent of Public Instruction
Special Education Section
Old Capitol Building
Olympia, WA 98504-7200
Contact: Douglas Gill (360) 753-6733

Department of Social and Health Services
Infant Toddler Early Intervention Program
P.O. Box 45201
Olympia, WA 98504
Voice: (360) 586-2810

WEST VIRGINIA
West Virginia Department Of Education
Office of Special Education
1800 Kanawha Boulevard
Charleston, WV 25305
Contact: Michael Valentine, (304) 558-2696

WISCONSIN
Department of Public instruction
Division of Learning Support
125 S. Webster
Madison, WI 53707-7841
Contact: Juanita S. Pawlisch (608) 266-1649

WYOMING
Wyoming Department of Education
Federal Programs Unit
2300 Capitol Avenue
Cheyenne, WY 82002-0050
Contact: Patti Muhlenkamp (307) 777-7417

EPILOGUE

I'd like to finish with the story of Molly, who recently died at the age of 16. Throughout her young life, Molly had brought much sunshine to those around her. Her family never lost an opportunity to see the humor in some of life's greatest tragedy. I always looked forward to their letters, which poked fun at nearly every mundane aspect of life with RS in the family. One photo of the family's yard sale showed a price sticker on Molly's head, put there by her brother and sister on a mischievous day. They were incredibly dedicated to Molly and she was an extraordinary part of their lives. When she died, her brother, Matt, and her sister, Annie, wrote:

When Molly was about 2 and she didn't talk, we tried to fix her. We took her to speech therapy and occupational therapy and any other therapy we could find. We went to conventional doctors and some doctors who weren't so conventional. When she got to be about 6 or 7, we pretty much gave up on fixing her and just accepted Molly for who she was, which became more important than what she could do. She was the light of our lives. Everything about her was genuine and real. We loved her and she loved us. And we had a good time with her. She was just plain fun to be with.

She taught us incredible patience and tolerance. In turn, she was patient and tolerated us, no matter what seemingly silly things we asked of her. She was an extremely emotionally together person. While we will never know how she perceived her surroundings, she conducted herself with a high degree of dignity.

The true measure of success is how well you play the hand you are dealt, and Molly played hers extremely well. We will miss her smile and her laughter, the twinkle in her eye and the occasional mischief she got into. We will miss her very presence. She will be a part of us forever.

When she died, Molly's mother was consumed with loss, yet she courageously called to make arrangements for autopsy, the ultimate gift of life for others. I explained how the process would go and assured her that I would follow the procedure from start to finish at the Harvard Tissue Bank. "Harvard", she said wistfully. And with her keen sense of humor still intact, she said through heavy tears, "She finally made it. We always wanted her to go to Harvard." And I responded, "Molly taught more in her little life than any prep school or college could have. She skipped over the formal education stuff and went right to work as a teacher."

It shouldn't have happened this way. Molly should have grown up and gone to college like her brother and sister will. She should be studying at Harvard instead of being studied. She had tremendous potential until RS took it away. And while our experience as special needs parents has brought us great joy and happiness, we know too well of the deep pain it also brings. It should never happen this way.

It is one thing to raise money for research, another to find willing researchers, and yet another to participate in the process that leads to the cure. We need to continually support research. We must feed the flames of this fire, to keep awareness heightened and make research a priority. No one can make this decision but us. No one will do it if we do not. Due to the generous contributions of families who have participated in research, we will ultimately bring about the cause, treatment and cure for a disorder that should never happen. It is a very courageous commitment. I ask you to tenderly consider the alternative—continued generations of RS. It's up to us.

Parents have an enormous task to seek and provide the best, to turn our trials to triumphs. Scientists have a complicated job to put answers to many questions. The work ahead is daunting and the journey sometimes arduous. But, like the sculptor chiseling rock into art, the hammer may hit the stone a thousand times before it finally breaks. And break it will.

"Some dreams seem impossible. Then they seem improbable. And when we summon the will, they become inevitable."

Christopher Reeve

I tiptoed softly into her darkened room and kissed her forehead. She stirred, turning her head toward me and slowly opened those beautiful, expressive eyes. A peaceful smile that held a full day's sunshine brightened the room with the sweetness of her being. I gently pulled the covers up to her smile and tucked her in. She closed her twinkling eyes with a deep, contented sigh and fell back into a blissful sleep.

My mind wandered to past years, so full of confusion as Stacie had remained such a mystery to everyone she met. I remembered the frustration of first finding no one who would listen that anything was wrong, and then as the years passed, finding no one who would believe that all had been right. I remembered asking myself the same questions over time and time again. How? When? Why? What?

Now almost fifteen years later, the confusion and frustration, the aloneness and, uncertainty are gone. They are replaced by hope and a world full of friends who care. Stacie is still somewhat a mystery, but we understand so much more about her. We have all come a long way down the path of unknowns. We stand on the threshold of new discoveries that will bring all of our precious daughters a better way of life.

I hope this book has made a bridge over the murky waters of the past uncertainties so that others may cross without having to live with so many unanswered questions. If so, it has been worth the effort.

I tiptoed quietly from her room, taking with me the sunshine of her smile and the warmth of this new hope.

Kathy Hunter

I wanted a perfect ending. Now I've learned, the hard way, that some poems don't rhyme, and some stories don't have a clear beginning, middle, and end. Life is about not knowing, having to change, taking the moment and making the best of it, without knowing what's going to happen next. Delicious Ambiguity.

Gilda Radner

it's not what
we carry with us in life
that's important,
but what
we leave behind...

COMING TO TERMS

A RETT SYNDROME GLOSSARY

Following is a list of common terms that you may come across in your search for information. Some of these terms are used to describe conditions that explain Rett syndrome. Other terms are used to rule out Rett syndrome.

abduction: movement of a limb or any other part away from the midline of the body.

absence seizure: a generalized seizure in which consciousness is altered, formerly called "petit mal."

adaptive behavior: skills needed by a child to function effectively and appropriately for her age in the school, family and community settings.

adduction: movement of a limb or any other part toward the midline of the body.

acetylcholine: a neurotransmitter chemical.

ADA (Americans With Disabilities Act): federal legislation enacted in 1990, intended to protect all people with disabilities from discrimination.

aerophagia: swallowing of air.

alternative communication: a method which replaces traditional forms or methods already used by someone to communicate.

ambulatory: able to walk.

amino acids: the building blocks or chief structure of proteins; several are essential in human nutrition.

Angelman Syndrome (Happy Puppet Syndrome): AS is a neurodevelopmental disorder caused by loss of paternally derived gene(s) on chromosome 15. It has many features that are similar to RS including ataxia, lack of speech, seizures and microcephaly. The majority of cases can be detected by an analysis of chromosome 15.

ankle-foot orthosis (AFO's): an orthopedic apparatus, most commonly splints or braces, used to support, align or correct deformities or to improve the function of the ankle/foot.

annual review: a review of a child's special education program to be held at least once a year to assess progress and determine whether any program changes are necessary in the following year.

anorexia: a severe loss of appetite.

anticonvulsant: any medication used to control seizures.

apnea: episodic arrest of breathing, seen during waking and not usually during sleep in RS.

appropriate education: an educational program that is capable of meeting the educational needs of a child who has an educational disability.

apraxia: inability to program the (usually automatic) planning done by the brain to execute movements.

arborization: branching.

aspiration pneumonia: a lung infection caused by inhaling a foreign body, such as food, into the lungs.

aspirated: inhaled.

asphyxia: interference with circulation and oxygenation of the blood that leads to loss of consciousness.

ataxia: an imbalance or lack of coordination of voluntary and involuntary muscles; shakiness on reaching or moving the trunk that is associated with malfunction in the cerebellum; unbalanced gait and jerky, uncoordinated movements.

atonic seizures: generalized seizures in which body tone is suddenly lost and the child falls to the ground or her head slumps forward.

atony: state in which muscles are floppy, lacking normal elasticity.

atrophy: wasting, from disuse; implies normal tissue to begin with.

atypical: not typical; different.

auditory evoked potential: a test to evaluate the processing of sound by the brain stem.

augmentative communication: all forms of communication that enhance, replace or supplement speech and writing.

aura: the start of a seizure—a peculiar feeling, sense of fear or funny sensation in one part of the body.

autism: a developmental disability that results in impairments in social interaction, verbal and nonverbal communication and unusual behaviors and responses to the environment.

automatisms: purposeless automatic movements that accompany a complex partial seizure, such as smacking the lips, chewing or picking at the clothes.

autonomic nervous system: the part of the nervous system that regulates certain automatic functions of the body, for example, heart rate, temperature and bowel movements.

autonomic responses: body functions that happen involuntarily, such as breathing, sweating, blood pressure, heart rate, flushing of the face.

autosomal dominant trait: a genetic trait carried on the autosomes. The disorder appears when one of a pair of chromosomes contains the abnormal gene; statistically, it is passed on from the affected parent to half of the children.

autosomal recessive trait: a genetic trait carried on the autosome. Both asymptomatic parents must carry the trait to produce an affected child. This child has two abnormal genes. The risk of recurrence is 25%. RS is not felt to be autosomal recessive.

autosome: any of the first 22 pairs of chromosomes; all chromosomes are autosomes except for the two sex chromosomes, X and Y.

axon: a nerve fiber.

Babinski reflex: extension of the big toe upon stimulation of the sole of the foot. This abnormal response is found in individuals with pyramidal tract damage.

Barrett's esophagus: damage to the normal skin-like lining of the esophagus, which is replaced with a lining that resembles that of the stomach. It is caused by persistent reflux of acid from the stomach. The new lining can resist the gastric reflux, but inflammation at the upper end of the new lining may narrow the interior passageway of the esophagus.

basal ganglia: several large masses of gray matter embedded deep within the white matter of the cerebrum.

behavior modification: the systematic application of the principles of learning theory to change behavior by modifying events that precede or follow the behavior.

beta endorphins: the body's own morphine-like substance.

biogenic amines: neurotransmitters dopamine, norepinephrine (also known as noradrenaline), serotonin and a few others.

biological marker: a scientific test which proves the presence of a condition.

body jacket: a molded, padded thin plastic brace designed to apply gentle pressure in the proper areas to straighten the spine.

bolus: 1) any mass of chewed food that is ready to be swallowed; 2) term used in tube feeding to indicate feeding given at one time.

brain stem: the primitive portion of the brain that lies between the cerebrum and the spinal cord.

brain stem auditory evoked response (BAER): a test to evaluate the processing of sound by the brain stem.

breath holding: quick inspiration of a single full breath, followed by delayed expiration during which breathing stops.

bruxism: tooth grinding, common in RS.

carnitine: an amino acid which helps to transport long-chain fatty acids.

central apnea: cessation of breathing movement at the end of expiration.

central nervous system (CNS): the portion of the nervous system that consists of the brain and spinal cord. It is primarily involved in voluntary movement and thought processes.

cerebrospinal fluid (CSF): the normally clear fluid that surrounds the brain and spinal cord.

cerebral palsy: a disorder of movement and posture due to a nonprogressive defect of the immature brain.

cerebral cortex: the outer part of the cerebrum.

cerebrum: the largest region of the brain, made up of 4 lobes and connected by the corpus callosum.

Child Find: the continuous efforts of a school district to identify all children from birth to age 21 in its area who may have educational disabilities and need special education.

chiropractic: a system of treating diseases by manipulation, mainly of the vertebrae of the backbone. It is based on the theory that nearly all disorders can be traced to the incorrect alignment of bones, with consequent malfunctioning of nerves and muscles throughout the body.

chromosome analysis: a study of the 46 potential chromosome structures that consist of the genetic code for our physical and biochemical traits.

chronological age: the child's actual age in years and months.

classic: typical.

clinical diagnosis: a conclusion based on findings from the patient's history and physical exam, usually not as "definitive" as a laboratory-made diagnosis would be. The term "clinical" as used here does not have the implication of "cold, analytical and detached" that it sometimes does in everyday conversation.

chromosomal analysis: a study of the 46 potential chromosome structures that consist of the genetic code for our physical and biochemical traits.

clonus: alternate muscle contraction and relaxation in rapid succession.

cognitive skills: thinking abilities, most often represented by IQ scores; difficult to assess in Rett syndrome.

complex partial seizure: a seizure which involves only part of the brain and which alters consciousness or awareness.

computerized axial tomography (CAT scan): an x-ray which is used to examine soft tissues in the body. The technique involves the recording of "slices" of the body with an X-ray scanner and then integrating them by computer to give a cross-sectional image. Within the skull, it can be used to reveal the normal anatomy of the brain, and to distinguish pathological conditions, such as tumors, abscesses and hematomas.

congenital: present at or before birth.

constipation: a condition in which bowel evacuations occur infrequently, or in which the feces are hard and small, or where passage of feces causes difficulty or pain.

contracture: irreversible shortening of muscle fibers that causes decreased joint mobility.

convulsion: older term for a seizure; it most commonly involves a series of involuntary contractions of voluntary muscles.

Corpus callosum: the bridge of white matter connecting the two hemispheres of the brain.

cortex: the gray matter that lies at the outer portion of the cerebrum.

cyanosis: a bluish discoloration of the skin and mucous membranes resulting from an inadequate amount of oxygen in the blood.

cytoplasm: the jellylike substance that surrounds the nucleus of a cell.

degenerative CNS disorder: a condition leading to progressive disability and death, usually associated with significant, identifiable changes in the brain. Rett syndrome is no longer thought to be a degenerative CNS disorder.

deletion: loss of genetic material from a chromosome.

dendrite: one of the shorter branching processes of the cell body of a neuron, which makes contact with other neurons at synapses and carries nerve impulses from them into the cell body.

deoxyribonucleic acid (DNA): a fundamental component of living tissue; it contains the genetic code.

dementia: marked decline in intellectual ability; loss of cognitive skills.

demyelinization: loss of myelinin around around an axon.

developmental delay: a delay in the development of skills and abilities which usually would have developed by a certain age.

diagnostic test: a test that provides an in-depth assessment of a skill area, including strengths and weaknesses and error patterns.

differential: a list of conditions that could possibly cause the patient's presenting problem. Differential diagnoses for RS include cerebral palsy and autism.

distal: situated away from the organ or point of attachment or from the median line of the body.

dorsiflexion: backward flexion of the foot or hand or the toes and fingers.

due process: a system of procedures designed to ensure that individuals are treated fairly and have an opportunity to contest decisions made about them. The due-process requirements of Public Law 94-142 and Section 504 are intended to safeguard the right of children who have disabilities to a free appropriate public education.

duodenum: upper part of the small intestine.

dyspraxia: impairment of the ability to perform coordinated motor movements.

dystonia: alteration in muscle tone, usually referring to muscle cramps/spasms of muscles close to the midline of the body (neck, shoulders, hips).

early intervention: the provision of educational services at an early age for children with learning difficulties to avoid more serious problems later in life.

electrocardiogram (EKG or ECG): the tracing made by an instrument for recording the changes of electrical potential occurring during the heartbeat.

electroencephalogram (EEG): a test to measure and record brain waves. In Rett syndrome, the EEG is almost always abnormal, although clinical seizures are not always present.

electromyelogram (EMG): a test in which wire probes which detect muscle contraction are inserted into a muscle. The muscle is then stimulated electrically to initiate a contraction and the response is recorded. The test allows monitoring of muscle contractions timing and efficiency of the response to a known stimulus.

electronic communication device: a communication system which is computer chip based and contains messages which are words or phrases designed for the user of the device. Pictures, small objects or words are placed on the device as cues to where messages are located.

encephalopathy: an indication that something is wrong in the brain.

endometrial ablation: a laser procedure to remove the lining of the uterus, which results in total or partial cessation of menstrual bleeding.

endorphins: the body's natural opiates, probably involved in the perception of pain and pleasure.

endoscopy: the use of an instrument to visualize the interior of a hollow organ, such as the esophagus; used to detect gastroesophageal reflux (GER).

epiglottis: a lidlike structure that hangs over the entrance to the windpipe and prevents aspiration into the lungs during swallowing.

epilepsy: recurrent seizures, excluding ones caused solely by fever.

epileptiform patterns: patterns which resemble those of a seizure.

epiglottis: a thin, leaf-shaped flap of cartilage covered with mucous membrane, situated immediately behind the root of the tongue.

equilibrium: balance.

equinus: involuntary extension of the foot downward, due to a tight or overactive heelcord.

esophagus: tube extending from the pharynx to the stomach.

esophagitis: inflammation of the esophagus.

etiology: cause.

evaluation: the process by which a team of professionals gathers information about a child's skills, deficits, aptitudes, interests and personality variables from a variety of sources, including testing, observation, and other procedures, to guide decisions about the child's educational program. Often used interchangeably with "assessment."

expressive language: communication that is given out to others.

fine motor coordination: the ability to use the small muscles to accomplish tasks requiring precision.

flexion: the bending of a joint so that the bones forming it are brought toward each other.

flexor: a muscle whose primary function is flexion at a joint.

formal test: a standardized evaluative measure, namely one that has explicit methods for administration and scoring and for which norms are available.

forme fruste: incompletely expressed (a 'frustrated form'), as in a RS variant who has most, but not all, of the classical characteristics.

fortunate activation: females usually randomly inactivate one of the two copies of the X-chromosome in each cell. Fortunate activation refers to a situation where a female who carries an abnormal gene on one X-chromosome silences the abnormal copy, leaving the normal copy to function. It protects her from symptoms of the X-linked disease, but does not prevent her from passing it on.

frontal lobe: front part of the cerebrum; important for voluntary muscle movement and memory.

fundoplication (fundal plication): an operation in which the opening from the esophagus to the stomach is closed.

gagging: voluntary or involuntary rhythmic movements of the back of the mouth near the epiglottis; protects airway from a bolus; usually triggered by food near the back of the tongue that does not trigger the swallowing reflex.

gait: manner or style of walking.

Gastroesophageal reflux disease (GER): the backward flow of stomach contents from the stomach back into the esophagus.

gastroenterologist: a doctor who specializes in disorders of digestion.

gastrostomy (G-tube): a surgical creation of an artificial opening into the stomach through the wall of the abdomen.

generalized seizure: a seizure involving the whole brain.

genotype: the genetic composition of an individual.

GI: gastrointestinal.

gliosis: elaborate term for scar tissue in the form of excess astrocytes, also called astroglia.

grand mal: old term for tonic-clonic; a form of seizure in which there is a sudden loss of consciousness immediately followed by a generalized convulsion.

gray matter: the parts of the brain that contain the cell bodies of nerve cells (neurons).

gross: on a large scale; not to be confused with the common term for "yucky." "Grossly normal," means "after less than in-depth inspection, this appears to be normal." "Gross anatomy" refers to the study of organs as they appear to the naked eye, without the benefit of a microscope.

gross motor coordination: the ability to use the large muscles in a coordinated, purposeful manner to engage in such activities as walking and running.

gyri: convolutions of the surface of the brain.

handicapped child: the term used in federal and state law to designate a child who has a specific cognitive, physical or emotional disability to the extent that specially designed instruction is necessary for her to learn effectively.

habilitation: teaching of new skills.

head circumference: the size of the head, usually plotted on a growth curve to compare with other children of the same age; the increase in the head circumference in infancy and early childhood is a reflection of normal brain growth.

hip dislocation: occurs at the ball-and-socket joint of the hip, when the ball is completely pulled out of the socket.

hip subluxation: occurs at the ball-and-socket joint of the hip, when the ball is partially pulled out of the socket.

hippotherapy: therapeutic horseback riding.

homebound instruction: temporary instruction at home, provided if a child is unable to attend school for medical reasons or if the school is in the process of arranging a special education placement.

hydrotherapy: water therapy, such as provided in a whirlpool bath or warm pool.

hyperventilation: exaggerated inspirations followed immediately by equally exaggerated expirations (fast, deep breaths), contributing to a central apnea at the end.

hypertonia: high muscle tone, muscle tightness or spasticity.

hypoplasia: underdeveloped tissue. Both "atrophy" and "hypoplasia" can lead to smaller than normal amounts of tissue, but atrophy implies that normal tissue was once present and hypoplasia implies that normal tissue never developed. Both processes appear to occur in the brains of girls with RS.

hypotonia: decreased muscle tone, not to be confused with muscle weakness. Diminished resistance of muscles to passive stretching.

hypsarrhythmia: an abnormality of the EEG, a wildly chaotic pattern with multiple spikes and slow waves.

hypoxia: reduction of oxygen content in body tissues.

ictal (ictus): an event. A seizure of any type is referred to as an ictus.

IDEA (Individuals With Disabilities Education Act): passed in 1997, this law was written to strengthen academic expectations and accountability for children with disabilities, and bridge the gap that has too often existed between what those children learn and the regular curriculum.

idiopathic: of unknown cause.

ileum: lower portion of the small intestine.

inclusion: the placement of a child who has an educational disability in an instructional setting in which most students do not have disabilities, in a manner that is educationally and socially beneficial to the child.

incontinence: absence of bowel or bladder control.

independent living skills: skills needed to care for oneself and to function effectively in a community setting (including for example, personal hygiene, money management, cooking, use of public transportation).

independent evaluation: evaluation of a child by one or more professionals who have no formal relationship with the school district. Parents can request this evaluation if they disagree with the school's evaluation.

individualized educational program (IEP): a written plan that a team composed of school staff, parents and the child, if appropriate, develops for every special education student. Must include, at a minimum, the child's current educational strengths and weaknesses, goals and objectives, educational services, start-up dates for those services, and procedures for program evaluation.

intelligence quotient (IQ): score on an intelligence test for which 100 is the mean. Indicates a child's test performance relative to other children of the same age.

intelligence test: a test used to measure overall capacity for learning. In RS, an adequate intelligence test has not been devised that can accurately measure understanding.

intussusception: the slipping of a length of intestine into an adjacent portion, usually producing obstruction.

intubation: the insertion of a tube through the nose or mouth into the trachea to provide artificial ventilation.

in utero: before birth.

invasive test: a procedure or examination that requires that the body be entered in some way, either through a needle or with a tube.

ischemic: an inadequate flow of blood to a part of the body caused by constriction or blockage of the blood vessels supplying it.

joy: what you experience when your daughter lights up the room with a smile.

karyotype: photograph of the chromosomal makeup of a cell; in humans, there are 23 pairs of chromosomes in a normal karyotype. Usually reported as "46, XX, normal female karyotype." The "46" refers to the number of chromosomes in each cell (23 pairs), the "XX" describes the sex chromosomes, in this case, female. A few girls with RS have had abnormal results.

ketosis: the buildup of acid in the body due to starvation; important in the ketogenic diet.

ketogenic diet: a diet which provides the minimal amount of protein necessary for growth, no carbohydrates and most of the calories from fats. The diet is used in seizure control.

kindred cases: recurrences of RS in a family, for example, sisters, cousins, etc.

kyphosis: a spinal curvature as seen from the side, often termed "hunch back."

least restrictive environment (LRE): a standard established by PL-94-142 for special education placement. A child who has an educational disability must be allowed to participate in as much of the regular education program as is appropriate in view of her educational needs. The law holds that children with special needs must not be separated from students who do not have disabilities any more than is educationally necessary.

lumbar puncture (spinal tap): the tapping of the subarachnoid space to obtain cerebrospinal fluid from the lower back region for examination.

lysosomal enzymes: enzymes normally involved in the process of digestion.

magnetic resonance imaging (MRI): imaging procedure that uses the magnetic resonance of atoms to provide clear images on interior parts of the body.

mediation: a process for settling disputes between parents and school districts through the intervention of a neutral third party who tries to negotiate an agreement acceptable to others.

medulla: the brain stem.

melatonin: a naturally occurring hormone produced in the pineal gland, involved in regulation of sleep. It is now available as an over-the-counter sleep aid.

meninges: the three connective tissue membranes that line the skull and vertebral canal and enclose the brain and spinal cord.

mental age (MA): a form for expressing a child's performance on an intelligence test. A child who receives an MA of 8-4 has achieved a score comparable to an "average" child of 8 years, 4 months.

mental retardation: a significant delay in the development of cognitive (problem solving) skills that is associated with a significant delay in adaptive (use of intelligence in daily living) skills that occurs during childhood. The term "significant" refers to "statistically significant" when compared to other children of the same age. Usually measured by intellectual functioning at least two standard deviations below the mean, or average.

metabolites: the products of metabolism; in RS articles, often seen in the phrase "biogenic amine metabolites," which refers to the normal breakdown products of the neurotransmitters dopamine, norepinephrine and serotonin. These can be measured in the cerebrospinal fluid directly.

microcephaly: head circumference below normal for age (two standard deviations below the average); usually reflects lack of brain growth.

mitochondria: a structure in the cytoplasm of every cell which is the site of the cell's energy production.

mucopolysaccharides: product of metabolism that may accumulate in cells and cause a progressive neurological disorder known as mucopolysacharidosis; usually ruled out before the diagnosis of Rett syndrome is given.

music therapist: someone who is trained to use musical activities to teach non-music skills, such as communication, socialization, choice-making and motor skills.

mutation: a change in the genetic material that occurs by chance; it can be passed on to future generations.

myelination: the production of a coating called myelin around an axon, which quickens neurotransmission.

myoclonic: repetitive contraction of muscles; occurs in infantile spasms.

myopathy: condition affecting the muscles.

nasogastric tube (Ng tube): a temporary plastic feeding tube placed through the nose down the esophagus and into the stomach for introduction of high caloric foods.

negative test result: the test was normal (usually perceived by the patient to be a "positive" event).

neurologist: a physician skilled in the diagnosis and treatment of disease of the nervous system.

neuronal packing density: closeness of neurons within cerebral cortex (gray matter). Technically, number of neurons per .001 cubic millimeter.

neurons: the nerve cells of the brain.

neuropathy: any disease of the peripheral nerves, causing weakness and numbness.

neurotransmitters: the chemicals used by nerves to "talk" to each other; released at the synapse that permits transmission from one nerve to another.

nociception: the perception of pain, impaired in girls with RS.

non-specific findings: those physical or laboratory results that can be seen in a variety of conditions, for example, "seizures" are a non-specific finding because they occur in many neurological diseases, not just Rett syndrome.

nystagmus: rapid involuntary movements of the eyes.

obstipation: severe and obstinate constipation; leads to fecal impaction.

occipital lobe: one of the major divisions of each cerebral hemisphere of the brain.

occupational therapy: treatment by an occupational therapist to improve an individual's ability to integrate different mental and motor processes in a purposeful and efficient manner. The occupational therapist concentrates on promoting, maintaining or restoring use of the body for daily living skills.

opthamalogical: anything related to the eye.

organic acids: error in metabolism of organic acids can cause the child to develop symptoms of acidosis, coma, developmental and psychomotor retardation. Some forms of this disorder have been successfully treated by vitamin therapy both before and after birth. Not seen in RS.

organomegaly: enlarged internal organs, not seen in RS.

oropharyngeal dysfunction: improper function of the mouth and pharynx.

orotic acids: excessive excretion or orotic acids is indicative of a genetic metabolic disorder, characterized by physical and mental retardation; ruled out in Rett syndrome.

orthopedic: relating to bones or joints.

orthosis: an orthopedic appliance used to support, align, prevent or correct deformities or to improve the functioning of movable parts of the body.

osteotomy: surgical realignment of the bone; used for hip subluxation.

osteoarthritis: inflammation of joints characterized by degenerative changes and sometimes increasing bulk in the bone and cartilage.

palmar grasp: immature hand movement in which the palm rather than the fingertips makes contact with an object.

parietal lobe: one of the major divisions of each cerebral hemisphere, lying behind the frontal lobe, above the temporal lobe and in front of the occipital lobe. It contains the sensory cortex and association areas of the brain.

peripheral nervous system: the parts of the nervous system that are outside the brain and spinal cord.

petit mal: old term for absence seizures.

pharynx: a muscular tube lined with mucous membrane which extends from the beginning of the esophagus up to the base of the skull.

phProbe: a test for gastroesophageal reflux (GER), in which a probe in place near the esophageal sphincter, and acid reflux is measured.

phenotype: the clinical appearance of a patient, her historical and/or physical findings; in contrast to a patient's genotype, which is the genetic profile of a patient. Patients with the same phenotype can have different genotypes. Or just because patients share the same clinical findings doesn't mean that they were caused by the same thing.

physical therapy: Treatment by a physical therapist to improve an individual's motor skills and increase the strength and endurance of body parts.

pincer grasp: refined, mature hand movement in which the thumb and first finger are used to pick up a small object.

placement: the educational setting in which a student receives instruction.

plantar flexion: bending of the toes or fingers downward, toward the sole or palm.

positioning: physical management of posture and body alignment for daily living skills such as eating and standing up.

positive findings: an abnormal test or finding (although usually not a "positive" event from the patient's point of view, a consistently "positive" test result in girls with RS would lead to a diagnostic test for this disorder).

positron emission tomography (PET scan): imaging study which uses radioactive labeled chemical compounds to study the metabolism of an organ.

prognosis: outcome or outlook of a medical condition; what is likely to happen.

procedural safeguards: legal regulations intended to safeguard the right of a child who has an educational disability to a free appropriate public education, and ensure that both child and parents receive the due process of law.

progressive: the problem gets worse with time. In RS, this means that symptoms continue to develop over time; it is not clear whether or not the underlying disease process is actively getting worse with time or whether the new symptoms represent the result of previous involvement of the brain.

prolonged Q-T interval: the resting period between heart beats is elongated.

pronation: turned inward.

prone stander: a piece of equipment that holds a person upright in a standing position. The support is under the front of the body and the individual is tipped forward slightly.

Public Law 94-142: the primary federal legislative act involving the education of children who have educational disabilities. Called the Education for All Handicapped Act of 1975, this law aims to assure the availability of a "free appropriate public education" for every eligible child. It sets forth a range of school and parental responsibilities as well as procedural safeguards to ensure the due process of law.

pulmonary: pertaining to the lungs.

pyramidal tract: a collection of nerve tracts in the brain stem.

pseudo arthritis: failure of bone to fuse, sometimes requiring bone graft.

range of motion: the amount of movement available in a joint, measured in degrees. May be reduced in RS, as is seen in spasticity (as in tight heel cords) or by the rigidity or fixing (as in the shoulders and elbows). The motion may be temporarily reduced. If motion is limited for a long time, the limitation becomes structural because muscles and tendons become shortened.

receptive language: communication that is received.

related services: support services needed by a child to benefit from special education.

residential placement: a placement, usually arranged and paid for by a state agency or the parents, where a child with special needs resides and typically receives academic instruction.

retinopathy: disease of the retina (the back of the eye that registers visual signals); NOT seen in RS.

righting response: ability to return to upright after tilting.

rigidity: abnormal stiffness of muscle.

rotation: turning of a body part about its long axis as if on a pivot; i.e. of the head to look over the shoulder.

rumination: after swallowing, the regurgitation of food followed by chewing another time.

salivation: the secretion of saliva by the salivary glands of the mouth, increased in response to the chewing action of the jaws or to the thought, taste, sight or smell of food.

scoliosis: spinal curvature caused by a rotation of spinal vertebrae, appearing as a side-to-side or S curve.

section 504: a federal civil rights law passed in 1973 to eliminate discrimination against people with disabilities in federally funded programs. Requires that children with disabilities receive educational services and opportunities equal to those provided other children.

segmental rolling: rolling over where there is rotation (twisting) between the shoulders and hips, often difficult for the child with RS.

seizure: an episodic electrical discharge of nerve cells in the brain resulting in alteration of function or behavior.

self-help skills: skills related to the care of oneself such as eating, dressing and grooming.

sensory modalities: specific channels through which a person receives information about the environment, including sight, sound, touch, taste and smell.

serial casting: a series of casts on the feet to correct shortened heelcords.

sex chromosomes: those chromosomes that determine gender, the X and Y chromosomes.

short-term instructional objective: precise statement, described in terms of overt behavior, of what a child is expected to accomplish over a short period in a specific educational area. An intermediate step between the student's current skill level and the annual goal.

siblings: the other kids who live at your house. Before you had a daughter with RS, they were called brothers and sisters.

side lyer: a piece of equipment that supports and stabilizes the child on her side. It may be used to provide change of position for the very inactive child or may be used as part of a therapy program to correct scoliosis.

simple partial seizures: local seizures involving a single area of the brain.

sleep myoclonus: sudden massive jerks of the body when going to sleep. These are normal.

spatial disorientation: a person's perception of where she is in space is distorted and not accurate. This is observed in RS when the girl's perception of midline is disturbed, causing her to lean.

spastic: increased muscle tone so that muscles are still and movements are difficult.

special education: specialized instruction for children who have educational disabilities based on a comprehensive evaluation. The instruction may occur in a variety of settings, but must be precisely matched to their educational needs and adapted to their learning styles.

splint: a material or device use to protect or immobilize a body part.

sporadic: occurrence by chance, with little risk of recurrence.

SSI (Supplemental Security Income): federal and state funded program that provides money to offset expenses for children with disabilities who come from low-income families under the age of 18, and all individuals with disabilities after the age of 18.

static: unchanging; a "static encephalopathy" refers to a brain disorder that does not get worse with time. It does not mean or imply that the child will remain "static" or "unchanging." A child with a static encephalopathy, such as cerebral palsy, can continue to learn and develop.

stereotypies: repetitive, patterned movements; in RS, usually referring to the hands.

storage diseases: a number of metabolic diseases in which some material, usually a breakdown product of normal tissue, cannot be further metabolized and is stored within nerve cells of the brain, which produces malfunction.

strabismus: inability of one eye to attain binocular vision with the other because of imbalance of the muscles of the eyeball.

subluxation: partial dislocation.

sulci: crevices on the surface of the cerebrum.

synapse: the minute spacing separating one neuron from another; neurochemicals breach this gap.

syncope: fainting; dizziness, pallor, sweating and loss of consciousness.

systemic illness: illness affecting the body as a whole instead of one part.

temporal lobe: one of the main divisions of the cerebral cortex in each hemisphere of the brain, lying at the side within the temple of the skull and separated from the frontal lobe by a cleft (sulcus).

tonic: continuous increased muscle tone.

tonic-clonic seizures: once called "grand mal," seizures associated with stiffening followed by rhythmic jerking.

tongue thrust: oral-motor feeding problem; voluntary tongue motions are not controlled; tongue extends in front of the lips when touched with spoon or food; interferes with moving food from the front of the mouth to the back for swallowing.

transitional movements: movements which allow us to change position, for example rolling, pulling to stand.

translocation: the transfer of a fragment of one chromosome to another chromosome.

trophic foot disturbances: Trophic literally means growth so this means poor growth of the feet, likely resulting in poor circulation.

truncal ataxia: ataxia is poor coordination resulting most often from poor function of a part of the brain called the cerebellum. Truncal ataxia describes limitation or exaggeration of the symptoms to the muscles of the torso. If the torso is unsteady and poorly balanced, the limbs have to overwork to maintain posture.

unconditional love: love with no conditions, as seen through your daughter's eyes.

unfortunate activation: females usually randomly inactivate one of the two copies of the X-chromosome in each cell. Unfortunate activation refers to a situation when a female who carries an abnormal gene on one X-chromosome silences the normal copy of the gene. This allows females to manifest symptoms of X-linked recessive diseases like Duchenne muscular dystrophy or hemophilia.

upper motor neuron: refers to the nerve cell that starts in the cerebral cortex, winds its way down through the brain and then into the spinal cord and that carries information about movement to the lower motor neuron. Damage to the upper motor neuron results in spasticity and deep tendon flexes (like the knee jerk) that are too brisk, while damage to the lower motor neurons results in weakness and decreased reflexes.

vacant spells: may be confused with seizures, but are usually associated with irregular breathing patterns instead.

vagus nerve: the tenth cranial nerve which supplies motor nerve fibers to the muscles of swallowing and parasympathetic fibers to the heart and organs of the chest cavity and abdomen.

vagal tone: impulse from the vagus nerve.

valgus: turned outward, usually referring to the ankle in Rett syndrome.

Valsalva's manoeuver: long inspirations (breath holds) capable of raising blood pressure and heart rate changes.

varus: turned inward, usually referring to the ankle in Rett syndrome.

vasomotor disturbance: relating to the nerves or the centers from which they arise that supply the muscle fibers of the walls of blood vessels, which regulate the amount of blood passing to a particular body part or organ. In Rett syndrome, used to describe cold, bluish hands and feet.

vestibular: movements which give the body input about posture and movements in space which allow coordination and balance.

video EEG: the use of video cameras to capture visually the onset and characteristics of seizures while simultaneously monitoring the EEG to see electrical changes.

volvulus: a twisting of the intestine upon itself which causes obstruction.

weight shift: the movement of the body's center of gravity in any direction. Most movement sequences are initiated by this and it is a significant concern because this may be very difficult for the girl with RS to do.

white matter: the parts of the brain made up of axons, the long "extension cords" of the nerve cells that carry messages from one cell to another. These extensions are wrapped in an insulating substance called myelin and when the axons are grouped together, they appear white.

X-linked dominant disorder: a disorder caused by a gene located on the X chromosome; also called sex-linked; passed on by one parent.

zero reject: all children are to be provided a free appropriate education.

INDEX

acetylcholine 35, 113, 289
agitation 28, 32, 36, 110, 120, 228
allergies 85, 108, 231
Americans With
Disabilities Act 271, 293
anesthesia 110, 125, 144, 162, 231, 240
anticonvulsant 109, 33, 294
  Ativan 109
  Depakene 109
  Depakote 33, 94, 109, 235
  Dilantin 106, 109, 110, 112
  Felbatol 109
  Klonipin 108
  Lamictal 109
  Mysoline 110
  Neurontin 109
  Phenobarbital 109, 110, 238
  Tegretol 94, 106, 108, 109, 110, 268
  Topamax 110
  Tranzene 94, 108
  Valium 93, 108, 112
  Zarontin 109, 110
apraxia 150-154, 169, 170, 172
     175, 176, 179, 189, 209
arousal and calm 81
ataxia 154, 169, 172, 175, 299, 300, 312
atypical RS 27
augmentative devices 31, 223
autism 26, 27, 304
autonomic nervous system 35, 113, 116
     122, 151, 300
autonomic responses 104, 107, 300
balance 153, 154
bathing 141
behaviors 83-94, 303
biological marker 26, 36, 300
blood 26, 309
books and magazines ....ix, 283-288
bowel 125-133, 306
brain 35, 37, 113, 305
  axons 113, 315
  basal ganglia 115, 304
  brain stem 35, 106, 113-116, 121, 304, 305
  Broca's area 114
  caudate 34
  cerebellum 34, 113-116, 304, 314
  cerebral hemisphere 115, 311
  cerebrospinal fluid ...26, 115, 305, 310
  corpus callosum 114, 305, 306
  cytoplasm 113, 306, 310

dendrites 113, 304
frontal lobe 34, 114, 307, 311, 314
gray matter 113, 115, 304, 306
hippocampus 34, 35, 115
hypothalamus 34, 35, 115
medulla 35, 115, 310
meninges 115, 310
neurons 31, 34, 35, 113, 115, 116
    118, 306, 308, 311, 314
neurotransmitters 32, 35, 37, 113, 114
    303, 304, 310, 311
occipital lobe 114, 311
parietal lobe 114, 311
putamen 34
substantia nigra 35
temporal lobe 34, 114, 311, 314
thalamus 115
white matter 113, 115, 304, 306, 315
breathing 116
  aerophagia 117, 303
  apnea 28, 107, 116-118
    121, 122, 164, 303, 305, 308
  breath holding 28, 29, 37, 107, 116-122
    254, 305
  hyperventilation 28, 29, 37, 116, 117, 119
    120, 121, 122, 164, 170
    188, 194, 232, 254, 308
  oxygen 69, 72, 106, 111, 117-120
    177, 254, 306, 309
  valsalva manoeuvre 118, 120, 127
bruxism 28, 90, 305
catalogs 138, 162, 182, 227, 272, 280
central nervous system 31, 35, 113
    114, 116, 305
cerebral palsy 188, 194, 256, 289
    290, 305, 306, 314
chewing 28, 91, 122, 138, 172, 176, 209
    231, 232, 233, 235, 236, 239, 304, 313
choking 34, 130, 233, 236, 238, 239, 244
circulation 28, 35, 115, 133, 157
    158, 163, 177, 303, 314
classic RS 27
cognition 30, 34, 178, 197, 204
communication 209
  augmentative 31, 153, 211, 223, 224, 304
  alternative 211, 224, 303
  body language 176, 202, 209, 211, 213, 229
  choice-making skills 94, 177, 211, 310
  choosing vocabulary 212, 221
  communication boards 211, 216, 221

communication digest 227
computers 142, 211, 215, 218, 221
                          224, 227, 287
eye blinks 105, 215, 225
eye gaze frame 225, 226, 229
eye gaze vest 215, 230
eye pointing 212, 214, 215, 229
facilitated communication 193, 210, 214
                          216, 217, 220
  head pointers 217
  helpful hints 229
  IEP objectives 225
  switches 218-220
  using words 221
  using yes/no 212
  voice output devices 219
community resources 279
Community Supported
Living Arrangements (CSLA) 263
  guardianship 259
  programs for 263
  residential care 263
comprehension 187
congenital onset RS 27
constipation ..119, 120, 125-128, 131, 306, 311
contractures 306
crying 84-89
deep pressure 76, 81
degenerative disorder 26, 28, 35, 170, 306
dehydration 232, 240, 241
depth perception 76, 78
developmental delay 26, 27, 113, 306
diagnostic criteria 27, 28, 187
digestion 156, 163, 231
discriminative touch 80
drooling 134
drugs 32
  bromocriptine (Parlodel®) 32
  Depo-Provera® 144, 145
  L-dopa (dopamine®) 32
  naltrexone (Revia®) 32, 89, 94, 121
  Reglan® 240
  tyrosine 32
  tryptophan 32
dyspraxia 26, 36, 152, 306
ear infections 79
education 187
  inclusion 202-207, 309
  placement 197, 199, 200, 256, 312, 313
  state special education departments ..293-297
EEG 104, 105
emotions 84, 90
equilibrium 34, 154

equipment 280-282
exclusion criteria 28
eyes 26, 214, 215
eye gaze 229, 230
facial movements 90
fecal impaction 126, 130, 311
feet 157
  ankle foot orthosis 157, 172, 311
  equinus 157, 307
  pronation 157, 172, 312
  serial casting 157, 158, 313
  surgery 158, 163-165
  valgus 157, 315
  varus 157, 315
Feldenkrais integration (FI) 77
fluctuations 83
free materials 287-288
functional assessment 199
gait 308
gastroesophageal reflux (GER) 37, 236
                          238, 308
gastrostomy (G button) 241-243, 308
gas 132
gastrointestinal tract 133
genetics 247, 248, 250
genes
  chromosomes 247, 248
  dominant 248, 304, 315
  inherited 247, 248, 250
  recessive 248, 304
  risk 249, 250
  sporadic 250, 313
glossary 303-314
glutamate 35
government agencies 289-290
grief 69
hands 95
  movements 95-99
  skills 95, 100
  splints 98, 99
head growth 308
heart 122
heartburn 238
hips
  adduction 159, 303
  dislocation 159, 308
  osteotomy 159, 311
  subluxation 159, 308, 314
horseback therapy (hippotherapy) .179, 308
hotlines 290
hydrotherapy 179, 308
hypertonia 151, 308
hyperventilation 120, 308